PUBLICATIONS OF THE
SCOTTISH COUNCIL FOR RESEARCH IN EDUCATION
60

A BIBLIOGRAPHY OF
SCOTTISH EDUCATION
BEFORE 1872

A BIBLIOGRAPHY OF
SCOTTISH EDUCATION

BEFORE 1872

JAMES CRAIGIE, OBE, MA, PhD, FEIS

UNIVERSITY OF LONDON PRESS LTD

ISBN 0 340 11763 x

University of London Press Ltd
St Paul's House, Warwick Lane, London EC4

Printed and bound in Great Britain by
T & A Constable Ltd, Hopetoun Street, Edinburgh EH7 4NF

Preface

Dr R R Rusk, when Director of the Scottish Council for Research in Education, began the collection of materials for a bibliography of writings relating to education in Scotland which should cover the history of the subject from its beginnings to the present time. After his retiral the Executive Committee of the Council decided that his work should be continued and completed, and set up a special committee for this purpose. The present volume is the first fruits of its work.

As work on the undertaking proceeded it became apparent that more than one volume would be needed to accommodate all the material bearing on the subject, and the question arose of where the division should be made. Finally, since the year 1872 marked a great watershed in the history of Scottish education, it was decided to concentrate first on producing a volume which should contain all the material referring to the period before that date. The present volume is the result of that decision. It lists not only the books, pamphlets and articles in periodicals which were published before 1872, but also those which appeared after that date but which dealt either wholly or in part with Scottish education before it.

Because of limitations of space and because of the tremendous amount of time which would be required to track it all down, many types of material have had to be excluded. No manuscript material, for example, is listed, except that Appendix C directs the student and the researcher to papers in HM General Register House, Edinburgh, and elsewhere which might otherwise be overlooked. Also omitted are reports of parliamentary debates, important though they are, since they are both easy to trace and easy of access. Newspaper reports on educational matters, whether national or local, school prospectuses, annual reports for schools and other educational institutions, school magazines, and so forth have also had to be passed over in silence. Local histories too have been ignored unless they contain a section specifically devoted to education, or to schools and schoolmasters. Those interested to know what local histories have been written will find many of them listed in the Bibliographies contained in the various volumes of the *Fasti Ecclesiae Scoticanae*.

Even after exclusions so extensive as those indicated in the previous paragraph the amount of printed material bearing on the history of education in Scotland before 1872 is still not inconsiderable. It is also too varied in its subject matter to be presented as a single undifferentiated mass. Various arrangements are possible, and it is unlikely that any two editors would produce schemes of arrangement which were identical in all respects for a certain subjective element must enter into all. The arrangement offered here is based partly upon the way in which much of the material seemed to organise itself round a focal point according to its subject matter, and partly upon what seemed likely to serve best the interests and the needs of those who will use the volume. The general difficulty involved in arranging so much material as is presented here and of the kind that it is, is further complicated by the fact that many items could appear in more than one place since they deal with more than one topic or with one topic under several aspects, and in either case it is not always easy to determine what should be regarded as the dominant theme. To save a multiplicity of cross-references the Index of Subjects has been made very full, and it is believed that it will enable the student to follow through with some completeness those particular aspects of the subject in which he is especially interested.

The Scottish universities are an integral part of the Scottish educational system but their inclusion in a work of this type presents certain difficulties. There are three aspects of them to be considered. There is, first, their internal history; then, there is their relation to the educational system as a whole; and, lastly, there is their relation to the life of the nation. To deal at all adequately with the first of these would require a very large volume to itself, and to prepare it seems a task more suited to the universities than to the Scottish Council for Research in Education. Accordingly, the section devoted to the Scottish universities deals only with the second and third aspects of the subject as indicated above.

The form of the entries follows generally that found in the British Museum catalogue of printed books. While consistency has been aimed at, it has not always been achieved, because of the intractability of the material. But it is believed that the deviations from consistency are few and not such as to cause difficulty to anyone consulting the volume. Within sections, the order followed is normally an alphabetical one; it should be noted, however, that though the definite and the indefinite article are printed where they occur in the titles of anonymous writings, they are disregarded in determining the alphabetical order, which is based upon the initial letter of the first significant word in the title. In certain sections, however, a chronological order has been followed since it seemed to bring out better the significance of the material in them.

It is almost as important for the student or the researcher to know where the literature on his subject is to be found as it is to know what that literature is. Accordingly, one library where it may be found is given for every item listed here. Since much of the research on which the bibliography is based was done in the National Library of Scotland, because it contains far more of the material than any other library in Scotland or elsewhere, it has not been thought necessary to indicate it in every case where it would apply; no location therefore means that that particular item will be found in the collections of the National Library of Scotland. The other libraries whose collections have been drawn upon are indicated according to the following table:

APL	Aberdeen Public Library
AUL	Aberdeen University Library
Ba	Baillie's Institute, Glasgow
BM	British Museum, London
DPL	Dundee Public Library
DUL	Dundee University Library
Df	Dunfermline Public Library
EIS	Educational Institute of Scotland Library, Edinburgh
EPL	Edinburgh Public Library
EUL	Edinburgh University Library
Fi	Fife County Library, Kirkcaldy
GUL	Glasgow University Library
Ha	Haddington Public Library
Inv	Inverness Public Library
Jor	Jordanhill College of Education Library, Glasgow
Ki	Kirkcaldy Public Library
Lei	Institute of Education Library, Leicester University
Mid	Midlothian County Library, Musselburgh
Mit	Mitchell Library, Glasgow
Mo	Moray House College of Education Library, Edinburgh
New Coll	New College Library, Edinburgh
Pe	Sandeman Library, Perth
StAUL	St Andrews University Library

To the librarians and their staffs in all these institutions the warmest thanks of the Scottish Council for Research in Education and of the editor of this Bibliography are due for their advice, their co-operation and their encouragement, all of which were always most willingly given. Special thanks are due to Mr R M Strathdee, Midlothian County Library, and to Mr M C Pottinger, Scottish Central Library, for their help in tracing rare items. I should also like to express my thanks to the members of the Advisory Committee for their helpful advice and assistance in tracing appropriate material.

It will, of course, be understood that the assignment of a particular item to a library other than the National Library of Scotland does not necessarily mean that that other library is the only one where a copy may be found, since a number of others may have it in their collections. But no attempt has been made to compile a census of all the existing copies of all the items in the Bibliography it being felt that this would delay publication almost indefinitely.

Completeness is not claimed for this work, but to have delayed its publication till every writing relating to the history of education in Scotland before 1872 had been located, examined and listed would have meant postponement till some date in the distant future. It is, however, claimed that this volume, which represents the results of more than eight years' work, is more comprehensive than anything of the same nature that has previously been attempted. Such omissions as there are are due to circumstances beyond editorial control, but they are believed to be inconsiderable compared with what is presented here. It is likely, too, that when identified they will not change much the picture that can be drawn from the material presented here; this is true even for local history, where the omissions are likely to be most numerous. All that the new information could provide would be additional details about attitudes and practices whose existence had already been fairly clearly established.

James Craigie

Abbreviations

DNB	*Dictionary of National Biography*
Educ News	*Educational News*
PP	*Parliamentary Papers*, cited by year, volume, and number
SEJ	*Scottish Educational Journal*
SHR	*Scottish Historical Review*
TES	*Times Educational Supplement*

Contents

J Craigie, OBE, MA, PhD, FEIS, Vice-President, The Scottish Council for Research in Education

Convener

T R Bone, MA, MEd, PhD, Principal Lecturer in Education, Jordanhill College of Education

J Clarke, OBE, MA,* *formerly* Rector, Paisley Grammar School

J J Fowler, MA,† *formerly* Principal Teacher in Modern Languages, Carrick Academy, Maybole

A Law, OBE, MA, PhD, *formerly* HM Inspector of Schools, Scottish Education Department

R R Rusk, MA, BA, PhD, *formerly* Director of the Council

D J Withrington, MA, MEd, Senior Lecturer in History, Aberdeen University

David A Walker, OBE, MA, MEd, PhD, FRSE, FEIS, Director of the Council

Gerard J Pollock, MA, MEd, InstP, Depute Director

John L Powell, MA, MEd, Assistant Director

Jessie M Gray, MA, Secretary

* Died 1963 † Died 1966

Part One

BROWN, P HUME *History of Scotland*. 3 vols. Cambridge: At the University Press, 1911. 8vo.

CRAIK, SIR HENRY *A Century of Scottish History, from the Days before the '45 to those within living Memory*. Second edition. Edinburgh and London: William Blackwood and Sons, 1911. 8vo.

DICKINSON, WILLIAM CROFT *Scotland from the Earliest Times to 1603*. Second edition, revised. (*A New History of Scotland*, vol I.) London and Edinburgh: Thomas Nelson and Sons Ltd, 1965. 8vo.

DONALDSON, GORDON *Scotland. James V– James VII*. (*The Edinburgh History of Scotland*, vol III.) Edinburgh and London: Oliver & Boyd, 1965. 8vo.

FERGUSON, WILLIAM *Scotland: 1689 to the Present*. (*The Edinburgh History of Scotland*, vol IV.) Edinburgh and London: Oliver & Boyd, 1968. 8vo.

LANG, ANDREW *A History of Scotland from the Roman Occupation*. 4 vols. Edinburgh and London: William Blackwood and Sons, 1900-7. 8vo.

PRYDE, GEORGE S *Scotland from 1603 to the Present Day*. (*A New History of Scotland*, vol II.) London and Edinburgh: Thomas Nelson and Sons Ltd, 1962. 8vo.

SMOUT, T C *A History of the Scottish People, 1560-1830*. London: Collins, 1969.

INNES, COSMO *Scotland in the Middle Ages. Sketches of Early Scottish History and Social Progress*. Edinburgh: Edmonston and Douglas, 1860. 8vo.

MACKINTOSH, JOHN *The History of Civilisation in Scotland*. A new edition, partly rewritten and carefully revised throughout. 4 vols. Paisley: Alexander Gardner, 1892. 8vo.

BELLESHEIM, ALPHONSE *History of the Catholic Church of Scotland*, translated by David Oswald Hunter Blair. 4 vols. Edinburgh and London: William Blackwood and Sons, 1887. 8vo.

BURLEIGH, JOHN H S *A Church History of Scotland*. London: Oxford University Press, 1960. 8vo.

MILLAR, JOHN HEPBURN *A Literary History of Scotland*. (The Library of Literary History.) London: T Fisher Unwin, 1903. 8vo.

DAWSON, JAMES H *An Abridged Statistical Account of Scotland, parochially arranged*. Edinburgh: W H Lizars, 1853. 8vo.

The New Statistical Account of Scotland. By the Ministers of the respective Parishes. 15 vols. Edinburgh and London: William Blackwood and Sons, 1845. 8vo.

The Statistical Account of Scotland. Drawn up from the Communications of the Ministers of the different Parishes, by Sir John Sinclair, Bart. 21 vols. Edinburgh: Printed by William Creech, 1791-9. 8vo.

The accounts of the different parishes are not arranged in any particular order, but seem to have been printed as they were received by the editor from the authors. There is, however, an Index of Parishes in vol 21, 555-86. An *Analysis of the Statistical Account of Scotland* by Sir John Sinclair, Bart, was published by John Murray at London in 1826.

BLACK, GEORGE F *A List of Works relating to Scotland*. New York: The New York Public Library, 1916. 8vo.

MITCHELL, SIR ARTHUR, and CASH, C G *A Contribution to the Bibliography of Scottish Topography*. (Publications of the Scottish History Society, 2nd series, 14 and 15.) 2 vols. Edinburgh: Printed at the University Press by T and A Constable for the Scottish History Society, 1917. 8vo.

General Histories of Scottish Education

BARCLAY, HUGH *A Sketch of the History of Schools in Scotland.* Glasgow: J Tweed, 1880. 8vo. Pp 23.   BM

EDGAR, JOHN *History of Early Scottish Education.* Edinburgh: James Thin, 1893. 8vo. Pp xii, 333. Index.

G, J S 'Scottish Popular Education. A Historical Sketch'; *The Museum*, new series, 1 (1865), 177-81, 294-8, 331-6.

GIBSON, WILLIAM J *Education in Scotland: A Sketch of the Past and the Present.* London: Longmans, Green, and Co, 1912. 8vo. Pp xi, 151. Bibliography.

GRANT, JAMES *History of the Burgh and Parish Schools of Scotland.* Vol I— Burgh Schools. London and Glasgow: William Collins, Sons, and Co, 1876. 8vo. Pp xvi, 571. Index.

NOTE No further volumes were ever published.

HOLMES, EILEEN M *Education in Scotland. A Survey of its Historical Development, its Characteristic Qualities and its Problems.* Fabian Society Research Series, 66. London: Victor Gollancz Ltd, 1942. 8vo. Pp 31. Bibliography.

KERR, JOHN *Scottish Education: School and University from Early Times to 1908.* Cambridge: At the University Press, 1910. 8vo. Pp xvi, 442. Index.

— —. With an Addendum, 1908-1913. Cambridge: At the University Press, 1913. 8vo. Pp xvi, 454. Index.

KNOX, HENRY M *Two Hundred and Fifty Years of Scottish Education, 1696-1946.* Edinburgh and London: Oliver and Boyd, 1953. 8vo. Pp xiv, 253. Index.

MACKINTOSH, MARY *Education in Scotland: Yesterday and Today.* Glasgow: Robert Gibson & Sons, Glasgow, Ltd, 1962. 8vo. Pp viii, 248. Chapter bibliographies. 7 illustrations. Index of Names. Index of Topics. End maps.

MIDDLETON, DAVID *A Glance at the History of Scottish Education.* Edinburgh: Thomas Laurie, 1866. 8vo. Pp 24.   GUL

MORGAN, ALEXANDER *Rise and Progress of Scottish Education.* Edinburgh and London: Oliver and Boyd, 1927. 8vo. Pp xi, 234. Index.

SMITH, JOHN 'Scottish Education in Earlier Days'; *Secondary School J,* Oct 1914, 7, 78-81; Feb 1915, 8, 8-11.   BM

STEWART, GEORGE *The Story of Scottish Education.* London: Sir Isaac Pitman & Sons, Ltd, 1927. 8vo. Pp vii, 164. Bibliography.

STRONG, JOHN *The Story of Secondary Education in Scotland. An Account of Scottish Secondary Education from Early Times to the Education Act of 1908.* Oxford: At the Clarendon Press, 1909. 8vo. Pp viii, 288.

WRIGHT, ALEXANDER *The History of Education and of the Old Parish Schools of Scotland.* Edinburgh: John Menzies & Co; Portobello: Thomas Adams & Sons; Musselburgh: A C Gordon, 1898. 8vo. Pp viii, 292. Index.

YOUNG, ROBERT 'On the History of Education in Scotland'; *Transactions of the Hawick Archaeological Society for 1879,* pp [16].

BRENNER, EDUARD *Betrachtungen zur Schottischen Erziehungsgeschichte.* Erlanger Forschungen, Reihe A, Band 13. Erlangen, 1962. 4to. Pp 60.

YOUNG, THOMAS P *Histoire de l'Enseignement primaire et secondaire en Écosse, plus spécialement de 1560 à 1872.* Paris et Londres: Librairie Hachette et Cⁱᵉ, 1907. 8vo. Pp xii, 403. 13 plates. Bibliography. Map. Index.

Part Two

From *Acts of the Parliaments of Scotland, 1124-1707.* Edited by Thomas Thomson and Cosmo Innes. 12 vols. Record Commission, 1844, 1814-75. Fol.

General Acts

1496. 13 June, c 3 **2, 238**
That all barronis and frehaldaris of substance put thair eldest sonis and airis to the sculis.

NOTE The suggestion sometimes made, that this act was inspired by Bishop William Elphinstone, the founder of King's College, Aberdeen, seems to rest on no surer foundation than an unverifiable conjecture by Sir Alexander Grant, *Story of the University of Edinburgh* (1884), **2**, 27.

1567. 20 Dec, c 11 **3, 24**
Anent thame that salbe teicheris of the ȝouth in Scuilis.

NOTE This Act merely repeats No 16 of 'Articlis concerning the Kirk', printed at *Acts of the Parliaments of Scotland*, 3, 38.

1579. 11 Nov, c 58 **3, 174**
For instructioun of the ȝouth in musik.

1581. 29 Nov, c 1 **3, 210**
The ratificatioun of the libertie of the trew kirk of god and religioun with confirmatioun of the lawis and actes maid to that effect of before.

Confirms, *inter alia*, the Act of 20 Dec 1567.

1584. 22 Aug, c 2 See under SCOTTISH UNIVERSITIES, p 22, below.

1587. 29 July, c 8 **3, 433**
Annexatioun of the temporalities of benefices to the croun.

1593. 21 July, c 14 **4, 18**
Anent annuellis payit out of the propirtie of the croun to prelattis or beneficit personis.

1594. 8 June, c 98 **4, 94**
Anent hospitallis and schooles.

1598. 29 June, c 2 **4, 160**
Anent ane pastyme day oulklie.

1607. 11 Aug, c 9 **4, 374**
Commissioun anent grammer & teacheris therof.

1609. 24 June, c 3 **4, 428**
Act anent the cheising of pedagoges to children passing furth of Scotland to schooles.

1633. 2 June, c 5 **5, 21**
Ratification of the Act of Counsall Anent plantatione of Schooles.

1633. 28 June, c 34 **5, 48**
Anent Mr David Wedderburnes grammer.

1639. 6 Sept **5, 594**
The Supplicatioune presented by the Commissioners of the Assemblie for . . . erectioune of schooles etc as containing many pointis of greate importance takin for farder consideratioune and advisement.

1640. 6 June, c 20 **5, 277-8**
Act Rescissorie.

1641. 20 Aug **5, 646**
Articles and desires gevine in be the Commissionaris of the kirk to the estates of Parliament: Overtours for universities and schooles.

1641. 8 Sept **5, 657**
Overture for intertayning and erecting of Manufactories for cloathe.

NOTE Included in the proposals put forward here was a detailed apprenticeship scheme.

1641. 9 Sept, c 15 See under SCOTTISH UNIVERSITIES, p 22, below.

1641. 5 Oct **5, 679**
The Commissione anent the kirk and teindis being Red the nobilitie present observit thir remarkis following anent the plantatioune of schooles.

1644. 28 July, c 191 See under SCOTTISH UNIVERSITIES, p 22, below.

1646. 2 Feb, c 167 **6, pt 1, 552-3**
Overtouris [concerning schools] from the commissionaris of the Generall Assemblie with the parliamentis ordinance thairanent.

1646. 2 Feb, c 171 **6, pt 1, 554**
Act for founding of Schooles in euerie paroche.

1647. 26 Mar, c 411   **6**, pt 1, 495
Act anent the educatioune of childrene
vnder popish parentis or tutors.

1655. 30 Mar   **6**, pt 2, 126-7
Instructions given by his Highness the
Lord Protector to . . . his Highness
Councell in Scotland for the Government
of that Nation.

Two of the Instructions, nos 2 and 12,
deal with schools and schoolmasters.
The second of them was repeated in
identical terms as no 13 of the Instructions of 16 June 1658, for which see *Acts
of the Parliaments of Scotland*, **6**, pt 2, 877.

1655. 21 Dec   **6**, pt 2, 837
An Order and Declaration of His Highness Council in Scotland for the Government thereof; for the more equal raising
the assessment of Ten thousand pounds
by the moneth from the last of December
1655 to the first of July 1656.

NOTE One clause in the Order exempted
from the assessment the salaries of all
persons engaged in any form of education.
A similar exemption was contained in the
'Act for Raising of Fifteen Thousand
Pounds Sterling in Scotland' of 17 Sept
1656, for which see *Acts of the Parliaments
of Scotland*, **6**, pt 2, 849.

1661. 28 Mar, c 126   **7**, 860-7
Act Rescinding & annulling the pretendit
Parliaments in the yeers 1640, 1641, &c.

1662. 24 June, c 13   **7**, 379
Act concerning Maisters of vniversities
Ministers &c.

1672. 11 Sept, c 147   **8**, 206
Ratification in favors of Andrew Ander-
sone Printer to the College & City of
Edinburgh and his Co-Partners of the
gift of sole & chieff Printer to his Majestie.

1689. 11 Apr, c 28   **9**, 39
The Declaration of the Estates of the
Kingdom of Scotland containing the
Claim of Right.

1690. 4 July, c 25   **9**, 163
Act for the Visitation of Universities
Colledges and Schoolls.

1693. 12 June, c 38   **9**, 303
Act for Setling the Quiet & Peace of the
Church.

1696. 9 Oct, c 26   **10**, 63-4
Act for Settling of Schools.

1700. 8 Nov   **10**, Appendix, 48
Some things humblie offerred by the
Commissione of the Generall Assembly
to the consideration of his Grace his
Majesties high Commissioner and the
high court of Parliament.

NOTE No 4 of the 'things humblie
offerred' has to do with schoolmasters.

1700. 23 Nov, c 3   **10**, 215-16
Act for preventing the grouth of Popery.

1707. 16 Jan, c 6   **11**, 402-3
Act for Securing the Protestant Religion
and Presbyterian Church Government.

Local Acts
ARGYLLSHIRE

1661. 9 Apr   **7**, Appendix, 33-4
The humble petition of the poore schollers
haueing the Irish language presently
maintaind att Schooles & Colledges by
the Synod of Argyll.

1661. 9 Apr, c 167   **7**, 130
Act anent the poore Schoolers in Argyle.

1663. 17 Sept, c 38   **7**, 478
Act appointing some schollers to be
enterteaned out of the vacant stipends of
Argyll.

1690. 19 July, c 54   **9**, 197
Act concerning vacant Stipends in the
Synod of Argyle.

1695. 12 July, c 48   **9**, 448
Act & Remit in favours of the Synod of
Argyle.

Dunoon

1641. 17 Nov, c 274   **5**, 508
Ratificatione in favours of the Minister
of Donoone.

NOTE Among other provisions is one
obliging him to pay two hundred merks
Scots money to the schoolmaster annu-
ally.

EAST LOTHIAN
Prestonpans

1606. 11 July, c 29   **4**, 302
Erectioun of the Kirk of Prestoun.

NOTE A School for teaching Latin, Greek, and Hebrew was also to be established.

FIFESHIRE
Auchtertool

1641. 17 Nov, c 232   **5**, 477
Ratificatione to the Schoolmaister of Auchtertuill.

Ceres

1633. 28 June, c 101   **5**, 109
Act in favour of Sir Thomas hope of Craighall knicht baronett.
NOTE The income from the vicarage of Kinninmonth was to be used for the maintenance of the schoolmaster at Ceres.

Drummeldrie

1661. 29 May, c 231   **7**, 215
Ratification in favours of the Hospitall of Largo and Grammar School at Drummeldrie of the Mortificatione made be John Wood esquire.

Wemyss

1649. 1 Aug, c 313   **6**, pt 2, 514
Act in favores of Mr Thomas Irland Minister at Wemyss.
NOTE Among other provisions is one obliging him to pay half of the vacant stipend of Logierait for the training of Irish boys at school.

HIGHLANDS AND ISLANDS

1641. 20 Aug   **5**, 646
Overtours from the Generall Assemblie for universities and schooles.

1644. 23 July, c 189   **6**, pt 1, 195
Act declareing vacand stipendes should be imployed upon pious uses.

NOTE It was enacted, *inter alia*, that the vacant stipends of Highland kirks should be used for the training in schools and colleges of youths that have the Irish tongue.

1649. 1 Aug, c 313 See under FIFESHIRE, *Wemyss*.

1658. 4 May   **6**, pt 2, 875
An Ordinance appropriating £1,200 for education in the Highlands.

1663. 17 Sept, c 39   **7**, 478
Act appointing some Scollers to be enterteaned out of the vacant Stipends of the Yles.

MORAYSHIRE
Kinloss

1633. 17 Sept, c 40   **7**, 478
Act allowing a yeers vacant stipend of the kirk of Kinloss for biging a Schoole ther.

PERTHSHIRE
Dunkeld

1606. 11 July, c 53   **4**, 313
Ratificatioun of the erectioun of the schole of dunkeld.

Meigle

1641. 30 Oct, c 51   **5**, 377
Ratification in favoures of the reeder and schoolmaister of Megle kirke.

SUTHERLAND
Dornoch

1641. 17 Nov, c 275   **5**, 509
Ratificatione in favoures of the minister of Dornoche.
NOTE Among other provisions is one obliging him to pay two hundred merks yearly to help to provide a schoolmaster for the grammar school.

WIGTOWNSHIRE
Glenluce

1641. 17 Nov, c 278   **5**, 512
Ratificatione to the Kirk of Glenluce.

1641. 17 Nov   **5**, 586-7
Protestatioun for the Universitie and Colledge of Glasgoue againes the Ratificatioun in favoures of the minister and Schoolmaister of Glenluce.

SCOTTISH UNIVERSITIES

1563. 4 June, c 26   **2**, 544
Anent ane Commissioun to visie the Collegeis of Sanctandros and utheris

within this realme and to reporte to the nixt Parliament.

1567.   20 Dec, c 13   3, 25
Anent the dispositioun of Prouestreis, prebendareis, and Chaplanereis, to Bursaris to be fundit in Collegeis.

1567.   20 Dec   3, 37
Articlis concerning the Kirk.
Article 9.   That prouisioun may be maid for instructioun of the yowth.

1574.   5 Mar   3, 87
Anent the pvnisement of strang and ydle beggaris.
NOTE Among these were included 'all vagaboundis scollaris of the vniversiteis of sanctandrois glasgow and abirdene not licencit be the rector and dene of faculte of the vniversitie to ask almous'. The clause is repeated in the similar Act of 26 Oct 1579, for which see *Acts of the Parliaments of Scotland*, 3, 140.

1578.   25 July, c 5   3, 98
Anent the visitation of the vniversiteis and collegis.

1579.   26 Oct, c 9   3, 138
Anent the ʒouth and vtheris beʒond scy suspectit to have declinit from the trew religioun.

1580.   26 Feb   3, 190
Taxatioun.
NOTE Educational establishments were to be exempted from taxation. This exemption was repeated on 19 Apr 1584, for which see *Acts of the Parliaments of Scotland*, 3, 330.

1584.   22 Aug, c 2   3, 347
Ane Act for ane vniforme ordour to be obserwit be the beneficit men ministeris reiddaris and maisteris of colleges and scuilis in obedience to the kingis maiesteis lawis and thair ordinaris.

1585.   10 Dec, c 24   3, 395
Act for repossessioun of ministaris and maisteris of collegis and scuilis.

1587.   29 July, c 8 See under **General Acts**, p 19, above.

1592.   5 June, c 89   3, 586-7
Anent provestries and prebendaries being laic patronages.

1593.   21 July, c 14   4, 18
Anent annuellis payit out of the propirtie

of the croun to prelattis or beneficit personis.

1594.   8 June, c 33   4, 70
For pvnischement of sum disorderis of studentis and bursaris.

1598.   29 June, c 2 See under **General Acts**, p 19, above.

1625.   1 Nov   5, 177
Letter from his Majestie Anent the childrene of noblemen remaning beyond sea.

1625.   1 Nov   5, 179
Ane Act anent the childrene of noblemen and otheris remaning in seminaryis of popish religioun beyond sea and aganis Jesuitis and messe preistis.

1641.   9 Sept, c 16   5, 350
Act anent raising of malisious Suspensiones against ministeres colledges schooles and hospitalles.

1644.   28 July, c 191   6, pt 1, 196
Act in favoures of . . . Wniversities hospitalls and Schooles Anent Malignantes rentes.

1644.   28 July, c 192   6, pt 1, 196-7
Act anent the Universities of Standrois Glasgou Aberdene and Edinburgh.

1645.   6 Aug, c 34   6, pt 1, 453-6
Continouatione of the act anent pryme places in Wniversities.

1647.   26 Mar, c 411   6, pt 1, 795
Anent the educatioune of childrene vnder popish parentis or tutors.

1652.   4 June   6, pt 2, 810
[Ordinance] By the Commissioners for visiting and Regulating Universities and other matters relating to the Ministry in Scotland.

1653.   16 June   6, pt 2, 750
Instructions to the Commissioners for visiting the Universities in Scotland.

1653.   24 Oct   6, pt 2, 779-80
Authority to the Commissioners on the disposal of vacant places.

1654.   8 Aug   6, pt 2, 831-2
An Ordinance for the better Support of the Universities in Scotland, and encouragement of Publick Preachers there.

1661.   9 July, c 331   7, 303
Act in favours of Laik Patrons of Provestries Prebendaries Chaplanries & Altarages.

1661. 30 May   **7**, Appendix, 76
Commission past for visiteing the Col-
ledges & Vniversities of St Andrews
Glasgow & Edinburgh.

1662. 24 June, c 13   **7**, 379
Act concerning Masters of Vniversities
Ministers etc.

1663. 2 Oct, c 62   **7**, 491
Act for additional provision in favours of
the Universities.

1672. 10 Sept, c 46   **8**, 94-5
Act for imploying Vacand Stipends for
the Universities.

1685. 22 May, c 22   **8**, 474
Act concerning Vacant Stipends.

1689. 5 June   **9**, Supplement, 126,
                               ... note 16
Instructions to the King's Commissioners
for calling the first session of the Parliament of 1689.

NOTE Instruction 16 directs the Commissioners to pass an Act for regulating
the universities in Scotland.

1690. 4 July, c 25   **9**, 163
Act for visitation of Universities Schools
and Hospitals.

1696. 9 Oct, c 14   **10**, 58
Act in favours of Universities Schools
and Hospitalls.

1707. 16 Jan, c 6   **11**, 403
Act for Securing the Protestant Religion
and Presbyterian Church Government.

1707. 16 Jan, c 7   **11**, 414
Act ratifying and approving the Treaty
of Union of the Two Kingdoms of Scotland and England.

Acts of the Parliament and of the Privy
Council of Scotland, relative to the establishment and maintaining of schools, from

the year MCCCCXCVI to the year
MDCXCVI. *Maitland Club Miscellany*,
II, pt 1 (Edinburgh, 1840), 1-37.

13 June 1496. That all Baronis and fre-
halderis of Substance put thair eldest
sonis and airis to the Sculis.

4 June 1563. Anent ane commissioun to
visie the Collegeis of Sanctandrois and
utheris within this realme and to report
to the next Parliament.

3 Dec 1567. Anent the instruction of the
youth. Anent reformation of Scoles and
Collegis.

20 Dec 1567. Anent thame that salbe
teicheris of the youth in Sculis. Anent the
disposition of Provestries Prebendaries
and Chaplanereis to Bursaris to be fundit
in Collegeis.

25 July 1578. Anent the Visitation of the
Universities and Collegis.

11 Nov 1579. For instruction of the Youth
in Musik.

11 Aug 1607. Commission anent Grammer
and teacheris thairof.

10 Dec 1616. Act of the Privy Council of
Scotland appointing a Schoole to be
erectit in euery Parroche.

25 Aug 1626. Letter from King Charles I
to the Archbishops and Bishops for
Schooles to be in euerie Parochin.

28 June 1633. Ratification of the Act of
Secreit Counsall anent plantatione of
Schooles.

2 Feb 1646. Act for founding Schooles in
everie paroche.

4 July 1690. Act for Visitation of Universities Colledges and Schoolls.

9 Oct 1696. Act in favors of Universities
Schools and Hospitalls.

9 Oct 1696. Act for Settling of Schools.

Register of the Privy Council of Scotland

First Series, 1545-1625. 14 vols.
Edinburgh: HM General Register House,
1877-98.

Second Series, 1625-1660. 8 vols.
Edinburgh: HM General Register House,
1899-1908.

Third Series, 1661-1689. 15 vols.
Edinburgh: HM General Register House,
1908-33, 1967.

1561. 15 Feb   **1,** 202
Chaplainries and Friaries in burghs, if
undemolished, to be used for Schools.

1567. 25 July   **1,** 535
Repeats the entry in *Acts of the General
Assembly of the Kirk of Scotland* of 26
June 1565, for which see p 52 below.

1567. 25 July   **1,** 536-7
A band to reform schools colleges and
universities throughout the realm, and to
remove idolaters from them.

1571. 15 Jan   **2,** 107
'Of the dispositioun of Provestreis,
Prebendareis in College Kirkis, fundit
upon temporall landes or annuellis, as
alsua of Chapellanreis, being of the like
foundatioun, for support of the scoles
and increase of letters.'
See under *Acts of the General Assembly of
the Kirk of Scotland*, 16 Jan 1571, p 52
below.

1575. 15 Dec   **2,** 478
One form of [latin] grammar only to be
taught in grammar schools.

1593. 20 Dec   **5,** 110-12
Act anent the teaching of grammar, one
authorised grammar only to be used in
schools in future.

1598. 29 June   **5,** 462
Act establishing Monday as a weekly
half holiday.

1609. 13 Jan   **8,** 550-2
Letter from His Majesty to the Convention of Estates concerning . . . the
education of Scottish youths in foreign
countries, and staying the increase of
popery.

1611. 25 Oct   **9,** 272-3
Act prescribing the Grammar and Rudiments prepared by Mr Alexander Hume
to be the only Grammar and Rudiments
used in grammar schools after 1st November, 1612.
See also **9,** 275-6, 414.

1616. 22 May   **10,** 521-2
Commission to the Archbishops of St
Andrews and Glasgow and to the Bishops
of Galloway and Caithness to examine
a book entitled 'God and the King' and
to report on its fitness for publication.

1616. 13 June   **10,** 534-8
Act making imperative the use in Schools
and Universities throughout Scotland of
the Book entitled 'God and the King',[1]
already similarly made imperative
throughout England and Ireland, and
requiring the doctrines of the book to be
taught by all ministers and schoolmasters,
and copies of the book to be bought by
all families any member of which can
read; granting also a monopoly of the
printing and sale of the said book within
Scotland for twenty-one years to Mr
James Primrose, Clerk of the Council.

1616. 10 Dec   **10,** 672
Act requiring all parents, under specified
penalties, to use the ordinary means of
instruction for their children.

1623. 17 June   **13,** 264-5
Petition of Mr Alexander Ross, schoolmaster at Dunbar, for a renewal of his
privilege of having his Latin grammar
universally used in schools, and appointment of a commission to examine and
report on the new edition of the book
which Mr Hume has prepared.

1623. 31 July   **13,** 318-19
Charge to certain named schoolmasters
to appear before the Council on the 10th
of September next, each bringing some of
his scholars with him, in order to settle
a dispute as to the propriety of granting
the request of Mr Alexander Hume for
a monopoly of his Latin grammar.

1625. 1 Nov   *Second Series,* **1,** 157
Letter from His Majesty to the Council
ordering proclamation for the recall
before 1st May next of all Scottish
children that have been sent to foreign
colleges or other Roman Catholic seminaries for their education.

1625. 1 Nov   *Second Series,* **1,** 162
Act of Convention carrying out His Maj-

---

1. The authorship of this work is usually attributed
to Dr Richard Mockett, an Oxford divine who died
in 1618. It is cast in the form of a dialogue between
two speakers, Theodidactus and Philalethes, and
inculcates most strongly the doctrine of the King's
absolute prerogative in all matters spiritual, ecclesiastical and temporal. Its circulation in Scotland
seems to have met with very great passive resistance,
and the *Register* makes mention of actions by
Primrose against ministers and others for non-payment of the copies supplied to them; see **11,** 392;
12, 42, 118, 229, 601; **13,** 144-5, 164; *Second Series,*
1, 433.

esty's instructions for a proclamation against the education of Scottish children in foreign Popish seminaries.

1629. 27 Jan   Second Series, 3, 20
Charge to noblemen suspected of being popishly inclined to send their sons to be educated at the universities of Glasgow, Edinburgh, or St Andrews.
Entries relating to proceedings against certain noblemen under this charge will be found at *Second Series, 3,* 45, 69-70, 88-9, 91, 98, 99-100, 117, 119, 145, 156, 232-3, 247, 328-9, 331.

1629. 31 Mar   Second Series, 3, 121
Letter to His Majesty anent the education of noblemen's sons in the true religion.
For another letter on the same subject, see *Second Series, 3,* 126.

1629. 29 Oct   Second Series, 3, 328
The Acts of Parliament of 1579 and 1609 anent the education of the children of Papists to be put into force.
This replaced an earlier instruction of the same year to the same effect; see *Second Series, 3,* 246.

1630. 8 July   Second Series, 3, 596-7
Commission to the Bishop of Dunkeld to examine and report on Mr Alexander Hume's Latin grammar.

1631. 10 Mar   Second Series, 4, 163
Commission to the Bishop of Dunkeld and others to arrange for the publication of a Latin grammar to be exclusively used in schools.

1631. 15 Mar   Second Series, 4, 168
Act granting to Mr David Wedderburn, master of the grammar school of Aberdeen, the sole right for twenty-one years of printing his Latin grammar.
Further entries referring to Wedderburn's Latin grammar will be found at *Second Series, 4,* 172, 176, 242, 287-8, 310, 454, 500-1.

1632. 7 June   Second Series, 4, 493
Letter from Charles I anent a new Latin grammar by Mr Robert Williamson, master of the grammar school at Cupar-Fife.

1632. 19 July   Second Series, 4, 514
Letter from Charles I granting to Mr Robert Williamson and his partners the liberty of printing his Latin grammar for twenty-one years.
Williamson and Wedderburn had had earlier in the year an argument about the merits of Wedderburn's grammar: see *Second Series, 4,* 432, 436, 437.

1661. 10 Dec   Third Series, 1, 119
Supplication by the printers and booksellers of Edinburgh anent the printing of schoolbooks.

1672. 1 Feb   Third Series, 3, 450
Act prohibiting the teaching of philosophy and Greek by unauthorised persons outside of the universities.

1674. 28 July   Third Series, 4, 249
Charge to the Archbishops and Bishops to enquire who are acting as chaplains, teachers, and tutors without licence from the ordinary of the diocese.

1674. 2 Oct   Third Series, 4, 292
Monopoly of nineteen years granted to Mr James Kirkwood for the printing of his grammar either in Latin or in any other language.

1675. 13 July   Third Series, 4, 425
Charge to the Archbishops and Bishops anent unlicensed chaplains, teachers, and tutors.

1683. 1 Mar   Third Series, 8, 70
Directions from His Majesty for action against unlicensed schoolmasters and their employers.

1683. 20 Mar   Third Series, 8, 97-8
Instructions to James Crawford, baillie of Carrick, for his dealings with unlicensed schoolmasters.

1683. 4 June   Third Series, 8, 178-9
Royal proclamation prohibiting the employment of chaplains, tutors and schoolmasters who have not taken the Test.

1684. 11 Nov   Third Series, 10, 24
School kept by an unlicensed schoolmaster reported to have been demolished.

1686. 15 Sept   Third Series, 12, 465
Act in favour of Robert Blaw, one of the doctors of St Cuthbert's Grammar School, Edinburgh, for his vocabulary entitled, *Fraus elusa* or *Tenebrae Repulsae.*

1686. 8 Oct   Third Series, 12, 483
Petition by William Maclean anent teachers of dancing.

EDINBURGH

1576. 4 May   **2, 528-9**
Ordinance giving effect to the will of the
late Bishop of Orkney in which he left a
legacy to 'big ane college, in the quhilk
wes appointed to be thre scolis, ane
thairof for the bairnis in grammar, and
[*sic*] uther for thame that leirnis poetre
and oratore, and chalmeris to the
Regentis, with ane hall and uthers
houssis necessar: the thrid scole for
the techeing of the civile and canon
lawis' on the south side of Edinburgh.

1580. 9 Sept   **3, 305-6**
Complaint by the Bailies, Council, and
Kirk of the burgh of Canongate that their
school has been closed by the action of
Mr William Robertson, schoolmaster of
Edinburgh.

1582. 11 Apr   **3, 472-3**
Caution by the Provost, Bailies, and
Council of Edinburgh that they will do
their utmost to recover the money left
by the late Bishop of Orkney for founding a college in Edinburgh.

1675. 22 July   *Third Series*, **4**, 432, 435
Order to the magistrates of Edinburgh
anent 'outed' schoolmasters.

1679. 2 Jan   *Third Series*, **6**, 90-1
Order to the Bishop of Edinburgh to
take the Oaths of Allegiance and
Supremacy from the Principal and Professors of Edinburgh University, and
from all the schoolmasters in that burgh.

1679. 6 Feb   *Third Series*, **6**, 120
Decreet anent the report of the Bishop
of Edinburgh that one professor and six
schoolmasters in Edinburgh had refused
to take the Oaths of Allegiance and
Supremacy.

1680. 11 Nov   *Third Series*, **6**, 572
Order forbidding the keeping of private
schools in Edinburgh. Repeated on 2
June 1681; see *Third Series*, 7, 123.

1681. 2 June   *Third Series*, **7**, 123
Act anent certain Edinburgh schoolmasters, imprisoned because they had
refused to take the Oaths of Allegiance
and Supremacy.

1681. 2 June   *Third Series*, **7**, 123-4
Order for the release of the imprisoned
Edinburgh schoolmasters.

1685. 17 Dec   *Third Series*, **11**, 251
Supplication by Isobel Cumming, who
kept a girls' school in Edinburgh, to be
free of all public burdens.

FIFE
Ballingry

1670. 23 Aug   *Third Series*, **3**, 220
Supplication by the heritors and parish-
ioners of Ballingry, Fife, craving that a
portion of the stipend of the parish be
devoted to erecting a school and schoolhouse there.

Dunfermline

1573. 14 Oct   **2, 288-9**
John Henryson, master of the Grammar
School of Dunfermline, confirmed in his
office after suspension by the Minister of
Dunfermline.

HIGHLANDS AND ISLANDS

1610. 27 July   **9, 28-9**
'Statutes of Icolmkill
   '. . . The quhilk day, it being undirstand
that the ignorance and incivilitie of the
saidis Iles hes daylie incressit be the
negligence of guid educatioun and
instructioun of the youth in the knowledge of God and good letters for remeid
quhairof it is inactit that everie gentilman
or yeaman within the said Ilandis, or
ony of thame, haveing childreine maill
or famell, and being in goodis worth
thriescore ky, sall put at the leist thair
eldest sone, or haveing no childrene
maill thair eldest dochter, to the scuillis
on the Lawland, and interteny and bring
thame up thair quhill thay may be found
able sufficientlie to speik, reid and wryte
Inglische.'
   NOTE This is the sixth of the nine Statutes
of Icolmkill, assented to by the leading
Islesmen at a conference held at Iona on
23 Aug 1609, under the chairmanship of
Andrew Knox, Bishop of Argyll and the
Isles. For an account of the conference,
see GREGORY, DONALD *History of the
Western Highlands and Isles of Scotland*
(Edinburgh, 1836; second edition, Lon-
don, 1881), 326-34; also MACLEAN,
MAGNUS *Historical Development of the
Different Systems of Education in the*

Highlands, The Old Highlands (Glasgow, 1908), 174.

This particular statute had already been printed in BURT, EDWARD *Letters from a Gentleman in the North of Scotland to his Friend in London*, fifth edition, ed JAMIESON, R (London, 1822), **2**, 245, and in 'Collectanea de Rebus Albanicis'; *Transactions of the Iona Club* (Edinburgh, 1834), **1**, pt 1, 119-20.

1616. 17 July   **10**, 777-8
Act ordaining that the children of all the Island Chiefs and of their principal clansmen be sent for their education to schools in the inland country.

NOTE This act had already been printed in 'Collectanea de Rebus Albanicis'; *Transactions of the Iona Club* (Edinburgh, 1834), **1**, pt 1, 121-2, with textual and spelling differences.

A provision to this effect was from time to time inserted in bonds entered into between Crown and individual Islesmen, eg, that of 22 Mar 1617 with Lauchlan MacLean of Duart (*RPCS*, **11**, 74), that of 17 July 1617 with Sir Donald Gorme of Sleat (*RPCS*, **11**, 192), and that of 22 July 1619 with John Macdonald of Ilanteram (*RPCS*, **12**, 34).

1616. 10 Dec   **10**, 671-2
Act ordering that there be an English school in every parish of the Kingdom, and charging the Bishops to see to their provision, [and] that . . . the English tongue [may be] universally planted, and the Irish or Gaelic extirpated.

1629. 16 June   *Second Series*, **3**, 172
'Anent the articlis gevin in be the Bishop of the Ilis aganis the Ilanderis, and first, anent the planting of scoolis, the Lordis remittis to the bishop and Ilanders to consult of the meanes how and of the placeis quhair the scoolis salbe select, and to reporte.'

1661. 1 Aug   *Third Series*, **1**, 21-2
Supplication by two Highland students for assistance by means of vacant stipends to enable them to prosecute their studies.

1664. 1 Mar   *Third Series*, **1**, 518-19
Act in favour of the Bishop of Argyll for the collection of vacant stipends in his diocese to be modified[1] to eight expect-ants[1] who have passed their course in philosophy and to eight scholars who are to be trained at schools and universities.

1665. 28 Mar   *Third Series*, **2**, 38
Supplication by the Earl of Argyll anent certain stipends in the bishopric of Argyll which had been allocated to eight expectants and eight scholars to enable them to continue their studies in schools and colleges.

1666. 20 Dec   *Third Series*, **2**, 240
Supplication by the students in divinity, maintained by the vacant stipends in the diocese of Argyll, anent these stipends.

1669. 26 Nov   *Third Series*, **3**, 97-8
Supplication from a student in divinity in the College of Glasgow anent a modification from the vacant stipends in the bishopric of Argyle and the Isles.

Entries relating to similar applications will be found in the *Third Series*, **3**, 113, 155, 232-3, 379, 495, 578 (*bis*); **4**, 129, 312, 620; **5**, 490; **8**, 337-8.

ORKNEY
Kirkwall

1683. 20 Oct   *Third Series*, **8**, 266-7
Order anent a complaint by the Bishop of Orkney against Mr James Arbuthnot for teaching a school in Kirkwall without licence.

PERTHSHIRE
Coupar-Angus

1685. 19 May   *Third Series*, **11**, 55
Order for a new school to be built at Coupar-Angus.

SCOTTISH UNIVERSITIES

1576. 8 Nov   **2**, 565
Patrons of provostries, etc, may present them to bursars to study at a college in any university in the realm.

1579. 8 Aug   **3**, 199-200
Order for enforcing an Act of the last Parliament for the reformation of the Scottish universities, with special reference to St Andrews, and commission to that effect.

---

1. ie, paid.

1. ie, a candidate for the ministry who has not yet received a licence to preach the gospel.

1584. 18 Dec **3, 713**
Order that there be no married Regents in colleges.

1637. 16 Jan   Second Series, 6, 364
Commission appointed to enquire into the state of the universities.

1665. 22 June   Third Series, 2, 60
Supplication by Alexander Cunningham anent vacant stipends allocated for the use of universities.

1666. 28 June   Third Series, 2, 173-4
Act enjoining that all students at the universities take the Oath of Allegiance before receiving their degree.

1667. 5 Dec   Third Series, 2, 374
Appointment of commissioners to superintend the collection of vacant stipends which are to be appropriated to the benefit of the universities.

1669. 8 July   Third Series, 3, 38
Appointment of a committee for the allocation of vacant stipends for the benefit of the universities.

1672. 4 Mar   Third Series, 3, 482
Escheats of Papists put to the horn to be given to the universities and to the witnesses against them.

1676. 1 Mar   Third Series, 4, 550
Charge to the Archbishops of St Andrews and Glasgow and to the Bishops of Edinburgh and Aberdeen to call before them the principals in the universities and to exact the Oaths of Allegiance and Supremacy from them.

1677. 6 Mar   Third Series, 5, 133-4
Act anent the subscription of the Oaths of Allegiance and Supremacy by the principals and professors of the universities.

1680. 25 Nov   Third Series, 6, 592
Supplication on behalf of the heritors of the parish of Airth for warrant to uplift the vacant stipend of the parish, ordinarily appointed to be paid to the colleges and universities, for the repair of the manse.

1681. 8 Nov   Third Series, 7, 246-7
Masters and doctors of the universities to take the Test before the bishop of their diocese.

Parliament of Great Britain

Acts

1 Geo 1, c 54. An Act for the more effectual securing the Peace of the Highlands in Scotland.   (1715)

Sect 16 made provision for the setting up of a commission to lay before His Majesty 'an Account of the Proper Places for establishing Schools, and of the necessary Salaries for the maintenance of them', since ' "the Want of Schools in proper Places for the Education of Youth within the Bounds aforesaid [ie, in § 1 of the Act] is a great Cause of the Ignorance and Rudeness of the meaner sort of People in those Parts" '.

4 Geo 1, c 8. An Act for vesting the . . . Forfeited Estates in Great Britain and Ireland in Trustees, to be sold for the Use of the Publick.   (1717)

By sect 32 a capital sum of £20,000 was to be set aside out of the proceeds of the sale and the income derived from it was to be used to erect schools in the Highlands of Scotland.

6 Geo 1, c 11. An Act for . . . applying Money arising out of the clear Produce (by Sale of the Forfeited Estates) towards answering His Majesty's Supply.   (1719)

Sect 42 declared that nothing in the Act was to invalidate the grant of £20,000 for Highland schools.

19 Geo 2, c 39. An Act for the more effectual disarming the Highlands in Scotland . . . and for obliging the Masters and Teachers of Private Schools in Scotland, and Chaplains, Tutors, and Governors of Children or Youth, to take the Oaths to His Majesty, his Heirs and Successors, and to register the same [ie, the private schools]. (1746)

21 Geo 2, c 34. An Act to amend and enforce so much of an Act made in the nineteenth Year of His Majesty's Reign, as relates to the more effectual disarming the Highlands in Scotland, . . . and to Masters and Teachers of Private Schools, and Chaplains. (1748)

37 Geo 3, c 103. An Act to raise and embody a Militia Force in that part of the Kingdom of Great Britain called Scotland. (19 July 1797)

Sect 16, 18, 22, and 25 state the duties and rights of parochial schoolmasters under the Act. Minor changes in these were made by the amending Acts of 38 Geo 3, c 44, and 39 Geo 3, c 62.

42 Geo 3, c 73. An Act for the Preservation of the Health and Morals of Apprentices and others, employed in Cotton and other Mills, and Cotton and other Factories. (22 June 1802)

Sect 6 laid down that 'apprentices shall be instructed in Writing, Reading, and Arithmetic, &c.'

42 Geo 3, c 91. An Act to raise and establish a Militia Force in Scotland. (26 June 1802)

Sect 20, 21, 25, 29, and 31 state the duties and rights of parochial schoolmasters under the Act. For amending legislation see 48 Geo 3, c 150.

43 Geo 3, c 54. Parochial Schools (Scotland) Act, 1803. An Act for making better Provision for the Parochial Schoolmasters, and for making further Regulations for the better government of the Parish Schools in Scotland. (11 June 1803)

47 Geo 3, sess 2, c lxxxv. An Act for raising and securing a Fund for the Relief of Widows and Children of Burgh and Parochial Schoolmasters in Scotland. (Private Act, 8 Aug 1807)

6 Geo 4, c 22. An Act to regulate the Qualifications and the Manner of enrolling Jurors in Scotland. (20 May 1825)

Sect 22 exempted all parochial school-masters from the liability to serve as jurors.

10 Geo 4, c 7. An Act for the Relief of His Majesty's Roman Catholic Subjects. (13 Apr 1829)

Sect 16 still excluded them from schools and other educational establishments.

3 & 4 Will 4, c 103. An Act to regulate the Labour of Children and Young Persons in the Mills and Factories of the United Kingdom. (29 Aug 1833)

Sect 20-4 made Regulations on School Attendance.

4 & 5 Will 4, c 84. An Act to apply a Sum of Money out of the Consolidated Fund and the Surplus of Grants to the Service of the Year 1834, and to appropriate the Supplies granted in this Session of Parliament. (15 Aug 1834)

Sect 17 provided, *inter alia*, for a grant not exceeding £10,000 to enable His Majesty to issue money for the erection of schoolhouses, in aid of private subscriptions for that purpose, for the education of the children of the poorer classes in certain great towns in Scotland, and for the erection of Model Schools in England.

1 Vict, c 83. An Act to compel Clerks of the Peace for Counties and other Persons to take the Custody of such Documents as shall be directed to be deposited with them under the Standing Orders of either House of Parliament. (17 July 1837)

Parochial schoolmasters in Scotland are enumerated among the 'other persons'.

1 & 2 Vict, c 87. Highland Schools Act, 1838. An Act to facilitate the Foundation and Endowment of additional Schools in Scotland. (10 Aug 1838)

3 & 4 Vict, c 48. An Act to enable Proprietors of entailed Estates in Scotland to feu or lease on long leases Portions of the same for the building of Churches and Schools, and for Dwelling Houses and Gardens for the Ministers and Masters thereof. (4 Aug 1840)

4 & 5 Vict, c 38. An Act to afford further facilities for the Conveyance and Endowment of Sites for Schools. (21 June 1841)

6 Vict, c xxv. An Act for better raising and securing the Fund for the Relief of Widows and Children of Burgh and Parochial Schoolmasters in Scotland.
(Private Act, 9 May 1843)

6 & 7 Vict, c lxxxvi. An Act to render valid an Act for better raising and securing the Fund for the Relief of Widows and Children of Burgh and Parochial Schoolmasters in Scotland.
(Private Act, 28 July 1843)

7 Vict, c 15. An Act to amend the Laws relating to Labour in Factories.
(6 June 1844)

Sect 38 and 39 made additional Regulations for the attendance of children at school.

7 & 8 Vict, c 37. An Act to secure the Terms on which Grants are made by Her Majesty out of the Parliamentary Grant for the Education of the Poor; and to explain the Act of the Fifth Year of the Reign of Her present Majesty, for the conveyance of Sites for Schools.
(19 Aug 1844)

8 & 9 Vict, c 29. An Act to regulate the Labour of Children, Young Persons, and Women, in Print Works. (30 June 1845)

Sect 23-6 dealt with the attendance of children at school.

8 & 9 Vict, c 33. An Act for consolidating in One Act certain Provisions usually inserted in Acts authorising the making of Railways in Scotland. (21 July 1845)

Sect 7 laid down that plans for proposed railways were to be deposited with parochial schoolmasters.

8 & 9 Vict, c 40. An Act for amending an Act for making Provision for Parish Schoolmasters in Scotland.
(21 July 1845)

8 & 9 Vict, c 83. An Act for the Amendment and better Administration of the Laws relating to the Relief of the Poor in Scotland. (4 Aug 1845)

9 & 10 Vict, c 18. An Act to amend Two Clerical Errors in an Act of last Session, for regulating the Labour of Children, Young Persons, and Women in Print Works. (18 June 1846)

9 & 10 Vict, c ccxxvi. An Act for better

Raising and more securely constituting the Fund for the Relief of Widows and Children of Burgh and Parochial Schoolmasters in Scotland.
(Private Act, 16 July 1846)

12 & 13 Vict, c 49. An Act to extend and explain the Provisions of the Acts for the Granting of Sites for Schools.
(28 July 1849)

13 Vict, c 13. An Act to render more simple and effective the Titles by which Congregations or Societies associated for the Purposes of Religious Worship or Education in Scotland hold Real Property required for such purposes.
(17 May 1850)

14 & 15 Vict, c 24. An Act to amend the Acts for the Granting of Sites for Schools.   (24 July 1851)

17 & 18 Vict, c 74. An Act to render Reformatory and Industrial Schools in Scotland more available for the Benefit of Vagrant Children.   (7 Aug 1854)

17 & 18 Vict, c 86. An Act for the better Care and Reformation of Youthful Offenders in Great Britain.
(10 Aug 1854)

17 & 18 Vict, c 98. An Act to regulate the Salaries of the Parochial Schoolmasters of Scotland.   (10 Aug 1854)

18 & 19 Vict, c 87. An Act to amend the Act for the better Care and Reformation of Youthful Offenders, and the Act to render Reformatory and Industrial Schools in Scotland more available for the Benefit of Vagrant Children.
(14 Aug 1855)

19 & 20 Vict, c 109. An Act to amend the Mode of Committing Criminal and Vagrant Children to Reformatory and Industrial Schools.   (29 July 1856)

24 & 25 Vict, c 132. The Industrial Schools (Scotland) Act, 1861. An Act for consolidating and amending the Law relating to Industrial Schools in Scotland.
(6 Aug 1861)

25 Vict, c 10. An act for continuing for a further limited Time, and for extending the Operation of Orders made under . . . 'The Industrial Schools (Scotland) Act, 1861'.   (11 Apr 1862)

29 & 30 Vict, c 117. The Reformatory

Schools Act, 1866. An Act to consolidate and amend the Acts relating to Reformatory Schools in Great Britain. (10 Aug 1866)

29 & 30 Vict, c 118. The Industrial Schools Act, 1866. An Act to consolidate and amend the Acts relating to Industrial Schools in Great Britain. (10 Aug 1866)

32 & 33 Vict, c 39. Endowed Institutions (Scotland) Act, 1869. An Act to make provision for the better Government and Administration of Hospitals and other Endowed Institutions in Scotland. (26 July 1869)

34 & 35 Vict, c 112. The Prevention of Crimes Act, 1871, § 14, 'Custody of the Children of Women convicted of Crimes'. (21 Aug 1871)

35 & 36 Vict, c 62. The Education (Scotland) Act, 1872. An Act to amend and extend the provisions of the Law of Scotland on the subject of Education. (6 Aug 1872)

SCOTTISH UNIVERSITIES

16 & 17 Vict, c 89. An Act to regulate the Admission of Professors to the Lay Chairs in the Universities of Scotland. (20 Aug 1855)

21 & 22 Vict, c 83. An Act to make provision for the better Government and Discipline of the Universities of Scotland, and improving and regulating the Course of Study therein, and for the Union of the two Universities and Colleges of Aberdeen. (2 Aug 1858)

Bills
EDUCATION AND SCHOOLS

1 Vict. Schools (Scotland). A Bill to facilitate the Foundation and Endowment of additional Schools in Scotland. (6 Feb 1838)   *PP*, 1837/8, vi, 114

8 Vict. Education. A Bill, intituled, An Act to secure the Terms on which Grants are made by Her Majesty out of the Parliamentary Grant for the Education of the Poor; and to explain the Act of the Fifth Year of the reign of Her Majesty for the Conveyance of Sites for Schools. (20 June 1844)   *PP*, 1844, ii, 399

13 Vict. School Establishment (Scotland). A Bill to reform and extend the School Establishment of Scotland. (1 May 1850)   *PP*, 1850, viii, 296

14 Vict. School Establishment (Scotland). A Bill to reform and extend the School Establishment of Scotland. (24 Feb 1851)   *PP*, 1851, vi, 77

17 Vict. Education (Scotland). A Bill to make further Provision for the Education of the People in Scotland, and to amend the Laws relating thereto. (3 Mar 1854)   *PP*, 1854, ii, 37

18 Vict. Schools (Scotland). A Bill to amend the Laws relating to the Parish Schools in Scotland. (9 Feb 1855)   *PP*, 1854/5, vi, 22

18 Vict. Education (Scotland). A Bill to provide for the Education of the People in Scotland. (28 Mar 1855)   *PP*, 1854/5, ii, 69, 211

19 Vict. Education (Scotland). A Bill to make Provision for Education within Burghs in Scotland. (9 Apr 1856)   *PP*, 1856, iii, 94

19 Vict. Parochial Schools (Scotland). A Bill to regulate and make further Provision for Parochial Schools in Scotland. (9 Apr 1856)   *PP*, 1856, v, 95, 203, 257

24 Vict. Parochial and Burgh Schools (Scotland) (No 2). A Bill to alter and amend the Law relating to Parochial and Burgh Schools, and to the Test required to be taken by Schoolmasters in Scotland. (7 June 1861)   *PP*, 1861, iii, 166, 243
NOTE Bill no 1 was never printed.

25 Vict. Education (Scotland). A Bill to make further Provision for Education of the People in Scotland. (21 Mar 1862)   *PP*, 1862, ii, 56

32 Vict. Parochial Schools (Scotland). A Bill, intituled, An Act to extend and improve the Parochial Schools of Scotland, and to make further Provision for the Education of the People of Scotland. (14 June 1869)   *PP*, 1868/9, iv, 164, 215, 265

34 Vict. Education (Scotland). A Bill to amend and extend the Provisions of the Law of Scotland on the Subject of Education. (Apr 1871)   *PP*, 1871, i, 17, 205

35 Vict. Education (Scotland). A Bill to amend and extend the Provisions of the Law of Scotland on the Subject of Education. (Feb 1872)
PP, 1872, i, 31, 204, 210, 264

COMMITTEE OF COUNCIL ON EDUCATION

19 Vict. A Bill intituled An Act for the Appointment of a Vice-President of the Committee of Council on Education. (25 Feb 1856)   *PP*, 1856, vi, 51

ENDOWED HOSPITALS

32 Vict. Endowed Hospitals, &c (Scotland). A Bill to make Provision for the better Government and Administration of Hospitals and other endowed educational institutions in Scotland, and for carrying into effect the main designs of the founders and benefactors thereof. (14 Apr 1869)   *PP*, 1868/9, li, 79, 110, 124

34 & 35 Vict. Endowed Hospitals (Scotland). A Bill to continue and amend the Provisions of the Act of the thirty-second and thirty-third years of Victoria, chapter thirty-nine, intituled, 'An Act to make Provision for the better government and administration of Hospitals and other endowed institutions in Scotland'. (13 July 1871)   *PP*, 1871, ii, 248

SCHOOL ATTENDANCE

4 Vict. A Bill for regulating the Employment of Children and Young Persons in Factories. (26 Mar 1841)
PP, 1841, ii, 184

10 Vict. Print Works. A Bill to amend the Law as to the School Attendance of Children employed in Print-Works. (16 June 1847)   *PP*, 1847, iii, 511

SCHOOLMASTERS

42 Geo 3. A Bill (as amended by the Committee) for bettering the Condition of the Schoolmasters in Scotland, as regulated by an Act made in the Sixth Session of the First Parliament of Scotland, in the reign of King William, intituled 'Act for settling of Schools'. (21 June 1802)   *PP*, 1801/2, i, 21

43 Geo 3. A Bill for making better Provision for the Parochial Schoolmasters, and for the better Government of Public Schools in Scotland. (6 May 1803)
PP, 1802/3, i, 17

47 Geo 3. Schoolmasters (Scotland). A Bill for raising and securing a Fund for Relief of Schoolmasters' Widows and Children in Scotland. (6 May 1807)
PP, 1806/7, i, 134

9 Vict. Schoolmasters (Scotland). A Bill, intituled, An Act for amending an Act for making Provision for Parish Schoolmasters in Scotland. (4 July 1845)
PP, 1845, v, 446

11 Vict. Schoolmasters (Scotland). A Bill to facilitate the Removal of Burgh and Parochial Schoolmasters in Scotland. (29 Mar 1848)   *PP*, 1847/8, vi, 221

17 Vict. Parochial Schoolmasters (Scotland). A Bill to regulate the Salaries of the Parochial Schoolmasters of Scotland. (2 June 1854)   *PP*, 1854, v, 129

20 & 21 Vict. Parochial Schoolmasters (Scotland). A Bill, intituled, An Act concerning the Parochial Schoolmasters in Scotland. (7 Aug 1857)
PP, 1857, iii, 182

20 & 21 Vict. Parochial Schoolmasters (Scotland) (Bill No 2). A Bill concerning the Parochial Schoolmasters in Scotland. (13 Aug 1857)   *PP*, 1857, iii, 194

24 Vict. Parochial and Burgh Schools (Scotland) (No 2). See EDUCATION AND SCHOOLS, above.

32 Vict. Parochial Schoolmasters (Scotland). A Bill to amend the Law relating to the Appointment of Parochial Schoolmasters in Scotland. (12 Apr 1869)
PP, 1868/9, iv, 72

SCHOOL SITES

3 Vict. Entailed Estates (Scotland). A Bill, intituled, An Act to enable Proprietors of Entailed Estates in Scotland to feu or lease on long leases portions of the same, for the building of Churches and Schools, and for Dwelling-houses and Gardens for the Ministers and Masters thereof. (6 June 1840)
PP, 1840, ii, 371

4 Vict. School Sites. A Bill, intituled, An Act for affording further facilities for the Conveyance and Endowment of Sites for Schools. (17 May 1841)
PP, 1841, iii, 322

4 Vict. School Sites. A Bill to afford further facilities for the Conveyance and Endowment of Sites for Schools. (25 May 1841)   *PP*, 1841, iii, 349, 375

8 Vict. Education. See EDUCATION AND SCHOOLS, above.

12 Vict. Sites for Schools. A Bill to extend and explain the Provisions of the Acts for the granting of Sites for Schools. (1 June 1849)   *PP*, 1849, vi, 332

14 & 15 Vict. School Sites Acts Amendment. A Bill, intituled, An Act to amend the Acts for the granting of Sites for Schools. (26 June 1851)
PP, 1851, vi, 444

15 Vict. Schools Sites Acts Extension. A Bill, intituled, An Act to extend the Provisions of the several Acts passed for the Conveyance of Sites for Schools. (17 June 1852)   *PP*, 1852, iv, 486

SCHOOLS, REFORMATORY, AND INDUSTRIAL

17 Vict. A Bill to render Reformatory and Industrial Schools in Scotland more available for the benefit of Juvenile Delinquents and Vagrant Children. (18 May 1854)   *PP*, 1854, vi, 136, 155, 237

18 Vict. A Bill to amend the Youthful Offenders Act. (4 June 1855)
PP, 1854/5, vi, 153

18 Vict. A Bill to amend the Act for the better Care and Reformation of Youthful Offenders. (18 June 1855)
PP, 1854/5, vi, 176, 262

19 Vict. A Bill to make further Provision for rendering Reformatory and Industrial Schools more available for the benefit of Vagrant Children. (19 Feb 1856)
PP, 1856, vi, 42, 70

19 Vict. A Bill to amend the Mode of Committing Criminal and Vagrant Children to Reformatory and Industrial Schools. (31 Mar 1856)
PP, 1856, vi, 75, 102, 140, 153, 220

C

23 & 24 Vict. A Bill to amend the Industrial Schools Act, 1857. (30 July 1860)
PP, 1860, iii, 301

24 Vict. A Bill for consolidating and amending the Law relating to Industrial Schools in Scotland. (8 June 1861)
PP, 1861, ii, 161, 175

25 Vict. A Bill for extending the operation of Orders made under 'The Industrial Schools Act, 1861', and 'The Industrial Schools (Scotland) Act, 1861'. (6 Mar 1862)   *PP*, 1862, ii, 31, 60

29 Vict. A Bill to consolidate and amend the Acts relating to Reformatory Schools in Great Britain. (17 May 1866)
PP, 1866, iii, 62, 184

29 Vict. A Bill to consolidate and amend the Acts relating to Industrial Schools in Great Britain. (17 May 1866)
PP, 1866, iii, 63, 185

SCOTTISH UNIVERSITIES

8 Vict. Universities of Scotland. A Bill to regulate Admission to the Lay or Secular Chairs of the Universities of Scotland. (5 May 1845)   *PP*, 1845, vi, 276

14 Vict. Universities of Scotland. A Bill to regulate Admission to the Lay or Secular Chairs in the Universities of Scotland. (9 May 1851)
PP, 1851, vi, 284

15 Vict. Universities of Scotland. A Bill to regulate Admission to the Lay or Secular Chairs in the Universities of Scotland. (19 Feb 1852)
PP, 1852, iv, 88

'A Bill to extend and improve the Parochial Schools of Scotland, and to make further Provision for the Education of the People of Scotland'; *Education (Scotland) Commission: Second Report* (1867), 88-106.

Reports of Commissions and Select Committees

Select Committee on the State of the Children employed in the Manufactories of the United Kingdom. Minutes of Evidence, 1816.   *PP*, 1816, iii, 397

Evidence on educational conditions in Scotland was given by Archibald Buchanan, 5-11, and Robert Owen, 91-2.

Select Committee on the Education of the Lower Orders in the Metropolis. Third Report: Minutes of Evidence, 1816.
PP, 1816, iv, 495

Evidence on the educational arrangements at New Lanark was given by Robert Owen, 238-42.

Select Committee on the Education of the Lower Orders. Second Report, 1818.
PP, 1818, iv, 356

Evidence on the parochial schools of Scotland, 1-3.

Select Committee on the Education of the Poor. A Digest of Parochial Returns: Scotland. Vol III (1819), 1275-1450.
PP, 1819, ix, 224

Select Committee on the 'Bill to regulate the Labour of Children in the Mills and Factories of the United Kingdom'. Report, with Minutes of Evidence, Appendix, and Index.
PP, 1831/2, xv, 706

Evidence on educational conditions in Aberdeen was given by Abercromby L Gordon, 214-26, in Glasgow by William Smith and James McNish, 235-67, and in Dundee by James Paterson, Peter Smart, and others, 338-94.

Select Committee on Education in England and Wales. Report, 1835.
PP, 1835, vii, 465

Report on the state of education in Glasgow, by Alexander J D Dorsey, 37-46, and in Edinburgh, by James Simpson, 121-206.

Municipal Corporations (Scotland) Commission. Local Reports—pt I (Arbroath to Fortrose). Pp 463.
PP, 1835, xxix, 31
Local Reports—pt II (Glasgow to Wigton). Pp 2, 441.
PP, 1836, xxiii, 32
Local Reports—pt III (Burghs of Regality and Barony, and Unincorporated towns). Pp 163.   *PP*, 1836, xxiii, 33

Scottish Universities Commission, 1826, 'Parochial Education in Scotland'; *Evidence*, I (1837), 233-8.
PP, 1837, xxxv, 92

Education Inquiry (Scotland). Abstract, dated 9 July 1834, of Answers and Returns, 1837. Pp 749.
PP, 1837, xlvii, 133

Select Committee on the State of Education in Scotland. Report, together with the Proceedings of the Committee and Appendix. Pp 15.   *PP*, 1837/8, vii, 715
The heading to the Appendix reads: Abstract of the Copies or Extracts from all the Presbytery Books in Scotland, including Orkney and Shetland, of all the Cases which have been brought before such Presbyteries respecting Parochial Schoolmasters, under Act 43 Geo. 3, c. 54, s. 21, Copies of the Libels served on such Schoolmasters, and Copies of Sentences or Deliverances passed on such Schoolmasters, likewise stating whether such Sentences have been carried into effect in the manner pointed out by the Act.

Select Committee on Emigration (Scotland). First and Second Reports, together with Minutes of Evidence, Appendix, and Index, 1841.   *PP*, 1841, vi, 182, 333
A considerable amount of information about education is scattered through the evidence of the various witnesses, but it can easily be located with the help of the index.

Children's Employment Commission. First Report (Mines)—Appendix, Part I; Report on the Employment of Children and Young Persons in Collieries and Iron-works, and on the State, Condition, and Treatment of such Children and Young Persons, 1842.
PP, 1842, xvi, [381]

Second Report (Trades and Manufactures)—Appendix, Part II.
PP, 1843, xv, [432]
Each volume contains a report on conditions in the West of Scotland, by Thomas Tancred, and one on those in the East of Scotland, by Robert Hugh Franks, in which there is a good deal of information about education; but the only systematic treatment of the subject is to be found in the report by R F Franks, 'Educational Returns'; *First Report* (1842), Appendix B, 425-9.

Select Committee on Schoolmasters' Widows' Fund (Scotland) Bill. Report;

with the Minutes of Evidence and Appendix. Fol. Pp 26.
PP, 1843, xi, 413

Select Committee on Criminal and Destitute Children. Report, together with the Proceedings of the Committee, Minutes of Evidence, and Appendix, 1853.
PP, 1852/3, xxiii, 674

Scottish evidence on the educational aspects of the problem was given for Edinburgh by the Rev Dr Thomas Guthrie, 29-56, and Appendixes 2 and 13, and for Glasgow by J Playfair and John Downie Bryce, 367-83.

Religious Education and Worship (Scotland). Report and Tables, 1854. Pp 121.
PP, 1854, lix, [1764]

Select Committee on Education (Inspectors' Reports). Report, together with the Proceedings of the Committee, Minutes of Evidence, and Appendix. Pp xii, 66, 75.
PP, 1864, ix, 468

—Index to the Report. Pp 19.
PP, 1864, ix, 468-I

Select Committee appointed to inquire into the Constitution of the Committee of Council on Education, and the System under which the Business of the Office is conducted; and also the Best Mode of extending the Benefits of Government Inspection and the Parliamentary Grant to schools at present unassisted by the State. Report, together with the Proceedings of the Committee, Minutes of Evidence, and Appendix, 1865. Pp xii, 478.
PP, 1865, vi, 403

—Index to the Report. Pp vi, 99.
PP, 1865, vi, 403-I

—[Second] Report, together with the Proceedings of the Committee, Minutes of Evidence, Appendix, and Index. Pp xx, 381.
PP, 1866, vii, 392

Scottish evidence, given on 13 Mar 1866 by Patrick Cumin, will be found in the Second Report, 57-68.

Education (Scotland) Commission. First Report, 1865. Minutes of Evidence. Pp 404.
PP, 1865, xvii, [3483]

—Appendix to First Report, being Answers to Heads of Examination, and Correspondence, 1867. Pp 139.
PP, 1867, xxv, [3858]

—Statistics relative to Schools in Scotland. Pp 256. Index.
PP, 1867, xxvi, [3845-V]

—Second Report, with an Appendix, 1867. Elementary Schools. Pp clxxxv, 112.
PP, 1867, xxv, [3845]

CONTENTS Introduction. Chapter I, Lowland Parishes of Scotland. Chapter II, The Towns of Scotland. Chapter III, The Hebrides and Western Highlands. Chapter IV, The Privy Council System and the Revised Code. Chapter V, Ages of the Scholars and Attendance at School. Chapter VI, School-buildings, Teaching, and Teachers. Chapter VII, Cost of Education, and Mode of defraying it. Chapter VIII, Recommendations. Appendix of Tables. Maps to illustrate the State of Education in the Hebrides and in Glasgow.

—Statistical Report on the State of Education in the Lowland Country Districts of Scotland, by C F Maxwell and A C Sellar, 1866. Pp 38.
PP, 1867, xxv, [3845-I]

—Report on the State of Education in Glasgow, by John Greig and Thomas Harvey, 1866. Pp 159.
PP, 1867, xxv, [3845-II]

—Report on the State of Education in the Country Districts of Scotland, by A C Sellar and C F Maxwell, 1866. Pp 238. 10 plates.
PP, 1867, xxv, [3845-III]

—Report on the State of Education in the Hebrides, by Alexander Nicolson, 1866. Pp 200.
PP, 1867, xxv, [3845-IV]

—Third Report, with an Appendix. Volume I—Burgh and Middle-Class Schools, together with the General Report of the Assistant Commissioners, 1868. Pp lxxviii, 271.
PP, 1867/8, xxix, [4011]

—Third Report. Volume II—Special Reports of the Assistant Commissioners on Burgh and Middle-Class Schools, 1868. Pp iv, 366.
PP, 1867/8, xxix, [4011-I]

Schools Inquiry Commission. Report on Certain Burgh Schools, and other Schools of Secondary Education in Scotland. By D R Fearon, 1868. Pp xii, 222.
PP, 1867/8, xxviii, pt V, [3966-V]

CONTENTS I. Cost of Education in Burgh Schools. (i) The Cost of keeping Master and Pupil in contact. (ii) Price paid for Instruction. II. Class of Scholars receiving Education. (i) Mixture of social classes in Scotch Burgh Schools. (ii) Length of time and age to which scholars remain. III. Character of the Buildings and Premises of Burgh Schools. IV. The Quality of the Teaching. (i) Qualifications of Scotch teachers—Their educational status and preparation for the office of teacher. (ii) Method of Instruction. V. The effects of education on the scholars. (i) As regards the education of boys. (ii) As regards the education of girls. Conclusion. ['Education to be good must be popular.']

Endowed Schools and Hospitals (Scotland) Commission. First Report, with Evidence and Appendix, 1873. Pp [viii] 771.   *PP*, 1873, xxvii, [C755,
—Second Report, with Evidence and Appendix, 1874. Pp viii, 696.
    PP, 1874, xvii, [C976]
—Third Report, 1875. Pp 255.
    PP, 1875, xxix, [C1123]
—Appendix to Third Report. Vol I. Detailed Statement of Hospital Endowments and of General and Mixed Endowments; Reports by Secretary and Assistant Commissioner; Evidence, 1875. Pp iv, 434.   *PP*, 1875, xxix, [C1123-I]
—Appendix to Third Report. Vol II. Statistics, 1875. Pp 6, 370.
    PP, 1875, xxix, [C1123-II]

STUART, JAMES 'Scotland'; *Report from each of the four Factory Inspectors on the Effects of the Educational Provisions of the Factories Act* (1839), 65-70.
    PP, 1839, xlii, 42

HOUSE OF LORDS

Report from the Select Committee appointed to inquire into the Duties, Emoluments, and present Condition of the Parochial Schoolmasters in Scotland, and the present state of the Law as it affects them; together with the Minutes of Evidence taken before the Committee. Pp 151.   *H of L Papers*, 1845, xix, 211
NOTE The Education Commission appointed in 1858, under the chairmanship of the Duke of Newcastle, to inquire into the state of popular education in England had no direct concern with education in Scotland. Its Recommenda-

tions, however, contained in its *Report*, vol I (1861), 542-52, were largely embodied in the Revised Code of 1862 and therefore had a considerable indirect influence on Scottish education. For criticisms of the Commission's *Report*, see the communications of Sir James Kay-Shuttleworth and of S Tremenheere in *Parliamentary Papers*, 1861, xlviii.

Parliamentary Papers

FINANCE

An Estimate of the sum required to be granted in the Year ending 31 March 1835, to enable His Majesty to issue Money for the Erection of School Houses, in aid of Private Subscriptions for that Purpose, for the Education of the Children of the Poorer Classes in certain great Towns of Scotland, and for the Erection of Model Schools in England. Ten Thousand Pounds.
    PP, 1834, xlii, 311, 1

An Estimate of the sum that will be required to be voted, to enable His Majesty to issue Money for the Erection of School-Houses, in aid of Private Subscriptions for that Purpose, for the Education of the Children of the Poorer Classes in certain Great Towns in Scotland; and for the Erection of Model Schools in Scotland. Ten Thousand Pounds.
    PP, 1836, xxxviii, 525, 6; 1837, xl, 148, 7

An Estimate of the sum that will be required to be voted in the year 1838, to enable Her Majesty to issue Money for the Erection of School Houses, in aid of Private Subscriptions for that Purpose, for the Education of the Children of the Poorer Classes in Scotland. Ten Thousand Pounds.
    PP, 1837/8, xxxvii, 313, 8
Supplementary Estimate, 1842-43. P 1.
    PP, 1842, xxvii, 492

A Return of the Applications made from Scotland, for Participation in the Grants of £10,000 voted in the Estimates of the Years 1835 and 1836, in aid of Education in that Country; specifying the Date of each Application, the Place from whence it came, the Parties by whom it was made, and the Date and Purpose of the Answer. Pp 9. *PP*, 1837, xxxix, 304

A List of Applications for Grants out of the £30,000 voted for Education in the Year 1839; similar Returns with reference to the sum of £10,000 voted in 1835, for Normal and Model Schools.
PP, 1840, xl, 124, 14-16; xl, 470, 3-4

List of Applications for Grants out of the Sums voted for Education in the Years 1840-41 and 1842-43:—also, of Applications still under Consideration. Pp 55.
PP, 1843, xl, 444

An Account of all Sums of Money granted in pursuance of an Act of last Session in Aid of the Erection of Schools in England and Scotland; stating the Places in which the Schools are situated, the Description of the School, and the respective Amounts contributed. *PP*, 1835, xl, 236, 8-9

An Account of all Sums of Money granted by Parliament in Aid of the Erection of Schools in Scotland in 1834-35; stating the Places in which the Schools are situated, Description of the School, and the respective Amounts applied for and contributed.
PP, 1836, xlvii, 502, 19; 1837, xli, 372, 8-9

An Account of the Expenditure of the Several Sums of £10,000 granted by Parliament in the Years 1834, 1835, 1836, 1837, and 1838 for the Erection of School-Houses or Model Schools in Scotland; together with the Names and Designations of all Parties from whom Applications have been received by the Lords of Her Majesty's Treasury for Aid out of the above Grants, stating whether for Parochial, or for what other Schools, with the Answers thereto: specifying the Dates of each. Pp 30.
PP, 1839, xli, 282

Detailed Account of the Manner in which the Sum of £30,000 voted for Education in the last Session of Parliament has been expended; Similar Returns with Reference to the Sum of £10,000, voted in 1835, for Normal and Model Schools.
PP, 1840, xl, 124, 14-16; 1840, xl, 470, 3-4

A Return of the Number and Locality of Schools in Scotland to which Aid has been granted by the Educational Com-

mittee of the Privy Council;—also, Correspondence relating to the Application for Aid towards the Erection of Schools in the Northern District of Edinburgh. Pp 19. *PP*, 1844, xlii, 309

Return of all Sums which have been granted under Authority of the Committee of Council for Educational Purposes in Scotland; showing the Date of each Grant, the special Purpose to which each Grant has been applied, the Names of the Places in which the Schools receiving Aid are situated, and the Religious Body with which they are connected. Pp 4. *PP*, 1847/8, 1, 197

Return of all Sums granted under the Authority of the Committee for Educational Purposes in each County in Scotland, 1848-49; distinguishing the Religious Bodies with which the Schools to which the Grants were made are connected. Pp 5. *PP*, 1849, xlii, 279

Return showing the Sums received on Account of the Parliamentary Education Grant each Year, 1839 to 1850, by the Committee of Council, and the Appropriation of such Sums, distinguishing various Particulars; Amount of Grants made to Training Schools; List of Applications made to the Committee for Aid to erect Schools, from 28 June 1847 to the present Time; List of Schoolbooks, for the Purchase of which Grants are made; Returns showing the Instructions issued from time to time to the Inspectors; Regulations respecting Pupil Teachers and Stipendiary Monitors. Pp 155. *PP*, 1851, xliii, 103

A Return of all Sums granted under the Authority of the Committee of Privy Council for Educational Purposes, in each County of Scotland, for each of the Years 1847, 1848, 1849, and 1850, stating the Names of the Places in which the Schools receiving Aid are situated, and the Religious Body with which each School is connected, and distinguishing the Parochial Schools from other Schools connected with the Established Church. Pp 9. *PP*, 1851, xliii, 446

Return of the Number of Schools in Scotland which have received Aid in connexion with the Minutes of Council; and, of Number of Apprenticed pupils connected with each Religious Body; stated separately as to the Number connected with each Religious Body, and how much paid to Apprentices; and to Teachers, separately stated, for having Apprentices. P 1.   *PP*, 1852, liii, 266

Tabular Statement of the Expenditure from the Grants for Public Education for Great Britain, in the Year ended 31 December 1854, with an Appendix. Pp 11.   *PP*, 1854/5, xli, 167

Return showing the Total Amount of Education Grants from the Privy Council to each County in Scotland, from 1833 to 1855; distinguishing the Object of the Grant, and the Religious Denomination to which it was paid. Pp 7.
    PP, 1854/5, xli, 316

Returns for the Years 1854, 1855, and 1856 respectively, of the Names of the Parishes in each County in Scotland within whose Bounds any School is situated, in respect of which any Money has been paid under the Authority of the Committee of Council of Education; stating the Number of such Schools in each Parish, and the Aggregate Amount paid in respect of such Schools in each Parish; and the names of the Places in each Parish in which such Schools are situated, and the Religious Body to which each is connected; distinguishing the Parochial Schools from other Schools connected with the Established Church, and specifying the Amount paid to each School in each Year. Pp 29.   *PP*, 1857/8, xlvi, 40

Return, for the Year 1857, of the Names of the Places in each Parish and each County in Scotland, in which any School is situated, in respect of which any Money has been paid under the Authority of the Committee of Council on Education, stating the Amount paid for each Parish and each County respectively: specifying the Religious Body with which each School is connected, and distinguishing the Parochial Schools from other Schools connected with the Established Church. Pp 15.
    PP, 1859, xxi—pt 2, 105; 1859, sess 2, xix, 149

Return showing the Amounts of Grants which have been made by the Committee of Her Majesty's Privy Council on Edu-

cation to Reformatories, Ragged Industrial Schools, or any other Institutions in England and Scotland under whatever Designation, in accordance with the Minute dated 2 June 1856, from that date to 31 December 1857. Pp 5.
    PP, 1859, xxi—pt II, 227

Return of the Amount Paid to each Parish or Place in 1860-61, under the Heads of Grants to Certificated Teachers, Assistant or Probationary Teachers, Pupil Teachers, and Gratuities to Masters and Mistresses, and Capitation Grants, and the Total Amount of all such Grants paid to each Parish or Place. Pp 103.
    PP, 1863, xlvi, 141

A Return of all Endowed Schools receiving Grants from Government in the Years 1862 and 1863; showing the Amount of such Grants, and also the Amount received by each School from all other sources.   *PP*, 1864, xliv, 204, 37-43

Number of Grants made in each Year, 1859-1866, for Building, Enlarging or Improving Elementary Day Schools, with the Total Amount of such Grants:— Number of Schools inspected, distinguishing Schools from Departments of Schools:—Average Number of Scholars attending the Schools inspected, and the Number of Scholars present on the Day of Inspection:—Number of Certificated Teachers acting in the Schools inspected. P 1.   *PP*, 1867, lv, [3832]

Salary

Returns of the Total Amount of School Salary payable by the Landward Heritors, in every Parish in Scotland, under the Act 43 Geo. 3, c. 54, as at the date of the passing of the Act 24 & 25 Vict. c. 107: Of the Total Amount of the Addition made to such Salaries under the last mentioned Act, including Allowances to Female Teachers: Of the Amount of the Annual Grants from the Committee of Council on Education in the Year 1861, to schools in every Parish, distinguishing 1. Parochial Schools; 2. Schools within Burghs; and, 3. Other Schools; and of the Amount of the Building Grants by the Committee of Council to such Schools in 1861, distinguishing the School as above. Pp 29.   *PP*, 1863, xlvi, 2

Schoolmasters

'Abstract from Return of Inquiries into the Misdemeanours committed by School-masters in Scotland'; *Report from the Select Committee on the State of Education in Scotland* (1838). Pp 9-15.
PP, 1838, vii, 715

Return of the Parochial Schoolmasters in Scotland who have retired, or have been removed, from their Situations, in consequence of their Secession from the Established Church, subsequent to the month of May, 1843. Pp 3.
PP, 1844, xlii, 610

Abstract of Returns of the Number of Parochial Schoolmasters in Scotland, showing the Offices other than that of Schoolmaster, which they may hold, and the Emoluments derived therefrom. Pp 2.
PP, 1847/8, l, 51

Return of Copies or Extracts from all the Presbytery Books in Scotland, including Orkney and Shetland, of all the Cases which have been brought before such Presbyteries, respecting Parochial School-masters, under the Act 43 Geo. 3, c. 54, s. 21, from 1838 to 1853 inclusive:—Of the Libels served on such Schoolmasters, and of Sentences or Deliverances passed upon them, likewise stating whether such Sentences have been carried into effect:— And, Abstract of the above Returns in the Form used in the Appendix to Report of the Select Committee on the State of Education in Scotland, 1838. Pp 180.
PP, 1854, lix, 511

See also STATISTICAL RETURNS. Return of the several Grammar Schools, High Schools, and other Burgh Schools in Scotland, subject to the Administration of the Magistrates and Council, and not falling under 43 Geo. 3, c. 54, or provided with Salaries to the Teachers thereunder.

SCHOOLS

Answers made by Schoolmasters in Scotland to Queries circulated in 1838, by Order of the Select Committee on Education in Scotland. Part I.— Schools not Parochial. Pp 789. Part II.— Parochial Schools. Pp 312.
PP, 1841, xix, 64

Schools, Highland

Proceedings taken by the Lords of the Treasury for carrying into Effect an Act of the 1st & 2nd Victoria, c. 87, 'for facilitating the Foundation and Endowment of additional Schools in Scotland'; showing the Schools endowed, and the Money invested, for the Purpose of carrying the Provisions of the Act into Effect. Pp 14.
PP, 1840, xl, 382

Account of Schools in the Highlands and Islands of Scotland, endowed under the Provisions of the Act 1 & 2 Vict., c. 87. P 1.
PP, 1841, sess 2, ii, 29; 1842, xxxiii, 543

Return of Sums payable in the Year 1866 on Account of Grants made to facilitate the Foundation and Endowment of additional Schools in Scotland, in pursuance of the Act 1 & 2 Vict., c. 87. P 1.
PP, 1867, lv, 15

Return pursuant to the Act 1 & 2 Vict. c. 87, s. 13, showing the Amounts Received and Paid during the Year ended 31st December 1870, for Facilitating the Foundation and Endowment of Schools in the Highlands and Islands of Scotland. P 1.
PP, 1871, lvi, 32

Return pursuant to the Act 1 & 2 Vict. c. 87, s. 13, showing the Sums of Money invested and Appropriated, and the Schools endowed under the Provisions of that Act, for the Year from 1st January to 31st December 1871. P 1.
PP, 1872, xlvi, 266

Schools, Inspection of

Correspondence between Her Majesty's Government and the General Assembly of the Church of Scotland, respecting the Appointment, &c, of Inspectors of Schools for Scotland. Pp 48.
PP, 1841, xx, 392

Schools, Parish (County of Edinburgh)

Return for the Year 1871, respecting the different parishes of the County of Edinburgh, showing the Total Amount paid or payable in that year by the Heritors, for all purposes connected with Parish-Schools and School-Houses, in-

cluding the Salaries and Houses of the Schoolmasters. Pp 4.
PP, 1872, xliv, 159

Schools, Parochial

Return of Number of Heritors qualified to attend and vote at any Meeting held pursuant to the Act of 43 Geo. 3, c. 54, s. 22, in all Parishes in Scotland, in which a Parochial School is established. Pp 10.
PP, 1868/9, xlvii, 411

Supplementary Return, showing the Number of Heritors qualified to attend and vote at any meeting held pursuant to the Act of 43 Geo. 3, c. 54, s. 22, in all Parishes in Scotland in which a Parochial School is established. P 1.
PP, 1870, liv, 40

STATISTICAL RETURNS

A General Table showing the State of Education in Scotland. Pp 3.
PP, 1820, xii, 224

Parochial Education, Scotland. Returns from the Sheriffs of the several Counties of Scotland, relative to the Parochial Schools of Nine Hundred and five Parishes, showing the State of the Establishments for Parochial Education in Scotland. Pp iv, 985.
PP, 1826, xviii, 95

Abstract of Returns relating to the Population, and Number of Schools &c, in each of the Counties, Cities, and Burghs, Scotland (according to the Census of 1851). Pp 22.   *PP*, 1854, lix, 502

Returns of the Parochial and Burgh Schools, with the Number of Scholars at each, in the Royal Burghs and Parliamentary Towns of Aberdeen, Airdrie, Ayr, Arbroath, Banff, Cupar, Dumfries, Dundee, Dunfermline, Dysart, Edinburgh, Elgin, Forfar, Falkirk, Glasgow, Greenock, Haddington, Hamilton, Inverness, Kilmarnock, Kirkcaldy, Leith, Montrose, Perth, Port Glasgow, Paisley, Portobello, Peterhead, Rutherglen, Stranraer, Wigton and Wick. Pp 4.   *PP*, 1854, lix, 512

Census of Great Britain, 1851. Religion, Worship, and Education. Pp 111.
PP, 1854, lix, [1764]

Return showing the Proportion of Scholars (or Children attending School) to the Population in each County of Scotland, so far as it can be exhibited by the Census of 1851. P 1.   *PP*, 1854/5, xli, 302

Return of the Number of Schools which have been erected under the Minute of Her Majesty's Most Honourable Privy Council of Education of the 2nd Day of April 1853, as well as those erected by the Minute of the 14th Day of July 1855; from the 1st day of January 1854 to the 31st day of December 1859. Fol. Pp 14.
PP, 1860, liii, 508

Return of the Several Grammar Schools, High Schools, and other Burgh Schools, in the Burghs of Scotland, subject to the Administration of the Magistrates and Council, and not falling under 43 Geo. 3, c. 54, or provided with Salaries to the Teachers thereunder; setting forth the Number of Teachers in every such School and specifying how many of the present Teachers are members of the Church of Scotland; the Number of appointments of Teachers in every such School during the last sixty Years; and the Number of Instances in which the Teachers appointed during that period were examined and passed by the Presbytery of the Bounds, and subscribed the Confession of Faith and Formula; and also the Number of Instances during such period in which any such Teachers have been removed or dismissed from their Office, with the Number of Instances in which the Removal or Dismissal has been by Sentence of such Presbytery. Fol. Pp 5.
PP, 1861, xlviii, 139

Return of the Number of Schools (other than Burgh Schools, or Schools within a Royal Burgh, and other than Adventure Schools) in every Parish in Scotland, stating the Area of each Parish, and the Distance of the Schools in such Parish from each other, and specifying the Description of each School, whether Parochial or connected with any Committee, or Society, or Religious Denomination; and also showing the Number of Pupils in ordinary Attendance at every such School at the Date of the Return. Fol. Pp 136.   *PP*, 1862, xliii, 67

Returns of the Time to the 31st day of July 1866, during which the examinations of the Revised Code have been in Operation in England and Scotland respectively. Pp 4.   *PP*, 1867/8, liii, 54

See also FINANCE. Number of Grants made in each Year, 1859-1866; also, Education Commission (Scotland). *Statistics relative to Schools in Scotland* (1865); *Statistical Report* (1866).

SCHOOLS, REFORMATORY AND INDUSTRIAL

Return of the Number and Names, and in what County situated, of the Private Reformatory Schools which have been certified by Government; whether for Boys or Girls; and the Number of Boys or Girls which each School is capable of containing. P 1.   *PP*, 1854/5, xli, 269

Abstract of Return of the Number of Children under Fifteen Years of Age (distinguishing Boys from Girls) in Prison Schools at the latest date for which the same can be given; and, similar Return of Children in Industrial, Ragged, and Reformatory Schools assisted within the past year as Schools of Industry by the Committee of Privy Council for Education, showing the Number in each School at the latest date, and the Amount of Grant in each case. Pp 5.
PP, 1856, xlix, 164

Return of all Reformatories which have been certified in England and Scotland, and of any Reformatories which have been refused Certification; and the Grounds, in each case, of such refusal. Pp 2.   *PP*, 1856, xlix, 47

Returns showing the Number of Reformatory and Industrial Schools certified and sanctioned by the Secretary of State, under the Acts 17 & 18 Vict. c. 86, and 17 & 18 Vict. c. 74, respectively; and of the Number of Children, distinguishing Boys from Girls, which each of such schools is capable of accommodating, and the number contained in each at the latest date. Pp 12.   *PP*, 1857, sess 1, xiii, 153

Reformatory Schools certified and sanctioned by the Secretary of State under the Statutes 17 & 18 Vict. c. 74, and 17 & 18 Vict. c. 86, respectively, with the Date of Certificate; Number of Juveniles (distinguishing Boys from Girls) which each of such Schools is capable of accommodating; and the numbers contained in each. Pp 3.
PP, 1857/8, xlvii, 204

Return showing the Amount of Grant which has been made by the Committee of the Privy Council on Education, to Reformatories, Industrial Schools, or other Institutions in England and Scotland, in accordance with the Minute dated 2 June 1856, from that date to 31 December 1857. Pp 5.
PP, 1860, xxi, pt ii, 227

Return for the Year 1860, giving a Tabulated list, alphabetically arranged in their respective Counties, of all Reformatory Schools which have been certified and sanctioned by the Secretary of State, under the Statutes 17 & 18 Vict. c. 74 and 86, and the 21 Vict. c. 103[1] respectively, with the Date of Certificate; also, the Number of Juveniles (distinguishing Boys from Girls) which each of such Schools is capable of accommodating; and the Number contained in each at the latest date for which the Return can be given, according to the Forms of similar Return of 1859:—And, of the Amount of Money contributed by the Parents of Inmates towards their Maintenance in such Reformatory Schools, during the Twelve Months ending 31 March 1860. Pp 5.   *PP*, 1860, lvii, 444

Reports of the Inspector, appointed under the Provisions of the Act 5 & 6 Will. IV, c. 38,[2] to visit the different Reformatory and Industrial Schools of Great Britain.
PP, 1857/8, xxix, [2426]; 1859, sess 2, xiii, pt 2, [2537]; 1860, xxxv, [2688]; 1861, xxx, [2874]; 1862, xxvi, [3034]; 1863, xxiv, [3194]; 1864, xxvi, 9764; 1865, xxv, 12373; 1866, xxxviii, 15677; 1867, xxxvi, 18946; 1867/8, xxxvi, 1868/9, xxx, [4183]; 1870, xxxvi, [c 170]; 1871, xxviii, [c 373]; 1872, xxx, [c 628].

Minutes of the Committee of Council on Education

Papers on Education, dated 4, 6 and 9 February 1839. Pp 3.
PP, 1839, xli, 16

1. This Act applied only to Ireland.
2. 5 & 6 Will 4, c 38. An Act for . . . appointing Inspectors of Prisons in Great Britain. (25 Aug 1835)

Order in Council, dated 10 April 1839, appointing a Committee of Council to superintend the Application of any Sums voted by Parliament for the Purpose of promoting Public Education. P 1.
PP, 1839, xli, 287

Scheme, dated 13 April 1839, for the Guidance of the Committee of Council on Education. Pp 3.
PP, 1839, xli, 177

Report, dated 3 June 1839, of the Committee of Council appointed to superintend the Application of any Sums voted by Parliament for the purpose of promoting Public Education. P 1.
PP, 1839, xli, 284

Minutes, with Appendices, and Plans of School-houses, 1839-40. Pt II. Pp 206.
PP, 1840, xl, 254

Extracts from Minutes of 4 January and 15 July 1840. Pp 3.   *PP*, 1840, xl, 490

Minutes, with Appendices
1840/1. *PP*, 1841, xx, [317]
1841/2. *PP*, 1842, xxxiii, [442]
1842/3. *PP*, 1843, xl, [520]
1843/4. *PP*, 1845, xxxv, [622]
1845.   *PP*, 1846, xxxii, [741]
1846/7. *PP*, 1847, xlv, [787]
1847/8. *PP*, 1848, l, [998]

Minutes passed subsequently to August 1840.   *PP*, 1843, xl, [25]

Supplementary Minute dated 10 July 1847, on Religious Instruction in Schools.
PP, 1847, xlv, 660

Minutes in August and December, 1846.
PP, 1847, xlv, [787]

Minutes, with Appendices, with Maps and Plans, 1846.   *PP*, 1847, xlv, [866]

Minutes, with Correspondence, &c, 1848-49.
PP, 1849, xlii, [1090]

Minute, with Correspondence, Tabular Statements of Grants, &c, and Reports by Her Majesty's Inspectors of Schools, 1848-49-50. Vol I. 1850, xliii, [1215]; Vol II. 1850, xliv, [1216]

Minutes, with Correspondence, Financial Statements, and Reports of Her Majesty's Inspectors of Schools
1850/1, vol I. 1851, xliv, [1357]: vol II. 1851, xliv, [1358]; 1851/2, vol I. 1852,

xxxix, [1479]: vol II. 1852, xl, [1480]; 1852/3, vol I. 1852/3, lxxix, [1623]: vol II. 1852/3, lxxx, [1624]; 1853/4, vol I. 1854, li, [1787]: vol II. 1854, lii, [1788]; 1854/5. 1855, xlii, [1926]: 1855/6. 1856, xlvii, [2058]; 1856/7. 1857, sess 2, xxxiii, [2237]; 1857/8. 1857/8, xlv, [2380]

Reports, with Appendices
1858/9. 1859, sess 1, xxx, pt I, [2510]; 1859/60. 1860, liv, [2681]; 1860/1. 1861, xlix, [2828]; 1861/2. 1862, xlii, [3007]; 1862/3. 1863, xlvii, [3171]; 1863/4. 1864, xlv, [3349]; 1864/5. 1865, xlii, [3533]; 1865/6. 1866, xxvii, [3666]; 1866/7. 1867, xxii, [3882]; 1867/8. 1867/8, xxv, [4051]; 1868/9. 1868/9, xx, [4139]; 1869/70. 1870, xxii, [165]; 1870/1. 1871, xxii, [406]; 1871/2. 1872, xxii, [601, 601-I]; 1872/3. 1873, xxiv, [812, 812-I]

Regulations as to the Distribution of the Parliamentary Grant for the Promotion of Education in Great Britain. Minute, dated 22 November 1843. Pp 7.
PP, 1844, xxxviii, 84

Copies of all Minutes, arranged in Chronological Order, with Marginal Headings of Subjects. Pp 128.
PP, 1854/5, xli, 158

Continuation, up to the Present Time, of a Return (No. 158, Session 1855) of all Minutes, arranged in Chronological Order, with Marginal Headings of Subjects. Pp 14.   *PP*, 1857/8, xlvi, 191

Consolidation of Minutes and Regulations now in Force. Pp 79.
PP, 1857/8, xlvi, 192

Copy of all Minutes, arranged in Chronological Order, with Marginal Headings of Subjects. Pp 5.   *PP*, 1860, liii, 141

Copy of Minutes and Regulations reduced into the Form of a Code. Dated 19 April 1860. Pp 34.   *PP*, 1860, liii, 252

Minute, dated 29 July 1861, establishing a Revised Code of Minutes and Regulations; Reprinted, with proposed alterations, and marked to show which Articles are retained from the Code of 1860. Pp 37.   *PP*, 1862, xli, [2924]

Changes proposed to be introduced into the Revised Code, as last printed. Pp 3.
PP, 1862, xli, [2968]

Minute, dated 9 May 1862, confirming the alterations of the Revised Code of Regulations, and specifying the course to be adopted for putting it into effect. P 1.
Report, 1861/2, xv

Memorials and Letters addressed to the Committee of Council on Education on the Subject of the Revised Code by the Authorities of any Educational Society, Board, or Committee, or of any Training School. Three parts. Pp 147, 221, 47.
PP, 1862, xli, 81, 81-I, 81-II

Revised Code: Supplementary Rules. Pp 3.   *PP*, 1864, xliv, 293

Revised Code of Minutes and Regulations, with a Schedule of all Articles cancelled or modified, and of all new Articles.
Report, 1861/2, xvi-xliv; 1863/4, xxix-lxvii; 1864/5, xxxviii-lxxv; 1865/6, xx-liv; 1866/7, lvii-xcvi; 1867/8, xlvii-lxxxvii; 1868/9, xlvii-lxxxv; 1869/70, xxvi-lxi.

Extension of the Application of the Parliamentary Grant under the Revised Code to Schools in small Parishes, and to Evening Scholars. Minute, dated 8 February 1865. Pp 3.
PP, 1865, xliii, [3444]

Minutes excluding Scotland from the Capitation Grant in Elementary Schools, but continuing Inspection and Examination according to the Forms and Instructions of the Revised Code.—
13 Feb 1860. *Report*, 1859/60, xxvi
9 May 1862. *Report*, 1861/2, xv
21 Mar 1863. *Report*, 1862/3, xlvii
11 June 1864. *Report*, 1864/5, lxxvi
11 May 1865. *Report*, 1864/5, lxxxi-lxxxii
18 June 1867 and 21 May 1868. *Report*, 1867/8, lxxxviii
13 July 1869. *Report*, 1869/70, lxxv
5 July 1870. *Report*, 1870/1, cxxvii

Instructions, dated September 1862, to Her Majesty's Inspectors of Schools upon the Administration of the Revised Code.
Report, 1862/3, xvii-xxxi

WOODFORD, EDWARD. The New Code.
Report, 1865/6, 310-25

—Effects of the New Code.
Report, 1867/8, 411-21

Instructions, dated 4 January 1840, to Inspectors of Schools.
Minutes, 1839/40, 11-16

Instructions, dated August 1840, to Inspectors of Schools.
Minutes, 1840/1, 1-12

Explanatory Letter, dated July 1847, to Her Majesty's Inspectors of Schools on various questions relating to the Administration of Grants, under the Minutes of August and December 1846, and of 10 July 1847.
Minutes, 1846, 19-24; also in *PP*, 1851, xliii, 103, 89-92; 1854/5, xli, 158, 29-32.

Inspection of Schools. Minute, dated 25 July 1850.
Minutes, 1850/1, I, ix-xiii; Also in *PP*, 1854/5, xli, 158, 37-9

Inspection of Schools. Special Instructions, dated 24 May 1852, to Her Majesty's Inspectors of Schools.
Minutes, 1852/3, vol I, 15-16

Letter of Instructions, dated February 1848, to Her Majesty's Inspectors of Schools in Scotland, as to the Proceedings to be adopted by them in carrying into Execution the Minutes of the Committee of Council on Education of August and December 1846.
PP, 1851, xliii, 103, 93-5

Minute, dated 19 May 1863, on Duties and Remuneration of Inspectors under the Revised Code.
Report, 1862/3, xlviii-xlix

Proposed Inspection of Church of Scotland Schools together with Correspondence with the Education Committee of the General Assembly of the Church of Scotland. Minute, dated 4 January 1840.
PP, 1840, xl, 490, 1-2; 1854/5, xli, 158, 5-6; 1857/8, xlvi, 192, 34-5

Free Church of Scotland: Administration of the Parliamentary Grant for Education in Scotland. Report by the Deputation

from the Education Committee of the Free Church of Scotland of what passed in Interview between them and the Right Honourable the Lord President of the Privy Council, 1847.
Minutes, 1847/8, xxxii-xxxv; 1848/9, 77-93; also in *PP,* 1854/5, xli, 158, 25-8; 1857/8, xlvi, 192, 55-8

Correspondence relating to the Inspectorship of Free Church Schools in Scotland.
Minutes, 1850/1, I, lv-lviii

Appointment of Inspectors of Episcopal Schools. Minute, dated 12 June 1852.
Minutes, 1853/4, I, 40-1; also in *PP,* 1854/5, xli, 158, 47-8; 1857/8, xlvi, 192, 74-7

Day-Schools of Industry: Grants in Aid. Minute, dated 21 December 1846.
Minutes, 1846, 8-9

Schools of Industry. Circular Letter, dated 26 August 1850, to Her Majesty's Inspectors of Schools relating to Grants in Aid of Day-Schools of Industry.
Minutes, 1850/1, xxi-xxviii; also in *PP,* 1851, xliii, 103, 118-21; 1854/5, xli, 158, 95-6

Offer of Grants for promoting Schools wherein Children of Criminal and Abandoned Classes may be reformed by Industrial Training. Minute, dated 2 June 1856.
Minutes, 1856/7, 17-25; also in *PP,* 1856, xlvi, 259, 3-4; 1857/8, xlvi, 191, 6-7

Grants to Schools of Industry. Circular Letter, dated 18 October 1854, to Her Majesty's Inspectors of Schools.
Minutes, 1854/5, 120

Withdrawal of Aid from Reformatory Schools, out of Education Grant, except for Training of Teachers; and Conditions on which Certified Industrial and Ragged Schools may be added. Minute, dated 31 December 1857.
Minutes, 1857/8, 10-12; also in *PP,* 1857/8, xlvi, 191, 12-14; 192, 22-4

Industrial Schools—Ragged Schools.
Report, 1858/9, xxxiii-xxxviii

WOODFORD, EDWARD 'Report on Industrial Schools.'   *Minutes,* 1850/1, 731-4

Evening Schools for Labouring Classes.
Minutes, 1852/3, I, 54-6

Minute, dated 1 March 1855, approving Draft Circular to Her Majesty's Inspectors of Schools, explanatory of Minutes affecting Night Schools, and setting forth Conditions on which further Annual Aid will be granted towards Payment of Teachers in Such Schools.
Minutes, 1854/5, 109-12

Model Schools: Letter from the Glasgow Educational Society.
PP, 1839, xli, 216, 1

Correspondence with the Glasgow Educational Society respecting a Grant to the Normal and Model School of that Society at Glasgow, together with two Reports from John Gibson, Esq.
Minutes, 1841/2, 4-24

Correspondence with the Education Committee of the General Assembly of the Church of Scotland respecting the Establishment and Maintenance of Normal and Model Schools in Edinburgh and Glasgow, together with a Report from John Gibson, Esq., and a Minute of 31 December 1841. *Minutes,* 1841/2, 24-40

Correspondence with the Education Committee of the General Assembly of the Church of Scotland, regarding the transfer to it of the Glasgow Education Society's Normal School. Pp 5.
PP, 1843, xl, 25

Correspondence respecting the Grant to the Model and Normal Schools in Edinburgh and Glasgow.   *Minutes,* 1844, 1-22

Information required from Applicants for Aid towards the building of Normal Schools. Minute, dated 16 January 1844.
PP, 1844, xxxviii, 84, 2-7

Free Church in Scotland: Grants to Training Schools.
Minutes, 1851/2, I, 124-30

Normal Colleges in Scotland. Circular Letter, dated 1 March 1858.
Minutes, 1857/8, 35-6

of Female Pupil-Teachers, and Candidates for Queen's Scholarships, in Training Colleges under Inspection.
Report, 1858/9, xviii-xx

Syllabus of Subjects on which Students in Normal Schools will be examined.
Report, 1862/3, xxxii-xliii

Grants to Certificated Teachers in Training Schools. Minute, dated 6 August 1851.
Minutes, 1851/2, I, 24, 28-9

Effect of the Minutes which require that all Teachers of Schools receiving Annual Aid from Parliamentary Grants for Education, either hold 'Certificates of Merit', or be recognised as competent. Circular Letter, dated 10 May 1855, to Her Majesty's Inspectors of Schools.
Minutes, 1855/6, 7-10

A Table of the Conditions on which the Salaries of Certificated Schoolmasters and Schoolmistresses are augmented.
PP, 1857/8, xlvi, 192, 12-13

Augmentation of Salaries of Schoolmasters and Schoolmistresses who have obtained Certificates of Merit.
Minutes, 1857/8, 24

Grants to Normal Schools. Minute, dated 21 March 1863.
Report, 1862/3, xliv-xlvii

Teachers in Endowed Schools and Augmented Grants. Minute, dated 29 April 1854.
Minutes, 1853/4, I, 31-3

Certificated Teachers: Engagement of Teachers direct from Training Colleges at Christmas, though School-year may not end in December or January. Circular Letter, dated 14 August 1856, to Her Majesty's Inspectors of Schools.
Minutes, 1856/7, 36-7

KERR, JOHN Normal School Training and Parish Schools. *Report*, 1865/6, 303-9

—Joint University and Normal School Training. *Report*, 1867/8, 404-10

WILSON, CHARLES E The Normal School and University. *Report*, 1866/7, 339-42

Retiring Pensions to Schoolmasters and Schoolmistresses for long and efficient Service. Minutes, dated 25 August and 21 December 1846. *Minutes*, 1846, 3, 8

Grants for Retiring Pensions to Teachers. Minute, dated 6 August 1851.
Minutes, 1851/2, I, 25-6, 29-30

Retiring Pensions. Circular Letter, dated 17 November 1853, to Her Majesty's Inspectors of Schools.
Minutes, 1853/4, 59

Reports on Applications for Retiring Pensions. Circular Letter, dated 30 October 1854, to Her Majesty's Inspectors of Schools. *Minutes*, 1854/5, 122-3

Extract from Circular Letter, dated 12 June 1857, to Her Majesty's Inspectors of Schools, stating the Resolution of the Committee not to undertake any Scheme for the Superannuation of Teachers.
Minutes, 1857/8, 30-1; 1858/9, xxxviii-xl

Apparatus for School-rooms. Circular Letter, dated 7 August 1844.
PP, 1844, xxxviii, 84, 1; 1851, xliii, 103, 73-7

Grants towards the purchase of Lesson and Text-books, and Maps for Elementary Schools; with Schedule of Lesson Books for Scholars, and Text-books for Masters and Mistresses of Elementary Schools, and for Pupil-Teachers. Minute, dated 18 December 1847.
Minutes, 1847/8, x-xxv; also in *PP*, 1851, xliii, 103, 31-52

Book Grants. Correspondence with the Education Committee of the General Assembly of the Church of Scotland, relating to Grants in Aid of the Purchase of Books and Maps at reduced prices.
Minutes, 1851/2, I, 94-7

Supply Grants to Schoolmasters' Association for Books and Maps. Minute, dated 21 February 1853.
Minutes, 1852/3, 10-11; also in *PP*, 1854, xli, 158, 51; 1857/8, xlvi, 192, 8-9

Minute, undated, on Constructive Methods of Teaching Reading, Writing, and Vocal Music. *Minutes*, 1840/1, 18-34

Elementary Drawing. Minute, dated 26 January 1854. *Minutes*, 1853/4, 36-40

Exercises in Elementary Drawing. Circular

Letter, dated June 1854, to Her Majesty's Inspectors of Schools.
Minutes, 1854/5, 118-19

Elementary Drawing. Memorandum, dated 24 February 1857.
Minutes, 1856/7, 25-8; also in *PP*, 1857/8, xlvi, 191, 7-9; 192, 17-18

Instruction in Drawing. Circular Letter, dated 27 February 1858, to Her Majesty's Inspectors of Schools.
Minutes, 1857/8, 27-9

Grants towards Purchase of Scientific Apparatus. Minute, dated 22 November 1843. *PP*, 1857/8, xlvi, 192, 9

Area of Rooms designed for Scientific and Artistic Instruction to be reckoned in awarding Grants towards School Buildings. Minute, dated 20 January 1858.
Minutes, 1857/8, 22

Religious Instruction in Schools not connected with the Established Church. Supplementary Minute, dated 10 July 1847.
Minutes, 1846, 18; also in *PP*, 1854/5, xli, 158, 28-9; 1857/8, xlvi, 192, 30

Schoolmasters' Houses. Minute, dated 22 November 1843. *PP*, 1844, xxxviii, 84, 1

Endowments for Education. Minute, dated 1 May 1865. P 1.
PP, 1865, xliii, [3493]

Conditions on which the Parliamentary Grant of last Session for the Promotion of Education in Great Britain is distributed; with a List of Schools to which Grants of Money have been made by the Committee up to the present period.
PP, 1840, xl, 18, 1-17

Forms and Instructions for conducting Applications for Aid to build Schools.
PP, 1854/5, xli, 158, 71-90

Half-time System of School Attendance as a Condition of Capitation Grants. Minute, dated 21 June 1856.
Minutes, 1856/7, 35-6

Mode of Conducting Applications for Aid from the Parliamentary Grant. Supplementary Minute, dated December 1840.
Minutes, 1840/1, 12-14

Grants to promote Voluntary Assessments towards the Expense of erecting School Buildings in rural areas. Minute, dated 2 April 1853. *Minutes*, 1853/4, 9-16

Extension of Minute of 2 April 1853, for promoting Voluntary Assessments towards Expenses of Schools, to urban as well as rural areas. Minute, dated 14 July 1855. *Minutes*, 1855/6, 5

School Incomes. Circular Letter, dated 13 August 1844, to Her Majesty's Inspectors of Schools. *PP*, 1851, xliii, 103, 77-9

Statistics of Applications for Aid from the Parliamentary Grant, which have been considered and determined by the Committee.
Minutes, 1840/1, 40-51; 1845, 456-95

Return of Applications for Aid from the Parliamentary Grant, which have been considered and determined in the Year 1842-43. *Minutes*, 1842/3, 256-307

Statistics of Applications for Aid from the Parliamentary Grant for Education.
Minutes, 1843/4, 334-433; 1845/6, 576-603; 1847/8, clxiv-clxvii

Schools in Small Rural Areas, Apprenticeship of Pupil-Teachers, Position of Teachers between the end of Training and the date of Certification, Night-Schools. Minute, dated 26 July 1858. Also, Instructions, dated 24 November 1858, to Her Majesty's Inspectors of Schools thereon. Pp 3.
PP, 1859, xxi, pt II, 2496

Correspondence with the Board of Trade, relating to a Proposal to establish a connexion between Elementary Schools and Schools of Design, in the Study of Drawing. *Minutes*, 1850/1, I, lxi-lxvi

Order in Council, transferring the Direction of the Department of Science and Art from the Board of Trade to the Education Department. Dated, 25 February 1856.
Minutes, 1855/6, 1-3

Department of Practical Art. First Report.
PP, 1852/3, liv, [1615]

Department of Science and Art. Annual Reports
First. *PP*, 1854, xxviii, [1783]
Second. *PP*, 1854/5, xvii, [1962]
Third. *PP*, 1856, xxiv, [2123]

Fourth. *PP*, 1857, sess 2, xx, [2240]
Fifth. *PP*, 1857/8, xxiv, [2385]
Sixth. *PP*, 1859, sess 1, xxi, pt II, [2502]
Seventh. *PP*, 1860, xxiv, [2626]
Eighth. *PP*, 1861, xxxii, [2847]
Ninth. *PP*, 1862, xxxi, [3022]
Tenth. *PP*, 1863, xvi, [3143]
Eleventh. *PP*, 1864, xix, pt I, [3335]
Twelfth. *PP*, 1865, xvi, [3476]
Thirteenth. *PP*, 1866, xxv, [3728]
Fourteenth. *PP*, 1867, xxiii, [3863]
Fifteenth. *PP*, 1867/8, xxvii, [4049]
Sixteenth. *PP*, 1868/9, xxiii, [4136]
Seventeenth. *PP*, 1870, xxvi, [c 174]
Eighteenth. *PP*, 1871, xxiv, [c 318]
Nineteenth. *PP*, 1872, xxiv, [c 613]
Twentieth. *PP*, 1873, xxviii, [c 783]

Aid to Science Instruction. Minute, dated 2 June 1859.
Sixth Report, 13-14, footnote

Supply of Instruments, Apparatus, &c. Minute, dated 23 March 1860.
Seventh Report, 25-6

Local and National Scholarships. Minute, dated 3 March 1863.
Tenth Report, 4-5

Summary of the Nature and Amount of Assistance afforded by the Science and Art Department to the Industrial Classes in procuring Instruction in Science. Minute, dated 21 September 1863.
Eleventh Report, 1-5

—Minute, dated 16 February 1865.
Twelfth Report, 1-5

Circular Memorandum to Science Schools and Classes.   *Thirteenth Report*, 19

Local Exhibitions and Scholarships. Minute, dated 21 December 1867.
Fifteenth Report, 2-7

Whitworth Scholarships in Aid of Advanced Scientific Instruction.
Fifteenth Report, 7-11; *Sixteenth Report*, 12-21; *Seventeenth Report*, 22-7; *Eighteenth Report*, 21-4

Science Examinations. Minute, dated 24 August 1868.   *Sixteenth Report*, 1-9

Building Grants for Science Schools. Minute, dated 24 April 1868.
Sixteenth Report, 9

Correspondence relative to the Inspection of Science Schools and Classes.
Sixteenth Report, 9-12

Science Directory. January, 1870.
Seventeenth Report, 6-22; Aug 1870.
Eighteenth Report, 1-20; Nov 1871.
Nineteenth Report, 1-21

Modification of Rules of Science Directory. Dated February 1870.
Seventeenth Report, 1-6

Grants towards the Cost of Chemical Apparatus and of Practical Laboratory Instruction. Minute, dated 17 March 1870.   *Eighteenth Report*, 24-5

Elementary Drawing as Part of General Education.   *Second Report*, 27-32

Payments on Results of Teaching Drawing in Schools for the Poor. Minute, dated 24 October 1862.   *Tenth Report*, 1-2

Payments on Results to Art Masters. Minute, dated 24 February 1863.
Tenth Report, 3-4

Payment on Results of Instruction in Schools of Art. Minute, dated 17 March 1863.   *Tenth Report*, 6-7

Building Grants for Schools of Art. Minute, dated 8 July 1863.
Eleventh Report, 8-10

Conditions for obtaining Aid towards the Encouragement of Art-Instruction. Dated 8 July 1863.
Eleventh Report, 10-11

Art Schools and Art Instruction. Minute, dated 9 January 1865.
Twelfth Report, 13-19

Art Schools—Increased Payments. Minute, dated 1 June 1865.
Thirteenth Report, 23-6

Art. Minute, dated 10 October 1866.
Fourteenth Report, 11-12

Art Directory. Revised to March 1868.
Sixteenth Report, 26-45

Report upon the School of Art, Edinburgh.
Sixth Report, 195-8

BRYCE, JAMES 'The Minutes of Council viewed in connexion with Scottish Conditions'; *Transactions of the National Association for the Promotion of Social Science, 1860* (1861), 335-9.   EUL

DEMAUS, ROBERT Letter to the Right Hon. Earl Granville, on the recent Alterations in the Minutes of the Committee of

Council on Education. Edinburgh: Johnstone and Hunter, 1856. 8vo. Pp 22.

EWING, ALEXANDER A Letter to the very Rev. E. B. Ramsay, Dean of Edinburgh, on the Co-operation of the Church Society with the Committee of Council on Education. London: Hope and Co; Edinburgh: Grant; Aberdeen: Messrs Brown; Glasgow: Messrs Ogle, 1853. 8vo. Pp 13.

LAURIE, SIMON SOMERVILLE 'Report of the Privy-Council on Education'; *The Museum*, Oct 1861, **1**, 333-45; Oct 1862, **2**, 286-95.

'Report of the Committee of Council on Education for 1862-63'; *The Museum*, Oct 1863, **3**, 273-87.

'The Scottish Education Report again'; *The Museum*, new series, 1 Aug 1867, **4**, 165-70.

INSPECTION OF SCHOOLS:
INSPECTORS' REPORTS

Elementary Schools
(a) *General*

GIBSON, JOHN Report on Schools in Scotland. *Minutes*, 1843/4, 154-66

GORDON, JOHN On Deficiencies in the Means of Elementary Education in Scotland. *Minutes*, 1843/4, 167-78

(b) *Reports on Schools connected with the Church of Scotland*

BLACK, JOHN On Schools inspected in the Counties of Aberdeen, Forfar, and Kincardine. *Report*, 1865/6, 280-94; 1867/8, 378-93

GIBSON, JOHN On the State of Elementary Education in the Presbyteries of Aberdeen and Fordyce. *Minutes*, 1841/2, 213-51
On Schools within the Presbyteries of Tongue and Tain. *Minutes*, 1842/3, 192-201
On Schools within the Presbyteries of Chirnside, Dunse, and Lauder. *Minutes*, 1842/3, 202-19

GORDON, JOHN On the State of Education in the Counties of Stirling, Clack-

mannan, Linlithgow, and Renfrew. *Minutes*, 1845, **II**, 409-24
On Schools inspected in the Presbyteries of Hamilton, Meigle, Langholm, and Kintyre. *Minutes*, 1847/8, 326-40
General Report on Schools connected with the Established Church. *Minutes*, 1848/9/50, **II**, 548-57
On Schools inspected in the West of Scotland. *Minutes*, 1855/6, 569-95; 1856/7, 636-60
On Schools inspected in the South Western Division of Scotland. *Minutes*, 1857/8, 663-93; *Report*, 1858/9, 219-35; 1859/60, 236-46
On Schools inspected in the Counties of Ayr, Dumfries, Kirkcudbright, Lanark, Renfrew, and Wigton. *Report*, 1860/1, 222-34; 1861/2, 204-18; 1862/3, 144-152; 1863/4, 237-48
On Schools inspected in the Counties of Lanark, Renfrew, Dumfries, and Bute. *Report*, 1864/5, 222-33; 1866/7, 291-312; 1867/8, 290-312; 1868/9, 325-42
On Schools inspected in the Counties of Edinburgh, Haddington, Linlithgow, Peebles, Selkirk, Roxburgh, and Berwick. *Report*, 1871/2, 82-90

HALL, JOHN On Schools inspected in the Counties of Argyll, Ayr, Kirkcudbright, Wigtown, and in the Western Islands of Scotland. *Report*, 1868/9, 343-53
On Schools inspected in the Counties of Ayr, Dumfries, Kirkcudbright, and Wigtown. *Report*, 1870/1, 291-301

JACK, WILLIAM On Schools inspected in the Counties of Argyle, Ayr, Dumfries, Kirkcudbright, Lanark, Renfrew, Wigton, and in the Western Isles. *Report*, 1864/5, 234-60

JOLLY, WILLIAM On Schools inspected in the Counties of Banff, Moray, Nairn, Inverness, Ross, Cromarty, Sutherland, and Caithness. *Report*, 1870/1, 307-22

KERR, JOHN On Schools inspected in the Counties of Banff, Moray, Nairn, Inverness, Ross, Cromarty, Sutherland, Caithness, Orkney and Shetland. *Report*, 1865/6, 295-303; 1867/8, 394-404
On Schools inspected in the Counties of Banff, Moray, Nairn, Inverness, Ross, Cromarty, Sutherland, Caithness, Orkney, Shetland, and parts of Aberdeen and Kincardine. *Report*, 1869/70, 380-93

D

On Schools inspected in the Counties of Aberdeen, Kincardine, Orkney, and Shetland. *Report*, 1871/2, 91-100

MIDDLETON, DAVID On Schools inspected in the North-eastern Division of Scotland. *Report*, 1858/9, 236-50; 1859/60, 247-261

On Schools inspected in the North of Scotland and in the Orkney and Shetland Islands. *Report*, 1860/1, 235-48; 1861/2, 219-28; 1862/3, 153-63

On Schools inspected in the Counties of Perth, Dumbarton, and Clackmannan. *Report*, 1864/5, 261-76

On Schools inspected in the Counties of Perth, Stirling, Dumbarton, Linlithgow, and Clackmannan. *Report*, 1866/7, 313-28; 1868/9, 354-66

On Schools inspected in the Counties of Lanark and Renfrew. *Report*, 1870/1, 302-6

OGILVIE, R On Schools inspected in the Counties of Stirling, Kinross, Clackmannan, Dumbarton, Argyll, and the South-west half of the County of Perth. *Report*, 1871/2, 101-4

WALKER, ALEXANDER On Schools inspected in the Counties of Fife, Forfar, and Perth. *Report*, 1871/2, 105-15

WOODFORD, EDWARD General Reports on Schools inspected. *Minutes*, 1850/1, II, 736-53; 1851/2, II, 659-724; 1852/3, II, 757-815; 1853/4, II, 917-87; 1854/5, 699-713; 1855/6, 549-56; 1856/7, 618-653; 1857/8, 647-62

On Schools inspected in the Midland Division of Scotland and in the Western Isles. *Report*, 1858/9, 212-18; 1859/60, 228-35; 1860/1, 212-21; 1861/2, 194-203; 1862/3, 134-43; 1863/4, 249-58

On Schools inspected in the South-east of Scotland. *Report*, 1865/6, 318-28

On Schools inspected in the Counties of Berwick, Edinburgh, Fife, Haddington, Kinross, Peebles, Roxburgh, and Selkirk. *Report*, 1867/8, 411-31

(c) Schools connected with the Free Church of Scotland

CUMMING, JAMES Reports on Schools inspected. *Minutes*, 1851/2, II, 725-59; 1852/3, II, 817-69; 1853/4, II, 988-1043; 1854/5, 716-25; 1855/6, 596-607; 1856/7, 661-73; 1857/8, 694-703; *Report*, 1858/9, 251-56; 1859/60, 262-7

On Schools inspected in the North and East of Scotland and in Orkney and Shetland. *Report*, 1860/1, 249-56; 1861/2, 229-32;[1] 1862/3, 164-8; 1863/4, 259-64

On Schools inspected in the East of Scotland. *Report*, 1864/5, 277-81

On Schools inspected in the South-eastern Division of Scotland. *Report*, 1866/7, 329-33; 1868/9, 367-71; 1869/1870, 394-7; 1871/2, 116-19

GIBSON, JOHN General Report on Schools not in connexion with the Established Church. *Minutes*, 1848/9/50, II, 607-41

SCOUGALL, JAMES On Schools inspected in the North and North East of Scotland. *Report*, 1865/6, 329-53; 1867/8, 432-444; 1871/2, 120-33

WILSON, CHARLES E On Schools inspected in the West of Scotland. *Report*, 1858/9, 257-64; 1859/60, 268-73

On Schools inspected in the West of Scotland and in the Western Isles. *Report*, 1860/1, 257-62; 1861/2, 233-9; 1862/3, 169-75; 1863/4, 265-73; 1864/1865, 282-7; 1866/7, 334-9; 1868/9, 372-80; 1870/1, 323-9

(d) Roman Catholic Schools

LYNCH, HENRY J *Report*, 1862/3, 130-3; 1863/4, 219-21; 1864/5, 208-10; 1868/1869, 310-11

MARSHALL, T W M General Report on Roman Catholic Schools in Great Britain. *Minutes*, 1848/9/50, II, 502-47; 1850/1, II, 659-91; 1852/3, II, 707-55

MORELL, J R Report on Roman Catholic Schools inspected in the North-East Division of Great Britain. *Minutes*, 1857/8, 641-6; *Report*, 1858/9, 206-11

On Roman Catholic Schools inspected in the North of England and in Scotland. *Report*, 1859/60, 218-27

STOKES, SCOTT N On Roman Catholic Schools inspected in the North-Western District of Great Britain. *Minutes*, 1853/4, II, 885-916

On Roman Catholic Schools inspected in the North-Eastern District of Great Britain. *Minutes*, 1854/5, 665-80

1. For the original form of his Report for 1861, see Select Committee on Education, [Second] Report (1866), Appendix, 26-7. In *PP*, 1866, ix, 468.

On Roman Catholic Schools inspected in the Northern District of Great Britain. *Minutes,* 1855/6, 529-48; 1856/7, 602-617

(c) *Scottish Episcopal Church Schools*

WILKINSON, THOMAS *Minutes,* 1853/4, vol II, 1045-75; 1854/5, 726-37; 1855/6, 608-619; 1856/7, 674-81; 1857/8, 704-18; *Report,* 1858/9, 265-72; 1859/60, 274-279; 1860/1, 263-6; 1861/2, 240-4; 1862/3, 176-80; 1863/4, 274-6; 1864/5, 288-92; 1865/6, 354-7; 1866/7, 343-52; 1867/8, 445-8; 1868/9, 381-5; 1869/70, 398-402; 1870/1, 330-4

Training Colleges
(a) *Church of Scotland Training Colleges*

GIBSON, JOHN Report on the Glasgow Normal Seminary. *Minutes,* 1840/1, 412-24

GORDON, JOHN Report on the Edinburgh and Glasgow Normal Schools. *Minutes,* 1846, 526-48
Report on the Established Church Normal College, Glasgow. *Minutes,* 1856/7, 806-21; 1857/8, 817-25; *Report,* 1858/9, 387-400; 1859/60, 443-53; 1860/1, 403-17; 1861/2, 375-84; 1862/1863, 297-314; 1863/4, 388-97; 1864/5, 413-23; 1865/6, 461-75; 1866/7, 517-528; 1867/8, 585-96; 1868/9, 474-84
Report on the Established Church Normal School, Edinburgh. *Report,* 1869/70, 497-510; 1870/1, 404-9; 1871/2, 207-11

MIDDLETON, DAVID Report on the Church of Scotland Normal School, Glasgow. *Report,* 1869/70, 511-16; 1870/1, 410-415; 1871/2, 212-18

WOODFORD, EDWARD Report on the Edinburgh and Glasgow Normal Schools. *Minutes,* 1850/1, II, 693-730; 1854/5, 683-98
Report on the Edinburgh Normal School. *Minutes,* 1855/6, 564-5
Report on the Established Church Training College, Edinburgh. *Report,* 1858/1859, 376-86; 1859/60, 439-42; 1860/1, 395-402; 1861/2, 369-74; 1862/3, 290-6; 1863/4, 385-7; 1864/5, 410-12;

1865/6, 457-60; 1866/7, 513-16; 1867/1868, 581-4

(b) *Free Church Training Colleges*

CUMMING, JAMES Report on the Free Church Training College, Edinburgh. *Report,* 1858/9, 401-6; 1859/60, 454-9; 1860/1, 418-22; 1861/2, 385-94; 1862/3, 315-318; 1863/4, 398-405; 1864/5, 424-7; 1865/6, 477-9; 1866/7, 529-37; 1867/8, 597-9; 1868/9, 485-91; 1869/70, 517-522; 1870/1, 416-19; 1871/72, 219-23

GORDON, JOHN Special Report on the Free Church Normal Training School, Edinburgh. *Minutes,* 1848/9/50, II, 737-806

WILSON, CHARLES E Report on the Free Church Training College, Glasgow. *Report,* 1858/9, 407-15; 1859/60, 460-468; 1860/1, 423-33; 1861/2, 395-403; 1862/3, 319-29; 1863/4, 406-14; 1864/1865, 428-35; 1865/6, 480-90; 1866/7, 538-43; 1867/8, 600-6; 1868/9, 492-7; 1869/70, 523-36; 1870/1, 420-7; 1871/1872, 224-30

(c) *Scottish Episcopal Training College, Edinburgh*

WILKINSON, THOMAS *Report,* 1858/9, 416-20; 1859/60, 469-72; 1860/1, 434-8, 1861/2, 404-8; 1862/3, 330-4; 1863/4, 415-18; 1864/5, 436-8; 1865/6, 491-4; 1866/7, 544-6; 1867/8, 607-10; 1868/9, 498-501; 1869/70, 537-40; 1870/1, 428-9

CUMMING, JAMES and WILSON, CHARLES E Tabulated Reports on Schools not connected with the Church of Scotland, inspected in Scotland, 1853-54. London: HMSO, 1855. 8vo. Pp 56.   GUL

—Tabulated Reports on Schools, not connected with the Church of Scotland, inspected in Scotland, 1855-56. London: HMSO, 1857. 8vo. Pp 74.   New Coll

MIDDLETON, DAVID General Report on the Schools connected with the Established Church and other schools inspected in the North-East of Scotland during the year 1858. Edinburgh: Thomas Constable and Co; London: Hamilton, Adams, and Co, 1859. 12mo. Pp 19.

Acts of the General Assembly

1560 TO 1618

None of the original records of the General Assemblies of the Church of Scotland which met before 1618 has survived, nor had any of them been printed before they disappeared. The modern printed editions of the proceedings of these early Assemblies have therefore had to be based upon transcripts which were made when the original records were still in existence.[1] These modern printed editions are three in number.

(1) and (2) *The Booke of the Universall Kirk of Scotland*, ed THOMSON, THOMAS. 3 vols. Edinburgh: Bannatyne and Maitland Clubs, 1839-45. These two editions are identical in every respect, and the references here to the Bannatyne edition are equally valid for the Maitland one.

(3) *The Booke of the Universall Kirk of Scotland*, ed PETERKIN, ALEXANDER. Edinburgh: The Edinburgh Printing and Publishing Co, and William Blackwood and Sons, 1839. This edition was not printed from the same manuscript as that used by Thomson for the Bannatyne and Maitland editions. Textually it is almost identical except that, while everything that is in the other two is also here, it omits some entries that they include. Orthographically, however, they differ considerably. For convenience, references are also given below to this edition.

(a) Schools

1562. 1 July (1) **1**, 17; (3) not printed
'To prefer supplication for the poor and their support; for maintainance of schools for instruction of the ʒouth in every parish; and the same to be taken of the twa part of the teinds and within burrows of the annual rents, and other such things as before served to idolatrie.'

---

1. See SHAW, DUNCAN *The General Assemblies of the Church of Scotland, 1560-1600: Their Origin and Development* (Edinburgh: The St Andrew Press, 1964), 1-12.

1563. 26 June (1) **1**, 33-4; (3) 16
'Ordainit that the instructioun of ʒouth be committit to none within this realme, neither in universities nor without the samein, but to them that professe Chrysts true religioun, now publicklie preached; and that sick as now occupie the places, not professing as said is, be removed fra the samein, and to remember that same[1] ordour be made for the sustentatioun of poore scholers.'

1565. 16 June (1) **1**, 60; (3) 29
Tenor of the Articles [to be sent to the Queen's Majesty]. Thridlie, that none be permittit to have charge of schooles, colledges or universities, or ʒet privatlie or publicklie to instruct the ʒouth, but such as salbe tryed be the superintendents or visitors of the church, found sound and abill in doctrine, and admittit be them to ther charges.
This Act was re-enacted in identical terms on 23 June 1567. See (1) **1**, 108: (3) 66.

1571/2. 16 Jan (1) **1**, 214-15; (3) not printed
Of the dispositioun of Prouestreis Prebendareis in College Kirkis, foundit vpoun temporall landes or annuellis, as alsua of Chapellanreis, being of the like foundatioun, for support of the scholes and incres of Letters.

1574. 11 Aug (1) **1**, 311; (3) not printed
[A Commission appointed to visit the Counties of Caithness and Sutherland and to visit schools and plant schoolmasters there.]

1578. 24 Oct (1) **2**, 425-6; (3) 184
[On the education of children of popish parents.]

1579. July, sess 7ᵃ (1) **2**, 432-3; (3) 188
[Suspension of Master Ninian Dalyell from the post of master of the Grammar School, Dumfries.]

1581. Oct, sess 11ᵃ (1) **2**, 535; (3) 227
'To sute that the tryall and admissioun of all masters of schooles, be now joynit to the Presbyteries.'

---

1. *Peterkin*, some.

1582. Oct, sess 16ª   (1) **2**, 603; (3) 267
That remedie may be found how spirituall[1] livings and teynds transferritt in temporall lordschips, may be restorit againe for the sustentatioune of the Ministers, poore, and schooles.

1583. Oct, sess 14ª   (1) **2**, 640; (3) 285
[No authors to be read in schools or universities whose writings impugn the Christian faith.]

1587/8. 20 Feb   (1) **2**, 723; (3) 328-9
Greives of the Kirk, assembled in Edenburgh, givin in to his Majestie.

1592. 30 May, sess 10ª   (1) **2**, 788; (3) 359
[*Ane Forme of Examinatioun befor the Communioun* to be used in schools instead of the *Little Catechism*.[2]]

1595. 28 June   (1) **3**, 856; (3) 422
Anent Gramer Schooles in Townes.

1601. 14 May   (1) **3**, 965; (3) 492
[Lack of schoolmasters one cause of the decay of religion and education.]

1616. 15 Aug   (1) **3**, 1120; (3) 592
[No one to keep a school for teaching the young without episcopal and presbyterial authority.]

(b) Scottish Universities

1582. Oct, sess 10ª   (1) **2**, 593-4; (3) 262-3
Anent Colledges and Vniversities within this realme.

1582. Oct, sess 16ª   (1) **2**, 601; (3) 266
That of the temporall lands of every Abbacie, Pryorie, Bischoprick, Nunrie, &c. so meikle may be applyit to the schooles as may sufficientlie mantaine ane sufficient number of Masters and Bursers, according as the living may beare, in place of Cannons, Monkes, Nunnes, or other idle bellies.

1. *Peterkin,* speciall.
2. *Ane Forme of Examinatioun befor the Communioun* was an abridgement by John Craig of an earlier work of his own, entitled *A shorte Summe of the Whole Catechisme*; the General Assembly of Aug 1590 had ordered him to prepare it, and that of July 1591 had ordered it to be printed. (*Booke of the Universall Kirke,* 2, 774, 784.) The *Litle Catechism* which it replaced was *The Maner to examine Litle Children,* found at the end of Calvin's Catechism and in use since 1562. See *A Shorte Summe of the Whole Catechisme by John Craig,* ed LAW, T GRAVES (Edinburgh, 1883), vii-viii.

1583. Apr, sess 2ª   (1) **2**, 614; (3) not printed
Anent visitatione of Universities conforme to the directione of the late Assemblie.

1587. June, sess 9ª   (1) **2**, 693; (3) 318
[All university students to subscribe the true religion presently established within the realm of Scotland.]

1595. 28 June   (1) **3**, 856; (3) 422
Anent Colledges.

1638 TO 1842

The page references are to *Acts of the General Assembly of the Church of Scotland, M.DC.XXXVIII-M.DCCC.XLII.* Reprinted from the original Edition, under the Superintendence of the Church Law Society. Edinburgh: The Edinburgh Printing and Publishing Company, 1843.

(a) Schools

1638. 17 and 18 Dec, sess 23 and 24   21-2
Reviving and ratifying several former Acts, &c.
IV. Anent the visitation of Kirks, Schooles, and Colledges.
VI. Anent the planting of Schools in Landward.

1638. 20 Dec, sess 26   31
Concerning the subscribing the Confession of Faith.

1639. 30 Aug, sess 23   42
Act ordaining the Subscription of the Confession of Faith, and Covenant.

1640. 5 Aug, sess 10   45
Act against Expectants refusing to subscribe the Covenant.

1642. 3 Aug, sess 8   63
Overtures anent the Schooles.

1645. 7 Feb, sess 14   117
Overtures for advancement of Learning, and good Order in Grammar Schools and Colledges.

1645. 13 Feb, sess ult   128
Act for censuring the Observers of Yule-day, and other superstitious dayes, especially if they be Schollars.

1649. 6 Aug, sess ult   217
Recommendation for Maintenance Schoolmasters and Precenters.

1699. 31 Jan, sess 11   282-3
X. Recommendation to Presbyteries and
Synods anent Schools.

1705. 5 Apr, sess 7   384
V. Act concerning Schools and Bursaries,
and for Instructing Youth in the Principles of Religion.

1707. 12 Apr, sess 5   399-400
V. Act anent Schools in every Parish,
and a Contribution thereanent.

1708. 20 Apr, sess 5   431
Acts concerning the Proposals about
Propagating Christian Knowledge, Sup-
pressing Popery, Erecting Schools, &c.

1713. 8 May, sess 7   483
VII. Act and Recommendation for Teaching the Common Tunes.[1]

1719. 18 May, sess 4   526-7
Act for the Settlement and Provision of
Schools.

1746. 22 May, sess 9   687
VIII. Act and Recommendation about
the Manner of Singing of Psalms.

1749. 20 May, sess 9   699
VI. Act appointing Presbyteries to hold
Visitations for Settling Parochial Schools.

1758. 3 June, sess 9   733-4
VI. Act anent Parochial Schools.

1767. 23 May, sess 3   766-7
IV. Proposals for more effectually exe-
cuting a Scheme for maintaining and
educating the Infants and Orphans of
Soldiers.

1794. 26 May, sess ult   846-7
IX. Act and Resolution respecting the
Religious Education of Youth.

1799. 3 June, sess ult   873-5
XII. Report concerning Vagrant Teachers
and Sunday Schools.

1800. 2 June, sess ult   880
VIII. Order and Injunction concerning
Teachers and Schoolmasters.
See also Act VIII of 30 May 1801, 886;
Act VI of 27 May 1802, 890-1; Act IX
of 30 May 1808, 914; Act VIII of 27
May 1809, 917; Act IX of 28 May 1810,
923; Act X of 31 May 1813, 937-8; and
Act VIII of 29 May 1819, 971-2.

1. For 'common tunes', see PATRICK, MILLAR *Four
Centuries of Scottish Psalmody* (Oxford, 1949), 66-8.

1817. 26 May, sess 4   958-9
V. Judgement of the General Assembly
on the Reference from the Presbytery of
Brechin, respecting the Examination of
the Schools of Montrose.

1820. 27 May, sess 5   976-8
VII. Report of the Committee appointed
to class the Returns from Presbyteries of
the Examination of Schools.
See also 2 June 1823, 987-8; 30 May 1825,
992-3; 27 May 1826, 995-6; 28 May
1827, 1001-2; 2 June 1828, 1003-5;
30 May 1829, 1006-7; 31 May 1830,
1010-11; 30 May 1831, 1016-18; 28
May 1832, 1021-2; 27 May 1833, 1025-7;
31 May 1834, 1040-2.

(b) Schoolmasters

1699. 3 Feb, sess 17   285
XIII. Act anent subscribing the Confession of Faith.

1700. 16 Feb, sess 15   294
X. Act anent Schoolmasters, Chaplains,
Governors, and Pedagogues.

1706. 13 Apr, sess 12   395
XIII. Recommendation and Act concerning Schoolmasters and Schools.

1800. 2 June, sess ult   881
XII. Recommendation by the General
Assembly, for promoting a Subscription
towards defraying the Expense of the
Appeal in the Cause relating to the School-
master of Bothwell; and Order for Print-
ing the Appeal Case prepared by the
Procurator.

1802. 27 May, sess 7   891
VII. Declaration and Instruction of the
General Assembly in favour of the
Parochial Schoolmasters in Scotland.

(c) Highlands and Islands

1646. 18 June, sess ult   142
Overtures presented to the Assembly.
IV, 3. That Scots schools be erected in all
parishes there, according to the Act of
Parliament, where conveniently they can
be had.

1648. 4 Aug, sess 29   189
Overtures concerning the Education of
the Hieland Boys in the Province of
Argyle.

1648. 11 Aug, sess 40 197
Exemption of Murray, Rosse, and
Caithness, from the contribution granted
to the Boyes of Argyle, with a Recommendation to Presbyteries to make up
what is taken of them by that exemption.

1649. 6 Aug, sess ult 216
Act for a Collection for entertaining
Highland Boyes at Schools.

1690. 11 Nov, sess 24 227
XI. Act approving Overtures.
3. That it be recommended to the Kirk-
sessions, heritors, and others concerned
in the Highlands, to see the Act of Parliament anent erecting of schools in every
parish duly executed, and the funds
established by law for the same made
effectual.

1699. 30 Jan, sess 10 282
IX. Act anent Planting of the Highlands.
4. That English schoolmasters be erected
in all Highland parishes according to
former acts of Parliament and General
Assemblies.

1699. 4 Feb, sess 18 et ult 288
XVI. Overtures for promoting the Knowledge of God in the Highlands, and for
rendering the Act made Sess. 10 of this
Assembly the more effectual.

1704. 27 Mar, sess 10 330
XIV. Act anent erecting Schools in the
Highlands.

1704. 29 Mar, sess 12 332
XVII. Act anent Libraries in the Highlands.
Other Acts of the same tenor were passed
on 10 Apr 1705, 388; 16 Apr 1706, 396;
26 Apr 1709, 438.

1709. 19 Apr, sess 5 433-4
VI. Act and Recommendation for fur-
thering the Design of propagating
Christian Knowledge.

1710. 10 May, sess 13 445-6
XI. Representation of the Society in
Scotland for Propagating Christian
Knowledge, with an Act and Recommen-
dation thereupon.

1711. 21 May, sess 11 452
IX. Instructions by the General Assembly
to their Commission.
13. The said Commission are to
endeavour to make effectual whatever
hath been by this or preceding Assemblies

agreed upon, concerning the erecting of
schools in the North, the Highlands and
Islands . . . according to the 11th Act of
the late General Assembly thereanent,
which is hereby renewed.
14. The said Commission are appointed and empowered to use their
endeavours for getting a legal school
erected in every parish, according to law,
for putting in execution the 5th Act of
the General Assembly, held *anno* 1707,
entitled, 'Act anent a School in every
Parish'.

1712. 7 May, sess 6 462-4
V. A Representation of the Committee
of the Society in Scotland for Propagating
Christian Knowledge, with an Act of the
General Assembly thereupon.
Acts to the same effect were passed on
5 May 1713, 481-2; 17 May 1714, 492-4;
17 May 1715, 504-5; 7 May 1716, 509-10;
8 May 1717, 514-15; 19 May 1719, 527-9;
18 May 1727, 589-91; 8 May 1728, 600-1;
3 May 1729, 605-6; 12 May 1732, 617-18.

1717. 13 May, sess 11 516
VI. Instructions by the General Assembly to their Commission.
8. The said Commission are appointed
to use their best endeavours to obtain a
fund for erecting schools in the Highlands
and Islands, and to get the same rightly
proportioned, and to keep a correspondence with the Society for Propagating
Christian Knowledge . . . according to
the Acts of this and former Assemblies.

(d) Scottish Universities

1638. 17 and 18 Dec, sess 23 and 24
See *(a) Schools,* above, p 53.

1638. 20 Dec, sess 26
See *(a) Schools,* above, p 53.

1639. 30 Aug, sess 23
See *(a) Schools,* above, p 53.

1641. 3 Aug, sess 9 46-7
Act approving Overtures anent the
Universities and Colledges of this King-
dom.

1645. 7 Feb, sess 14
See *(a) Schools,* above, p 53.

1646. 18 June, sess ult 142
Overtures presented to the Assembly.
[Overtures III and V are concerned with
university teaching.]

1705. 5 Apr, sess 7
See (*a*) *Schools*, above, p 54.

1711. 23 May, sess 13 et ult   457
XIV. Act concerning the Inspection of
Universities and Colleges.

GILLAN, ROBERT 'Schools and Schoolmasters'; *An Abridgement of the Acts
of the General Assembly of the Church of
Scotland from the Year 1638 to the Year
1820 inclusive* (Edinburgh: Printed for
the Author, 1821), 52-4.   EUL

PETERKIN, ALEXANDER 'Schools and Schoolmasters'; *A Compendium of the Laws of
the Church of Scotland* (Edinburgh:
Robert Buchanan), 2nd pt (1830), 273-81.

WILSON, JOHN 'Schools and Schoolmasters';
*Index to the Acts and Proceedings of
the General Assembly of the Church of
Scotland from the Revolution to the
Present Time* (Edinburgh and London:
William Blackwood and Sons, 1863),
107-9, 231-5.

Reports of the Education Committee, etc

General Assembly's Education Committee.[1]
Abstract of Parochial Returns of School
Examinations made by the several Pres-
byteries of the Church of Scotland for
the Year ending 15th April. 1849. np
[Edinburgh], nd [1849]. 8vo. Pp 56.
                              New Coll

—Abstract of the Report, May 1827[-28].
Edinburgh: Printed J and D Collie,
1827[-28]. 8vo.   New Coll
    1827—pp 36   1828—pp 57

—Abstract of Reports of Presbyteries on
Schools examined by them during the
year 1860[-70]. np [Edinburgh], nd
[1860-70]. 8vo.   New Coll
    1860—pp 74   1866—pp xii, 79
    1861—pp xiii, 72   1867—pp x, 88
    1862—pp x, 68   1868—pp x, 84
    1863—pp x, 66   1869—pp x, 77
    1864—pp x, 75   1870—pp x, 84
    1865—pp xiv, 80

1. This was its commonly used short title. When
first set up in 1825 it was called 'The Committee for
increasing the Means of Education and Religious
Instruction in Scotland'; from 1827 to 1835 the
words, 'particularly in the Highlands and Islands',
were added after 'Scotland'; from 1836 to 1872 it
was called simply 'The Committee for increasing the
Means of Education in Scotland'.

—'Copy Interim Report on the Means of
Education in Parishes, *quoad sacra*';
Report of the Education Committee, 1839,
31-3.

—'Correspondence relative to Certain
Articles of the Revised Code'; *Report of
the Education Committee*, 1863, 26-8.

NOTE The Articles in question were 40 (a)
on grants to Highland and Island
Schools, and 51 (e) on the teaching of
Needlework.

—Educational Statistics of the Highlands
and Islands of Scotland. Prepared from
Returns made by the Parochial Ministers.
Edinburgh: J and D Collie, 1833. 8vo.
Pp 24, 29.   New Coll

—'Extract from Regulations issued to the
General Assembly's Schoolmasters'; *Report of the Education Committee*, 1863,
23-5.

—Extracts from the Reports of the Ministers of Parishes in some Synods of
Scotland, made in 1818 and 1819, as to
Parochial Schools. Edinburgh: Printed
by Duncan Stevenson, 1824. 8vo. Pp
viii, 36, 6.   New Coll

—General Assembly's Schools. Edinburgh:
Printed by J and D Collie, 1836. 8vo.
Pp 15.   New Coll

—'Memorial addressed to the Right
Honourable the Committee of Her Majesty's Privy-Council on Education';
Report of the Education Committee, 1843,
36-7.

NOTE Asked that Royal Burghs, specifically excluded from the Act of 1803 by
one of its own clauses, be now brought
within its scope.

—'Narrative of the Rise and Progress of
the Scheme of the General Assembly, for
promoting Education and Religious
Instruction throughout Scotland, and
particularly in the Highlands and
Islands'; *Abstract of the Education
Committee's Report*, May 1828, 19-32.

—'Notes relative to the Government
Scheme of Education'; *Report of the
Education Committee*, 1849, 47-54.

—Presbyterial and Parochial Reports on
the State of Education in Scotland, 1842.
Edinburgh: Printed by John Stark, 1843.
8vo. Pp vii, 168.   New Coll

—Presbyterial Reports on the State of Education in Scotland, 1852[-54]. Edinburgh: Printed by William Blackwood and Sons, 1852[-54]. 8vo.   New Coll

1852—pp x, 47   1853—pp x, 51
        1854—pp x, 56

—Reports, 1826-72. Edinburgh: Printed by A Balfour & Co, 1829; Printed by J and D Collie, 1830-5; Printed by John Stark, 1836-42; Printed by Stark and Company, 1843-7; Printed by Paton and Ritchie, 1848-9; Printed by Robert Inches, 1850-1; Printed by Neill & Company, 1852; Printed by William Blackwood and Sons, 1853-72. 8vo.
        New Coll

1826—pp 19, 10	1850—pp 83
1827—pp 18	1851—pp 91
1829—pp 40	1852—pp 74
1830—pp 38	1853—pp 108[1]
1831—pp 31	1854—pp 80
1832—pp 40	1855—pp 99
1833—pp 28	1856—pp 127[2]
1834—pp 38	1857—pp 110[2]
1835—pp 60	1858—pp 122[2]
1836—pp 32	1859—pp 130[2]
1837—pp 66	1860—pp 62
1838—pp 60	1861—pp 61
1839—pp 67	1862—pp 72
1840—pp 57	1863—pp 83
1841—pp 55	1864—pp 57
1842—pp 59	1865—pp 66
1843—pp 66	1866—pp 64
1844—pp 47	1867—pp 68
1845—pp 51	1868—pp 53
1846—pp 43	1869—pp 71
1847—pp 44	1870—pp 61
1848—pp 119	1871—pp 88
1849—pp 90	1872—pp 66

—Report as to the General Assembly's Schools, by the Very Reverend Principal Baird and Mr J. Gordon. np [Edinburgh], 1828. 8vo. Pp 7.   New Coll

—Reports of Presbyteries on schools examined in the Year 1871[-72]. Abstract and Tables. Edinburgh: Printed by William Blackwood and Sons, 1871[-72]. 8vo.   New Coll

1871—pp x, 88   1872—pp x, 78

1. Includes also Reports of Assembly Schools, by ministers of the parishes.
2. Include Abstracts of Presbyterial Reports.

—Report of the Assembly Schools inspected in 1831. np [Edinburgh], 1831. 8vo. Pp 8.   EUL

—'Report of the Proceedings of the Deputation from the General Assembly's Education Committee to London, in reference to the Arrangement proposed by the Privy Council Committee, in regard to the Normal Seminaries, and to the General Scheme of Education prepared by the Government'; *Report of the Education Committee*, 1849, 38-46.

—Report on the Returns from Presbyteries regarding the Examination of Schools in the Year 1838[-40]. Edinburgh: Printed by John Stark, 1838[-40]. 8vo.
        New Coll

1838—pp 32
1839—pp 43
1840—pp 57

—Report on the Returns from Presbyteries on the State of Schools in the Year 1841. Edinburgh: Printed by John Stark, 1841. 8vo. Pp 112.   New Coll

—'Report on School Endowments in Scotland'; *Report of the Education Committee*, 1854, 24-31.

—'Resolutions upon the Report made by their Deputation to London, and with reference to the Government's Education Scheme'; *Report of the Education Committee*, 1849, 19-37.

—'Results of a Recent Inquiry concerning the Means of Education in Scotland'; *Report of the Education Committee*, 1850, 43-53.

—'Rules and Regulations'; *Report of the Education Committee*, 1835, 33-41.

—Statement of Deficiencies in the Means of Education for the Poor in certain of the large Towns of Scotland, etc. Edinburgh: Printed by John Stark, 1836. 8vo. Pp 14.   New Coll

—Special Report [on Report of Royal Commission on Education]. np [Edinburgh], 1868. 8vo. Pp 18.   New Coll

—Special Report showing the Nature and Effect of the Recommendations and Draft Bill of the Royal Commission appointed to inquire into Schools in Scotland published May 1867. Edinburgh: Printed by William Blackwood and Sons, 1867. 8vo. Pp 26.

New Coll

Presbytery of Glasgow. *Report of Proceedings on 25th March, 1868, on the Subject of Education in Scotland.* Glasgow: Thomas Murray & Son, 1868. 8vo. Pp 42.   EUL

Synod of Aberdeen. *Memorandum on the Reports of the Royal Commission on Schools in Scotland.* 9th October, 1867.

Aberdeen: Printed by Arthur King and Company, 1868. 8vo. Pp 16.   BM

'The Church and [Private] Schools, 1824'; *Records of the Scottish Church History Society,* 1929, **3**, 79-80.

'General Assembly's Schools'; *Presbyterian Rev,* Jan 1836, **7**, 555-71.

GORDON, JOHN *The Education Scheme of the Church of Scotland from its Origin, 1825 to 1872.* Edinburgh and London: William Blackwood and Sons, 1878. 8vo. Pp 62.   GUL

Free Church of Scotland

Acts of the General Assembly

From *Acts of the General Assembly of the Free Church of Scotland.* Edinburgh: Printed for the Free Church of Scotland by John Greig, 1843-72.

1843. 29 May, sess 17 Act XV. Act anent the Education of Students for the Ministry, and the Establishment of a System of Schools.   *Acts,* 1843, 37

1844. 24 May, sess 14 Act XII. Acts anent the Education Scheme.   *Acts,* 1844, 20

1846. 1 June, sess 5 Act XIII. Act anent the Education Scheme.   *Acts,* 1846, 30

1847. 26 May, sess 5 Act IV. Acts anent the Government Scheme of Education.   *Acts,* 1847, 14-16

1860. 25 May, sess 15 Act VIII. Act anent the Terms of Admission of Schoolmasters to Office.   *Acts,* 1860, 229

Reports of the Education Committee

FREE CHURCH OF SCOTLAND [Candlish, Robert S] Appeal to the People of the Free Church of Scotland on behalf of the Education Scheme. np [Edinburgh], 1855. 8vo. Pp 4.   New Coll

—Correspondence with the Privy Council and Report of Deputation to London in

connection with the Omission of Religious Subjects from the Syllabus of Study in Normal Schools for 1871. Edinburgh, 1871. 8vo. Pp 11.   New Coll

—Education Bill. np [Edinburgh], nd [1854]. 8vo. Pp 14.   New Coll

—Education Committee. Annual Reports. In *Proceedings of the General Assembly of the Free Church of Scotland.* Edinburgh: William Whyte and Co, 1843-4; John Greig & Son, 1845-56; James Nichol, 1857-70; Printed by Ballantyne & Co, 1871-2. 8vo.   New Coll
1843, May, 113-18, 158-9; 1843, Oct, 61-8; 1844, 167-80; 1845, 49-56; 1846, 180-7; 1847, 123-43; 1848, 297-305; 1849, 248-70; 1850, 195-237; 1851, Appendix III, 8; 1852, 321-8; 1853, Report No XVI, Appendix, 245-50; 1854, *See* Speeches of Dr Candlish *and others,* below; 1855, 268-74; 1856, 153-163; 1857, 256-65; 1858, 250-7; 1859, Appendix, Miscellaneous Reports No V, 20; 1860, 177-85, and Appendix, Report No XXII, 28; 1861, Appendix, Report No XXI, 24; 1862, Appendix, Report No XXIV, 24; 1863, Appendix, Report No XXIV, 20;

— —. 1864—Appendix, Report No XXIV, 30; 1865—Appendix, Report No XXIV, 30; 1866—Appendix, Report No II, 34; 1867—Appendix, Report

No II, 28; 1868—Appendix, Report
No II, 11; 1869—Appendix, Report
No II, 4; 1870—Appendix, Report
No II, 10; 1871—Appendix, Report
No II, 17; 1872—Appendix, Report
No II, 19.

— —. Education Bill. Report of the Standing Education Committee. np [Edinburgh], nd [?1868]. 8vo. Pp 15.
New Coll

— —. Explanatory Minute of the Acting Education Committee. np [Edinburgh], 1850. 8vo. Pp 16. New Coll

— —. 'The Lord Advocate's Education Bills'; *Proceedings*, 1856, 110-31; Appendix No XXIII (*Appendix*, 114); Appendix No XXVIII (*Appendix*, 132-3).

— —. National Education and the Parish Schools. *Proceedings*, 1859, 285-8.

— —. National Education and Tests. *Proceedings*, 1861, 289-96.

— —. Overture relative to the Constitution of Schools; *Acts of the General Assembly of the Free Church of Scotland*, 1847, 98-100; 1848, 87-90. New Coll

— —. Report on the Public Schools (Scotland) Bill; *Proceedings*, 1869, Appendix, Report No II, 5-16.

— —. Special Report to the Commission of the General Assembly, 8th August 1855. np [Edinburgh], nd [1855]. 8vo. Pp 16. New Coll

— —. Speeches of Dr Candlish, Lord Panmure, and Professor Miller, in the General Assembly, Thursday, 25th May 1854. Edinburgh: Printed by Johnstone and Hunter, 1854. 8vo. Pp 16.
New Coll

—Government Education; *Proceedings*, 1847, 150-79.

—National Education; *Proceedings*, 1849, 105-23; 1850, 199-236.

—National Education Committee. Reports. In *Proceedings of the General Assembly of the Free Church of Scotland*. 1862, 300-15; 1869, 188-202; Appendix, Report No XXX, 3; 1870, 77-92; Appendix, Report No XXV, 8; 1871, 208; Appendix, Report No XXVI, 3; 1872, Appendix, Report No XXVI, 15.

—Parish Schools; *Proceedings*, 1853, 208-218.

—Parish Schools and National Education. np [Edinburgh], nd [1853]. 8vo. Pp 12.
New Coll

—Reasons for the Education Scheme. np [Edinburgh], nd [1849 and various subsequent years]. 8vo. Pp 4. New Coll

—Report anent Constitution of Schools; *Proceedings*, 1848, 162-3.

—Report of the Committee appointed by the General Assembly of 1867, on the Report of the Royal Commissioners on Elementary Schools. May, 1868; *Proceedings*, 1868, Appendix, Report No XXIII, 4.

—Report on Education Bills: *Proceedings*, 1855, 257-64.

—The Royal Commissioners' Report on National Education; *Proceedings*, 1867, 208-39.

NOTE Some at least of the Reports of the Education Committee were published separately and printed by a printer other than the printer of the *Proceedings*, but so far only the following have been seen; they are all in New College Library.
1843. Edinburgh: Printed by Balfour and Jack. Pp 8.
1846. Edinburgh: Printed at the *Witness* Office. Pp 24.
1847. With Appendix. Edinburgh: John D Lowe. Pp 118.
1849. With Appendix. Edinburgh: Printed by Johnstone, Ballantyne, and Co. Pp 32.

BROWN, THOMAS 'The Schools'; *Annals of the Disruption* (Edinburgh: MacLaren and MacNiven, 1877), pt 2, 103-26.

— '—'; — new edition (MacNiven & Wallace, 1890), 309-26.

CANDLISH, ROBERT S 'Educational Scheme of the Free Church.' From the *Northern Warder* of 10 Sept 1846. Dundee: McCosh, Park, and Dewars, 1846. 8vo. Pp 16.

—*Speech before the General Assembly of the Free Church of Scotland on the Report of the Education Committee and relative Overtures*. Edinburgh: Printed by Miller and Fairly, 1850. 8vo. Pp 16.

'Education'; *Home and Foreign Missionary Record for the Free Church of Scotland,* Oct 1846, **2**, 497-500.

FRASER, WILLIAM *The Educational Work of the Free Church of Scotland.* Paisley: Printed by J and J Cook, nd [?1862]. 8vo. Pp 8.   New Coll

'The Free Church Education Scheme'; *Free Church Mag,* July 1846, **3**, 193-7; Dec 1848, **5**, 360-3.   New Coll

GUNN, JOHN 'The Free Church "Education" Scheme'; *Maurice Paterson: A Memorial Biography* (1921), 84-111.

A Memorial on Education to General Assembly of the Free Church. By the Son of a Clergyman. Edinburgh: W P Kennedy, 1844. 8vo. Pp 42.   GUL

MILLER, HUGH 'The Educational Question'; *The Witness,* 2 Mar 1850, **11**, 2.

NOTE This article deals exclusively with the salaries of Free Church schoolmasters.

'The Proposed fate of our [Free Church] Education Scheme; The Position of its Founders'; *The Watchword,* 1 Apr 1872, **7**, 25-8.   New Coll

STOW, DAVID *Scheme for Free Church Schools and the Training of Schoolmasters.* Glasgow, 1846. 4to. P 1.   New Coll
An offprint of a letter to the editor of the *Scottish Guardian.*

STUART, ALEXANDER MOODY *An Inquiry into the Character of the Present Educational Connexion between the Free Church and the Government.* Edinburgh and London: John Johnstone, 1848. 8vo. Pp 102.

WITHRINGTON, DONALD J 'The Free Church Educational Scheme, 1843-50'; *Records of the Scottish Church History Society, 1963-65,* **15** (1966), 103-15.

From 'The First Book of Discipline' (1560)

First Book of Discipline, 'For the Schollis. I. The Necessitie of Schollis. II. The Tymes appointed to everie Course. III. The Erectioun of Universiteis. IV. Off Reidars, and of the Greis, off Tyme, and Studye [and of Principals and Rectors, and of Bursars]. V. Off Stipendis and Expensses necessarie. VI. Of the Privilege of the Universitie'; *The Works of John Knox,* collected and edited by David Laing (Edinburgh: Printed for the Wodrow Club, 1848), **2**, 208-21.
The Bannatyne Club edition of Knox's *Works,* also published in 1848, was also edited by David Laing, and is identical with this one. The *First Book of Discipline,* with the orthography modernised, is to be found in *John Knox's History of the Reformation in Scotland,* ed DICKINSON, WILLIAM CROFT (London, Edinburgh, and New York: Thomas Nelson and Sons, Ltd, 1949), **2**, 280-325.

CRAIGIE, JAMES 'Knox's Book of Discipline'; *SEJ,* 14 Oct 1960, **42**, 720-2.

GORDON, DONALD C BRYCE 'The Political and Educational Ideas and Ideals of John Knox.' Unpublished PhD thesis, Edinburgh University, 1926. Typescript. 4to. Pp 267.   EUL

KISTLER, MILTON S 'John Knox's services to Education'; *Education* (Boston, Mass), 1898, **19**, 105-16.   Not seen

LINDSAY, THOMAS M 'What John Knox did for Scottish Education'; *Macmillan's Mag,* Oct 1870, **22**, 461-71.

MACFARLAND, HENRY S N 'The Book of Discipline'; *Aberdeen University Rev,* Spring 1960, **38**, 246-8.

TURNBULL, JAMES *An Examination of the Antecedents and Influence of the Educational Proposals of the First Book of Discipline in the Period bounded by the Education Acts of 1496 and 1633.* Unpublished EdB thesis, Aberdeen University, 1946. Typescript. 4to. Pp 163. Bibliography.   AUL

Extracts from Accounts of the Common Good of various burghs, 1557 and 1634: Reports on the State of Certain Parishes in 1627

Extracts from the Accounts of the Common Good of various Burghs in Scotland relative to Payments for Schools and Schoolmasters, between the years 1557 and 1634. *Maitland Club Miscellany*, **2**, pt 1 (Edinburgh, 1840), 39-50.

Covers the burghs of Aberdeen, Arbroath, Annan, Anstruther, Ayr, Banff, Burntisland, Cupar, Crail, Cullen, Dumbarton, Dumfries, Dunbar, Dundee, Elgin, Forfar, Forres, Haddington, Inverkeithing, Inverness, Inverurie, Irvine, Jedburgh, Kinghorn, Kirkcudbright, Lanark, Lauder, Linlithgow, North Berwick, Peebles, Perth, Renfrew, Rothesay, Rutherglen, St Andrews, Selkirk, Stirling, Tain, and Wigton.

Reports on the State of Certain Parishes in Scotland, made to His Majesty's Commissioners for Plantation of Kirks, &c. in pursuance of their Ordinance, dated April XII, M.DC.XXVII. Edinburgh: Maitland Club, 1835. 4to. Pp xii, 232.
Berwickshire: Bonkle and Preston, Chingilkirk,[1] Coldstream, Hume, Lang-

1. ie, Channelkirk.

ton, Ligertwood, Longformacus, Mordington, St Bothans,[1] Swinton.
Clackmannanshire: Tillicoultry.
Dumfriesshire: Dalgarno and Closeburn.
Edinburghshire: Borthwick, Cockpen, Cranstoun, Crichton, Currie, Fala and Soutra, Heriot, Inveresk *alias* Musselburgh, Kirknewton, Newbattle, Neaton,[2] Temple.
Haddingtonshire: Oldhamstocks, Barrow,[3] Bothan,[4] Dirleton, Humbie, Ormiston, Pencaitland, Saltoun, Tranent.
Stewartry of Kirkcudbright: Lochrutton, Terregles, Urr.
Perthshire: Dull, Forgandenny, Kenmore, Killin, Lecropt, Weem.
Renfrewshire: Greenock, Houston.
Roxburghshire: Ednam, Stitchill.
Stirlingshire: Logie.
Wigtonshire: Kirkcowan, Kirkinner.
Zetland: Nesting.

1. now Abbey St Bathans.
2. ie, Newton.
3. now incorporated in Garvald.
4. now Yester.

The State of every Burgh within the Kingdom of Scotland in the Year 1692

Register containing the State of every Burgh within the Kingdom of Scotland in the Year 1692. Printed in *Miscellany of the Scottish Burgh Records Society* (Edinburgh: Printed for the Scottish Burgh Records Society, 1881), 49-157.

Information about the salaries paid to the schoolmasters and about the sources whence the moneys to pay were derived is given about these burghs in this order: Perth, Dundee, Aberdeen, Stirling, Linlithgow, St Andrews, Glasgow, Ayr, Haddington, Dysart, Montrose, Cupar-Fife, Dumfries, Inverness, Burntisland, Inverkeithing, Kinghorn, Brechin, Irvine, Jedburgh, Kirkcudbright, Wigton, Pittenweem, Dunfermline, Anstruther Wester, Selkirk, Dumbarton, Renfrew, Dunbar, Lanark, Arbroath, Elgin, Peebles, Crail, Tain, Banff, Culross, Whithorn, Forfar, Rothesay, Nairn, Rutherglen, Cullen, Lauder, Annan, Lochmaben, Sanquhar, South Queensferry, Kintore, Inverurie, Stranraer.

Part Three

Part Three

Abstract of the Minutes of the Committee of Council on Education: For the guidance of Managers of Schools, Teachers, Pupil-Teachers, Candidates for Queen's Scholarships, Students in Training Colleges, and others interested in the promotion of education. By a Correspondent of the Committee of Council. London: Thomas Nelson and Sons, 1856. 12mo. Pp 6, 122. Index.   New Coll

BELL, GEORGE JOSEPH 'Schoolmaster's Salary and House'; *Principles of the Law of Scotland* (Edinburgh: William Blackwood; London: T Cadell, 1829), 279-80.

— —; —. Second edition (Edinburgh: William Blackwood; London: T Cadell, 1830), 291-2.

— —; —. Third edition (Edinburgh: Oliver and Boyd; London, Simpkin & Marshall, 1833), 304.

—'Schools'; *Principles of the Law of Scotland,* fourth edition (Edinburgh: Thomas Clark, 1839), 415-16, 794-5.

— —; —, Fifth edition, by Patrick Shaw, Advocate (Edinburgh: T and T Clark, 1860), 423-4, 812-13.

— —; —, Sixth edition, edited by William Guthrie, Advocate (Edinburgh: T and T Clark, 1872), 483-5, 546-7.   EUL

COOK, JOHN 'Schoolmasters and Schools'; *Styles of Writs, and Forms of Procedure in the Church Courts of Scotland* (Edinburgh: T and T Clark, 1850), 218-39.

— —; —, second edition (Edinburgh: T and T Clark, 1850), 218-39.   Pe

— —; *Styles of Writs, Forms of Procedure and Practice of the Church Courts of Scotland,* third edition (Edinburgh: T and T Clark, 1856), 184-203.

— —; —, fourth edition (Edinburgh: T and T Clark, 1870), 211-31.

—'Nature and Amount of Aid given to Schools by the Committee of the Privy Council on Education'; *Styles of Writs, Forms of Procedure, and Practice of the Church Courts of Scotland,* fourth edition (1870), 317-21.

DUNCAN, JOHN M 'On Schools and School-masters'; *Treatise on the Parochial Ecclesiastical Law of Scotland* (Edinburgh: Bell and Bradfute, 1864), 596-662.

— —, second edition (Edinburgh: Bell and Bradfute, 1869), 754-832.

DUNDAS, JOHN *The Method of Procedure by Presbyteries, in Settling of Schools in every Parish . . . in Pursuance of the Acts of Parliament Impowering them to these Effects.* Edinburgh: Printed by the Heirs and Successors of Andrew Anderson, 1709. 12mo. Pp [6], 120.

DUNLOP, afterwards MURRAY-DUNLOP, afterwards COLQUHOUN-STIRLING-MURRAY-DUNLOP, ALEXANDER 'Schools'; *Parochial Law* (Edinburgh: William Blackwood; London, T Cadell, 1830), 292-344.

— —; —, second edition (Edinburgh: William Blackwood and Sons; London: T Cadell, 1835), 454-508.

— —; —, third edition (Edinburgh and London: William Blackwood and Sons, 1841), 480-535.

LAURIE, SIMON SOMERVILLE *Classified Abridgment of the Minutes of the Committee of Council on Education for the Use of School Managers and Teachers.* Edinburgh: Thomas Constable and Co, 1856. 8vo. Pp 48.

MACDONALD, ALEXANDER *Education (Scotland) Act, 1872.* Compendium of the Law relative to Schoolmasters and National Education in Scotland; with Digest of all the Acts of Parliament, relating to Education. And an Appendix containing the Education Act of 1872. Glasgow and London: W R McPhun and Son, 1872. 8vo. Pp 132, 8.   GUL

Parochial and Burgh Schools Acts of Parliament, 1696 to 1861. Edinburgh: William Blackwood and Sons, 1861. 8vo. Pp iv, 44, 4.   EUL

CONTENTS 1696. Act for Settling of Schools. William III, c. 26. 1803. Act for making better Provision for the Parochial Schoolmasters, and for making further Regulations for the better Government of the Parish Schools in *Scotland.*

43 Georgii III, c. 54. 1838. Act to facilitate the Foundation and Endowment of additional Schools in *Scotland*. 1 & 2 Victoriae, c. 87. 1845. Act for amending an Act for making Provision for Parish Schoolmasters in Scotland. 8 & 9 Victoriae, c. 40. 1854. Act to regulate the Salaries of the Parochial Schoolmasters of Scotland. 17 & 18 Victoriae, c. 98. 1861. Act to alter and amend the Law relating to the Parochial and Burgh Schools in Scotland, and to the Test required to be taken by Schoolmasters in *Scotland*. 24 & 25 Victoriae, c. 107.

SIMPSON, ALEXANDER B 'An Historic Law Case—Presbytery of Elgin v Magistrates and Town Council of Elgin'; *SEJ*, 2 May 1952, **35**, 269-70.

Suggestions for the Administration of the Privy Council Grant for Education in Scotland. With a New Plan for a National System. By an Educationist. Edinburgh: John Maclaren, 1870. 8vo. Pp 32.   EUL

TURNER, STANLEY HORSFALL 'Parochial Taxation: Schools'; *History of Local Taxation in Scotland* (Edinburgh and London: William Blackwood and Sons, 1908), 62-81.

WRIGHT, ALEXANDER 'Bothwell Case, 1798'; *History of Education and of the Old Parish Schools of Scotland* (1898), 124-7.

Biography

Collective Work

MORGAN, ALEXANDER *Makers of Scottish Education*. London: Longmans, Green, and Co, 1929. 8vo. Pp ix, 282. 8 portraits. Bibliography.

CONTENTS George Buchanan; John Knox; Andrew Melville; George Heriot; George and Thomas Hutcheson; Mary Erskine; George Watson; James Gillespie; Robert Gordon; John Watson; James Donaldson; Louis Cauvin; John Morgan; James Dick; Andrew Bell; Robert Owen; David Stow.

Individual Lives

ADAM, Alexander (1741-1809), rector, the High School of Edinburgh.

ANDERSON, WILLIAM 'Adam, Alexander'; *The Scottish Nation* (Edinburgh and London: A Fullarton & Co, 1863), **1**, 21-3; (Edinburgh: Thomas C Jack, 1882), **1**, 21-3.

ARNOT, JAMES 'Dr Alexander Adam, Edinburgh High School'; *Educ News*, 10 June 1899, **24**, 394-5.

CHAMBERS, ROBERT 'Adam Alexander'; *Biographical Dictionary of Eminent Scots-men* (Glasgow and Edinburgh: Blackie & Son, 1835), **1**, 13-17; new edition (1855), **1**, 16-18; new edition (1868), **1**, 12-13; revised throughout (1875), **1**, 12-13. Portrait.

HENDERSON, ALEXANDER *An Account of the Life and Character of Alexander Adam, LL.D.* Edinburgh: Printed by D Schaw and Son, 1810. 8vo. Pp 162, xiv.

PAUL, SIR JAMES BALFOUR 'Adam, Alexander'; *DNB*, **1** (1908), 84.

ALVES, Robert (1745-94), schoolmaster at Banff and teacher of languages in Edinburgh.

ALVES, ROBERT 'Short Biographical Account of the Author'; in Alves' posthumously published *Sketches of a History of Literature* (Edinburgh: Printed by Alex Chapman and Co, 1794), vi-ix.

ESPINASSE, FRANCIS 'Alves, Robert'; *DNB*, **1** (1908), 349.

ANDERSON, Alexander (1808-84), Chanonry School, Aberdeen.

CORMACK, ALEXANDER A *Alexander Anderson, M.A., LL.D. (1808-84)*. Reprinted from *Banffshire Journal* of 21 Feb 1956. Banff: Printed by the *Banffshire Journal* Ltd, 1956. 8vo. Pp 30. Frontispiece and portraits.

BEATTIE, James (*circa* 1860), schoolmaster, Gordonstone, Aberdeenshire.

KERR, JOHN *Lessons from a Shoemaker's Stool*. London: Alexander Strahan, 1865. 8vo. Pp 32. Portrait.
Reprinted from *Good Words* (1865), 279-86; reprinted in all editions of Kerr's *Memories Grave and Gay* as chapter X.

BELL, Andrew (1753-1832), educational pioneer.

ANDERSON, WILLIAM 'Bell, Andrew'; *The Scottish Nation* (Edinburgh and London: A Fullarton & Co, 1863), **1**, 271-2; (Edinburgh: Thomas C Jack, 1882), **1**, 271-2.

B, J C 'An Educational Ozymandias'; *SEJ*, 6 Oct 1933, **16**, 1138.

CHAMBERS, ROBERT 'Bell, Andrew'; *Biographical Dictionary of Eminent Scotsmen* (Glasgow and Edinburgh: Blackie & Son, 1835), **4**, 478-83; new edition (1855), **1**, 196-9; new edition, **1** (1868), 114-15; revised throughout (1875), **1**, 114-15.

KNOX, HENRY M 'An Old Scottish Educational Reformer'; *SEJ*, 20 Nov 1953, **36**, 714-15.

LEITCH, JAMES 'Dr Andrew Bell'; *Practical Educationists and their Systems of Teaching* (Glasgow: James Maclehose, 1876), 121-48.

MCDONELL, GEORGE PAUL 'Bell, Andrew'; *DNB*, **2** (1908), 149-52.

MEIKLEJOHN, JOHN M D *An Old Educational Reformer: Dr Andrew Bell*. Edinburgh and London: William Blackwood and Sons, 1881. 8vo. Pp [8], 182.

SOUTHEY, ROBERT *The Life of the Rev. Andrew Bell*. 3 vols. London: John Murray; Edinburgh: William Blackwood & Sons, 1844. 8vo. Pp xx, 531; ix, 693; ix, 736. Frontispiece to vol 1.

BELL, James (1818-79), master at the High School of Glasgow.

In Memoriam of the late James Bell, English Master in the High School, Glasgow. Glasgow: David Bryce and Son, 1879. 16mo. Pp 97. Portrait.

BIRKBECK, George (1776-1841), educational pioneer.

GODARD, JOHN GEORGE *George Birkbeck, the Pioneer of Popular Education*. London and Derby: Bemrose & Sons, 1884. 8vo. Pp xvi, 242, vi. Portrait. Index.

KELLY, THOMAS *George Birkbeck, Pioneer of Adult Education*. Liverpool: At the University Press, 1957. 8vo. Pp [xiii], 380. Frontispiece and 18 plates. Bibliography. Index.

WOOD, SIR HENRY TRUEMAN 'Birkbeck, George, M.D.'; *DNB*, **2** (1908), 542-3.

BRAIDWOOD, Thomas (1715-1806), teacher of the deaf and dumb.

GORDON, ALEXANDER 'Braidwood, Thomas'; *DNB*, **2** (1908), 1107-8.

BUCHANAN, George (1506-82), humanist scholar.

ANDERSON, WILLIAM 'Buchanan, George'; *The Scottish Nation* (Edinburgh and London: A Fullarton & Co, 1863), **1**, 462-72; (Edinburgh: Thomas C Jack, 1882), **1**, 462-72. Portrait.

BROWN, P HUME *George Buchanan and his Times*. Edinburgh and London: Oliphant, Anderson & Ferrier, 1906. 8vo. Pp 96. Frontispiece and 20 illustrations.

—*George Buchanan. Humanist and Reformer. A Biography*. Edinburgh: David Douglas, 1890. Pp xix, 388. Portrait. Index.

'George Buchanan'; *Scottish Rev*, Jan 1855, **3**, 1-14. BM

IRVING, DAVID *Memoirs of the Life and Writings of George Buchanan*. Edinburgh: Bell and Bradfute, and A Lawrie; London: Longman, Hurst, Rees, and Orme, 1807. 8vo. Pp xxx, 318. Index.

— —, second edition. Edinburgh: William Blackwood; London: T Cadell and W Davies, 1817. 8vo. Pp xvii, 436. Frontispiece and 2 plates. Index.

'Lives of Eminent Preceptors—George Buchanan'; *Scottish Educational and Literary J*, May-July 1853, **1**, 347-54, 407-16, 450-8.

MACKAY, AENEAS 'Buchanan, George'; *DNB*, **3** (1908), 186-93.

BUCHANAN, James (1784-1857), teacher at New Lanark.

RUSK, ROBERT R 'James Buchanan'; *History of Infant Education* (London: University of London Press Ltd, 1933), 135-45. Portrait.

SALMON, DAVID and HINDSHAW, WINIFRED 'James Buchanan'; *Infant Schools: Their Theory and History* (London: Longmans, Green, and Co, 1904), 35-40.

CARSON, Aglionby Ross (1789-1850), rector, High School of Edinburgh.

ANDERSON, WILLIAM 'Carson, Aglionby Ross, M.A., LL.D.'; *The Scottish Nation* (Edinburgh and London: A Fullarton & Co, 1863; Edinburgh: Thomas C Jack, 1882), 1, 599.

CAUGHIE, David (1802-74), teacher in Glasgow.

C, D 'A Great Educationist, David Caughie'; *SEJ*, 7 Sept 1928, 11, 951.

CAUVIN, Louis (1745-1825), educational philanthropist.

LE ROI, DAVID 'Burns's French Teacher. Louis Cauvin and his Edinburgh School'; *SEJ*, 29 July 1933, 16, 972-3.

NEIL, SAMUEL 'Louis Cauvin: A Biographical Sketch'; *Educ News*, 16 Nov 1889, 14, 783-4; 23 Nov 1889, 14, 799-801; 30 Nov 1889, 14, 816-17; 7 Dec 1889, 14, 831-3.

—*Louis Cauvin and the Institution he founded.* Issued by the Governors of Cauvin's Hospital, for private circulation only. Edinburgh: Printed by Morrison & Gibb, 1891. 8vo. Pp 40.   EUL

CHALMERS, Charles (1792-1864), founder of Merchiston Castle School, Edinburgh.

MARWICK, WILLIAM H 'Charles Chalmers'; *SEJ*, 17 Jan 1936, 19, 63.

CHALMERS, James K (1803-74), teacher at Paisley.

Dinner and Presentation to J. K. Chalmers, Esq., Teacher, Paisley, by his Old Scholars, Tuesday, 19th May, 1870. Paisley: Printed for private circulation by J & J Cook, 1870. 8vo. Pp 44.   GUL

CHAPMAN, George (1723-1806), schoolmaster at Dumfries and Elgin, and writer on education.

ANDERSON, WILLIAM 'Chapman, George'; *The Scottish Nation* (Edinburgh and London: A Fullarton & Co, 1863), 1, 634-5; (Edinburgh: Thomas C Jack, 1882), 1, 634-5.

B, D 'Memoirs of the late Dr Chapman'; *Scots Mag*, June 1806, 68, 404-5.

CHAMBERS, ROBERT 'Chapman, George'; *Biographical Dictionary of Eminent Scotsmen* (Glasgow and Edinburgh: Blackie & Son, 1835), 1, 513-14.

HENDERSON, T F 'Chapman, George'; *DNB*, 4 (1908), 53.

Sketch of the Life of the late George Chapman, LL.D. Edinburgh: John Moir, 1808. 8vo. Pp 30.   BM

COMBE, George (1788-1858), writer on education.

ANDERSON, WILLIAM 'Combe, George'; *The Scottish Nation* (Edinburgh: Thomas C Jack, 1882), 3, 697-9.

CHAMBERS, ROBERT 'Combe, George'; *Biographical Dictionary of Eminent Scotsmen*, new edition (Glasgow, Edinburgh, and London: Blackie & Son, 1868), 1, 385-6; revised throughout (1875), 1, 385-6.

GIBSON, CHARLES *The Life of George Combe.* 2 vols. London: Macmillan and Co, 1878. 8vo. Pp xvi, 335; viii, 404. 2 portraits. Bibliography. Index.

STEPHEN, SIR LESLIE 'Combe, George'; *DNB*, 4 (1908), 883-5.

DALE, David (1739-1806), philanthropist and educational pioneer.

ESPINASSE, FRANCIS 'Dale, David'; *DNB*, 5 (1908), 384-5.

LIDDELL, ANDREW *Memoir of David Dale, Esq., Merchant, Glasgow.* np, [Glasgow: Blackie & Son], 1854. 8vo. Pp 16.   GUL The verso of the front cover carries the following note: 'The subjoined article was written for, and forms part of, the Supplementary Volume of Chambers' *Biographical Dictionary of Eminent Scotsmen*, now in course of publication by Messrs Blackie and Son. A limited number of copies has been printed from the stereotype plates in this form, by special request of the friends of the deceased.'

—'Dale, David'; *Biographical Dictionary of Eminent Scotsmen*, originally edited by Robert Chambers, new edition (Glasgow, Edinburgh, and London: Blackie and Son, 1855), 5, 161-77; new edition, 1 (1868), 422-5; revised throughout (1875), 1, 422-5.

DALGARNO, George (?1626-87), writer on sign language.

CHAMBERS, ROBERT 'Dalgarno, George'; *Biographical Dictionary of Eminent Scotsmen* (Glasgow and Edinburgh: Blackie & Son, 1835), **2**, 44; new edition (1855), **2**, 44; new edition, **1** (1868), 425; revised throughout (1875), **1**, 425.

GOODWIN, GORDON 'Dalgarno, George'; *DNB*, **5** (1908), 389-90.

'Sketch of the Author's Life and Writings'; *The Works of George Dalgarno of Aberdeen* (Edinburgh: Maitland Club, 1834), v-xii.

DEMAUS, Robert (?1829-74), schoolmaster, Aberfeldy, Perthshire.

CARLYLE, EDWARD I 'Demaus, Robert'; *DNB*, **22** (1909), 552.

DICK, James (1743-1828), educational benefactor.

DOUGLAS, ROBERT 'James Dick and the Dick Bequest'; *Aberdeen University Rev*, Mar 1926, **13**, 97-109. Portraits.   EUL

'James Dick Memorial'; *SEJ*, 30 Nov 1928, **11**, 1282-3.

SKINNER, ROBERT T 'The Friend of Preceptors—James Dick'; *Figures and Figureheads* (Edinburgh: Printed privately by T and A Constable, Ltd, 1931), 23-7.

—'James Dick of Forres. The Dominie's Maecenas'; *Yesterday and Today* (Edinburgh: Printed privately by T and A Constable, Ltd, 1929), 74-80.

DOIG, David (1719-1800), master of Stirling Grammar School.

CHAMBERS, ROBERT 'Doig, David'; *Biographical Dictionary of Eminent Scotsmen* (Glasgow and Edinburgh: Blackie & Son, 1835), **2**, 79-82; new edition (1855), **2**, 82-5; new edition, **1** (1868), 449-50; revised throughout (1875), **1**, 449-50.

GOODWIN, GORDON 'Doig, David'; *DNB*, **5** (1908), 1091-2.

IRVING, DAVID 'David Doig'; *Lives of Scottish Writers* (Edinburgh: Adam and Charles Black, 1839), **2**, 313-24.

GILLESPIE, James (1726-97), founder of James Gillespie School, Edinburgh.

TAIT, JAMES 'Gillespie, James'; *DNB*, **7** (1908), 1240.

GORDON, Robert (1665-1732), founder of Robert Gordon's Hospital, Aberdeen.

ANDERSON, WILLIAM 'Gordon, Robert'; *The Scottish Nation* (Edinburgh and London: A Fullarton & Co, 1863), **2**, 334; (Edinburgh: Thomas C Jack, 1882), **1**, 334.

BURNETT, G W 'Gordon, Robert'; *DNB*, **8** (1908), 227-8.

CHAMBERS, ROBERT 'Gordon, Robert'; *Biographical Dictionary of Eminent Scotsmen* (Glasgow and Edinburgh: Blackie & Son, 1835), **2**, 470-4; new edition (1855), **2**, 475-9.

GUNN, William Maxwell (1806-51), schoolmaster at Haddington and Edinburgh.

GRAY, WILLIAM FORBES and JAMIESON, JAMES H 'Gunn, William Maxwell'; *East Lothian Biographies* (Haddington: Printed for East Lothian Antiquarian and Field Naturalists' Society, 1941), 59.

HERIOT, George (1563-1624), founder of George Heriot's Hospital, Edinburgh.

ANDERSON, WILLIAM 'Heriot, George'; *The Scottish Nation* (Edinburgh and London: A Fullarton & Co, 1863), **2**, 469-70; new edition (Edinburgh: Thomas C Jack, 1882), **2**, 469-70.

'Biographical Sketch of the Life of George Heriot'; *Scots Mag*, Feb 1802, **64**, 95-9. Portrait.

CHAMBERS, ROBERT 'Heriot, George'; *Biographical Dictionary of Eminent Scotsmen* (Glasgow and Edinburgh: Blackie & Son, 1835), **3**, 42-5; new edition (1855), **3**, 43-6; new edition, **2** (1869), 256-7; revised throughout (1875), **2**, 256-7.

CONSTABLE, ARCHIBALD *Memoirs of George Heriot*, Jeweller to King James VI, with an Historical Account of the Hospital founded by him at Edinburgh. Edinburgh: Archibald Constable and Co; London: Hurst, Robinson and Co, 1822. 8vo. Pp viii, 228. Frontispiece and 3 plates.

ERSKINE, DAVID STEUART, 11th Earl of Buchan, 'Sketch of the Life of George Heriot; with a Portrait'; *The Bee, or Literary Weekly Intelligencer*, ed ANDERSON, JAMES, 9 Nov 1791, **6**, 1-4.
Reprinted in ERSKINE, DAVID STEUART *Anonymous and Fugitive Essays* (Edinburgh: J Ruthven and Co, 1812), **1**, 283-8.

ESPINASSE, FRANCIS (2) 'Heriot, George'; *DNB*, 9 (1908), 695-7.

GRAY, WILLIAM FORBES 'George Heriot, Jeweller to James VI'; *An Edinburgh Miscellany* (Edinburgh: Robert Grant & Son, 1925), 55-66.   EPL

STEVEN, WILLIAM *Memoir of George Heriot: with the History of the Hospital, founded by him in Edinburgh; and an Account of the Heriot Foundation Schools* (Edinburgh: Bell & Bradfute; London: Smith, Elder, & Co, 1845), 1-40.

HUME, Alexander (?1560-?1630), schoolmaster at Edinburgh and Dunbar.

WHEATLEY, HENRY B 'Alexander Hume'; in HUME, ALEXANDER, *Of the Orthographie and Congruitie of the Britan Tongue* (London: Early English Text Society. Original Series, 5, 1865), vi-viii.

HUTCHESON, George (?1580-1639), and Thomas (1589-1641), founders of Hutchesons' Hospital, Glasgow.

HENDERSON, T F 'Hutcheson, George', and 'Hutcheson, Thomas'; *DNB*, 10 (1908), 335.

JENKINS, Tom (c 1820), teacher at Teviothead, Roxburghshire.

BARTON, E 'The Negro Prince, "Tom Jenkins" '; *Transactions of the Hawick Archaeological Society, 1936*, 62-3.

CRAIGIE, JAMES 'The Strange Story of Tom Jenkins, Negro Teacher'; *SEJ*, 22 Jan 1965, 48, 80-2.

'Intelligent Negroes: Tom Jenkins'; *Chambers's Miscellany of Useful and Entertaining Tracts* (Edinburgh: W and R Chambers, 1844-7), 8, no 3, 1-7.   BM

—*Chambers's Miscellany of Instructive and Entertaining Tracts*, new and revised edition (London and Edinburgh: W and R Chambers, 1869-72), 8, no 3, 2-7.   EUL

KENNEDY, JOHN W 'A Negro Prince in Teviotdale; "Tom Jenkins" '; *Transactions of the Hawick Archaeological Society, 1926*, 15.

KENNEDY, W NORMAN 'Tom Jenkins'; *Transactions of the Hawick Archaeological Society, 1870*, 52-6.

MACGILL, ALEXANDER 'The Black Dominie of Teviothead'; *SEJ*, 29 Oct 1948, 31, 620-1.

SCOTT, ROBERT E 'The Strange Case of Tom Jenkins'; *Scots Mag*, new series, Oct 1959, 72, 51-4.

KIRKWOOD, James (1) (?1650-1708), advocate of parochial libraries.

SECCOMBE, THOMAS 'Kirkwood, James'; *DNB*, 11 (1909), 225-6.

KIRKWOOD, James (2) (?1654-1720), schoolmaster at Linlithgow and Kelso.

COLVILLE, JAMES 'A Scottish Schoolmaster of the Seventeenth Century'; *Some Old-fashioned Educationists* (Edinburgh and London: William Green & Sons, 1907), 98-108.

STRONACH, GEORGE 'Kirkwood, James'; *DNB*, 11 (1909), 226-7.

KNOX, William (1799-1874), schoolmaster at St Ninians, Stirlingshire.

POLLOCK, ALEXANDER J 'William Knox, Schoolmaster and General Factotum'; *SEJ*, 19 July 1957, 40, 434-5.

LANCASTER, Joseph (1778-1838), educational pioneer.

LEITCH, JAMES 'Joseph Lancaster'; *Practical Educationists and their Systems of Teaching* (Glasgow: James Maclehose, 1876), 149-65.

SALMON, DAVID *Joseph Lancaster*. London: Published for the British and Foreign School Society by Longmans, Green, and Co, 1904. 8vo. Pp viii, 76. Frontispiece and 4 plates. Bibliography. Index.

LAURIE, John (1800-72), schoolmaster, Invershin, Sutherlandshire.

KEMP, DANIEL W *John Laurie; An Eccentric Sutherland Dominie*. Edinburgh: Norman Macleod; Wick: W Rae; Bonar Bridge: J A Polson, 1892. 8vo. Pp viii, 38.
Reprinted from the *Northern Ensign* (Wick), April-May 1892.

LINDSAY, Robert (c 1830), schoolmaster in Kincardineshire.

MACGILLIVRAY, WILLIAM *Rob Lindsay and his School*, by one of his old Pupils. A Reminiscence of Seventy-five Years ago. Edinburgh: William J Hay; London: Samuel Bagster & Sons, Ld, 1905. 8vo. Pp 45. Frontispiece and 9 illustrations.
Reprinted in the same author's *Memories of my Early Days* (London and Edinburgh: T N Foulis, 1912), 3-49.

MACDONALD, John (1748-1832), school-master, Tongue, Sutherlandshire.

Autobiographical Journal of John Macdonald Schoolmaster and soldier, 1770-1830. With Introduction, Illustrations, and Notes by the Rev. Angus Mackay, M.A. Edinburgh: Norman Macleod; Halkirk: D Y Forbes, 1906. 8vo. Pp 119.

MACDONALD, John (1828-83), school-master, Huntly, Aberdeenshire.

M, J L *A Notable Aberdeenshire Schoolmaster.* By an Old Pupil. Banff: The *Banffshire Journal* Office; Huntly: Joseph Dunbar, 1908. 8vo. Pp 15. Portrait.
Reprinted from the *Banffshire Journal* of 24 Nov 1908.

ALLARDYCE, JOHN 'Rev. John Macdonald, M.A.'; *Byegone Days in Aberdeenshire* (Aberdeen: The Central Press, 1913), 144-50.

MACLACHLAN, Ewen (1775-1822), rec-tor, Old Aberdeen Grammar School.

ANDERSON, PETER J *Ewen Maclachlan.* Aberdeen: At the University Press, 1918. 8vo. Pp 32. 4 plates. Bibliography.
Reprinted from *The Aberdeen University Library Bulletin*, May 1918, 3, 643-72.

ANDERSON, WILLIAM 'Maclachlan, Ewen'; *The Scottish Nation* (Edinburgh and London: A Fullarton & Co, 1863), 3, 35; (Edinburgh: Thomas C Jack, 1882), 3, 35.

MACDONALD, J RAMSAY 'Maclachlan, Ewen'; *DNB*, 12 (1909), 634.

MAIR, John (1795-1853), schoolmaster at Ayr and Perth.

SUTHERLAND, DAVID J S 'John Mair: The Pioneer of Science Teaching in Scotland'; *SEJ*, 4 July 1952, 35, 422.

MELVIN, James (1795-1853), rector, Aber-deen Grammar School.

'Biographical Sketch of Dr James Melvin, Rector of the Grammar School, Aber-deen'; *Scottish Educational and Literary J*, Oct 1853, 2, 3-9.

MASSON, DAVID *James Melvin, Rector of the Grammar School of Aberdeen.* A Sketch, with Appendices. Aberdeen: Printed for the [Grammar School] Centenary Committee, 1895. 4to. Pp [8], 112. Frontispiece and 3 plates.
Pp 1-46 first appeared in *Macmillan's Mag*, Jan 1864, 9, 225-39, under the title,

The Aberdeen Grammar School—Dr James Melvin; they were reprinted in *Bon Record*, ed SIMPSON, HENRY F M (Aberdeen: D Wyllie & Son, 1906), 204-30, and in MASSON, DAVID *Memories of Two Cities* (Edinburgh and London: Oliphant, Anderson & Ferrier, 1911), 234-70.

SECCOMBE, THOMAS 'Melvin, James'; *DNB*, 13 (1909), 247.

MILNE, John (1775-1842), educational benefactor.

SMITH, JOHN *Memoir of John Milne, M.D.* Aberdeen: A Brown & Co; Edinburgh: John Menzies & Co; London: Long-man & Co, 1871. 8vo. Pp viii, 134. Frontispiece.

NAPIER, John (1550-1617), mathemati-cian.

NAPIER, MARK *Memoirs of John Napier of Merchiston,* with a History of the Inven-tion of Logarithms. Edinburgh: William Blackwood; London: Thomas Cadell, 1834. 4to. Pp xvi, 534. Plates and Facsimiles.

MACDONALD, W RAE 'Napier, John'; *DNB*, 14 (1909), 59-65.

NEWLAND, John (1737-99), founder of Bathgate Academy, West Lothian.

GRAHAM, DAVID *John Newland: An Account of the Founder of Bathgate Academy.* Arbroath: Brodie & Salmond, 1901. 8vo. Pp 144. 8 plates.

NORVALL, James (1765-1847), school-master, Montrose, Angus.

LAWRANCE, ROBERT M 'James Norval—Schoolmaster, Playwright, and Author'; *Aberdeen Book-Lover*, Nov 1926, 5, 95-111. Portrait.   BM

OWEN, Robert (1771-1858), educational pioneer.

COLE, GEORGE D H *The Life of Robert Owen.* London: Macmillan and Co, Limited, 1930. 8vo. Pp x, 350. Frontispiece and 2 plates. 2 bibliographies. Index.
A reprint of the volume of 1925.

—*Robert Owen.* London: Ernest Benn Limited, 1925. 8vo. Pp ix, 267. 2 bibliographies. Index.

COLE, MARGARET *Robert Owen of New Lanark.* London: The Batchworth Press, 1953. Pp vii, 230. Frontispiece. Bibliography. Index.

JONES, LLOYD *The Life, Times, & Labours of Robert Owen*. Vol I—London: The Labour Association, 1889. 8vo. Pp xix, 239. Vol II—London: Swan Sonnenschein and Co, 1890. 8vo. Pp viii, 203.
BM

—*The Life, Times, and Labours of Robert Owen*, edited by William Cairns Jones. Second edition. London: Swan Sonnenschein and Co; New York: Charles Scribner's Sons, 1895. 8vo. Pp xii, 443.

— —. Third edition. London: Swan Sonnenschein & Co, Lim; New York: Charles Scribner's Sons, 1900. 8vo. Pp xii, 443.

OWEN, ROBERT *The Life of Robert Owen, by himself*. Reprinted. London: G Bell & Sons Ltd, 1920. 8vo. Pp xiii, 352. Index.

PODMORE, FRANK *Robert Owen, A Biography*. With 44 illustrations, 2 photogravure plates, and facsimiles. London: Hutchinson & Co, 1906. 8vo. Vol 1, pp xv, 1-346; vol 2, pp xii, 347-688. Bibliography. Index.

— —. London: George Allen & Unwin Ltd, 1923. 8vo. Pp xv, 688. Bibliography. Index.
A reprint of the edition of 1906.

RUSK, ROBERT R 'Robert Owen'; *A History of Infant Education* (London: University of London Press, Ltd, 1933), 119-34. Portrait.

SALMON, DAVID and HINDSHAW, WINIFRED 'Robert Owen'; *Infant Schools: Their History and Theory* (London: Longmans, Green, and Co, 1904), 8-34.

STEPHEN, SIR LESLIE 'Owen, Robert'; *DNB*, 14 (1909), 1338-46.

WILSON, DAVID 'Robert Owen'; *SEJ*, 31 Aug 1928, 11, 910-12.

PAIP, Gilbert (?-1769), schoolmaster at Broughty Ferry, Angus, and Dundee.

WILLSHER, H M 'An Eighteenth Century Schoolmaster'; *Scots Mag*, new series, Jan 1933, 18, 301-4.

PILLANS, James (1778-1864), rector, the High School of Edinburgh; *later* Professor of Humanity, Edinburgh University.

GORDON, ALEXANDER 'Pillans, James'; *DNB*, 15 (1909), 1188-91.

RICHARDSON, ALEXANDER *Memoir of the late James Pillans, LL.D.*, Professor of Roman Literature in the University of Edinburgh. By an Old Student. Edinburgh: Maclachlan & Stewart, 1869. 8vo. Pp 56.

RUDDIMAN, Thomas (1674-1757), grammarian.

AITKEN, GEORGE A 'Ruddiman, Thomas'; *DNB*, 17 (1909), 381-3.

ANDERSON, WILLIAM 'Ruddiman, Thomas'; *The Scottish Nation* (Edinburgh and London: A Fullarton & Co, 1863), 3, 386-7; (Edinburgh: Thomas C Jack, 1882), 3, 386-7. Portrait.

CHALMERS, GEORGE *The Life of Thomas Ruddiman, A.M.* London: Printed for John Stockdale; and William Laing, Edinburgh, 1794. 8vo. Pp [8], 466. Portrait.

CHALMERS, ROBERT 'Ruddiman, Thomas'; *Biographical Dictionary of Eminent Scotsmen* (Glasgow and Edinburgh: Blackie & Son, 1835), 4, 182-7; new edition (1855), 4, 207-12; new edition (1870), 3, 311-14; revised throughout (1875), 3, 311-14.

DUNCAN, DOUGLAS *Thomas Ruddiman*. A Study in Scottish Scholarship of the Eighteenth Century. Edinburgh & London: Oliver & Boyd, 1965. 8vo. Pp xi, 178. Index.

'Lives of Eminent Preceptors—Thomas Ruddiman'; *Scottish Educational and Literary J*, Sept 1853, 1, 542-51.

SCHMITZ, Leonhard (1807-90), rector, Royal High School, Edinburgh.

STRONACH, GEORGE 'Schmitz, Leonhard'; *DNB*, 17 (1909), 907-8.

SCOTT, George (1777-1853), schoolmaster, Lilliesleaf, Roxburghshire.

G, A T 'An Old Parochial'; *Border Mag*, June 1899, 4, 108-10.

SIMPSON, James (1781-1853), educational pioneer.

CARLYLE, EDWARD I 'Simpson, James'; *DNB*, 18 (1909), 270.

MARWICK, WILLIAM H 'James Simpson'; *SEJ*, 22 Jan 1932, 15, 113-14.

SNELL, John (1629-79), educational benefactor.

ADDISON, W INNES 'The Founder'; *The Snell Exhibitions* (1901), 1-13.

CAMPBELL, G W 'Snell, John'; *DNB*, **18** (1909), 614-15.

MILROY, ANTHONY *John Snell, his Schools, Schoolmasters, and Scholars.* Reprinted from the *Ayr Advertiser.* np [Ayr], 1923. 12mo. Pp 186.

STOW, David (1793-1864), educational pioneer.

CHAMBERS, ROBERT 'Stow, David'; *Biographical Dictionary of Eminent Scotsmen*, new edition (London, Glasgow and Edinburgh: Blackie and Son, 1870), **3**, 404-9; revised throughout (1875), **3**, 404-9.

CRUICKSHANK, MARJORIE 'David Stow, Scottish Pioneer of Teacher Training in Britain'; *British J of Educational Studies*, May 1966, **14**, 205-15.

FITCH, SIR JOSHUA 'Stow, David'; *DNB*, **19** (1909), 1-2.

FRASER, WILLIAM *Memoir of the Life of David Stow.* Founder of the Training System of Education. London: James Nisbet and Co, 1868. 8vo. Pp xvi, 320. Portrait.

INSH, GEORGE PRATT *The Life and Work of David Stow.* Edinburgh: Lindsay and Company, Limited, 1938. 8vo. Pp 16.

LEITCH, JAMES 'David Stow'; *Practical Educationists and their Systems of Teaching* (Glasgow: James Maclehose, 1876), 186-238.

RUSK, ROBERT R 'David Stow'; *A History of Infant Education* (London: University of London Press, Ltd, 1933), 158-64. Portrait.

SALMON, DAVID, and HINDSHAW, WINIFRED 'David Stow'; *Infant Schools: Their History and Theory* (London: Longmans, Green, and Co, 1904), 67-75.

THOMSON, JOHN G *David Stow: Author of 'The Training System'.* Centenary Address. Edinburgh: Printed by John Lindsay, 1893. 12mo. Pp 24. Frontispiece and 1 plate.   GUL

TELFER, James (1797-1862), schoolmaster, Saughtrees, Roxburghshire.

HILSON, OLIVER 'An Old Border Schoolmaster'; *Transactions of the Hawick Archaeological Society*, 1922 (Hawick: Printed at *The Hawick Express & Advertiser* Office, 1922), 35-8.

WATSON, William (1796-1878), pioneer of industrial schools.

ANGUS, MARION *Sheriff Watson of Aberdeen:* The Story of his Life, and his Work for the Young. Aberdeen: D Wyllie & Son, 1913. 8vo. Pp xiii, 101. Portrait. Index.

WEDDERBURN, David (1580-1646), master of the Grammar School of Aberdeen.

CHAMBERS, ROBERT 'Wedderburn, David'; *Biographical Dictionary of Eminent Scotsmen* (1835), **4**, 428-30; new edition (1855), **4**, 450-2; new edition, **3** (1870), 509-10; revised throughout (1875), **3**, 509-10.

MILLAR, A H 'Wedderburn, David'; *DNB*, **20** (1909), 1045-7.

WILDERSPIN, Samuel (?1792-1866), educational pioneer.

LEITCH, JAMES 'Samuel Wilderspin'; *Practical Educationists and their Systems of Teaching* (Glasgow: James Maclehose, 1876), 166-85.

RUSK, ROBERT R 'Samuel Wilderspin'; *A History of Infant Education* (London: University of London Press, Ltd, 1933), 146-57. Portrait.

—'An Educational Missionary'; *SEJ*, **11**, 27 July 1928, 828-9.

SALMON, DAVID, and HINDSHAW, WINIFRED 'Samuel Wilderspin'; *Infant Schools, Their History and Theory* (London: Longmans, Green, and Co, 1904), 41-66.

WRIGHT, John (1797-1884), schoolmaster, Kirkholm, Wigtownshire.

ANDERSON, R M 'The "Whaleback" Dominie'; *Glasgow Herald*, 6 Apr 1935.

'The Art of Reading, and the Method of teaching it'; *Scottish Educational and Literary J*, Aug 1854, **2**, 586-93.

[BAIN, ALEXANDER] *Dr Clark's Spelling Reform*. Aberdeen, nd. 8vo. Pp 8. BM

BLACKIE, JOHN STUART 'The Importance of the German Language, and Reasons for its more general cultivation in this country'; *Edinburgh Literary J*, 22 Aug 1829, **2**, 163-6.

—*On the Studying and Teaching of Languages*. Two Lectures delivered in the Marischal College of Aberdeen. Edinburgh: Sutherland & Knox; London: Simpkin, Marshall, & Co; Aberdeen: George Davidson, 1852. 8vo. Pp 36.

BUCHANAN, C *Observations on Schools, and on Teaching some of the Common Branches of Education*. viz, 1. English; 2. Different Styles of Current-Hand Writing; 3. Arithmetic as an Art and as a Science; 4. The Advantages of learning Book-keeping; 5. The Possibility of Teaching Drawing as a Branch of General Education; 6. Popular Geography, and the Propriety of making Young People acquainted with Ancient Geography, etc. Edinburgh: Sold by Oliver & Boyd, 1824. 8vo. Pp 57.
GUL

BUCHANAN, ROBERT *Prospectus of a System of Initiatory Lessons in Drawing*, designed for the use of young people in our elementary schools. np, nd [1824]. 8vo. Pp 11. GUL

CALDWELL, CHARLES *Thoughts on Physical Education*, and the true mode of improving the condition of man, and on the study of the Greek and Latin Languages. With notes by Robert Cox, and a recommendatory Preface by George Combe. Edinburgh: Adam & Charles Black, 1836. 8vo. Pp xv, 190. BM

——. Second British edition. Edinburgh: Maclachlan, Stewart, & Co, 1844. 8vo. Pp iv, 36. EUL

COMBE, GEORGE *On Teaching Physiology and its Application in Common Schools*. Edinburgh: Maclachlan and Stewart:

London: Simpkin, Marshall, & Co, 1857. 8vo. Pp 16.

DUBUC, E 'Lecture on the Study of Physiology, as a part of General Education'; *Scottish Educational and Literary J*, Nov 1852, **1**, 68-74.

DUN, FINLAY 'On the Advantages of Studying the Theory along with the Practice of Music'; *Scottish Educational and Literary J*, Oct 1852, **1**, 31-7.

ESPINASSE, FRANCIS 'The Place which the Study of the Modern Languages ought to hold in a System of Education'; *Scottish Educational and Literary J*, Dec 1852, **1**, 118-28.

HADDEN, J CUTHBERT 'Music in Early Scotland'; *Scottish Rev*, Oct 1888, **12**, 221-44.

ILLSLEY, WILLIAM ALLEN *Studies in the History of the Teaching of English in Scotland*. Unpublished PhD thesis, St Andrews University, 1966. Typescript. 4to. Pp [4], 454. 11 plates. Bibliography. DUL

'Inaptness in Learning to Read'; *Scottish Educational and Literary J*, June 1853, **1**, 393-7.

J, A 'Art and Art Teaching'; *The Museum*, new series, 1 Nov 1866, **3**, 288-94.

KNIGHT, GEORGE 'The *Phonic* System of Teaching to read English'; *Scottish Educational and Literary J*, 2 July 1855, **3**, 227-34.

LAWSON, G 'Botany as a Branch of School Education; with some Observations on the Teaching of Science in General'; *Scottish Educational and Literary J*, Nov 1852, **1**, 57-65.

LEES, GEORGE *An Address in Defence of Euclid's Elements of Geometry as a Class-book for Students*. Edinburgh: Edmonston & Douglas, 1870. 8vo. Pp 27.

MCNAB, HENRY *A Plan of Reform, in the Mode of Instruction, at present practised in English Schools*. Glasgow: Printed by Andrew Foulis, for the Author, 1786. 8vo. Pp 24. GUL

MACPHERSON, ANGUS *English Education*; being an Attempt to place the Teaching and Study of the English Language on a truer and broader basis than is at present recognised. Second edition. Glasgow: David Robertson; Edinburgh: Oliver & Boyd, 1854. 8vo. Pp 38.

MEIKLEJOHN, JOHN M D *On the best & the worst Methods of Teaching Geography*. London: Williams and Norgate, 1869. 8vo. Pp 24.

NICOL, JAMES *On the Study of Natural History as a Branch of General Education*. Edinburgh: Oliver & Boyd; London: Simpkin, Marshall, & Co, 1853. 8vo. Pp 32.

PHILLIPS, JOHN *A Guide to the Physical Training of Both Sexes*. Glasgow: David Robertson, 1848. 8vo. Pp 46.
GUL

ROBERTSON, GEORGE *The Science Education Movement*. Edinburgh: Printed by Neill and Company, 1868. 8vo. Pp 29.

WADE, W M *Summary of a Course of Lectures on the Art of Reading*. Dundee: Printed by Colville and Son, 1813. 8vo. Pp vi, 52, x.

BEATTIE, JAMES 'Remarks on the Utility of Classical Learning'; *Essays on the Nature and Immutability of Truth* (Edinburgh: Printed for William Creech, 1776), 707-757.
EUL

— —; — (Edinburgh: Printed for the Author; and sold by Edward and Charles Dilly, in London; and William Creech, Edinburgh, 1777), 707-57.

— —; — (Dublin: Printed for C Jenkin, 1778), **2**, 433-94.

— —; *Essays. On Poetry and Music* (Edinburgh: William Creech; London E and C Dilly, 1776), 489-555.
BM

— —; *Essays: On Poetry and Music* (Edinburgh: Printed for Edward and Charles Dilly, in London; and William Creech, Edinburgh, 1778), 489-555.

—'Remarks on the Usefulness of Classical Learning'; *Essays: On Poetry and Music*. Third edition, corrected (London: Printed for E and C Dilly; and W Creech, Edinburgh, 1779), 455-515.

—*Remarks on the Usefulness of Classical Learning*. New Edition. London: Edward Roper, 1822. 12mo. Pp vii, 88.
BM

CHAPMAN, GEORGE *Advantages of a Classical Education:* The Importance of Latin, in particular; and its Usefulness for the Attainment of the English Language. Edinburgh: J Moir, 1804. 8vo. Pp 48.
BM

The Claims of Classical Studies whether as Information or as Training. By a Scotch Graduate. Aberdeen: John Adam; Edinburgh: Oliver & Boyd; London: Simpkin, Marshall, & Co, 1869. 8vo. Pp [4], 44.

CLARKE, MARTIN L 'Scotland from the Sixteenth to the Eighteenth Century'; *Classical Education in Britain, 1500-1900* (Cambridge: At the University Press, 1959), 133-45.

—'Greek in Scotland'; *Greek Studies in England, 1700-1830* (Cambridge: At the University Press, 1945), 40-7.

'Classical Education'; *Edinburgh Rev*, July 1821, **35**, 302-14.

'Estimate of "Classical Learning"; with a View towards a new arrangement of the Grammar Schools, and of education therein'; *Edinburgh Mag and Literary Miscellany*, Sept 1824, **15**, 336-8; Oct 1824, **15**, 398-9.

GEDDES, SIR WILLIAM D *Classical Education in the North of Scotland*. Edinburgh: Edmonston & Douglas; Aberdeen: John Smith, 1869. 8vo. Pp 69. EUL

'Greek Literature in Scotland'; *Westminster Rev*, Jan 1832, **16**, 90-110.

H, G 'On the Disadvantages of a Classical Education'; *Scots Mag*, July 1803, **65**, 452-6; Aug 1803, **65**, 521-5.

HAMILTON, SIR WILLIAM 'Pillans on Classical Education'; *Edinburgh Rev*, Oct 1836, **64**, 106-24.
Under the title, 'On the Conditions of Classical Learning. With relation to the Defence of Classical Instruction by Professor Pillans', this article was reprinted in HAMILTON, SIR WILLIAM, *Discussions on Philosophy and Literature, Education and University Reform* (1852), 328-47; (New York, 1853), 325-44;

second edition, enlarged (1853), 341-62; third edition (1866), 337-57.

HODGSON, WILLIAM B *'Classical' Instruction: Its Use and Abuse.* London: John Chapman, 1854. 8vo. Pp 71.
No 14 in 'Chapman's Library for the People'. It was a reprint of an article in the *Westminster Rev*, new series, 1 Oct 1853, 4, 450-98, where it was entitled 'The School Claims of Languages, Ancient and Modern'.

'Importance of Classical Education'; *Edinburgh Mag and Literary Miscellany*, Mar 1826, 18, 273-9.

An Inquiry whether the Study of the Ancient Languages be a necessary Branch of Modern Education? Edinburgh: Printed by Sands, Murray, and Cochran, 1769. 8vo. Pp xiv, 66.   New Coll

'Our Classical Education'; *Free Church Mag*, Dec 1848, 5, 563-7.

PILLANS, JAMES *A Discourse on the Latin Authors read and the Order of reading them in the earlier Stages of Classical Discipline.* Edinburgh: Maclachlan, Stewart, and Co; London: Taylor and Walton, and J W Parker, 1847. 12mo. Pp 48.   EUL

— 'How to improve the Preliminary Stages of Classical Education'; *The Museum*, Apr 1861, 1, 14-20.
Reprinted in PILLANS, JAMES *Educational Papers* (1862), 53-65, under the title, 'Hints for improving the preliminary Stages of a Classical Education'.

RUSSELL, MICHAEL *Observations on the Advantages of Classical Learning*, viewed as the Means of cultivating the Youthful

Mind, and more especially as compared with the Studies which it has been proposed to substitute in its stead. Edinburgh: Oliver & Boyd; London: Simpkin, Marshall, & Co, 1836. 8vo. Pp 56.   BM

— —. Second edition. Edinburgh: Oliver & Boyd; London: Simpkin, Marshall, & Co, 1836. 8vo. Pp 56.

—'Ueber die Vortheile der altclassischen Studien als eines Bildungsmittels des junglichen Geistes, in Vergleich mit den Real- und Natur- Wissenschaften'; *Paränesen für die Studirende Jünglinge auf Deutschen Gymnasien und Universitäten*, gesammelt durch F A Friedemann (Braunschweig, 1848), Vierter Band, 13-58.   BM
On p 13 the name of the translator is given as Fr Geiger.

SCHMITZ, LEONHARD 'On the Place which the Study of the Classics ought to hold in Education'; *Scottish Educational and Literary J*, Oct 1852, 1, 22-31.

SELLAR, WILLIAM Y *Theories of Classical Teaching.* Edinburgh: Edmonston and Douglas, 1867. 8vo. Pp 30.

'Should Boys learn Latin'; *Chambers's Edinburgh J*, 13 Aug 1842, 11, 239-40.

SUTTON, G M *The History of the Teaching of Classics in Scotland till 1872.* Unpublished PhD thesis, St Andrews University, 1956. 4to. Typescript. Pp 239. Bibliography.   DUL
See also CHRISTISON, ALEXANDER *The Diffusion of Knowledge, one great cause of the Prosperity of Great Britain.*

Education

Adult

BARCLAY, JOHN B *Adult Education in South-East Scotland.* Unpublished PhD thesis, Edinburgh University, 1960. Typescript. 4to. Pp 4, 424. Bibliography.   EUL

BROUGHAM, HENRY, LORD BROUGHAM *Practical Observations upon the Education of*

the People, addressed to the Working Classes and their Employers. London: Printed by Richard Taylor, and sold by Longman, Hurst, Rees, Orme, Brown and Green, for the Benefit of the London Mechanics' Institution, 1825. 8vo. Pp 33.
The greater part of this pamphlet origin-

ally appeared in the *Edinburgh Rev*, Oct 1824, **41**, 96-123, as a review of DAVID, WILLIAM, *Hints to Philanthropists: or, A Collective View of Practical Means of Improving the Condition of the Poor and Labouring Classes of Society*; its title there was *Scientific Education of the People*.
Twenty editions of this pamphlet were called for in 1825. The twentieth edition was reprinted at Boston, USA, in 1826, and a German translation of the same edition appeared at Berlin in 1827.

'Brougham on the Education of the People'; *Blackwood's Edinburgh Mag*, May 1825, **17**, 534-51.

BURNS, DAVID *Mechanics' Institutions; Their Objects and Tendency*. Glasgow: Thomas Murray; Edinburgh: Adam and Charles Black, 1837. 12mo. Pp xii, 72.
EUL

CHALMERS, THOMAS 'On Mechanic Schools, and on Political Economy as a Branch of Popular Education'; *The Christian and Civic Economy of Large Towns* (Glasgow: Printed for William Collins), 3 (1826), 378-408.

The Consequences of a Scientific Education to the Working Classes of the Country pointed out, and the Theories of Mr Brougham on that Subject confuted. By a Country Gentleman. London: Printed for T Cadell, 1826. 8vo. Pp [4], 77.
EUL

DICK, THOMAS 'Mechanics' Institutions'; *On the Mental Illumination and Moral Improvement of Mankind* (1835), 581-600.
EUL

GRIFFIN, JOHN *A Study of the Development of Adult Education in Scotland*. Unpublished PhD thesis, St Andrews University, 1953. Typescript. 4to. Pp 408, 12. Bibliography.
StAUL

HOLE, JAMES *An Essay on the History and Management of Literary, Scientific & Mechanics' Institutions:* and especially how far they may be developed and combined, so as to promote the moral wellbeing and industry of the country. London: Longman, Brown, Green, and Longmans, 1853. 8vo. Pp viii, 183.

HUDSON, JAMES WILLIAM *The History of Adult Education*, in which is comprised a full and complete History of the Mechanics' and Literary Institutions, Athenaeums, Philosophical, Mental and Christian Improvement Societies, Literary Unions, Schools of Design, etc., of Great Britain, Ireland, America, etc. etc. London: Longman, Brown, Green, & Longmans, 1851. 8vo. Pp xvi, 238. Index.

KELLY, THOMAS *A History of Adult Education in Great Britain*. Liverpool: Liverpool University Press, 1962. 8vo. Pp xli, 352. Index.

MCCONECHY, JAMES *An Introductory Address* delivered on the 19th of March, 1825, on the Formation of a Literary and Scientific Institution among the workmen of the University Printing Office, Glasgow: with an account of the Institution and some preliminary remarks on Popular Education. Glasgow: Printed at the University Press, 1825. 8vo. Pp 39.

MACKENZIE, SIR GEORGE S, BART *General Observations on the Principles of Education*: for the use of Mechanics' Institutions. Edinburgh: John Anderson, Jun; Glasgow: John McLeod, 1836. 8vo. Pp 95.
EUL

MARWICK, WILLIAM H 'Adult Educationalists in Victorian Scotland'; *J of Adult Education*, Apr 1933, **6**, 130-8.

—'Early Adult Education in the West of Scotland'; *J of Adult Education*, Apr 1930, **4**, 191-202.

—'Mechanics' Institutes in Scotland'; *J of Adult Education*, Oct 1933, **6**, 292-309.

Observations on Public Education, &c. &c. with a hint to those who are preparing Speeches for the Public Dinner to Henry Brougham, Esq., M.P. Edinburgh: Printed by G Mudie and Co, 1825. 8vo. Pp 20.

—Edinburgh: Printed by W Stewart, 1826. 8vo. Pp 20.
BM

'On the Power of Association applied to the Formation of Popular Literary and Scientific Institutions'; *Tait's Edinburgh Mag*, new series, Nov 1835, **2**, 753-8.

POLE, THOMAS *A History of the Origin and Progress of Adult Schools*. Bristol: Printed for the Author, 1814. 8vo. Pp [2], ii, 106.

Roman Catholic

ANDERSON, WILLIAM JAMES 'The College for the Lowland District of Scotland at Scalan and Aquhorties: Registers and Documents'; *Innes Rev*, 1963, **14**, 89-212.

—'Some Notes on Catholic Education for Scottish Children in Pre-Emancipation Days'; *Innes Rev*, 1963, **14**, 38-45.

BARRETT, MICHAEL 'On the Pioneer R.C. Seminary at Scalan, Glenlivet, Banff-shire'; *American Catholic Quarterly Rev*, 1909, **34**, 215-24.   Not seen

BLUNDELL, ODO 'Scalan Seminary'; *The Catholic Highlands of Scotland* (Edinburgh and London: Sands & Co, 1909), **1**, 24-39.

DEALY, MARY B *Catholic Schools in Scotland*. Washington, DC: The Catholic University of America Press, 1945. 8vo. Pp xii, 305. Bibliography. Index.

HANDLEY, JAMES EDMUND 'French Influences on Scottish Catholic Education in the Nineteenth Century'; *Innes Rev*, 1950, **1**, 22-34.

—'Provision of Schools'; *The Irish in Scotland, 1798-1845* (Cork University Press, 1943), 259-63; second edition (Cork University Press, 1945), 279-83.

—'Education of the Immigrants'; *The Irish in Modern Scotland* (Cork University Press, 1947), 191-239.

Elementary

ALMOND, HELY HUTCHINSON *Mr Lowe's Educational Theories examined from a practical point of view*. Edinburgh: Edmonston & Douglas, 1868. 8vo. Pp 40.

COLQUHOUN, JOHN CAMPBELL 'On the Advantages which accrue to Elementary Education in Scotland, from the System of the Committee of Privy Council on Education'; *Transactions of the National Association for the Promotion of Social Science, 1860* (1861), 356-60.

CURRIE, JAMES *The Principles and Practice of Common-School Education*. Edinburgh: James Gordon; London: Hamilton, Adams, & Co, 1861. 8vo. Pp xv, 504.

— — Second edition. Edinburgh: James Gordon; London: Hamilton, Adams, & Co, 1862. 8vo. Pp xv, 504.   EUL

—*The Principles and Practice of Early and Infant School-Education*. Edinburgh: Thomas Constable and Co; London: Hamilton, Adams, and Co, nd [?1857]. 8vo. Pp xvi, 310.

'Elementary Education in Scotland'; *Quarterly J of Education*, Oct 1834, **9**, 1-26.

'Elementary Instruction in Scotland'; *Quarterly J of Education*, Jan 1831, **1**, 16-24.

'Elementary Teaching'; *Quarterly Rev*, Jan 1829, **39**, 99-143.

FRASER, WILLIAM 'On the Present State of Elementary Education in Scotland, with Suggestions as to a Commission of Inquiry'; *Transactions of the National Association for the Promotion of Social Science, 1863* (1864), 303-8.

GLASGOW, UNIVERSITY OF *Report of Committee of Senate on Elementary Schools in their relation to the Universities*. Glasgow: James Maclehose, 1868. 8vo. Pp 24.   EUL

GORDON, JOHN *Letter to the Right Honourable the Lord Advocate of Scotland on Elementary Education in Scotland*. Edinburgh, 1835. 8vo. Pp 34.   EUL

—'Elementary Instruction. Its Character'; *Minutes of the Committee of Council on Education, 1855-56*, 582-93.

GREGORY, ALEXANDER *Destitution of Elementary Education in Scotland. Its two Aspects; and our Present Duty*. Edinburgh and London: Johnstone and Hunter, 1850. 8vo. Pp 23.   New Coll

HOME, DAVID MILNE *Legislation for Elementary Schools in Scotland with reference to the Report of the Royal Commissioners*. Edinburgh and London: William Blackwood and Sons, 1867. 8vo. Pp 103.

—*Sketch of Arrangements suggested for Elementary Schools in Scotland*. With explanatory Notes. Edinburgh and London: William Blackwood and Sons, 1868. 8vo. Pp 31.

Infant Play-School, for the Development of the Five Senses. From the German. With a Plate. Aberdeen: A Watson, 1829. 8vo. Pp 40.   APL

KERR, H J N *An Address on the Duty and Benefits of Early Education*, delivered in the Infant School of Brechin, 1st. August 1845. Brechin: Printed by Alexander Black, 1845. 12mo. Pp 24.

LAURIE, SIMON SOMERVILLE *On Primary Instruction in relation to Education*. Edinburgh and London: William Blackwood and Sons, 1867. 8vo. Pp xii, 223.
                                                      EUL
On p ix it is said that this work was originally written as part of a report made to the Trustees of the Dick Bequest which was printed at Edinburgh in 1865 but never published.

LOWE, ROBERT *Primary and Classical Education*. An Address delivered before the Philosophical Institution of Edinburgh, on Friday, November 1, 1867. Revised by the Author. Edinburgh: Edmonston and Douglas, 1867. 8vo. Pp 32.

MACGILL, STEVENSON *On Elementary Education*—A Discourse delivered before the Glasgow Society of Teachers (1810). Glasgow: John Smith & Sons, 1811. 8vo. Pp 41.   GUL

Memorial regarding Elementary Education in Scotland. Edinburgh, 1835. 8vo. Pp 32.   New Coll

NICHOL, JOHN PRINGLE *Moral Training in our Common Schools*. Suggestions of certain Practical Methods of increasing its Efficiency. London and Glasgow: Richard Griffin and Company, 1858. 8vo. Pp 56.

[NORVALL, JAMES] *Letters addressed to the Parochial Schoolmasters of Scotland, concerning the New Method of Tuition*. Containing Strictures on Professor Pillans' 'Principles of Elementary Teaching', and Suggestions respecting the Means of Accomplishing a strict Division of Labour in conducting Promiscuous Schools. By a Schoolmaster. Montrose: Sold by John Mitchell, at the *Review* Office; and by A Macredie, Edinburgh, 1829. 8vo. Pp viii, 117.   EUL
For the authorship see JESSOP, J C *Education in Angus* (1931), 113-15.

O, S G *Letters on the Education of Young Children*. Edinburgh: Edmonston and Douglas, 1866. 8vo. Pp 39.
                                                      New Coll

PILLANS, JAMES 'Hints on some prevailing Errors in the Educational Training of the Working Classes'; *Transactions of the National Association for the Promotion of Social Science, 1858* (1859), 284-90.

—*Principles of Elementary Teaching*, chiefly in reference to the Parochial Schools of Scotland: in two Letters to T. F. Kennedy, Esq., M.P. Edinburgh: Adam Black; and Longman, Rees, Orme, Brown, & Green, London, 1828. 8vo. Pp iv, 146.

— —. Second edition, with Corrections and Additions; and a Postscript, containing Answers to Objections, and additional Illustrations. Edinburgh: Adam Black; and Longman, Rees, Orme, Brown, & Green, London, 1829. 8vo. Pp iv, 186.

— '—'; In *Contributions to the Cause of Education* (1856), 3-102. Reprinted from the second edition with the title, *Two Letters on Teaching*.

NOTE The author of the *Memoir of the late James Pillans* (1869), 37, gave the date of the first edition of this work as 1827 and of the second as 1828, and in this he was followed by the writer of the article on Pillans in *DNB*. But since the dates on the title pages are as given here, and since the Preface is dated 'July 4, 1828', they must be both in error. This error may be due to the fact that the two letters to Kennedy are dated respectively 'Oct. 21, 1827', and 'Oct. 27, 1827'. Both also mention a third edition in 1855, but no trace of this has been found, and there may be here only a mistaken reference to the Inclusion of the *Principles* in the 1856 volume, *Contributions to the Cause of Education*.

PLAYFAIR, LYON *On Primary and Technical Education*. Two Lectures. Edinburgh: Edmonston and Douglas, 1870. 8vo. Pp 52.

S, J M 'Infant Schools'; *Edinburgh Christian Instructor*, June 1829, **28**, 401-6.

SHUTTLEWORTH, SIR JAMES KAY 'The Condition and Prospects of Elementary Education in Scotland'; *Public Education as affected by the Minutes of the Committee of Privy Council from 1846 to 1852; with Suggestions as to Future Policy*

(London: Longman, Brown, Green, and Longmans, 1853), 322-416.

WATSON, WILLIAM *Elementary Education.* np [?Aberdeen], 1863. 8vo. Pp 8.   APL

WEIR, A C *Primary Education considered in relation to the State*: Reply to the Address of the Right Hon. Robert Lowe, M.P., on 1st November, 1867, before the Philosophical Institution, Edinburgh. Edinburgh: Edmonston and Douglas, 1868. 8vo. Pp 28.

National

BEGG, JAMES 'Obstacles to a National System of Education in Scotland'; *Transactions of the National Association for the Promotion of Social Science, 1858* (1859), 282-4.

—*Recent Educational Struggles in Scotland*: The altered policy of the Free Church on the subject of National Education. Edinburgh: Johnstone, Hunter, & Co, 1872. 8vo. Pp 47.   New Coll

—*National Education for Scotland practically considered*: with Notices of certain recent Proposals on that subject. Edinburgh and London: Johnstone & Hunter, 1850. 8vo. Pp 36.   New Coll

— —. Second edition. Edinburgh and London: Johnstone and Hunter, 1850. 8vo. Pp 36.
Reprinted in the *Presbyterian*, new series, Apr 1872, **1**, 266-70; May 1872, **1**, 323-8.

BLACK, ADAM 'Plan for the conversion of the Parochial and Denominational Schools into National Schools'; *Education (Scotland) Commission: Second Report* (1867), 106-12.

—*Speech in favour of the Government's Scheme of Education.* Edinburgh: A Fullarton and Co, and P S Frazer and Co; Glasgow: William Lang, [1847]. 8vo. Pp 13.   EUL

CHURCH OF SCOTLAND: GENERAL ASSEMBLY 'Declaration by the General Assembly of the Church of Scotland on National Education'; *Report of the General Assembly's Education Committee*, 1849, 55-64.

—PRESBYTERY OF GLASGOW *Report of Proceedings on 25th March, 1868, on the subject of Education in Scotland. And on 11th March, 1869, on the Parochial Schools (Scotland) Bill.* Glasgow: Thomas Murray & Son, 1868. 8vo. Pp 42, [18].   New Coll

NOTE This is a re-issue of a pamphlet published in 1868 with the account of the 1869 Proceedings printed on 18 unnumbered pages which have been inserted between 40 and 41 of the original pamphlet. The second sentence in the title has been added to the original title-page of 1868.

COLQUHOUN, JOHN CAMPBELL *On the Measures to be now taken in order to secure a good National Education.* London: T Hatchard, and J Ridgway, 1853. 8vo. Pp 16.   New Coll

COMBE, GEORGE *Remarks on National Education.* Edinburgh: Maclachlan, Stewart & Co; London: Simpkin, Marshall, & Co; Dublin: James M'Glashan, 1847. 8vo. Pp 33.

— —. Second edition. Edinburgh: Maclachlan, Stewart & Co; London: Simpkin, Marshall, & Co; Dublin: James M'Glashan, 1847. 8vo. Pp 15.

— —. Third edition. Edinburgh: Maclachlan, Stewart & Co; London: Simpkin, Marshall, & Co; Dublin: James M'Glashan, 1847. 8vo. Pp 15.   New Coll

—*Remarks on National Education: being an Inquiry into the Right and Duty of Government to educate the People.* Fourth edition. Edinburgh: Maclachlan, Stewart & Co; London: Simpkin, Marshall, & Co; Dublin: James M'Glashan, 1847. 8vo. Pp 38.   EUL

— —. Fifth edition. Edinburgh: Maclachlan, Stewart & Co; London: Simpkin, Marshall, & Co; Dublin: James M'Glashan, 1848. 8vo. Pp 38.
Reprinted under the title, 'National Education', in *Moral and Intellectual Science: applied to the Elevation of Society*, ed WELLS, S R (New York: Fowler and Wells, 1848), 5-43.

EDMOND, JAMES *National Education and the Position of the Churches*, especially the Free Church. Aberdeen: John Smith, 1854. 8vo. Pp 38.   New Coll

EDMOND, JOHN *Voluntaryism in the House of its Friends*: being Review of Answers by the United Presbyterian Synod to Reasons of Dissent from Resolutions on the Subject of National Education. Glasgow: Robert Stark; London: Ward & Co; Edinburgh: W Oliphant & Son, 1855. 8vo. Pp 24.   New Coll

ELLIOT, WILLIAM HUGH, Lord Melgund, 3rd Earl of Minto. *Remarks on the Government Scheme of National Education, as applied to Scotland.* Edinburgh: A & C Black; London: Longman, Brown, Green & Longmans, 1848. 8vo. Pp 46.

FRASER, WILLIAM *National Education: Reasons for the Rejection in Britain of the Irish System.* A brief Exposition for Christian Educationists. London: James Nisbet and Co, 1861. 8vo. Pp 48.   BM

— —. Fourth edition. Paisley: Robert Stewart; London: James Nisbet and Co, 1861. 8vo. Pp 48.

—'Suggestions as to a Legislative Basis for a National System, suited to the educational Condition of Scotland'; *Transactions of the National Association for the Promotion of Social Science, 1860* (1861), 347-56.

The Free Church Education Scheme, National or Denominational, as indicated by the Rejection of Dr Gunn? Being five Letters reprinted from the *Caledonian Mercury* Newspaper. With additional Remarks. By a Free Churchman. Edinburgh: A & C Black, 1851. 8vo. Pp 31.

GLASGOW COMMITTEE ON NATIONAL EDUCATION *National Education in Scotland.* Glasgow, 1860. 8vo. Pp 15.   New Coll

GLASGOW PUBLIC SCHOOL ASSOCIATION *Memorial on behalf of a National System of Education.* Glasgow: James Maclehose, 1854. 8vo. Pp 17.   Mit

GORDON, ABERCROMBY LOCKHART *The System of National Education in Scotland, its Origin, its Nature, and Results.* Being the Substance of a Report of a Committee of the Synod of Aberdeen. With Notes and Illustrations. Aberdeen: Peter Gray; Edinburgh: John Johnstone; Glasgow: Wm Collins; London: Jas Nisbet & Co, 1839. 8vo. Pp 59.

'Government Education'; *Chambers's Edinburgh J*, new series, 8 May 1847, 7, 297-9.

'Government Education'; *Presbyterian Rev*, Apr 1847, **20**, 252-9.   New Coll

GRAY, ANDREW *National Education.* Speech delivered in the Free Church Presbytery of Perth, on the 26th December 1849. Perth: James Dewar & Son, 1850. 12mo. Pp 16.   New Coll

— —. Second Speech delivered in the Free Church Presbytery of Perth, on the 30th January 1850. Perth: James Dewar & Son, 1850. 12mo. Pp 16.   New Coll

GREGOR, WALTER *National Education and the Church of Scotland.* Edinburgh: Edmonston & Douglas, 1868. 8vo. Pp 32.

GUNN, WILLIAM M *Religion in Connexion with a National System of Instruction*: their Union advocated, the Arguments of non-Religionists considered, and a System proposed. Edinburgh: Oliver & Boyd; London: Simpkin, Marshall, & Co, 1840. 8vo. Pp xv, 444.

GUTHRIE, THOMAS *Letter on National Education.* Edinburgh and London: Johnstone and Hunter, 1850. 8vo. Pp 8.   New Coll

HETHERINGTON, WILLIAM M 'National Education in Scotland'; *Free Church Mag*, Mar 1850, 7, 65-71.   New Coll

—*National Education in Scotland, Viewed in its Present Condition, its Principles, and its Possibilities.* Edinburgh and London: Johnstone & Hunter, and Charles Ziegler, 1850. 8vo. Pp 75.   New Coll

— —. Second edition. Edinburgh and London: Johnstone and Hunter, and Charles Ziegler, 1850. 8vo. Pp 75.

— —. Third edition. With an Introduction and Notes. Edinburgh and London: Johnstone and Hunter, and Charles Ziegler, 1850. 8vo. Pp 62.   New Coll

HILL, FREDERIC 'Scotland'; *National Education; its Present State and Prospects* (London: Charles Knight, 1836), **1**, 284-319.

'Hints on a National System of Education for Scotland'; *The Museum*, new series, 2 Oct 1865, **2**, 241-7.

F

HOPE, JOHN *The Education Question from the Voluntary Stand-point*. Edinburgh, 1869. 8vo. Pp 7.   New Coll

—*National Education in Scotland.* A Letter to the Right Honourable the Earl of Aberdeen, embodying a New Suggestion for the harmonising of sound Religious Instruction, with the Claims of the Established and other Presbyterian Churches. Edinburgh: Alexander C Moodie; Glasgow: J Murray & Son; Aberdeen: J H Wilson; Perth: P Drummond; London: Arthur, Hall, Virtue, & Co; Dublin: W Cutty, Jun & Co, 1854. 8vo. Pp 24.

—*National Education.* The Individual System of National Education reconciles all Differences. np, 1872. 8vo. Pp 8.
                                      Mit

JOHNSTONE, W *A Voice from the Schoolroom,* or, Hints and Suggestions on the Education Question, as regards Scotland. Addressed to the Lord Advocate. Edinburgh: Shephard & Elliot; Glasgow: David Bryce; Dumfries: William F Johnstone; Dunfermline: W Clark, 1855. 8vo. Pp 69.   New Coll

LEE, ROBERT *National Education.* Edinburgh: Edmonston & Douglas; and Sutherland & Knox, 1856. 8vo. Pp 26.

LEE, WILLIAM 'National Education in Scotland'; *Blackwood's Edinburgh Mag*, May 1849, **65**, 567-76.

—*Lord Melgund and the Parish Schools.* By a Churchman. Reprinted with Additions from *Blackwood's Magazine*. Edinburgh and London: William Blackwood and Sons, 1849. 8vo. Pp 23.

—*National Education in Scotland. A Word or Two for the Parish Schools.* Reprinted from *Blackwood's Magazine*. Second edition, enlarged. Edinburgh and London: William Blackwood and Sons, 1854. 8vo. Pp 23.   New Coll

———. Third edition, enlarged. Edinburgh and London: William Blackwood and Sons, 1854. 8vo. Pp 23.

LEGGATT, WILLIAM *Scottish Education, and the Principles of the National Education League.* Glasgow: James Maclehose, 1870. 8vo. Pp 26.   GUL

'Lord Melgund on the Government Scheme

of Education'; *Free Church Mag*, Nov 1848, **5**, 343-5.

MACKAY, CHARLES *The Education of the People, and the Necessity for the Establishment of a National System.* Glasgow: William Lang; London: Simpkin, Marshall, & Co; Edinburgh: Fraser & Co; Dublin: James M'Glashan, 1846. 12mo. Pp 122.

'Manifesto on National Education. January, 1850'; in ANDERSON, JOHN *History of Edinburgh* (1856), 536-40.

MARTIN, HUGH *National Education.* Reply to the Lord Advocate's Speech at Stranraer. Edinburgh: John Maclaren; London: James Nisbet & Co; Glasgow: Thomas Murray & Son; Belfast: C Aitchison, 1872. 8vo. Pp 19.
                                 New Coll

MELGUND, LORD See ELLIOT, WILLIAM HUGH.

MILLIGAN, WILLIAM 'The Parish Schools of Scotland, and their Bearing upon the Question of National Education in Scotland'; *Transactions of the National Association for the Promotion of Social Science, 1863* (1864), 292-302.

MILNE, DAVID *Remarks on the Government Scheme of Education, as applicable to Scotland,* in a Letter addressed to the Secretary of the Education Committee of the Church of Scotland. Edinburgh: Edmonston and Douglas, 1849. 8vo. Pp v, 59.

'National Education'; *Church of Scotland Mag and Rev*, June 1853, **1**, 89-111; July 1853, **1**, 185-210.

'National Education'; *The Presbyterian,* new series, 1 Oct 1869, **1**, 144-8.

'National Education'; *The Watchword,* 2 Dec 1867, **2**, 293-4; 1 Apr 1872, **7**, 15-19.   New Coll

'National Education'; *Autobiography of Thomas Guthrie, D.D., and Memoir by his Sons, Rev. David K. Guthrie and Charles J. Guthrie* (London: Daldy, Isbister, & Co), **2** (1875), 284-307.

National Education. Glasgow, 1871. 8vo. Pp 8.   New Coll

'National Education'; (extracted from the *Presbyterian Review.*) np, nd [1837]. 8vo. Pp 20.   New Coll

First printed in the *Westminster Rev,*

Aug 1837, **10**, 1-15, under the title, 'Simpson on National Education'.

National Education. The Bible in the School. Authorised Report of the Public Meeting held in the City Hall, Glasgow, on Monday, 25th April, 1870. Glasgow: Thomas Murray and Son, 1870. 8vo. Pp 48.
New Coll

National Education. The Gunn Dinner analysed, and the Gunn Rejection vindicated, including Five Letters reprinted from the Caledonian Mercury Newspaper. By a Free Church Member. Edinburgh: John D Lowe, 1851. 8vo. Pp ?.
Mit
The first four letters are dated 30 Nov, 7, 14 and 21 Dec 1851. The fifth letter, dated 8 Jan 1851, had not in fact been previously printed in the *Caledonian Mercury*, 'the Proprietors of that paper thinking the continuance of the controversy unnecessary and undesirable'.

National Education. Report of the Proceedings at a Public Meeting held in the Mechanics' Hall, Aberdeen, on the 25th April, 1851, on the Important Subject of National Education. (From the *Aberdeen Herald*.) Aberdeen: Lewis Smith; Edinburgh: Maclachlan & Stewart; Glasgow: David Robertson, 1851. 8vo. Pp 19.

National Education. Report of the Proceedings at a Meeting of the Working Classes of Edinburgh, on the 21st January 1851. (From the *Scotsman*.) Second edition, revised. Edinburgh: Maclachlan & Stewart, 1851. 8vo. Pp 23.

National Education. Report of the Proceedings at a Meeting of the Glasgow Public School Association, held in the Merchants' Hall, Glasgow, on the 11th November, 1851, with the Address then delivered by Dr J. P. Nichol, on the existing Obstructions to the Institution of a National System of Education. (From the *North British Daily Mail*.) Glasgow: David Robertson; John Robertson, 1851. 8vo. Pp 22.

National Education. Report of the Proceedings at a Meeting of the Working Classes of Paisley, on Monday, September 29, 1851. (From the *North British Daily Mail*.) np, nd [1851]. 8vo. Pp 16.

'National Education—The Government Scheme'; *Free Church Mag*, Apr 1847, **4**, 105-14.

'National Education and the United Presbyterians'; *The Watchword*, 1 May 1869, **4**, 49-62.
New Coll

'National Education in Scotland'; *The Presbyterian*, new series, 2 Aug 1869, **1**, 85-8.

'The National School Question'; *Scottish Rev*, Apr 1854, **2**, 136-47.

National Education for Scotland. Proposed Basis for Legislation. Glasgow: W G Blackie and Co, 1859. 8vo. Pp 32.
New Coll

THE NATIONAL EDUCATION ASSOCIATION OF SCOTLAND *Report of Proceedings at a Public Meeting held in Edinburgh, on Tuesday, 9th April, 1850.* np, nd. 12mo. Pp 57.
New Coll

NICHOL, JOHN *Address on National Education.* Glasgow: James Maclehose, 1869. 8vo. Pp 43.

NICHOL, JOHN P See *National Education.* above.

'Notes on the Education Question. By Another Free Church Elder'; *The Watchword*, 1 Mar 1872, **6**, 549-53. New Coll

'On National Education'; *Voluntary Church Mag*, Aug 1835, **3**, 362-71.

'On National Education as to Quality'; *Voluntary Church Mag*, Oct 1835, **3**, 444-54.

'On National Education as to Superintendence. Claims of the Church Clergy'; *Voluntary Church Mag*, Nov 1835, **3**, 493-506.

'On National Education as to Superintendence. Legislative Interference'; *Voluntary Church Mag*, Dec 1835, 3, 529-38; Jan 1836, **4**, 7-16.

'On National Education as to Superintendence. Machinery of the System'; *Voluntary Church Mag*, Apr 1836, **4**, 171-5.

On National Education: An Essay, originally published in 'The British Educator'. Glasgow: Thomas Murray and Son, 1856. 8vo. Pp 47. New Coll
Appeared in 1856 in the *British Educator* in the following issues: No III (May),

97-106; No IV (June), 161-72; No V (July), 208-15; No VI (Aug), 273-9.

PARISH SCHOOLMASTER, A 'National Education—The proposed Tenure of Office'; *The Museum*, new series, 1 July 1867, 4, 138-9.

Proposal for a System of National Education in Scotland. Edinburgh: W P Kennedy, [1851]. 8vo. Pp 20, 2.   New Coll

RENTON, HENRY *The Principles of the United Presbyterian Church on National Education*, particularly in regard to Religious Education. Edinburgh: Andrew Elliot, 1869. 8vo. Pp 16.

Report of the Proceedings at the Public Meeting of the Friends of National Education in the Music Hall, Edinburgh, on Wednesday, January 25, 1854. Edinburgh: Adam and Charles Black, 1854. 8vo. Pp 98.   New Coll

Report of the Speeches delivered at the Public Meeting of the Inhabitants of Edinburgh opposed to the Government Scheme of Education, held on Wednesday evening, the 31st March 1847. Revised by the respective speakers. Edinburgh: Grant & Taylor, 1847. 8vo. Pp 34.
    New Coll

RICHARDSON, ALEXANDER 'Scottish National Education'; *Facts and Fallacies relative to Scottish Churches and Schools: Twelve Tracts for the Times.* By 'Freelance' (Edinburgh: Maclachlan & Stewart; Glasgow: Thomas Murray and Son; London: Simpkin, Marshall, and Co, 1871), 154-86.

RUSSELL, THOMAS *Government Scheme of Education.* Speech in the Edinburgh Town Council, April 6, 1847. Edinburgh: Printed and published by T and W M'Dowall, 1847. 8vo. Pp 8.

s 'On the Necessity of Pastoral Superintendence of the National Schools'; *Church of Scotland Mag*, Aug 1835, **2**, 247-54; Oct 1835, **2**, 333-6.

'Scottish National Education'; *North British Rev*, Feb 1850, **12**, 482-98.

Speeches on the Government Plan of National Education, delivered at a Public Meeting held in Edinburgh on Monday, the 8th of July 1839. Revised by the Speakers. Edinburgh: Thomas Paton; Glasgow: William Whyte and Co,

John Lindsay, J Gray, J Johnstone, D Bryce; Aberdeen: George King, 1839. 8vo. Pp 54.

—. Second edition. Edinburgh: George Paton; Glasgow: William Whyte and Co, John Lindsay, J Gray, J Johnstone, D Bryce; Aberdeen: George King, 1839. 8vo. Pp 54.   GUL

SIMPSON, JAMES *Anti-National Education*, or, The Spirit of Sectarianism morally tested by means of certain speeches and letters from the Member for Kilmarnock. With an appendix. Edinburgh: Adam & Charles Black; London: Longman & Co, 1837. 8vo. Pp 50.

—*Education*: Correspondence between Mr Simpson of Edinburgh and Mr Colquhoun of Killermont, M.P. Glasgow: Printed in the *Scottish Guardian* Office, 1837. 8vo. Pp 20.

Reprinted from the *Scottish Guardian* of Monday, 31 July and Thursday, 10 Aug 1837.

STOW, DAVID *National Education.* London, 1847. 8vo. Pp 90.

Strictures on the recent Public Meeting in Edinburgh on 25th January, 1854, on the Subject of a National System of Education in Scotland. By a Churchman. Edinburgh: Paton and Ritchie; Glasgow: T Murray and Son, and J Smith and Son, 1854. 8vo. Pp 36.

Strictures on the Rev. William Wilson's 'Plea for Congregational Schools'. By a Layman. Dundee: Frederick Shaw, 1854. 12mo. Pp 19.   New Coll

NOTE On the title-page of the copy in New College Library someone has pencilled in 'S. S. Laurie ?' under 'By a Layman'.

TULLOCH, JOHN 'The Parish Schools in relation to Plans of National Education for Scotland, to the Universities, and the Church'; *Transactions of the National Association for the Promotion of Social Science, 1860* (1861), 339-47.

A Voice from the Church, being a Review of the Resolutions and Speeches at the Public Meeting on National Education, 25 January, addressed to the Friends of a 'Religious System of National Education', with a Vindication of the Church of Scotland from the aspersions of Lord

Panmure, Drs Cunningham and Guthrie, and others. Edinburgh: Alexander C Moodie, 1854. 8vo. Pp 24.

—. Second edition. Edinburgh: Alexander C Moodie, 1854. 8vo. Pp 23.

'Voices from the Church on the Education Controversy'; *Church of Scotland Mag and Rev*, Mar 1854, **2**, 239-44.

WILSON, THOMAS 'National Education'; *The Freeman*, Aug 1851, 119-25. BM

WILSON, WILLIAM Education: A Plea for Congregational Schools. Dundee: William Middleton, 1854. 8vo. Pp 38.
New Coll

Of Handicapped Children

ALSTON, JOHN *First Specimen of Printing for the Use of the Blind.* Made in the Glasgow Asylum for the Blind. 21 Oct 1836. 4to. P 1. 4 plates. BM

—*Narrative of the Progress of Printing for the Blind at the Glasgow Institution.* Glasgow: Printed in the *Scottish Guardian* Office, 1838. 8vo. Pp 12. BM

—*Specimen of Type Printing in which the New Testament, Psalms and Paraphrases are printed for the Use of the Blind.* Glasgow: Printed by George Brookman, 1837. 4to. Pp 9.

—*Statements of the Education, Employment, and Internal Arrangements at the Asylum for the Blind, Glasgow.* With a short account of its Founder, and general observations applicable to similar institutions. January, MDCCCXXXV. Glasgow: John Smith & Son, 1835. 8vo. Pp 24. Illustrated. GUL

— —. Second edition, with an appendix. June 1835. Glasgow: Printed at the Asylum, nd [1835]. 8vo. Pp 27. Frontispiece and 4 plates. GUL

— —. Third edition, considerably enlarged, with lithographic illustrations. Jan 1836. Glasgow: John Smith & Son, nd [1836]. 8vo. Pp 40. Frontispiece.

— —. Also the Ninth Annual Report by the Directors of the Asylum. Fourth edition, considerably enlarged, with lithographic illustrations. June 1836. Glasgow: John Smith & Son, nd [1836]. 8vo. Pp 41, 24. Frontispiece.

— —. Sixth edition, considerably enlarged, with lithographic illustrations. Oct 1839. Glasgow: John Smith & Son, 1839. 8vo. Pp 44. 4 plates. BM

— —. —, With lithographic illustrations. Ninth edition, with an Appendix. June 1844. Glasgow: John Smith & Son; Edinburgh: John Johnstone, 1844. 8vo. Pp 68. BM

— —. —, With lithographic illustrations. Tenth edition, with an Appendix. Feb 1846. Glasgow: John Smith and Son, 1846. 8vo. Pp 80. Frontispiece.

— —. *To the Directors of the Asylum for the Blind, Glasgow.* Glasgow: Printed in the *Scottish Guardian* Office, 1838. 8vo. Pp 20. GUL

— —. *To the Directors of the Institutions for the Blind, in Great Britain and Ireland.* Glasgow: Printed in the *Scottish Guardian* Office, nd [?1838]. 8vo. Pp 11. EUL

ANDERSON, THOMAS *Observations on the Employment, Education, and Habits, of the Blind;* with a Comparative View of the Benefits of the Asylum and School Systems. London: Simpkin, Marshall, and Co, 1837. 8vo. Pp [2], ii, 103. EUL

ASYLUM FOR THE BLIND, GLASGOW *Public Examination.* Printing for the Blind. Glasgow: Printed in the *Scottish Guardian* Office, 1838. 8vo. Pp 4. BM
Reprinted from the *Scottish Guardian*, 10 May 1838.

Description of an Alphabet, the sole Invention of two of the Blind at the Asylum in Edinburgh, whereby Blind Persons can effectually communicate with each other. Edinburgh, 1821. 8vo. P 1. GUL

GALL, JAMES *An Account of the recent Discoveries which have made for facilitating the Education of the Blind,* with Specimens of the Books, Maps, Pictures, &c. for their Use. Printed on behalf of the Edinburgh School for the Blind. Edinburgh: James Gall, 1837. 8vo. Pp 106. 4 illustrations.

—*A historical Sketch of the Origin and Progress of Literature for the Blind*: and Practical Hints and Recommendations as to their education. With an appendix, containing directions for teaching reading and writing to the Blind, with and without a regular Teacher. Edinburgh: James Gall; London: Hamilton, Adams, & Co; Dublin: William Curry, Jun & Co, 1834. 4to. Pp xx, 388.

SOCIETY FOR THE ENCOURAGEMENT OF THE USEFUL ARTS IN SCOTLAND *Report on the best alphabet and method of printing for the use of the Blind.* np [?Edinburgh], 1837. 8vo. Pp [2], 34.

DALGARNO, GEORGE *Didascalocophus*, or, *The Deaf and Dumb Man's Tutor*, to which is added a Discourse of the Nature and Number of Double Consonants: both which Tracts being the first (for what the Author knows) that have been published upon either of the Subjects. Oxford: Printed at the Theater, *Anno Dom* 1680. 8vo. Pp 136.
                                                                    BM
Reprinted in *The Works of George Dalgarno of Aberdeen*, ed MAITLAND, THOMAS (Edinburgh: Maitland Club, 1834), 117-79; and see 'The Works of George Dalgarno', *Edinburgh Rev*, July 1835, **61**, 407-17.

ENGLAND, JOHN *A Treatise on the Education of the Deaf and Dumb.* Montrose: John Smith, 1819. 8vo. Pp xx, 48.

GREEN, FRANCIS '*Vox Oculis Subjecta*'; A Discourse on the most *curious* and important Art of imparting Speech, and the Knowledge of Language, to the *naturally* Deaf, and (consequently) Dumb; with a Particular Account of the Academy of Messrs Braidwood of Edinburgh, and a Proposal to perpetuate and extend the benefits thereof. London, 1783. 8vo. Pp xvi, 224.

'Education of Imbecile Youth'; *Scottish Rev*, Jan 1862, 53-62.

The Education of the Imbecile, and the Improvement of Invalid Youth. Edinburgh: Published for Behoof of the Home and School for Invalid Children, 10 Gayfield Square, Edinburgh, 1856. 8vo. Pp 20.   New Coll

SOCIETY FOR THE EDUCATION OF IMBECILE CHILDREN IN SCOTLAND *The Imbecile and*

their Training. Edinburgh: Johnstone, Hunter, & Co, 1861. 12mo. Pp 47.
Reprinted from the *Christian Treasury*.

WATSON, THOMAS J *A History of Deaf Education in Scotland, 1760-1939.* Unpublished PhD thesis, Edinburgh University, 1939. Typescript. 4to. Pp 4, 279. Bibliography.   EUL

Of the Poor

ALLAN, afterwards ALLAN-FRASER, PATRICK *On some of the Causes which at present retard the Moral and Intellectual Progress of the Working Classes.* A Lecture delivered to the Members of the Arbroath Scientific and Literary Association on 18th February 1857. Edinburgh: Edmonston and Douglas, 1857. 12mo. Pp 36.

ANDERSON, GEORGE *The Education of the Working Classes*, and the best Means of promoting it. Glasgow: Thomas Murray and Son, 1857. 8vo. Pp 15.

BUCHANAN, ROBERT *The Schoolmaster in the Wynds*; or, How to educate the Masses. Glasgow: Blackie and Son; Maurice Ogle and Son; Edinburgh: Robert Ogle, 1850. 8vo. Pp 32.
At least three editions of this pamphlet were called for in 1850.

CHALMERS, THOMAS *Churches and Schools for the Working Classes.* An Address on the practicability of providing moral and religious education for the Working Population of large towns, as illustrated by the success which has attended the Operation carried on in the West Port of Edinburgh. Delivered 27 Dec 1845. Edinburgh: John D Lowe; London: R Groombridge and Sons, and J Nisbet and Co, 1846. 8vo. Pp 31.

CHAPMAN, GEORGE *Hints on the Education of the Lower Ranks of the People: and the Appointment of Parochial Schoolmasters.* Respectfully submitted to the Proprietors of Land in Great Britain. Edinburgh: Printed by J Moir, 1801. 8vo. Pp 33.

COLQUHOUN, PATRICK *New and appropriate System of Education for the Labouring Poor.* London: J Hatchard, 1806. 8vo. Pp 93.   Not seen

ERSKINE, JOHN *The Education of Poor Children recommended*. Edinburgh: A Murray & J Cochran, 1774. 4to. Pp 29, [2].

FRASER, PATRICK ALLAN See ALLAN, afterwards ALLAN-FRASER.

'On the Education of the Poor'; *Blackwood's Edinburgh Mag*, July 1820, 7, 419-27.

PHILOPENETES 'Observations on the Provision made for the Education of the Lower Orders in the Metropolis, and other great cities of Scotland'; *Scots Mag*, Apr 1807, 69, 244-5.

PILLANS, JAMES 'On some prevailing Errors in the Educational Training of the Working Classes, and the Means of Cure'; *Educational Papers* (1862), 20-35.

Remarks on the Influence of Education on the Lower Classes of Society. By the Author of 'Independence, or, The Poor Man his own best Friend'. Glasgow: Young, Gallie, & Co, 1820. 12mo. Pp 12.   New Coll

THOMSON, JOHN (1) 'On the Education of the Poor'; in HUNTER, A *Georgical Essays* (York, 1804), 6, 437-79.   BM

TROUP, GEORGE *The Question of the Day. How are the Masses to be educated and evangelised?* Glasgow and London: R Griffin and Co, 1857. 8vo. Pp 48.
                                                      GUL

Of Women and Girls

COMBE, GEORGE 'The Education of Women'; *Lectures on Popular Education* (1833), 52-62; second edition (1837), 77-92; third edition (1848), 50-61.

ERSKINE, DAVID STEUART, 11th Earl of Buchan, 'On Female Education'; *The Bee, or, Literary Weekly Intelligencer*, 1791, 3, 22 June, 225-31; 29 June, 263-9; 6 July, 312-16; 4, 20 July, 54-6; 27 July, 81-9; 25 Aug, 233-8.

Reprinted in *Anonymous and Fugitive Essays of the Earl of Buchan* (1812), 1, 26-66.

GRANT, SIR ALEXANDER *Happiness and Utility as promoted by the Higher Education of Women*. Edinburgh: Edmonston and Douglas, 1872. 8vo. Pp 25.

LINDSAY, WILLIAM LAUDER 'The Education of Girls. Two Papers'; *The Development and Reform of Higher Education in Scotland* (1874), 14, 15.   GUL
Reprinted from the *Perthshire Constitutional* of 22 July and 5 Aug 1872.

MASSON, DAVID *University Teaching for Women*. Edinburgh: Edmonston and Douglas, 1868. 8vo. Pp 18.

MURRAY, EUNICE G 'The Education of Women in the Seventeenth and Eighteenth Centuries'; *Scottish Women in Bygone Days* (Glasgow and London: Gowans & Gray, Ltd, 1930), 162-94.

SANDFORD, DANIEL FOX 'On Female Education and Industrial Training'; *Two Short Lectures* (1855), 11-21.

WRIGHT, ALEXANDER 'Schools for Girls'; *History of Education and of the Old Parish Schools of Scotland* (1898), 244-53.

Quality and Quantity

BLACKIE, JOHN STUART *Education in Scotland. An Appeal to the Scottish People, on the Improvement of their Scholastic and Academical Institutions*. Edinburgh: William Tait; Aberdeen: Lewis Smith, 1846. 4to. Pp 16.

BLACKIE, WALTER G *Remarks on the East India Company's Civil Service Examination Papers*: as Illustrative of some defects in the course of academical education in Scotland. Glasgow: W G Blackie and Co, 1858. 8vo. Pp 24.

BORLAND, J W *Brief Hints in Aid of a Practical Solution of the Educational Problem*, on grounds common to all the friends of Education, without compromising the conscientious convictions of any. Glasgow: Printed by S and T Dunn, 1860. 8vo. Pp 20.

— —. Another edition. Glasgow: David Bryce; David Robertson; George Gallie; Edinburgh: W Oliphant: Andrew Elliott, 1860. 8vo. Pp 20.   GUL

BRUNTON, WILLIAM 'State of Intermediate Education in Scotland; the Burgh and Grammar Schools, with Suggestions for their Improvement and Extension'; *Transactions of the National Association for the Promotion of Social Science, 1860* (1861), 321-6.

BRYCE, REUBEN JOHN 'Hints for the Improvement of Education in Scotland'; *Sketch of a Plan for a System of National Education for Ireland* (London: George Cowie & Co, and Hatchard and Son, 1828), 38-41.   BM

—*Practical Suggestions for Reforming the Educational Institutions of Scotland*: being an attempt to point out the necessity for desectarianising the schools and universities simultaneously; and the means whereby this may be accomplished. In two letters to the Lord Viscount Lord Melgund, M.P. Edinburgh: William Oliphant and Sons; Glasgow: D Robertson; London: Hamilton & Co, 1852. 8vo. Pp 31.

CAMPBELL, JAMES A *The Education Question*: An Address delivered to the Glasgow Working Men's Conservative Association. Glasgow: Thomas Murray and Son, 1871. 8vo. Pp 24.   GUL

— —. Second edition. Glasgow: Thomas Murray and Son, 1871. 8vo. Pp 24.   GUL

COOK, JOHN (St Andrews) *Parish School Statistics.* Means of Education in Scotland. Carefully revised. Reprinted from *Church of Scotland Mag and Rev* for Feb 1854. Edinburgh: Alexander C Moodie, 1854. 8vo. Pp 16.

D, W S 'Educational Reform'; *Scottish Educational and Literary J*, Aug 1854, **2**, 577-85.

'Education in Scotland'; *Free Church Mag*, 1846, **3**, Apr, 97-101; May, 143-4; Sept 257-63; Oct, 289-91.

Education in Scotland: A Practical Movement. By a City Minister. (Reprinted from the *Edinburgh Evening Courant* [27 Nov, 4, 8 and 15 Dec 1855.]) Edinburgh: Paton and Ritchie, 1855. 12mo. Pp 26.

'Education—Secular or Religious'; *The British Educator Mag*, June 1856, 156-9.   Mit

'Educational Legislation'; *The Scottish Educational and Literary J*, 1 Sept 1855, **3**, 275-8.

'Educational Statistics'; *The Scottish Educational and Literary J*, 1 June 1855, **3**, 209-12.

'Educational Statistics—Episcopalian Children and Schools in Scotland'; *The Watchword*, 1 May 1869, **4**, 61-2.   New Coll

'The Education Question'; *The Free Church Mag*, Feb 1850, **7**, 33-7; Mar 1850, **7**, 71-6.   New Coll

'The Education Question'; *The Watchword*, 1 Jan 1870, **4**, 433-7; 1 Dec 1871, **6**, 381-9.   New Coll

'The Education Question and Present Duty'; *The Watchword*, 1 Aug 1871, **6**, 189-94.   New Coll

The Education Question in Scotland. (Being a reprint of articles which appeared in the *Fifeshire Journal*.) Cupar-Fife, 1853. 12mo. Pp 32.

'The Education Question in Scotland—its Present Aspect'; *The Watchword*, 2 Nov 1868, **3**, 274-7.   New Coll

[FLETCHER, ANDREW] *Proposals for the Reformation of Schools and Universities, in order to the better Education of Youth.* Humbly offer'd to the serious consideration of the High Court of Parliament. np [Edinburgh], 1704. 4to. Pp 11.

FRASER, WILLIAM *The Educational Condition of Scotland a National Disgrace.* Present Remedial Suggestions considered. Paisley: Robert Stewart, 1859. 8vo. Pp 31.   New Coll

—'Education in Scotland'; *The State of our Educational Enterprises. A Report of an Examination into the Working, Results, and Tendencies of the Chief Public National Experiments in Great Britain, and Ireland* (Glasgow, Edinburgh, and London: Blackie and Son, 1858), 91-163.

GIFFORD, WILLIAM *The Education Question considered.* Second edition (revised). Edinburgh: Edmonston & Douglas; Leith: J Macart; Dunfermline: W Clark & Son, and D Campbell, 1870. 8vo. Pp 35.   New Coll

GORDON, THOMAS *Education in Scotland: Its Actual Amount.* By a Country Minister. Edinburgh: Paton and Ritchie; Glasgow: T Murray and Son, and J Smith and Son, 1854. 8vo. Pp 43.

— —. Second edition. Embracing the Results of the Census. Edinburgh:

Paton & Ritchie; Glasgow: T Murray and Son, and J Smith and Son, 1854. 8vo. Pp 43.   GUL

HAMILTON, JOHN *Two Evils in our Present System of Education.* np, 1854. 4to. Pp 3.   GUL

KELLAND, PHILIP *The Scottish School System suited to the People.* Edinburgh: Adam and Charles Black, 1870. 8vo. Pp 16.

LEWIS, GEORGE *Scotland a Half-educated Nation,* both in the Quantity and Quality of her Educational Institutions. By the editor of the *Scottish Guardian.* Published under the Superintendence of the Glasgow Educational Association. Glasgow: William Collins, 1834. 8vo. Pp 95.

MACLAREN, CHARLES 'Suggestions for the Improvement of Popular Education'; *Select Writings* (Edinburgh: Edmonston and Douglas, 1869), **1**, 310-47.

A reprint of five articles which originally appeared in the *Scotsman* of 13, 17, 20 and 31 Dec 1828, and 7 Jan 1829.

MACTURK, JOHN 'A Plea for Compulsory Education'; *The Museum,* new series, 2 Apr 1866, **3**, 13-16.

MILLER, HUGH *Thoughts on the Educational Question;* or, 'The Battle of Scotland'. London and Edinburgh: Johnstone and Hunter, 1850. Pp 91. 8vo.

The chapters of this work originally appeared as articles in the *Witness*, which Miller himself edited, of 2, 9, 16, 23 and 27 Feb, and 9 and 16 Mar 1850. The work was reprinted in MILLER, HUGH *Leading Articles on Various Subjects,* ed DAVIDSON, JOHN (Edinburgh: William P Nimmo, 1870), 1-104.

MILLIGAN, WILLIAM *The Present Aspect of the Education Question in Scotland.* A Letter to his Grace the Duke of Argyll. Edinburgh: Sutherland and Knox, 1857. 8vo. Pp 32.

[MILNE, ROBERT] *The Churches and Education.* By a Parish Minister. Glasgow: Thomas Murray and Son, 1870. 8vo. Pp 52.   New Coll

MITCHELL, WILLIAM *Educational Destitution in Scotland.* Glasgow: David Bryce & Son, nd [?1871]. 8vo. Pp 8. New Coll

MULOCK, THOMAS *The Vindicated Value of Scottish Education*: being a series of articles reprinted from the Inverness Advertiser. Inverness: C Keith, 1850. 8vo. Pp 48.

R 'On the Advantages of Scotch Education'; *Literary and Statistical Mag for Scotland,* Aug 1817, **1**, 225-30.

The Present Aspects of the Scottish Education Question. With a Historical Survey. By a Layman. Edinburgh: Thomas Constable and Co; London: Hamilton, Adams, & Co, 1856. 8vo. Pp 40.

The Religious Difficulty in the Education Question. The Compulsory Principle in its bearing on that Difficulty. By a Parish Minister. Edinburgh and London: William Blackwood and Sons, 1872. 8vo. Pp 55.   GUL

SCOTT, HUGH *The Scottish Education Question.* Edinburgh: Bell & Bradfute, 1854. 8vo. Pp 14.   EIS

— —. London: Saunders and Otley, 1855. 8vo. Pp 29.

—*The Schools of the Scottish Episcopal Church.* 4 numbers. Aberdeen: A Brown & Co; Edinburgh: R Grant & Son; London: Longman & Co, 1870-2. 8vo. No 1—pp 13; no 2—pp 12; no 3—pp 13; no 4—pp 9.

'The Scottish Education Question'; *The Museum,* new series, 1 June 1867, **4**, 99-104.

'The Scottish Education Question: Its Present Position'; *The Presbyterian,* new series, 1 Sept 1869, **1**, 115-17.

SELLAR, ALEXANDER CRAIG 'Scotch Education Difficulties'; *Recess Studies,* ed GRANT, SIR ALEXANDER (Edinburgh: Edmonston and Douglas, 1870), 261-307.

SIMPSON, JAMES *Necessity of Popular Education, as a National Object.* Edinburgh: Adam & Charles Black; Longman, Rees, Orme, Brown, Green, & Longman, London, 1834. 8vo. Pp xii, 402.

—'Education in Scotland'; *Report from the Select Committee on Education in England and Wales* (1835), 121-206.

Speeches on the Education Question, delivered in their respective Presbyteries by the Rev. And. Gray, Perth; the Rev. Robert Bremner, Gorbals; the Rev.

James Lumsden, Barry; the Rev. David Crichton, Arbroath; the Rev. William Wilson, Dundee; and the Rev. William Nixon, Montrose. Perth: James Dewar & Son; Glasgow: David Bryce; Dundee: Wm Middleton; Montrose: George W Laird; Arbroath; James Adam, 1850. 8vo. Pp 70.   New Coll

'Statistical View of Education in Scotland'; *The Edinburgh Christian Instructor*, May 1819, **18**, 334-7; June 1819, **18**, 407-9; July 1819, **18**, 483-6; Aug 1819, **18**, 558-63; Sept 1819, **18**, 633-8.

Thoughts on the Scottish Education Question, suggested by the late Debates in Parliament and the opinions of the Press thereon. By a Member of the Church of England. Edinburgh: Johnstone and Hunter; London: Groombridge & Sons, 1855. 8vo. Pp 24.   New Coll

VEITCH, JAMES *Speech on the Education Question*, delivered in the General Assembly on Thursday, 29th May, 1851. Edinburgh: Fraser and Company, 1851. 8vo. Pp 15.   Mit

'What is Education doing?'; *The Scottish Rev*, Oct 1853, **1**, 363-70.

WILLM, JOSEPH *The Education of the People*: A Practical Treatise on the Means of extending its Sphere & Improving its Character. With a Preliminary Dissertation on some Points connected with the present Position of Education in this Country. By J. P. Nichol, LL.D. Glasgow: William Lang; London: Simpkin, Marshall, & Co; Edinburgh: A & C Black; Dublin: J M'Glashan, 1847. 8vo. Pp lxxxiii, 250.

WILSON, JOHN 'School Statistics of Scotland.' (Extracted from *Perth Constitutional* of 1 Mar 1854.) np, 1854. 8vo. Pp 4.
                                      New Coll

Religious

BROWN, JOHN (Biggar) *On the State of Scotland in reference to the Means of Religious Instruction*. Edinburgh: Printed for David Brown, [and others], 1819. 8vo. Pp 42.

CRAIK, ALEXANDER *A Letter to John Brown, in reply to his Sermon, 'On the State of Scotland in reference to the Means of*

Religious Instruction'. Edinburgh: Printed for Macreadie, Skelly, and Company, 1820. 8vo. Pp 31.   EUL

An Essay towards the Spiritual Instruction of Children. By a Well-wisher of Souls. Edinburgh: Printed by David Paterson, 1782. 8vo. Pp 24.   BM

The Foundation of National Prosperity: A Sermon preached lately in a Country Church, as a Plea for the Interests of Christian Education: By a Parish Minister. Glasgow: Thomas Murray & Son, 1870. 8vo. Pp 15.   New Coll

FOOTE, JAMES *The Duty of Training up the Young in the Way of Religion*. Aberdeen: Printed for the Aberdeen Gratis Sabbath Evening School Society by D Chalmers & Co, 1821. 8vo. Pp 16.   Mit

THOMSON, JOHN *On the Religious Education of the Rising Generation*. Aberdeen: Printed by J Chalmers and Co, 1807. 8vo. Pp 38.   APL

TORRY, PATRICK *The Duty, Pleasure, and Reward of educating religiously the Rising Generation*. Peterhead: Printed by P Buchan, 1828. 8vo. Pp 33.
                                      APL

ARNOT, WILLIAM *Suggestions as to Sabbath School Teaching in its Principles and Practice*. Glasgow: David Bryce, 1847; Edinburgh: W P Kennedy; Oliver and Boyd, and John Johnstone; Dundee: Wm Middleton; Paisley: Alex Gardner; Ayr: Wm Guthrie; London: Hamilton, Adams and Co, and James Nisbet and Co, 1847. 12mo. Pp 32.   GUL

BARCLAY, HUGH *Thoughts on Sabbath Schools*. Revised from the *Edinburgh Christian Mag* [vols 5-6 (1854-5)]. Edinburgh: Paton and Ritchie; London: Hamilton, Adams, and Co; Glasgow: Thos Murray and Son; Perth: Charles Paton, 1855. 8vo. Pp vi, 121.

BLYTH, R 'The Scottish Sabbath School System'; *Transactions of the National Association for the Promotion of Social Science, 1863* (1864), 376-7.

BROWN, JOHN (Langton) *The Testimony of Experience to the Utility and Necessity of Sabbath Schools*. Edinburgh: James Colston, 1826. 8vo. Pp 79.   New Coll

CHALMERS, THOMAS 'On Sabbath Schools'; *The Christian and Civic Economy of Large Towns* (Glasgow: Chalmers & Collins), **1** (1821), 305-56.

—*On the Advantages of Local Sabbath Schools*. Glasgow: Printed for Chalmers and Collins; Edinburgh: William Whyte and Co, and Wm Oliphant; Dublin: Wm Curry, Jun & Co; London: G & W B Whittaker, F Westley, and J Nisbet, 1824. 12mo. Pp 88.　　　BM

'The following little work contains the substance of the second, and a portion of the eighth numbers of "The Christian and Civic Economy of Large Towns" ', from the Preface.

GLOVER, WILLIAM *Journal through the Counties of Berwick, Roxburgh, Selkirk, Dumfries, Ayr, Lanark, East, West, & Mid Lothian, in the Year 1817; likewise an Account of the Sabbath Schools in the above Counties*. Edinburgh: Printed for the Author, 1818. 12mo. Pp 294. Index.

Local System of Sabbath Schools. Edinburgh: Printed by Hay, Gall, & Co, nd. 12mo. Pp 3.　　　EUL

POLLOCK, JOHN *An Enquiry into the Expediency of Sabbath Schools in Scotland*. Glasgow: Printed by James Hedderwick, 1815. 8vo. Pp 30.　　　New Coll

THE SABBATH SCHOOL UNION FOR SCOTLAND *Extracts from the Minutes of the General Committee regarding Mr Gall's pamphlet*; entitled 'Letter to the Secretary of the Committee for the Establishment of Local Sabbath Schools in Edinburgh'. Edinburgh: Printed by Anderson & Bryce, 1822. 8vo. Pp 10.　　　EUL

System of Local Sabbath Evening Schools. Edinburgh: Printed by Hay, Gall, & Co, 1821. 4to. Pp 3.　　　EUL

TASKER, W *Territorial Sabbath Schools*, or, Hints on Sabbath School Teaching. Edinburgh: John Maclaren; Glasgow: D Bryce; Dundee: W Middleton; Perth: J Dewar and Son; Ayr: D Guthrie; London: Hamilton, Adams & Co, and J Nisbet & Co, 1850. 8vo. Pp 32.　　　GUL

UNITED SECESSION CHURCH *Address on Sabbath Schools*, to the Presbyteries and Sessions of the United Secession Church.

By Committee of Synod. Edinburgh: Printed by Murray and Gibb, nd. 8vo. Pp 8.　　　EUL

WOOD, ROBERT J *A Plea for the Sabbath School;* or, The Sabbath School viewed in relation to Family Religion. Edinburgh: Thomas C Jack, 1858. 8vo. Pp 20.　　　New Coll

ALPHA 'The Religious Difficulty'; *The Museum*, new series, 1 Feb 1867, **3**, 421-3.

BLACK, P CAMERON *The Training of the Young*: A Discourse in support of the Principle of a Christian Education for the Young of the Land, and in Argument of the Mode by which such can be secured. Glasgow: Thomas Murray and Son, 1870. 8vo. Pp 18.　　　New Coll

The Churches and Education. By a Parish Minister. Glasgow: Thomas Murray and Son, 1870. 8vo. Pp 52.　　　GUL

COLQUHOUN, JOHN CAMPBELL *Church and School Extension*. Edinburgh: Printed by John Johnstone, nd. 8vo. Pp 12.　　　New Coll

COLVIN, WALTER LAIDLAW *A Plea for Scriptural Education*. A Sermon. Published by request. Edinburgh and London: William Blackwood and Sons, 1869. 8vo. Pp 16.

COMBE, ANDREW *On the Introduction of Religion into Common Schools*. Edinburgh: Printed by Neill & Co, nd. 8vo. Pp 8.

Part of an unposted letter written towards the end of 1846 to his brother, George Combe, the phrenologist, who printed it in his *Life and Correspondence of Andrew Combe* (Edinburgh 1850), 501-9.

COMBE, GEORGE *Secular Instruction, or Extension of Church Endowments?* Glasgow: John Robertson; Edinburgh: Maclachlan & Stewart; London: Simpkin, Marshall & Co, 1852. 8vo. Pp 7.

EASTON, THOMAS 'The Education Question and the Lord Advocate. (From the *Galloway Gazette*, January 13, 1872)'; *Religious Instruction in the National Schools of Scotland* (Newton-Stewart, 1872), 48-54.　　　BM

'Education—Secular or Religious'; *British Educator Mag*, June 1856, 156-9.　　Mit

FORBES, JOHN 'On the Necessity of Conducting the Education of Youth on Religious Principles'; *Church of Scotland Mag*, May 1837, **4**, 153-65.

FREE CHURCH TEACHER, A 'The Religious Difficulty'; *The Museum*, new series, 1 Jan 1867, **3**, 378-9; 1 Mar 1867, **3**, 454-5.

HUMPHREYS, E R *A Plea for the Spiritual Element of Education.* In two letters. Originally addressed to the Editor of the *Edinburgh Advertiser.* Edinburgh: Johnstone and Hunter, and Robert Seton, 1850. 8vo. Pp 12.   New Coll

LEE, JOHN *Evidence before the Commission on Religious Instruction, Scotland, in February and March 1836.* Printed verbatim from the Report of the Commissioners. Edinburgh: William Blackwood & Sons, 1837. 8vo. Pp 21.
New Coll

MACCALL, WILLIAM 'Religious Education'; *The Freeman*, Oct 1851, 141-51.   BM

MANN, HORACE *Report on Religious Worship and Education.* London: HMSO, 1854. Fol. Pp 111.

MANSON, JAMES B *The Bible in School.* A Vindication of the Scotch System of Education, in a series of Letters from 'A Practical Educator' to Mr George Combe. Edinburgh: Johnstone & Hunter, 1852. 8vo. Pp 32.

National Religious Education. *Full Report of the Public Meeting held in the City Hall, Perth, on Thursday evening, 21st December, 1871.* Perth: Printed by Dewar, Mitchell, and Co, *Perthshire Courier* Office, 1872. 8vo. Pp 44.   New Coll

NIXON, WILLIAM *Remarks on Christian Education*; or, The Union of Church and School. Edinburgh and Glasgow: William Whyte & Co, 1838. 8vo. Pp 19, 36.
BM

PAROCHIAL SCHOOLMASTER, A 'The Religious Difficulty'; *The Museum*, new series, 1 Dec 1866, **3**, 336-9; 1 Feb 1867, **3**, 423-4.

The Past and Present Education Acts of Scotland, in so far as they relate to Religious Teaching. Edited, with Observations thereon, by a Member of the College of Justice. Edinburgh: Andrew Elliot and John Maclaren; London: James Nisbet & Co; Glasgow: David Bryce and Son, 1872. 8vo. Pp 17.   BM

PURVES, JOHN *Religious Education: Can it be given in our Common Public Schools as now taught?* If not, by whom, when, where, and how? Edinburgh: John Maclaren; London: Hamilton, Adams, & Co; Glasgow: David Bryce & Son, 1871. 8vo. Pp 70.   New Coll

The Religious Difficulty in the Education Question. The Compulsory Principle in its Bearing on that Difficulty. By a Parish Minister. Edinburgh and London: William Blackwood and Sons, 1872. 8vo. Pp 55.   GUL

Religious Instruction in the National Schools of Scotland. Full Report of the great Public Meeting held in Stranraer, on 24th January, 1872. Newton-Stewart: Printed at the *Galloway Gazette* Office, 1872. 8vo. Pp 47.   BM

The Scotch Education Bill. Religious Instruction in Day Schools. Full Report of the Public Meeting held in the City Hall, Glasgow, on Wednesday evening, 20th December, 1871. Glasgow: Thomas Murray and Son, 1872. 8vo. Pp 55.
New Coll

Report of Speeches delivered at a Public Meeting of the Friends of the Established Church of Scotland, desirous of obtaining through the Aid of the State, an Extension of the Means of Religious Instruction and Parochial Superintendence, held in the Assembly Rooms, Wednesday, 15th March, 1835. Edinburgh: Fraser and Company, 1835. 12mo. Pp 46.   GUL

'Secular and Religious Education'; *Blackwood's Edinburgh Mag*, Feb 1839, **45**, 275-86.

SMITH, J FREDERICK *On teaching Religion in State Schools.* A Sermon preached in St Mark's Chapel, Edinburgh, on Sunday morning, April 3, 1870. Edinburgh: Edmonston and Douglas, 1870. 8vo. Pp 18.   New Coll

SOMERS, ROBERT *The Secular Theory of Education examined*; or, A Plea for the Bible in Schools. Edinburgh: Edmonston and Douglas; London: Hamilton, Adams, and Co; Glasgow: James Maclehose; Aberdeen: Lewis Smith, nd [1872]. 8vo. Pp 27.

STEWART, ROBERT *National Education: The Religious and Secular Aspects of the*

Education Question; or, In what sense Religion can, and in what sense it cannot, be excluded from ordinary school Instruction, with reference to recent Public Meetings and Correspondence. Glasgow: Thomas Murray and Son, 1868. 12mo. Pp 24.   New Coll

TEACHER, A 'The Religious Difficulty'; *The Museum*, new series, 1 Jan 1867, **3**, 375-8.

Revised Code

'Correspondence between the Association of Certificated Schoolmasters of Scotland and the Right Honourable Earl Granville, Lord President of the Privy Council'; *The Museum*, new series, 1 Mar 1866, **2**, 457-61.

An Exposure of the Revised Code. Aberdeen: Printed by A King & Co, nd [?1861]. 8vo. Pp 22.   New Coll

GRAHAM, GILBERT *The Revised Code tested in its Results.* Edinburgh: J Thin; Glasgow: R Gowanlock, 1868. 8vo. Pp 16   GUL

[KENNEDY, WILLIAM] *The Revised Code*: being the Resolutions agreed to at the Meeting of the Free Church Teachers' Association, September 20, 1861. With Notes and Explanations. Specially intended for School Managers, Teachers, and others interested in Elementary Education. By a Committee of the Association. Edinburgh: T Nelson & Sons, 1861. 8vo. Pp 24.

MEIKLEJOHN, JOHN M D *The Fundamental Error in the Revised Code*, with special reference to the Problem of teaching to read. London: E Stanford, 1870. 8vo. Pp 39.

PAROCHIAL SCHOOLMASTER, A 'The Revised Code in its Application to Scotland'; *The Museum*, new series, 2 May 1866, **3**, 61-3.

PURVES, JAMES 'The Educational Institute of Scotland and the Revised Code'; *The Museum*, new series, 1 Nov 1864, **1**, 290-4.

SCOTTISH SCHOOLMASTER, A 'The Revised Code in Scotland'; *The Museum*, new series, 1 May 1864, **1**, 60-1.

SHUTTLEWORTH, SIR JAMES KAY *Letter to Earl Granville, K.G., on the Revised Code*

of Regulations contained in the Minute of the Committee of Council on Education dated July 29th 1861. London: Smith, Elder, & Co, 1861. 8vo. Pp 80.

WEIR, A C *Tables showing the Comparative Progress of England and Scotland, under the Revised Code.* Edinburgh: Printed by Murray and Gibb, 1867. 8vo. Pp 9.

Technical

CHURCH OF SCOTLAND: GENERAL ASSEMBLY'S EDUCATION COMMITTEE 'Agricultural Schools'; *Report*, 1854, 32-40; 1855, 25-36; 1856, 18-25.   New Coll

—'Statement in regard to the proposed Schools of Agricultural Industry'; *Report*, 1853, 32-6.   New Coll

JOHNSTON, JAMES F W *Lectures on the Method of Teaching Agricultural Chemistry in the Parochial Schools of Scotland.* Edinburgh: Printed by Murray and Gibb, 1845. 8vo. Pp 16.   EIS

HUTCHISON, J A *Art and Education.* An Essay read before the National Social Science Congress. Glasgow: Printed for the Association for the Education of Females in Industrial Arts by James MacNair, 1861. 12mo. Pp 30.   GUL

KNOX, JAMES *On Commercial Training*, with Suggestions as to its Place in College and School Instruction. Edinburgh: Sutherland and Knox, 1858. 8vo. Pp 19.

Conference on Technical Education, held at Edinburgh, Friday, 20th March, 1868. Edinburgh: Printed by Hall and Company, 1868. 8vo. Pp 84.   GUL

GILL, ROBERT *Technical Education*: Importance of its Introduction into this Country. Edinburgh: Bell & Bradfute, 1870. 8vo. Pp 93.

PLAYFAIR, LYON *On Primary and Technical Education.* Edinburgh: Edmonston and Douglas, 1870. 8vo. Pp 52.

Schools Inquiry Commission: Report relative to Technical Education, 'Letter

from James Young, Esq., Bathgate';
PP, 1867, xxvi, [3898], 29-30.

Theory and Practice

BARCLAY, JAMES *A Treatise on Education*:
or, An Easy Method of Acquiring
Language, and introducing Children to
the Knowledge of History, Geography,
Mythology, Antiquities, &c. With Re-
flections on Taste, Poetry, Natural
History, &c. the Manner of Forming the
Temper, and Teaching Youth such Moral
Precepts as are necessary in the Conduct
of Life. Edinburgh: Printed by James
Cochran and Company, 1743. 12mo.
Pp vii, 240.

— —. London: P Vaillant, 1749. 12mo.
Pp vii, 240.   BM

BELL, ANDREW *The Complete Works*.
Published under the direction of the
Trustees of the Madras College, St
Andrews. Edinburgh: Oliver & Boyd;
J G & F Rivington, London; and John
Cumming, Dublin, 1832. 8vo. Pp 422.
                                         GUL

—*An Analysis of the Experiment in Education, made at Egmore, near Madras.*
Comprising a System, alike fitted to
reduce the Expense of Tuition, abridge
the Labour of the Master, and expedite
the Progress of the Scholar; and suggesting a Scheme for the better Administration of the Poor-laws, by converting
Schools for the Lower Orders of Youth
into Schools of Industry. Third edition.
London: Printed by T Bensley for Cadell
and Davies, 1807. 8vo. Pp xii, 115.

—*Elements of Tuition.* Part I. *The Madras
School*; or, The Report of the Military
Male Orphan Asylum, of Egmore, at
Madras, with its Original Proofs and
Vouchers, as transmitted from India in
1796, and published in London in 1797,
under the Title of An Experiment in
Education, &c. A new edition. To
which are subjoined additional Documents and Records, illustrative of the
Progress of the New System of Education
in the School in which it originated; and
of its Fruits in the Character, Conduct,
and Fortunes of its Pupils. London:
Reprinted for J Murray; and sold by

Rivingtons; Hatchard: Longman, Hurst,
and Co; W Blackwood, Edinburgh; and
J Cumming, Dublin, 1813. Pp xxx, 126,
[2]. Index. Part II. *The English School*;
or, the History, Analysis, and Application of the Madras System of Education
to English Schools. London: Printed
by Law and Gilbert, for Rivingtons:
J Murray: J Hatchard: Longman,
Hurst, and Co; T Underwood; W
Blackwood, Edinburgh; and J Cumming,
Dublin, 1814. 8vo. Pp xx, 448. Part
III. *Ludus Literarius*: The Classical and
Grammar School; or, An Exposition of
an Experiment in Education, made at
Madras in the Years 1789-1796: with a
view to its Introduction into Schools for
the Higher Orders of Children, and with
Particular Suggestions for its Applica-
tion to a Grammar School. London:
Printed for Rivingtons: Murray: Hat-
chard: Longman, Hurst, and Co; W
Blackwood, Edinburgh; and J Cumming,
Dublin, 1815. 8vo. Pp 226. 2 vols.
                                         BM

—*An Experiment in Education,* made at
the Male Asylum of Madras, suggesting
a System by which a School or Family
may teach itself under the Superintend-
ance [*sic*] of the Master or Parent.
London: Printed for Cadell and Davies;
W Creech, Edinburgh, 1797. 12mo.
Pp xii, 48.   GUL

—*An Experiment in Education,* made at the
Male Asylum at Egmore, near Madras.
Suggesting a System by which a School
or Family may teach itself under the
Superintendence of the Master or Parent.
Second edition. To which is prefixed the
Scheme of a School on the above Model,
alike fitted to reduce the Expense of
Education, abridge the Labour of the
Master, and expedite the Progress of the
Scholar. The Problem of teaching the
Alphabet in Sand, of reading, spelling,
and writing is explained; and a Board
of Education and Poor-rates suggested.
London: Printed for Cadell and Davies,
1805. 8vo. Pp 84.   BM

—*Instructions for Conducting a School,*
through the Agency of the Scholars
themselves: comprising the Analysis of
an Experiment in Education, made at
the Male Asylum, Madras, 1789-1796.
Extracted from the 'Madras School, or

Elements of Tuition'. For the Use of Schools and Families. Second edition, enlarged. London: Printed at the Free School, Gower's Walk, Whitechapel, for J Murray: Rivingtons: Hatchard; and Archibald Constable and Co, Edinburgh, 1809. 8vo. Pp 38.

—*Instructions for Conducting a School*, . . . Extracted from 'Elements of Tuition, Part 2. The English School'. Fourth edition, greatly enlarged. With an Historical Introduction, and Appendix. London: John Murray, 1813. 8vo. Pp 88.   BM

—*Instructions for Conducting a School*, . . . Compiled chiefly from Elements of Tuition, Parts 1, 2, and 3, viz.: The Madras, English, and Grammar Schools for the Use of Schools and Families. Sixth edition, greatly enlarged, with an Historical Introduction, on the Discovery, Progress, and Results of the new System of Education. London: Printed at the Free-School, Gower's Walk, Whitechapel, for Rivingtons: Murray: Hatchard: Longman, Hurst, and Co: T Underwood: W Blackwood, Edinburgh; and J Cumming, Dublin, 1817. 12mo. Pp 138.   BM

—*The Madras School, or Elements of Tuition*: comprising the Analysis of an Experiment in Education, made at the Male Asylum, Madras with its Facts, Proofs, and Illustrations; to which are added, Extracts of Sermons preached at Lambeth; A Sketch of a National Institution for Training up the Children of the Poor; and a Specimen of the Mode of Religious Instruction at the Royal Military Academy, Chelsea. London: Printed by T Bensley, for J Murray: Cadell and Davies: Rivingtons: Hatchard; and Archibald Constable and Co, Edinburgh, 1808. 8vo. Pp xv, 348.
                                        BM

—*Letters to the Rt. Hon. Sir John Sinclair, Bart. on the Infant School Society at Edinburgh*: The Scholastic Institutions of Scotland; and on the peculiar Facilities and Advantages of her Parochial Schools for the Adoption of the Intellectual Machinery for the Multiplication of Power and Division of Labour in the Moral and Religious World. London:

Printed for C J and F Rivington: Longman & Co, and Hatchard; and Bell & Bradfute, Edinburgh, 1829. 8vo. Pp 15, 3.

—*Manual of Public and Private Education*, founded on a Discovery, 'by which a School or Family may teach itself under the Superintendence of the Master or Parent', made, recorded, and promulgated at Madras in 1789-1796, published in London, 1797, and thence diffused over the World. Eighth edition, digested and abridged. With an Historical Introduction and Appendix. London: Printed for C and J Rivington, 1827. 8vo. Pp 60.

—*The Report of the Military Male Orphan Asylum at Madras*, with its Original Proofs and Vouchers. As transmitted from India in 1796, and published in London, 1797, under the Title of An Experiment in Education, &c. A new edition. To which are subjoined additional Documents and Records, illustrative of the Progress of the new System of Education, in the School in which it originated; and of its Fruits in the Character, Conduct, and Fortunes of its Pupils. London: reprinted for J Murray: W Blackwood, Edinburgh; and J Cumming, Dublin, 1812. 8vo. Pp xxxi, 126, [2]. Index.

BLACKIE, JOHN STUART *On Education*. Edinburgh: Edmonston & Douglas, 1868. 8vo. Pp 42.

BUDDO, JOHN *Progress of Education and Manners*. St Andrews: Printed by Francis Ray for the Author, 1801. 8vo. Pp xii, 180.

BURGH, JAMES *Thoughts on Education*, tending chiefly to recommend to the Attention of the Public, some Particulars relating to that Subject; which are not generally considered with the Regard their Importance deserves. Edinburgh, 1747. 8vo. Pp 60.

BURNET, GILBERT *Thoughts on Education*. Now first printed from an original Manuscript. London: Printed for D Wilson, 1761. 8vo. Pp xiii, 94.

CHAPMAN, GEORGE *A Treatise on Education*. With a Sketch of the Author's Method. Edinburgh: Printed for A Kincaid &

W Creech: sold, at London, by T Cadell, 1773. 12mo. Pp viii, 256.

— —. The second edition, corrected and enlarged. London: Printed for T Cadell, 1774. 12mo. Pp iv, 258, [2].

— —. The third edition, enlarged with an Appendix, containing Short Sketches of Books published on Education. London: T Cadell, 1784. 12mo. Pp vi, 258, 23.
BM

—*A Treatise on Education.* In two parts. With the Author's Method of Instruction while he taught the school of Dumfries, and a View of other Books on Education. The fourth edition, considerably enlarged. London: Published for the Author, 1790. 8vo. Pp xii, 242, 37.   EUL

— —. The fifth edition, improved and enlarged. London: Published for the Author, 1792. 8vo. Pp xiv, 176, 120.

—*Supplement to the Fifth Edition of Dr Chapman's Treatise on Education.* London: Sold by Cadell and Davies; Edinburgh: Mr Creech, 1796. 8vo. Pp 44.

CLARKE, CHARLES 'Education. A Lecture'; *The Freeman*, Apr 1851, 49-54.   BM

CLARKE, JOHN *Bishop Gilbert Burnet as Educationist*, being his '*Thoughts on Education*', with Notes and Life of the Author. Aberdeen University Studies, no 67. Aberdeen: D Wyllie & Son, 1914. 8vo. Pp xi, 244. Index.

COMBE, GEORGE *Discussions on Education.* London: Cassell and Company, Limited, 1893. 8vo. Pp 235.

CONTENTS On Popular Education. On National Education. On Secular Education. On Physiology.

—*Education. Its Principles and Practice as developed by George Combe.* Collated and edited by William Jolly. London: Macmillan and Co, 1879. 8vo. Pp lxxvi, 772. Index.

—*Lectures on Popular Education.* Edinburgh: John Anderson, Jun; London: Longman & Co, and Simpkin & Marshall; Glasgow: John Macleod, and Paterson & Rutherglen; Dublin: W Curry, Jun & Co; Liverpool: W Grapel. 1833. 8vo. Pp 76.   EUL

Reprinted serially under the title, 'Education', in *Chambers's Edinburgh J*, **3**, 1834, 15 Feb, 18-20; 1 Mar, 37-9; 29 Mar, 66-8; 12 Apr, 86-7; 3 May, 106-8.

— —. Second edition, corrected and enlarged. Edinburgh: Maclachlan and Stewart, and John Anderson, Jun; London: Longman & Co, and Simpkin, Marshall, & Co; Glasgow: John Macleod; Liverpool: W Grapel; Boston, USA: Marsh, Capen, & Lyon, 1837. 8vo. Pp viii, 126.

— —. Third edition, corrected and enlarged. Edinburgh: Maclachlan, Stewart, & Co; London: Longman & Co, Simpkin, Marshall, & Co, and W S Orr & Co; Glasgow: David Robertson; Dublin: James M'Glashan, 1848. 8vo. Pp viii, 82.

—*Secular Education.* Lecture on the Comparative Influence of the Natural Sciences and 'The Shorter Catechism', on the Civilisation of Scotland. Edinburgh: Maclachlan & Stewart; London: Simpkin, Marshall, & Co, 1851. 8vo. Pp 16.

—*What does Secular Education embrace?* Manchester: A Ireland and Co, 1851. 4to. Pp 4.

—*What should Secular Education embrace?* Edinburgh: Maclachlan, Stewart, & Co; London: Simpkin, Marshall, & Co; Dublin: James M'Glashan, 1848. 8vo. Pp [2], 34.

— —. Second edition, corrected and enlarged. Edinburgh: Maclachlan, Stewart, & Co; London: Simpkin, Marshall, & Co; Dublin: James M'Glashan, 1848. 8vo. Pp [2], 36.

NOTE The third edition, also published in 1848, is identical with the second.

CURRIE, JAMES *Principles of Teaching in their relation to Methods.* Edinburgh: Sutherland and Knox, 1854. 8vo. Pp 31.
BM

D, T 'General Remarks on Education'; *Edinburgh Christian Educator*, Mar 1822, **21**, 142-52; Feb 1823, **22**, 73-83.

DICK, THOMAS *On the Mental Illumination and Moral Improvement of Mankind*; or, An Inquiry into the means by which a general diffusion of knowledge and Moral principle may be promoted. Illustrated with engravings. Glasgow:

Printed for William Collins, 1835. 12mo. Pp 672. EUL

'A Directorie to be obserwed in teacheing off Grammar schooles and overseeing the same (1649)'; *Records of Elgin, 1234-1800* (Aberdeen: New Spalding Club, 2 (1908)), 432-6.

DONALDSON, SIR JAMES 'The Science of Education'; *The Museum*, new series, 1 Nov 1864, **1**, 281-6.

Reprinted in DONALDSON, SIR JAMES *Lectures on the History of Education* (1874), 167-85.

ERSKINE, DAVID STEUART, Earl of Buchan, 'On Education'; *The Scots Mag*, May 1782, **44**, 225-7; June 1782, **44**, 287-8.

An Essay on Practical Education: read before the Second Annual Meeting of the Friendly Society of Burgh and Parochial Schoolmasters of the County of Roxburgh. Held at Hawick, upon 30th May, 1812. By a Member of the Society. Hawick: Printed by R Armstrong, 1812. 12mo. Pp 69. Mit

GALL, JAMES *The Effects of the Lesson System of Teaching on Criminals, General Society, and on the Lowest Orders of the Human Intellect*, as ascertained by a Series of important Experiments. With an Appendix, containing a condensed View of the Nature and Design of the System, and a List of Books published to facilitate its Practice. Edinburgh: Published by James Gall, nd [1830]. 8vo. Pp 74. EUL

—*A Practical Inquiry into the Philosophy of Education*. Edinburgh: James Gall and Sons; London: Houlston & Stoneman; Glasgow: George Gallie; Belfast: William McComb, 1840. 8vo. Pp 348.

—*A Series of Educational Experiments in England, Ireland, and Scotland: for ascertaining the Effects of the Lesson System of Teaching*. Edinburgh: James Gall, 1834. 8vo. Pp 67, 16, [10].

GILLIS, JAMES *A Lecture on Education*, delivered in St Mungo's Parish Church, Glasgow, in behalf of its Catholic Boys' School. Edinburgh: Marsh & Beattie; London: Charles Dolman, 1856. 8vo. Pp 32.

HAMILTON, WILLIAM S *Remarks on Intellectual Education*: with Specimens of Composition, in Prose and Verse, by the Young Ladies attending the Classes conducted by him in Perth Academy. Perth: Printed by C G Sidey, 1830. 12mo. Pp xix, [32]. Pe

HOME, HENRY, LORD KAMES *Loose Hints upon Education*. Edinburgh: Printed for John Bell; and John Murray, London, 1781. 8vo. Pp xi, 381.

— —. Second edition, enlarged. Edinburgh: Printed for John Bell; Geo Robinson, and John Murray, London, 1782. 8vo. Pp xi, 419.

JOLLY, WILLIAM *George Combe as an Educationist*. np [?London], nd [?1879]. 8vo. Pp 56. BM
A separate edition of the Introduction to his *Education. Its Principles and Practice as developed by George Combe* (1879).

KNOX, HENRY M 'A Bishop's Thoughts on Education'; *The J of Education*, Jan 1952, **84**, 10-14.
The bishop was Bishop Gilbert Burnet.

A Letter from the Master of a Private School, to a reverend member of the General-Assembly, concerning the Education of Children, &c. np, 1705. 4to. Pp 5.

Letters addressed to the Parochial Schoolmasters of Scotland, concerning the New Method of Tuition. See NORVALL, JAMES.

M'COMBIE, WILLIAM *On Education in its Constituents, Objects, and Issues*. Aberdeen: George & Robert King; Hamilton, Adams & Co, and Ward & Co, London, 1857. 8vo. Pp vii, 422.

MACKENZIE, WILLIAM 'Notes on Education'; *Notes on Philosophy, Morality, and Education*. In three parts (Edinburgh: Printed for W & C Tait, 1822), 115-98.

—*Outlines of Education*; or, Remarks on the Development of Mind, and Improvement of Manners. Edinburgh: Archibald Constable and Co; and Hurst, Robinson, and Co, London, 1824. 12mo. Pp 245. GUL

MESTON, WILLIAM *A Practical Essay on the Manner of Studying and Teaching in Scotland*: or a Guide to Students at the University, to Parish Schoolmasters, and Family Tutors. In two parts. Edinburgh: Printed for Macredie, Skelly, and

G

Co; A Brown and Co, Aberdeen; and T and G Underwood, London, 1823. 8vo. Pp 5, vii, 302.

— —. Edinburgh: Printed for Alex Macredie; A Brown and Co, Aberdeen; T and G Underwood, London, 1825. Pp 5, vii, 303.

MORRISON, THOMAS *Manual of School Management*: For the Use of Teachers, Students, & Pupil Teachers. Glasgow: William Hamilton; John Menzies, and Oliver & Boyd, Edinburgh; Simpkin, Marshall, & Co, London, 1859. 8vo. Pp [5], 356.

— —. Second edition. Glasgow: William Hamilton; John Menzies, and Oliver & Boyd, Edinburgh; Simpkin, Marshall, & Co, London, 1860. 8vo. Pp viii, 371.

— —. Third edition. Glasgow: William Hamilton; John Menzies, and Oliver & Boyd, Edinburgh; Simpkin, Marshall, & Co, London, 1863. 8vo. Pp viii, 382.

NELSON, ROBERT J *Outlines of the Theory and Practice of Education*. Glasgow: Printed by Fullarton & Co, 1842. 8vo. Pp 28.
                                                    EIS

On Education; with Practical Hints. By an Old Dominie. Aberdeen: John Adam; London: Simpkin, Marshall, & Co; Edinburgh: Oliver & Boyd, 1869. 8vo. Pp 56.

PILLANS, JAMES *Three Lectures on the Proper Objects and Methods of Education in reference to the different Orders of Society*; and on the relative Utility of Classical Instruction. Edinburgh: Adam & Charles Black, Oliver & Boyd, and Alexander Macredie; and J Ridgway & Sons, London, 1836. 8vo. Pp 67.

— —. Second edition, corrected. Edinburgh: Maclachlan & Stewart; London: Walton & Maberly, and Simpkin, Marshall, & Co, 1854. 8vo. Pp 59.
                                                    EIS

The first edition was reprinted in PILLANS, JAMES *Rationale of Discipline* (1852), Appendix, 5-67, and the second edition in PILLANS, JAMES *Contributions to the Cause of Education* (1856), 251-304, where it was given a new title, *Three Lectures on the Relative Importance of Classical Training in the Education of Youth*.

Pleas for Education; being Addresses delivered to the Pupils of the Apprentice Schools of Edinburgh, at a Meeting held in the Music Hall, Edinburgh, February 7, 1849. Revised by the Speakers. Edinburgh: Sutherland & Knox; London: Simpkin, Marshall, & Co, 1849. 12mo. Pp 28.

POOLE, RICHARD *An Essay on Education, applicable to Children in General*; the Defective; the Criminal; the Poor; the Adult and Aged. Edinburgh: Printed for Waugh and Innes; M Ogle, Glasgow; Westley & Tyrrell, Dublin; and James Duncan, London, 1825. 8vo. Pp xv, 359.

According to the Preface, p vii, this work was originally written as a contribution to the *Encyclopaedia Edinensis*, and it duly appeared there in Volume Third (1827), 168-234.

RAMSAY, ANDREW MICHAEL *A Plan of Education*. The third edition, corrected according to a genuine manuscript. Glasgow: Printed for Robert Foulis, 1741. 8vo. Pp 28.
The first and second editions were printed at London in 1732 and 1736 respectively.

— —. The fourth edition. From a genuine manuscript. Glasgow: Printed by Robert Foulis, 1742. 8vo. Pp 28.

—*A Plan of Education*. By the Chevalier Ramsay. From a genuine Manuscript. The fifth edition. Glasgow: Printed by Robert and Andrew Foulis, 1766. 12mo. Pp 35.   New Coll

RUSSELL, MICHAEL *An abridged Edition of the Works of the Rev Andrew Bell*, comprehending a short Account of his Life as the Author of the Madras System. Edinburgh: Oliver & Boyd; J G & F Rivington, London; John Cumming, Dublin, 1833. 8vo. Pp 588.   GUL

[ST CLAIR, J] *A Faithful Appeal to Parents on the Education of their Children*. Edinburgh, Glasgow, and London: William Collins, Sons, & Company; John Menzies, Edinburgh, nd. 8vo. Pp 16.
                                                    GUL

SANDFORD, DANIEL FOX *Two short Lectures: I. On Female Education and Industrial Training. II. On the everyday Duties of Parents with regard to the Education and*

Training of their Children. Delivered in connection with the Opening of a new School-house at Alyth, in the diocese of Dunkeld. January, 1855. Edinburgh: R Grant & Son; J H Parker, London; and Robert Marshall, Alyth, 1855. 12mo. Pp 31.

SIMPSON, JAMES *The Philosophy of Education*, with its Practical Application to a System and Plan of Popular Education as a National Object. Second edition. Edinburgh: Adam & Charles Black; Longman & Co, Orr & Smith, Sherwood, Gilbert, & Piper, London; John Cumming, and Hodges & Smith, Dublin, 1836. 8vo. Pp xi, 288. Index.

SMITH, DAVID *On the Branches of Education which ought to be embraced in a School Curriculum*; their Adaptation, respectively, to develop the Mental Faculties and form the Character; and the Order in which they should be presented to the Mind. London: James Blackwood; Edinburgh: Johnstone & Hunter; Glasgow: Wm Hamilton, 1852. 8vo. Pp viii, 88.

STOW, DAVID *Moral Training, Infant and Juvenile*, as applicable to the Condition of Large Towns. Second edition, enlarged. Glasgow: Printed for William Collins, 1834. 12mo. Pp 320. 3 plates.
                                                    BM
MORGAN, ALEXANDER *Makers of Scottish Education* (1929), 100, note 3, says, 'the date of the first edition is doubtful', and no copy of it seems to have survived.

—*The Training System adopted in the Model Schools of the Glasgow Educational Society*; A Manual for Infant and Juvenile Schools, which includes a System of Moral Training suited to the Condition of Large Towns. Glasgow: W R McPhun; and H N Cotes, London, 1836. 12mo. Pp xi, 237. Frontispiece, plans, and sketches.

—*The Training System, established in the Glasgow Normal Seminary, and its Model Schools.* A new edition. Glasgow, Edinburgh, and London: Blackie and Son, 1840. 8vo. Pp 415. Frontispiece and 11 plates.   EIS

—*The Training System of Education, Religious, Intellectual, and Moral, estab-*

lished in the Glasgow Normal Training Seminary. Sixth edition, enlarged, with additions. Glasgow: Blackie and Son, 1845. 8vo. Pp xiv, 433, [17]. Frontispiece and 10 plates.   New Coll

—*The Training System of Education, for the Moral and Intellectual Elevation of Youth*, especially in large Towns and manufacturing Villages. Seventh edition, enlarged. Glasgow and London: Blackie and Son, 1846. 8vo. Pp 520. Frontispiece and 10 plates.   BM

—*The Training System, the Moral Training School, and the Normal Seminary.* Eighth edition, enlarged. London: Longman, Brown, Green, and Longmans, 1850. 8vo. Pp xi, 474. Frontispiece and 16 plates.   EIS

—*The Training System, Moral Training School, and Normal Seminary or College.* Ninth edition, enlarged. London: Longman, Brown, Green, and Longmans, 1853. 8vo. Pp xii, 516. Frontispiece and 16 plates.   EIS

—*The Training System, Moral Training School, and Normal Seminary for preparing School-Trainers and Governesses.* Tenth edition, enlarged. London: Longman, Brown, Green, and Longmans, 1854. 8vo. Pp xii, 536, 24. Frontispiece and 18 plates.   GUL

—*The Training System of Education, including Moral School Training for large Towns, and Normal Seminary, for Training Teachers to conduct the System.* Eleventh edition, enlarged. London: Longman, Green, Longman, and Roberts, 1859. 8vo. Pp xii, 564. Frontispiece, 18 plates, and 5 other illustrations.   EIS

—*Dr David Stow: System Christlicher Jugendbildung, wie es in den neuerrichteten Training-Schools in Schottland befolgt wird.* Auszugsweise übertragen von H A Jäschle. Stuttgart, 1844. 8vo. Pp 111.   BM

Strict Thoughts on Education, occasioned by Loose Hints on Education. A didactic poem, in four parts. Edinburgh: Printed for C Elliot, 1782. 8vo. Pp 27.

THOMSON, JOHN *Education: Man's Salvation from Crime, Disease, and Starvation.* Edinburgh: Ferrier & Trench, 1844. 8vo. Pp 56.   Mit

WITHERSPOON, JOHN *Four Letters on Education*. Glasgow: M Ogle, 1799. 12mo. Pp 58.   BM
There are, in fact, five letters, not four.

—'Letters on Education'; *Works* (Edinburgh: Printed for Ogle & Aikman; J Pillans and Sons; J Ritchie; and J Turnbull, 1805), **8**, 165-212.
Witherspoon's *Letters on Education*

originally appeared in the *Pennsylvania Mag*, **I** (1775) and **II** (1776). The first British edition was printed at Bristol in 1798.

WITTWOR, L O *Notes relating to Education*. London: Brown and Mitchell, 1850. 8vo. Pp 61.   EUL

— —. Edinburgh: Thomas Constable, 1851. 8vo. Pp 73.   EUL

The Education Bill Controversy, 1843-72

COOK, JOHN (ST ANDREWS) *Remarks on Lord Melgund's Bill and the Means of Education in Scotland*. Edinburgh and London: William Blackwood and Sons, 1851. 8vo. Pp 56.   New Coll

MILLER, HUGH 'Lord Melgund's Bill'; *The Witness*, 22 May 1850, **11**, 2.

SIMPSON, ALEXANDER L *Notes relative to Education in Scotland, more particularly with reference to the Bill now before Parliament, entitled 'A Bill for the Reform and Extension of the School Establishment of Scotland'*. np, nd [1850]. 8vo. Pp 11.   New Coll

Copy of the Correspondence between a Deputation from the Scottish Episcopal Church and the Lord President of the Council, May 12-17. Pp 2.
PP, 1854/5, xli, 286

Copy of Correspondence between Bishop Gillies and the Lord President of the Council, on the subject of the Lord Advocate's Education (Scotland) Bill. Pp 2.   *PP*, 1854/5, xli, 341

BRYCE, JAMES *Lord Advocate's Bill*. Speech before the Commission of the General Assembly, Wednesday, March 22, 1854. Edinburgh: Paton and Ritchie, 1854. 8vo. Pp 16.

BUCHANAN, ROBERT *The Scotch Education Bill*. Glasgow: Printed by W G Blackie and Co, 1854. 8vo. Pp 8.   New Coll

COLQUHOUN, JOHN CAMPBELL *A Letter on the Scotch Education Bill, its Principles*

and Results, addressed to the Hon. A. Kinnaird, M.P. London: Mackintosh, 1854. 8vo. Pp 12.   New Coll

—*Memorandum on a Bill 'To make further Provision for the Education of the People of Scotland'*. [London], 1854. 8vo. Pp 4.   New Coll

EDINBURGH TOWN COUNCIL *Education (Scotland) Bill. Report by the Lord Provost's Committee*. Edinburgh: Printed by Neill and Company, 1854. 8vo. Pp 15.
EUL

'The Educators and the Education Bill'; *The Scottish Educational and Literary J*, Apr 1854, **2**, 291-300.

'A Few Remarks upon the Education Bill'; *The Scottish Educational and Literary J*, May 1854, **2**, 333-40.

GILLIS, JAMES *A Letter to the Right Honourable Duncan Maclaren, Lord Provost of Edinburgh, on the proposed 'Voluntary' Amendment of the Lord Advocate's Educational Bill for Scotland*. Edinburgh: Marsh and Beattie, 1854. 8vo. Pp 38.

HUTCHISON, GEORGE *Remarks on the Education Bill for Scotland*. Aberdeen: John Smith; Edinburgh: Wm Blackwood & Sons; Glasgow: Griffin & Co, nd (?1854). 8vo. Pp 15.   New Coll

'Justice done to the Lord Advocate's Bill'; *Church of Scotland Mag and Rev*, Apr 1854, **2**, 311-24.

MCTAGGART, DAVID *Substance of the Speech, delivered in the Provincial Synod of Aberdeen, on the Lord Advocate's Educa-*

tional Bill, 12th April, 1854. Aberdeen: Printed by D Chalmers & Company, 1854. 8vo. Pp 20.   APL

MONCRIEFF, JAMES (Lord Moncrieff) *Speech in the House of Commons, Feb. 23. 1854, on the Bill for the Education of the People of Scotland.* London: Longman, Brown, Green, and Longman, 1854. 8vo. Pp 30.

Speeches at the County Meeting, held in Edinburgh on 1st May 1854 on the Lord Advocate's Education Bill. With an Appendix, containing Results of the Divisions of the other Counties. Edinburgh: Printed by Thomas Allan & Co, 1854. 8vo. Pp 31.   New Coll

STIRLING-MAXWELL, SIR WILLIAM *Scottish Education. Speech on the Second Reading of the Lord Advocate's Bill, for making Further Provision for the Education of the People in Scotland, in the House of Commons, on 12th May, 1854.* Perth: Printed by John Proudfoot, 1854. 12mo. Pp 16.   New Coll

[SWINTON, ARCHIBALD C] *Report by Sub-Committee of the Elders' Union of the Church of Scotland on the Lord Advocate's Education Bill, 1854.* Edinburgh, 1854. 8vo. Pp 10.

THOMSON, ALEXANDER *Remarks on the Lord Advocate's Education Bill.* Aberdeen: Printed by A King & Co, 1854. 12mo. Pp 16.   New Coll

---

COOK, JOHN (St Andrews) *Speech on the Lord Advocate's Education Bill,* delivered in the General Assembly of the Church of Scotland, May 30, 1855. Edinburgh & London: William Blackwood and Sons, 1855. 8vo. Pp 27.   BM
Reprinted from the *Witness*, 5 June 1855.

EDINBURGH TOWN COUNCIL *Education and Schools (Scotland) Bills.* Report by the Lord Provost's Committee. Edinburgh: Printed by Neill and Company, 1855. 8vo. Pp 7.   EPL

Eighteen Reasons for rejecting the Lord Advocate's Bill, for the Education of the People of Scotland. np, 1855. 8vo. Pp 6.   New Coll

[FRASER, PATRICK] *Domestic Economy, Gymnastics, and Music*: an omitted clause in the Education Bill. By a

Bystander. Edinburgh: W P Kennedy; London: Hamilton, Adams, & Co, 1855. 8vo. Pp 24.

FREE CHURCH OF SCOTLAND *Remarks of the General Assembly's Committee on Parish Schools and National Education,* on the 'Bill to provide for the Education of the People in Scotland', read a second time in the House of Commons, on Friday 27th April 1855. np, [1855]. 4to. Pp 4.   New Coll

A Help towards an Education Bill for Scotland. By a Layman. London: Simpkin, Marshall, & Co; Edinburgh: Edmonston and Douglas, & W P Kennedy; Aberdeen: D Wyllie & Son; Glasgow: Griffin, 1855. 8vo. Pp 41.

JOHNSTONE, JAMES *Letter to the Lord Advocate of Scotland, on the Education Bill.* By a Scotch M.P. Westminster: Vacher & Sons, 1855. 8vo. Pp 12.

'The Lord Advocate's Education Bill'; *Scottish Educational and Literary J,* 1 Aug 1855, 3, 251-6.

State Education at Variance with Civil and Religious Freedom. Report of the Speeches delivered at a Public Meeting held in the Merchants' Hall, Glasgow, on Thursday, May 31, 1855, to oppose the Lord Advocate's Education Bill for Scotland. Glasgow: Maurice Ogle & Son; Edinburgh: Oliphant and Sons, and Ogle and Murray, 1855. 8vo. Pp 39.   New Coll

---

COOK, JOHN (Haddington) and ROBERTSON, JAMES *Speeches upon the Parish Schools Bill as introduced by the Lord Advocate,* delivered at an Extraordinary Meeting of the Commission of the General Assembly of the Church of Scotland. Edinburgh: Printed by Paton and Ritchie, 1856. 8vo. Pp 28.   BM

KER, JOHN *Education in Scotland.* Speech at the meeting held in the Merchants' Hall, Glasgow, 15th May, 1856, to oppose the Lord Advocate's (Burgh) Education Bill. Glasgow: Printed by C L Wright, 1856. 8vo. Pp 8.
    New Coll

LEITCH, WILLIAM *The Scottish Education Question*; being a plea for the Denominational System, with objections to the

Parish Schools Bill of the Lord Advocate, in a Letter to the Right Honourable the Earl of Leven and Melville. Edinburgh: Paton & Ritchie; Glasgow: Murray & Son, 1856. 8vo. Pp 23.   New Coll

INGLIS, JOHN (Lord Justice General), and BUCCLEUCH, THE DUKE OF *Speeches upon the Parish Schools Bill*, as introduced by the Lord Advocate. Edinburgh: Printed by T Allan and Co, 1856. 8vo. Pp 32.   GUL

The Parish Schools and the Church of Scotland; or, A Few Words addressed to Members of the Legislature on the Lord Advocate's Parochial Schools Bill. By a Member of the General Assembly's Parish Schools Committee. Edinburgh and London: William Blackwood and Sons, 1856. 8vo. Pp 16.

ROBERTSON, JAMES See COOK, JOHN (Haddington), above.

SWINTON, ARCHIBALD CAMPBELL *Report on the Education Bills for Scotland* (now before Parliament) by a Sub-Committee of the Elders' Union of the Church of Scotland. Edinburgh: Printed by Paton and Ritchie, 1856. 8vo. Pp 10.   New Coll

CHURCH OF SCOTLAND: EDUCATION COMMITTEE OF THE GENERAL ASSEMBLY *Special Report showing the Nature and Effect of the Recommendations and Draft Bill of the Royal Commission appointed to inquire into Schools in Scotland published May 1867*. Edinburgh and London: William Blackwood and Sons, 1867. 8vo. Pp 26.   New Coll

COOK, JOHN (Haddington) *Remarks on the Recommendations and Draft Bill of the Royal Commissioners on Education*. Published by direction of the Education Committee of the Church of Scotland. Edinburgh and London: William Blackwood and Sons, 1868. 8vo. Pp 52.

NICOLSON, ALEXANDER *Recommendations of Her Majesty's Commissioners appointed to inquire into the Schools in Scotland*. With the text of the proposed Education Bill. And Introductory Note. Edinburgh: Duncan Grant, 1867. 8vo. Pp 32.   EUL

ABERDEEN, UNIVERSITY OF *Report of Committee of Senate on the Parochial Schools (Scotland) Bill*. Aberdeen, 1869. 4to. Pp 2.   APL

BEGG, JAMES *The Duke of Argyll's Bill on National Education considered*. With some remarks on Scotch Legislation and the Statement of the United Presbyterian Committee. Edinburgh: James Nichol, 1869. 8vo. Pp 32.   BM

CHURCH OF SCOTLAND: GENERAL ASSEMBLY'S EDUCATION COMMITTEE *Parochial Schools (Scotland) Bill*. Remarks on 'Return to an Order of the House of Lords, dated 10th May 1869'. Edinburgh, 1869. 8vo. Pp 27.   New Coll

— —. 'Parochial Schools (Scotland) Bill. Special Report'; *Report of the Education Committee*, 1869, 61-71.

—. PRESBYTERY OF GLASGOW *Report of the Proceedings on 11th March, 1869, on the Parochial Schools (Scotland) Bill*. Glasgow: Printed by William Macrone, 1869. 8vo. Pp 17.   New Coll

—. SYNOD OF GLASGOW AND AYR *Report of Proceedings on 13th April, 1869, on the Parochial Schools (Scotland) Bill*. Glasgow: Printed by William Gilchrist, 1869. 8vo. Pp 26.   New Coll

DYKES, THOMAS *The Duke of Argyll's Education Bill*. Its Designs and probable Results. Glasgow: James Maclehose; Edmonston and Douglas, Edinburgh, 1869. 8vo. Pp 33.

Education in the Country Districts of Scotland, with Suggestions for its Improvement and Extension, and Remarks on the Parochial School Bill. By a Parochial Schoolmaster. Edinburgh and London: William Blackwood and Sons, 1869. 8vo. Pp 20.

GLASGOW, UNIVERSITY OF: GENERAL COUNCIL *Parochial Schools (Scotland) Bill*. np [Glasgow], nd [1869]. 8vo. Pp 12.   New Coll

—*Report of Committee of Senate on the Scotch Education Bill 1869*. Glasgow: James Maclehose, 1869. 8vo. Pp 19.   EUL

HAY, WILLIAM *National Education in Scotland*, with Suggestions for the Extension of the Present System, and Remarks on

the Duke of Argyll's Bill. Edinburgh: William Blackwood & Sons; Aberdeen: A Brown & Co, 1869. 8vo. Pp 51.
APL

KIDSTON, WILLIAM *Report on the Scotch Education Bill*, delivered at the Free Church Commission, Edinburgh, 11th August, 1869. Glasgow: Printed by Aird and Coghill, 1869. 8vo. Pp 23.
New Coll

'The late Education Bill, as dealt with by the Free Church and the United Presbyterians'; *The Watchword*, 1 Oct 1869, 4, 289-99. New Coll

PAROCHIAL SCHOOLMASTERS OF SCOTLAND *Remarks by the General Committee on the Education (Scotland) Bill now before the House of Lords.* Edinburgh, 1869. 8vo. Pp 8. APL

'Scotch Legislation—The Education Bill'; *The Watchword*, 1 Sept 1869, 4, 241-8.
New Coll

CHURCH OF SCOTLAND: GENERAL ASSEMBLY'S EDUCATION COMMITTEE *Parochial Schools (Scotland) Bill.* Special Report by the Education Committee. np [Edinburgh], 1870. 8vo. Pp 19. New Coll

'The United Presbyterians and the Parochial Schools Bill'; *The Watchword*, 1 Jan 1870, 4, 460-70. New Coll

BRYSON, W G *Letter to Edward Strathearn Gordon, Esq., on the Education (Scotland) Bill, 1871.* Elgin: Printed at the *Courant* Office by James Black, 1871. 8vo. Pp 16. GUL

CHURCH OF SCOTLAND: GENERAL ASSEMBLY'S EDUCATION COMMITTEE 'Parochial Schools (Scotland) Bill. Special Report'; *Report of the Education Committee*, 1871, 75-88.

COOK, JOHN (Haddington) and HOME, DAVID MILNE *The Lord Advocate's Scotch Education Bill.* Speeches at the Commission of the General Assembly, held 1st March, 1871, and Resolutions of the Committee. Edinburgh and London: William Blackwood and Sons, 1871. 8vo. Pp 25. BM

'The Education Bill'; *The Watchword*, 1 Apr 1871, 6, 1-3. New Coll

Remarks on the Scotch Education Bill. By a Parish Minister. Glasgow: Printed by William Gilchrist, 1871. 8vo. Pp 8.
New Coll

The Scotch Education Bill. Religious Instruction in Day Schools. Full Report of the Public Meeting held in the City Hall, Glasgow, on 20th December, 1871. Glasgow: Thomas Murray and Son, 1872. 8vo. Pp 55. New Coll

'The Scotch Education Bill'; *Blackwood's Edinburgh Mag*, May 1871, 109, 660-72.

Scottish Education Bill. The Bible in the School. Report of a Public Meeting held in the City Hall, Glasgow on 13th April, 1871. Glasgow: Thomas Murray and Son, 1871. 8vo. Pp 55.
New Coll

'Some Thoughts on the Scotch Education Bill. By a Young Scotsman'; *The Watchword*, 1 Sept 1871, 6, 263-6.
New Coll

CHURCH OF SCOTLAND: GENERAL ASSEMBLY'S EDUCATION COMMITTEE *Report on the Lord Advocate's Bill to make further provision for Education in Scotland, 1872.* Edinburgh and London: William Blackwood and Sons, 1872. 8vo. Pp 17.
BM

—: — *Parochial Schools (Scotland) Bill, 1872.* Special Report. np [Edinburgh], 1872. 8vo. Pp 22. New Coll

DALE, ROBERT W *The Scotch Education Bill.* A Speech delivered at a Meeting of the Scottish Religious Education Society, held in Aberdeen. Printed from a revised verbatim report. Birmingham: Printed for the Central Non Conformist Committee by Hudson and Son, 1872. 8vo. Pp 15. BM

— —. Second edition. Birmingham, 1872. 8vo. Pp 15. BM

'The Education Bill—Free Church Deputation'; *The Watchword*, 1 Feb 1872, 6, 507-11. New Coll

GLASGOW, UNIVERSITY OF *Report by the Committee of Senate on the Scotch Education Bill (1872).* Glasgow: James Maclehose, 1872. 8vo. Pp 21. EUL

GUTHRIE, THOMAS *The Scotch Education Bill*. A Letter. Glasgow, 1872. 8vo. Pp 4.   GUL

KIDSTON, WILLIAM *On the Necessity of Retaining in our own Hands the Management and Control of our own Schools under the Scotch Education Bill*; Being Speech delivered at the Great Education Meeting in Aberdeen, on Thursday, 11th January, 1872. np, 1872. 8vo. Pp 15.
New Coll

—*Religious Instruction of the Young in Day Schools under the Scotch Education Bill*, being Speech delivered at the Great Education Meeting at Stirling, on Thursday, 4th January, 1872. np, 1872. 12mo. Pp 15.   New Coll

—*The New Education Bill*. What we have gained. Unionism and Voluntaryism illustrated. np, 1872. 8vo. Pp 8.
New Coll

MARTIN, HUGH *National Education. The Lord Advocate's Bill*. Edinburgh: Printed for the Scottish Educational Association by Ballantyne and Co, 1872. 8vo. Pp 8.
New Coll

MONCRIEFF, SIR HARRY WELLWOOD, Bart. *Notes on the History of the Scotch Education Bill in Parliament*. np, nd [1872]. 8vo. Pp 6.   New Coll

PLAYFAIR, LYON *Scotch Education Bill*: Speech on the Second Reading, 7th March, 1872. With an Appendix. Aberdeen: A Brown & Co; Edinburgh: Edmonston & Douglas, 1872. 8vo. Pp 24.

Scottish Education Bill. *Report of Parliamentary Debate on Mr Gordon's Resolution in favour of 'Instruction in the Holy Scriptures in the Public Schools'*, adopted by the House of Commons on Monday evening, 10th May, 1872. Glasgow: Printed by Arch K Murray, 1872. 8vo. Pp 56.   New Coll

MCLAREN, DUNCAN *Substance of a Speech in the House of Commons respecting 'The Endowed Hospitals (Scotland) Bill'*, on Monday, the 14th August 1871. Edinburgh: William Oliphant & Co, 1871. 8vo. Pp 15.   New Coll

Historical Studies

The Period before 1560

COISSAC, JEAN BAPTISTE *Les Institutions Scolaires de l'Ecosse depuis les Origines jusqu'en 1560*. Paris: Librairie Hachette, 1914. 8vo. Pp 79. Bibliography.

COULTON, GEORGE C *Monastic Schools in the Middle Ages*. Medieval Studies, 10. London: Simpkin, Marshall, Hamilton, Kent, and Co Ltd, 1913. 8vo. Pp 44.

—'Schools'; *Scottish Abbeys & Social Life* (Cambridge: At the University Press, 1933), 175-86.

DURKAN, JOHN *The Beginnings of Humanism in Scotland*. Glasgow, 1953. 8vo. Pp 20.
Offprint from *The Innes Rev* (Glasgow: The Scottish Catholic Historical Committee), 4 (1953), 5-24.

—'Education in the Century of the Reformation'; *Essays on the Scottish Reformation*, ed MCROBERTS, DAVID (Glasgow: Burns, 1962), 145-68.
Reprinted from *The Innes Rev* (Glasgow: John S Burns & Sons), 10 (1959), 67-90.

EASSON, DAVID E 'The Medieval Church in Scotland and Education'; *Records of the Scottish Church History Society* (Glasgow: Printed for the Society), 6 (1938), 13-26.

FLEMING, DAVID HAY *A Jesuit's Misconception of Scottish History* and a Fellow Jesuit's Apology for the Inexactitudes: Reprinted from 'The British Weekly' 27th January, 1916, with Notes and Additional Remarks. Knox Club Publication 39. Edinburgh: The Knox Club, 1916. 8vo. Pp 20.

FORBES-LEITH, WILLIAM *Pre-Reformation Scholars in Scotland in the XVIth Century.* Glasgow: James Maclehose and Sons, 1915. 8vo. Pp vii, 155. 18 plates. Bibliography.

FYFE, J C 'Sixteenth Century Schools'; *Glasgow Evening Citizen*, 15 Feb 1930.

Mit

GRAY, SIR ALEXANDER 'The Old Schools and Universities in Scotland'; *SHR*, Jan 1912, **9**, 113-18.

HILSON, J LINDSAY 'The Schoole of the Paroche'; *Transactions of the Hawick Archaeological Society, 1926* (1926), 46-8.

LINDSAY, THOMAS M 'Notes on Education in Scotland in Early Days'; *Transactions of the Glasgow Archaeological Society*, new series, **1** (1890), 13-48.

LOCKHART, WILLIAM 'On The Scolocs of the Thirteenth Century'; *The Church of Scotland in the Thirteenth Century* (Edinburgh and London: William Blackwood and Sons, 1892), 122-8.

MACCALLUM, ROBERT E 'The Blackfriars in Scotland'; *SEJ*, 30 Mar 1962, **45**, 251-2.

ROBERTSON, JOSEPH *On Scholastic Offices in the Scottish Church in the Twelfth and Thirteenth Centuries.* Printed for private circulation, 1853. 4to. Pp 28.
An offprint from *Miscellany of the Spalding Club*, **5** (1852), 56-77.

ROGERS, CHARLES 'Scholastic'; *Social Life in Scotland from Early to Recent Times* (Edinburgh: William Paterson, 1884), **3**, 65-104.

SHAW, DUNCAN 'The Universities and Schools'; *The General Assemblies of the Church of Scotland, 1560-1600.* Edinburgh: St Andrew Press, 1964, 180-202.

SKENE, WILLIAM F 'Learning and Language'; *Celtic Scotland* (Edinburgh: David Douglas, 1877), **2**, 419-63; second edition, **2** (1887), 419-63.

TUER, ANDREW W 'The Horn Book in Scotland'; *History of the Horn-Book* (London: The Leadenhall Press, Ltd, 1897), 123-31.

URQUHART, JEROME P *Pre-Reformation School Training in Scotland.* Edinburgh: The Catholic Truth Society of Scotland, nd. 8vo. Pp 31.

VALENTINE, JAMES 'On Ancient Music or Song Schools of Scotland, with a Plea for the Teaching of Music in Scotland'; *Transactions of the National Association for the Promotion of Social Science, 1863* (1864), 379-81.

The Period from 1560 to 1872

ALLAN, MARY D *Scottish Education in the Eighteenth Century.* Unpublished EdB thesis, St Andrews University, 1946. Typescript. 4to. Pp 56. Bibliography.

StAUL

BEALE, J M 'Scottish Education and the Act of 1696'; *Common Errors in Scottish History*, ed DONALDSON, GORDON (Historical Association Pamphlet, no G 32. London, 1956), 17-18.

BEDFORD, F W 'The Hospital System of Scotland'; *Transactions of the National Association for the Promotion of Social Science, 1863* (1864), 340-8.
George Heriot's. Merchant Maiden. Trades' Maiden. Orphan. Robert Gordon's. George Watson's. James Schaw's. Louis Cauvin's. George Stiell's. John Watson's. James Donaldson's. Daniel Stewart's.

BELFORD, ALEX J 'Education in the Forties'; *Centenary Handbook of the Educational Institute of Scotland* (1946), 34-59.

—'Education in the Sixties'; *Centenary Handbook of the Educational Institute of Scotland* (1946), 86-113.

BRANSTON, WILLIAM T 'A History of Parliamentary Grants for Education'; *SEJ*, 24 July 1953, **36**, 479-81.

BROWNLIE, W M 'Early French Teaching in Scotland'; *SEJ*, 8 Nov 1935, **18**, 1406-7.

BUNYAN, STEPHEN A *The Development of Scottish Schools, 1803-1872.* Unpublished BEd thesis, Edinburgh University, 1959. Typescript. 4to. Pp [2], 197. Bibliography.

EUL

BURNETT, J C 'The Election of a Schoolmaster by "A Comparative Trial" in 1715'; *SHR*, Oct 1926, **24**, 48-55.

C, W A 'A Parochial School of Fifty Years Ago'; *Educ News*, 27 June 1903, **28**, 493-4.

CHISHOLM, JAMES *Art Education in Scotland from the Reformation to 1902*. Unpublished BEd thesis, Edinburgh University, 1954. Typescript. 4to. Pp [6], 182, [2].
                                                    EUL

CRAMOND, W 'Extracts bearing on Education from Presbytery and Kirk Session Records'; *Educ News*, 29 Nov 1890, **15**, 811-13; 13 Dec 1890, **15**, 843-4.

CRAIK, SIR HENRY 'The Parish Schools'; *A Century of Scottish History, from the Days before the '45 to those within living memory* (Edinburgh and London: William Blackwood and Sons, 1911), 611-17.

CRUICKSHANK, MARJORIE 'The Argyll Commission Report, 1865-8. A Landmark in Scottish Education'; *British J of Educational Studies*, June 1967, **15**, 133-47.

CUMMING, ALEXANDER D 'Education in Olden Times. Schools and Schoolmasters'; *Old Times in Scotland* (Paisley: Alexander Gardner, 1910), 76-129.

CURTIS, STANLEY JAMES 'Education in Scotland to 1872'; *History of Education in Great Britain* (London: University Tutorial Press, 1948), 196-235; second edition (1950), 497-540; third edition (1953), 497-540.

DEAN, IRENE F M *Scottish Spinning Schools*. Scottish Council for Research in Education, Publication 1. London: University of London Press, Ltd, 1930. 8vo. Pp xi, 150. Frontispiece and 7 plates. Bibliography. Index.

DONALDSON, SIR JAMES 'The Burgh Schools of Scotland'; *The Museum*, new series, 1 Jan 1869, **5**, 378-84.

G, S J 'Scottish Popular Education. A Historical Sketch'; *The Museum*, new series, 1 Aug 1864, **1**, 177-81; 1 Nov 1864, **1**, 294-8; 1 Dec 1864, **1**, 331-6.

GARDINER, A KENNETH *A Short Historical Outline of the Latin Language in Scotland up to the 20th Century*—with special reference to its Study and Extent in Schools. Unpublished EdB thesis, St Andrews University, 1956. Typescript. 4to. Pp 44. Bibliography.   StAUL

GIBSON, GEORGE A 'Sketch of the History of Mathematics in Scotland to the end of the 18th Century'; *Proceedings of the Edinburgh Mathematical Society*, second series, **1**—1927-1929 (1929), 1-18, 71-93.

GRAHAM, HENRY GREY 'Education in Scotland—Schools and Schoolmasters'; *The Social Life of Scotland in the Eighteenth Century* (London: Adam and Charles Black, 1899), **2**, 151-81.
The second edition, issued in 1900, is identical with this.

— —. Third edition (London: Adam and Charles Black, 1901), 417-47.
This single-volume edition was re-issued without change in 1906, 1928, 1937, 1950, and 1964, except that the editions from 1928 onwards were illustrated by 8 plates.

HALDANE, ELIZABETH S 'The Education of the People'; *The Scotland of our Fathers. A Study of Scottish Life in the Nineteenth Century* (London: Alexander Maclehose & Co, 1933), 151-79.

INSH, GEORGE PRATT *School Life in Old Scotland from Contemporary Sources*. Edinburgh: The Educational Institute of Scotland, 1925. 8vo. Pp xv, 109.

CONTENTS A Sixteenth Century Schoolboy. An Eighteenth Century Schoolboy. Some Schoolmistresses of Long Ago. Queen Mary intervenes. A Sixteenth Century Schoolmaster. A Seventeenth Century Schoolmaster. Schoolmasters and Governing Bodies. A Standard Grammar. The Grammar of Mr Alexander Home. The Battle of the Grammar Books. Smoothing the Path. Select Documents.

LORIMER, JAMES 'The Burgh Schools of Scotland half a century ago'; *The Museum*, new series, 1 Oct 1864, **1**, 258-9.

LORIMER, JOHN G 'The Services which the Church of Scotland has rendered to the Cause of Education'; *Church of Scotland Mag*, June 1836, **3**, 212-20; July 1836, **3**, 227-39.

M, J 'Juvenile Delinquency a hundred years ago'; *SEJ*, 28 Dec 1951, **34**, 753-4.

MACANDREW, RONALD M 'Teaching in Scotland in 1845'; *SEJ*, 18 Mar 1960, **43**, 217; 25 Mar 1960, **43**, 237; 1 Apr 1960, **43**, 263; 8 Apr 1960, **43**, 281; 15 Apr 1960, **43**, 299; 22 Apr 1960, **43**, 311; 29 Apr 1960, **43**, 331.

MACDONAGH, FRANCIS *Scottish Sessional Schools*. Unpublished MEd thesis,

Glasgow University, 1966. Typescript. 4to. Pp 160. GUL

MACKINNON, JAMES 'The Eighteenth Century—Education and Culture'; *The Social and Industrial History of Scotland from the Union to the Present Time* (London: Longmans, Green, and Co, 1921), 35-44.

MCPHERSON, D 'The Origin of the Parish School System in Scotland'; *SEJ*, 7 Apr 1950, **33**, 236-7; 14 Apr 1950, **33**, 248-50.

MCROBERTS, ARTHUR E D 'Building a School Two Hundred Years Ago'; *SEJ*, 1 Jan 1932, **15**, 25.

MAIN, ARCHIBALD 'The Church and Education in the Eighteenth Century'; *Records of the Scottish Church History Society*, **3** (1929), 186-95.

MANN, HORACE 'Scotch Schools'; *Report of an Educational Tour in Germany, and Parts of Great Britain and Ireland* (London: Simpkin, Marshall, and Company; Liverpool: D Marples, 1846), 59-69.

MASON, JOHN 'Scottish Charity Schools of the Eighteenth Century'; *SHR*, Apr 1954, **33**, 1-13.

MECHIE, STEWART 'The Scottish Church and Education'; *The Church and Scottish Social Development, 1780-1870* (London: Oxford University Press, 1960), 136-53.

MILNE, ROBERT *The Churches and Education.* By a Parish Minister. Glasgow: Thomas Murray and Son, 1870. 8vo. Pp 52. GUL

DE MONTMORENCY, JAMES E G 'The Beginnings of State Education in Scotland'; *State Intervention in English Education* (Cambridge: At the University Press, 1902), 111-24.

NEIL, SAMUEL 'A Half-century of Educational Progress'; *Educ News*, 1 Dec 1883, **8**, 787-9; 8 Dec 1883, **8**, 807-9.

NISSEN, HARTVIG *Beskrivelse over Skotlands Almueskolevaesen tilligemed forslag til for skjellige Foranstaltninger til en videre Udvikling af det Norske Almueskolevaesen.* (En Indberetning i Anledning af en efter offentlig Foranstaltning foretagen Reise.) Christiania: P T Mallings, 1854. 8vo. Pp ix, 482. The account of the Scottish educational

system occupies the first 256 pages of the book.

'On the Present State of Education in Scotland, 1819'; *Edinburgh Annual Register for 1816* [*sic*], **9** (1820), ccxv-ccxlviii.

PETERKIN, ALEXANDER 'The Parochial Schools of Scotland'; *A Compendium of the Laws of the Church of Scotland* (Edinburgh: Robert Buchanan), second part (1831), 487-92.

PLANT, MARJORIE 'Education'; *The Domestic Life of Scotland in the Eighteenth Century* (Edinburgh: At the University Press, 1952), 7-18.

'Report on Scottish Education'; *North British Rev*, new series, June 1867, **7**, 504-30.

ROBB, W CUTHBERT 'School Life in Old Scotland'; *Transactions of the Hawick Archaeological Society, 1954* (1955), 6-20.

RUSK, ROBERT R 'Scottish Education One Hundred Years Ago'; *SEJ*, 27 July 1934, **17**, 984; 3 Aug 1934, **17**, 1002-3.

RUSSELL, JAMES A 'The Scottish Academy'; *SEJ*, 24 May 1957, **40**, 311-12.

SAUNDERS, LAURANCE JAMES 'Parochial and National Education'; *Scottish Democracy, 1815-1840. The Social and Intellectual Background* (Edinburgh and London: Oliver and Boyd, 1950), 241-303.

SAUNDERS, WILLIAM 'Quaker Schools in Scotland'; *SEJ*, 6 July 1934, **17**, 902-3; 13 July 1934, **17**, 928.

SINCLAIR, SIR JOHN, Bart, 'Education'; *Analysis of the Statistical Account of Scotland* (1826), Part Second, 65-140.

STENHOUSE, LAURENCE 'Hartvig Nissen's Impressions of the Scottish Educational System in the mid-Nineteenth Century'; *British J of Educational Studies*, May 1961, **9**, 143-54.

VOIGT, J A *Mittheilungen über das Unterrichtswesen Englands und Schottlands.* Halle: Eduard Anton, 1854. 8vo. BM The Scottish section occupies pp 145-58 of the book.

WILLIAMS, JAMES B 'Educational Legislation in Scotland from the 15th Century down to the Present Time'; *Educ News*, 26 Jan 1895, **20**, 61-2.

WILSON, DUNCAN K *The History of Mathematical Teaching in Scotland to the End of the Eighteenth Century.* Scottish Council for Research in Education, publication no 8. London: University of London Press, Ltd, 1935. 8vo. Pp viii, 99. Frontispiece and 1 plate. Bibliography. Indexes.

WITHRINGTON, D J 'Lists of Schoolmasters teaching Latin, 1690'; *Miscellany of the Scottish History Society,* **10** (1965), 119-142.

WYLLIE, B M *Church and State in Scottish School Education during the Reformation Period (1560-1700).* Unpublished MA thesis, London University, 1952.
Not seen

WYSE, HENRY T 'Art Teaching in Scottish Schools, 1837-1909'; *Educ News,* new series, 14 May 1909, **3**, 496; 11 June 1909, **3**, 602.

YOUNG, THOMAS PETTIGREW 'Some Notes on the Teaching of French in Early Times'; *Secondary School J,* Jan 1909, **2**, 10-12.
BM

Local History

Cities
ABERDEEN

BANNERMAN, THOMAS *Interim Report by the Committee of the Council of the City of Aberdeen on the Town's Public Schools.* 3rd November, 1834. 8vo. Pp 128. Aberdeen: Printed at the *Herald* Office by G Cornwall, 1834.   APL

BLACKIE, JOHN STUART *A Letter to the Citizens of Aberdeen, on the Improvement of their Academical Institutions.* Aberdeen: Lewis Tait; William Tait, Edinburgh, 1846. 8vo. Pp 58.

GORDON, ABERCROMBY LOCKHART *An Address to the Inhabitants of Aberdeen, on the Necessity of establishing Schools,* especially for the Poorer Classes, and on the Sessional System, in the six Parishes in which the City has been divided, and on the Funds applicable to their Support. Aberdeen: Printed by D Chalmers and Co, 1831. 12mo. Pp 50,   APL

LEDINGHAM, JAMES *A Lecture on Education,* delivered at the Annual Exhibition of his Pupils in Elocution. Aberdeen: Lewis Smith, 1835. 8vo. Pp 17.   AUL

A Letter to Thomas Bannerman, Esq. on the Aberdeen Committee on Education, and their 'Interim Report'. By Philologus. Aberdeen: Printed by John Davidson and Co, 1835. 8vo. Pp 36.

Aberdeen Asylum for the Blind

Royal Charter of Incorporation of the President and Managers. 1855. Aberdeen: Printed by Milne and Hutchison, 1856. 8vo. Pp 24.   APL

Aberdeen Boys' and Girls' Hospitals

Act Incorporating the Boys' and Girls' Hospitals of Aberdeen, 15 and 16 Victoria, cap 21. 30th June, 1852. Aberdeen: Printed by G Cornwall & Sons, 1856. 8vo. Pp 30. (Private Act.)   APL

BOTHWELL, GEORGE BENJAMIN *Report on the Removal of the Boys' and Girls' Hospitals.* np, [Aberdeen], 1865. 8vo. Pp 6.
APL

ENDOWED SCHOOLS AND HOSPITALS (SCOTLAND) COMMISSION 'Boys' and Girls' Hospitals, Aberdeen'; *First Report* (1873), 711-21; *Appendix to Third Report* (1875), **1**, 89-90.

Suggestions by Mr Aitken. np [Aberdeen], nd. 4to. Pp 3.   APL
Suggestions by Mr Reid. np [Aberdeen], nd. 4to. Pp 1.   APL

Aberdeen Education Society

GIBSON, JOHN 'Report to the Committee of Council on Education, respecting the [Lancastrian or] Aberdeen Education

Society's School in the County of Aberdeen'; *PP*, 1841, xx, 392, 17-25.

Report by the Directors to the Subscribers. Aberdeen: Printed by D Chalmers & Co, 1820. 8vo. Pp 16. AUL

Aberdeen English School

KENNEDY, WILLIAM 'Of the English School, &c.'; *Annals of Aberdeen* (London: Printed for A Brown and Co, Aberdeen; W Blackwood, Edinburgh; and Longman, Hurst, Rees, Orme, and Brown, 1818), **2**, 135-8.

Aberdeen Female Orphan Asylum

ENDOWED SCHOOLS AND HOSPITALS (SCOTLAND) COMMISSION 'The Aberdeen Female Orphan Asylum'; *First Report* (1873), 730-7; *Appendix to Third Report* (1875), **1**, 95-6.

GORDON, JOHN 'Report on the Female Orphan Asylum, Aberdeen'; *Minutes of the Committee of Council on Education, 1848-49-50*, 558-65.

WALKER, ALEXANDER *Mrs Elmslie and her Female Orphan Asylum.* Aberdeen: Printed by Lewis Smith & Sons, 1898. 8vo. Pp 21.

Aberdeen Grammar School

ABERDEEN TOWN COUNCIL '15 June 1659. Laws anent Visitatiouns, etc'; in SIMPSON, HENRY F M *Bon Record* (1906), 79-81.

—'23 October 1700. Laws and Maner of Teacheing to be observed in the Grammar-School of Aberdeen'; in SIMPSON, HENRY F M *Bon Record* (1906), 163-8.

—'23 October 1710. Act anent some Regulations in the Grammar Schooll'; in SIMPSON, HENRY F M *Bon Record* (1906), 91-2.

—'6 February 1711. Act anent some Regulations in the Grammar Schooll'; in SIMPSON, HENRY F M *Bon Record* (1906), 92-6.

—*Grammar School.* Observations by various parties on the Rector's Report as to the Curriculum, &c. 1854. Aberdeen: Wm Bennett, 1854. 8vo. Pp 55. APL

—*Memorandum and Queries with reference to the Curriculum proposed for the New Grammar School of Aberdeen.* np [Aberdeen], 1863. Fol. Pp 2. APL

—*New Grammar School.* Report containing the Answers to Queries on the Curriculum. 1863. Aberdeen: Printed by G Cornwall & Sons, 1863. 8vo. Pp 27, [6]. APL

—*[Second] Interim Report of the Education Committee of the Council.* 30th January, 1835. Aberdeen: Printed by D Chalmers and Co, 1835. 12mo. Pp 7. AUL

ANDERSON, SIR ALEXANDER *Memorandum by the Provost for the Consideration of the Magistrates and Town Council on the Emoluments of the Masters.* np [Aberdeen], 1863. Fol. Pp 4. APL

ANDERSON, PETER J 'Aberdeen Grammar School—Lists of the Rectors and Masters'; *Scottish Notes and Queries*, Sept 1897, **11**, 38-41.

Reprinted in SIMPSON, HENRY F M *Bon Record* (1906), 281-91.

CAMPBELL, PETER COLIN and BLACK, JOHN *Report on the Grammar School of Aberdeen* to the Lord Provost, Magistrates, and Town Council of Aberdeen, 29th October, 1866. Aberdeen: Printed by John Avery, *Northern Advertiser* Office, 1866. 8vo. Pp 22. Lei

Copy of Mortification by Dr Patrick Dune, Principal of Marischal College, of the Lands of Ferryhill, for maintaining four Masters in the Grammar School of Aberdeen. 3rd August, 1631. np, nd. 8vo. Pp 6. APL

ENDOWED SCHOOLS AND HOSPITALS (SCOTLAND) COMMISSION 'Grammar School. Old Machar'; *Second Report* (1874), 337-43.

FEARON, DANIEL R 'Aberdeen Grammar School'; *Schools Inquiry Commission Report* (1868), **6**, pt 5, 62-82.

GEDDES, SIR WILLIAM D *Report on the Grammar School, and other Educational Institutions,* under the Patronage of the Town Council of Aberdeen. 1854. Aberdeen: William Bennett, 1854. 8vo. Pp 116. AUL

GORDON, JAMES *A Letter to the Education Committee of the Town Council.* Aberdeen: Printed by D Chalmers & Co, 1835. 8vo. Pp 16.   AUL

GRAMMAR SCHOOL MASTERS *Curriculum for the New Grammar School as suggested by the Present Masters.* Aberdeen: Printed by G Cornwall and Sons, 1861. Fol. P 1.   APL

—*Memorandum by the Masters on the various Suggestions regarding the Curriculum.* np [Aberdeen], 1862. Fol. Pp 3.   APL

—*Revised Curriculum for the New Grammar School by the Present Masters.* Aberdeen: Printed by G Cornwall and Sons, 1862. Fol. Pp 3.   APL

GRAY, DAVID *A Letter to the Hon. Lord Provost and Magistrates of Aberdeen, Patrons of the Grammar School, on its Curriculum.* Aberdeen, 1854. 8vo. Pp 11.   EUL

HARROWER, JOHN (ed) *Trial Versions.* Aberdeen Grammar School, 1855. Aberdeen: The University Press, 1910. 8vo. Pp 30.   BM

HARVEY, THOMAS, and SELLAR, ALEX C 'Aberdeen Grammar School'; *Report on the State of Education in the Burgh and Middle-Class Schools in Scotland* (1868), **2**, 274-90.

KENNEDY, WILLIAM 'Of the Grammar School'; *Annals of Aberdeen* (London: Printed for A Brown & Co, Aberdeen; W Blackwood, Edinburgh; and Longman, Hurst, Rees, Orme, and Brown, London, 1818), **2**, 121-35.

MARTIN, ALEXANDER *Scheme for remodelling the Grammar School of Aberdeen.* Aberdeen: Printed by D Chalmers and Company, 1869. 8vo. Pp 8.   APL

MENZIES, ALLAN *Report on the Grammar School, and other Educational Institutions,* under the Patronage of the Town Council of Aberdeen. Aberdeen: William Bennett, 1854. 9vo. Pp 116, 18.   APL

MILNE, JOHN DUGUID *Grammar School Curriculum.* np [Aberdeen], 1861. Fol. Pp 4.   APL

—*Revised Sketch for Curriculum.* np [Aberdeen], 1863. Fol. Pp 3.   APL

MÜLLER, C F *Aberdeen Grammar School and its Management.* Aberdeen: Printed by Arthur King & Co, 1867. 8vo. Pp 15.   APL

Reports by the Examiners at the Visitation of the School. 1857. Aberdeen: Printed at the *Herald* Office, 1857. 8vo. Pp 9.   APL

SIMPSON, HENRY F M (ed) *Bon Record.* Records and Reminiscences of Aberdeen Grammar School from the Earliest Times. Printed for the Editor at the Ballantyne Press, Edinburgh; Aberdeen: D Wyllie & Son, 1906. 4to. Pp xix, 315. 2 photogravure portraits and 6 other illustrations. Index.

'Statuta et Leges Ludi Literarii Grammaticorum Abirdonensium'; in VAUS, JOHN *Rudimenta Artis Grammaticae* (Edinburgh: Robert Lepreuik, 1566), sigg. $0\text{-}0^{2r}$. Reprinted in *Miscellany of the Spalding Club*, **3** (1852), 399-402, from VAUS, JOHN *Rudimenta Artis Grammaticae* (Paris, 1553), and in SIMPSON, HENRY F M (ed) *Bon Record* (1906), 98-108. Renderings into English will be found in GRANT, J *History of the Burgh Schools of Scotland* (1876), 60-2, and in EDGAR, JOHN *History of Early Scottish Education* (1893), 122-4.

STIRLING, SIR JAMES *Education at the Aberdeen Grammar School, 1846-1851.* Aberdeen, 1916. 8vo. Pp 8.   AUL

WILLIAMSON, P *A Letter addressed to the Lord Provost, Magistrates, and Town Council, of the City of Aberdeen, containing some Hints for the Settlement of the Education Question on a truly National Basis.* Aberdeen: Lewis & James Smith; Edinburgh: William Blackwood & Sons; Glasgow: John Smith & Son, 1854. 8vo. Pp 15.   APL

Aberdeen Mechanics' Institution

Aberdeen Mechanics' Institution, for promoting the Instruction of Operative Tradesmen, in the Principles of their Profession. Aberdeen: Printed by D Chalmers and Co, 1824. 8vo. Pp 12.   AUL

Aberdeen Mechanics' Institution, for affording Scientific Instruction to Operative Tradesmen and others. Aberdeen: Printed by J Davidson & Co, 1837. 8vo. Pp 8.   AUL

ABERDEEN MECHANICS' INSTITUTION *Rules and Regulations.* Aberdeen: Printed by William Bennett, 1847. 8vo. Pp 12.   APL

NOTE The Reference Department of Aberdeen Public Library has a complete set of the Annual Reports of the Mechanics' Institution from its foundation in 1824 down to 1880.

Address to the Mechanics, Tradesmen, and Working-Classes in general of Aberdeen, respecting the proposed Building for the Mechanics' Institution. Aberdeen: Printed at the *Review* Office by G Mackay, 1844. 4to. Pp 4. APL

FRASER, GEORGE MILNE *Aberdeen Mechanics' Institute.* A Record of Civic and Educational Progress. Aberdeen: The University Press, 1912. 8vo. Pp [4], 68. BM

HUDSON, JAMES WILLIAM 'Aberdeen: The Mechanics' Institute'; *History of Adult Education* (1851), 58-62.

Aberdeen Music Schools

TERRY, CHARLES SANFORD 'The Music School of Old Machar'; *Miscellany of the Third Spalding Club* (Aberdeen: Printed for the Third Spalding Club, 1940), 225-48.

WALKER, WILLIAM 'Notes on the Song School'; *Extracts from the Commonplace Book of Andrew Melville, Doctor and Master in the Song School of Aberdeen* (Aberdeen: John Rae Smith, 1899), xvi-xlvi.

Aberdeen Schools of Industry

The Aberdeen Reformatory and Industrial Schools. Reprinted from the *Aberdeen Journal.* 1859. Aberdeen: Printed by D Chalmers and Company, 1859. 8vo. Pp 31. GUL

'Aberdeen Schools of Industry'; *Chambers's Edinburgh J*, new series, 27 June 1846, **5**, 408-9.

CHAMBERS, WILLIAM 'Visit to the Aberdeen Schools of Industry'; *Chambers's Edinburgh J*, new series, 15 Nov 1845, **4**, 305-8.

'Industrial Schools in Aberdeen'; *North British Rev*, May 1849, **11**, 73-82.

Alexander Shaw's Hospital

ENDOWED SCHOOLS AND HOSPITALS (SCOTLAND) COMMISSION 'Alexander Shaw's

Hospital'; *First Report* (1873), 722-4; *Appendix to Third Report* (1875), **1**, 91-2.

Bon-Accord Parish

COMMITTEE FOR THE ERECTION OF SCHOOLS IN BON-ACCORD PARISH Report, with Statement of Accounts, and List of Donations and Subscriptions. Aberdeen: Printed at the *Constitutional* Office, by G Cornwallis, 1839. 12mo. Pp 15. APL

Chanonry House School

[ALLAN, J BUCKLEY] *The Gym, or, Sketches from School.* By an Old Boy. Aberdeen: Printed by Taylor and Henderson, 1885. 4to. Pp 40. AUL

BLAIR, P J 'Recollections of the Gym'; *Aberdeen University Rev*, June 1919, **6**, 201-12. EUL

HARVEY, THOMAS, and SELLAR, ALEX C 'Gymnasium, Old Aberdeen'; *Report on the State of Education in the Burgh and Middle-Class Schools in Scotland* (1868), **5**, 319-23.

SHEWAN, ALEXANDER *Spirat adhuc Amor*: The Record of the Gym (Chanonry House School), Old Aberdeen. Aberdeen: The Rosemount Press, 1923. 8vo. Pp xviii, 494. Frontispiece, 38 plates, and 1 illustration. Index.

Deaf and Dumb Institution

Account of the General Institution for the Education of the Deaf and Dumb, on the Principles of the Abbé Sicard, established in Aberdeen. February 1, 1822. Aberdeen: Printed by D Chalmers and Co, 1822. 8vo. Pp 24. AUL

Orphan and Destitute Female Children's Hospital

ENDOWED SCHOOLS AND HOSPITALS (SCOTLAND) COMMISSION 'Hospital in Aberdeen for Orphan and Destitute Female Children'; *First Report* (1873), 725-9; *Appendix to Third Report* (1875), **1**, 93-4.

Old Aberdeen Grammar School

ANDERSON, PETER J 'The Old Aberdeen

Grammar School'; *Aberdeen University Rev*, Nov 1918, **6**, 40-5.   EUL

HARVEY, THOMAS, and SELLAR, ALEX C 'Old Aberdeen Grammar School'; *Report on the State of Education in the Burgh and Middle-Class Schools in Scotland* (1868), **2**, 24-6.

Robert Gordon's Hospital

ANDERSON, ROBERT *Auld Days in 'The Auld Hoose'*. Discipline in Robert Gordon's Hospital. Aberdeen: Printed for private circulation only, 1896. 8vo. Pp 17.   BM

—*The History of Robert Gordon's Hospital, Aberdeen, 1729-1881*. Aberdeen: D Wyllie and Son, 1896. 8vo. Pp xii, 199. Frontispiece and 4 plates. Index.

—*Some Reminiscences of Robert Gordon's Hospital*. Aberdeen: Printed for private circulation only, at the Free Press, 1894. 8vo. Pp 28.   APL

ENDOWED SCHOOLS AND HOSPITALS (SCOTLAND) COMMISSION 'Robert Gordon's Hospital'; *First Report* (1873), 702-10; *Appendix to Third Report*, **1**, (1875), 84-8.

FEARON, DANIEL R 'Gordon's Hospital, Aberdeen'; *Schools Inquiry Commission Report* (1868), **6**, pt 5, 183-6.

KENNEDY, WILLIAM 'Robert Gordon's Hospital'; *Annals of Aberdeen*. (London: Printed for A Brown and Co, Aberdeen; W Blackwood, Edinburgh; and Longman, Hurst, Rees, Orme, and Brown, 1818), **2**, 139-46.

KERR, JOHN *Report on Robert Gordon's Hospital, May 10, 1871*. Also, Supplementary Report, therein referred to, of date Nov. 22, 1870. Aberdeen: Printed by G Cornwall and Sons, 1871. 8vo. Pp 18.   APL

RAMSAY, JOHN 'Gordon's Hospital'; *Selected Writings* (John Rae Smith, Aberdeen; William Blackwood and Sons, Edinburgh, 1871), 182-201.

Robert Gordon's Hospital. Additional Endowment by Alexander Simpson, Esq. of Collyhill; with Agreement between the President and Governors of the Hospital, and Mr Simpson's Trustees: Also Minutes of the Trustees respecting new Buildings. Aberdeen: Printed by D Chalmers and Co, 1836. 8vo. Pp 8.   APL

NOTE The two copies seen of this pamphlet contain only the Trust Deed and Disposition of Simpson's Endowment.

—*Foundation, Statutes, and Rules*. Aberdeen: Printed by J Chalmers & Co, 1784. 8vo. Pp 116.   APL

—*Foundation, Statutes, and Rules*. Aberdeen: Printed by D Chalmers and Co, 1823. 8vo. Pp 118.   APL

—*General Regulations*, with Deeds and Charter of Robert Gordon's Hospital in Aberdeen. Founded 13th December, 1729. Aberdeen: Printed by John Avery, 1850. 8vo. Pp 126.   APL

—*Memorial and Queries for the President and Governors*, for the Opinion of Counsel; with Appendix. Aberdeen: Printed by G Cornwall and Sons, 1872. 8vo. Pp 19.   APL

—*Memorial for the President and Governors for the Opinion of Counsel*. Aberdeen: Printed by G Cornwall and Sons, 1873. 8vo. Pp 6.   APL

—I. *Queries, relative to the Hospital System*, transmitted to various Gentlemen of Experience, by a Committee of the Governors. II. *Answers*, received by the Governors. Aberdeen: Printed by D Chalmers & Company, 1857. 8vo. Pp 50.   New Coll

WALKER, ALEXANDER *Robert Gordon, 1665-1731, and his Hospital, 1750-1876*. Aberdeen: Printed for private circulation by Leslie and Russell, 1876. 8vo. Pp 36.   APL

According to a pencilled note on the flyleaf of the copy in Aberdeen Public Library, this work is 'very largely—if not mainly—a reproduction of articles in the *Aberdeenshire Herald* under the title 'Robert Gordon's Hospital: As it was, and is, and is like to be', 18 & 25 March, 1 & 8 April 1876'.

——. Second edition. Aberdeen: Printed by Milne and Hutchison, 1897. 8vo. Pp 40. Frontispiece.

—*Robert Gordon, 1665-1731, his Hospital, 1750-1876, and his College, 1880*. Aberdeen: J & J P Edmond & Spark, 1886. 8vo. Pp [8], 51.

Ross's School

Papers relating to Ross's School, Aberdeen. Aberdeen: Printed by D Chalmers & Company, 1864. 8vo. Pp iv, 9, 3.
APL

Sessional Schools

GORDON, JOHN 'Report on the Sessional Schools of Edinburgh, Glasgow, Aberdeen, Dundee and Perth'; *Minutes of the Committee of Council on Education, 1848-49-50* (1850), **2**, 570-605.

DUNDEE

DUNDEE TOWN COUNCIL *Report on the Mortifications and Educational Trusts under the Management of the Town Council of Dundee*, or Members of that Body; with particulars illustrative of the Mortifications and Designs of the Founders. By a Committee of the Town Council. Dundee: Printed by M'Cosh, Park, and Dewars, 1845. 8vo. Pp 34.   BM

ENDOWED SCHOOLS AND HOSPITALS (SCOTLAND) COMMISSION 'Dundee Educational Endowments'; *Appendix to Third Report* (1875), 363-423.

GRASSIE, M C *The Relationship between the Economic and the Educational Development of Dundee, 1800-1872.* Unpublished EdB thesis, St Andrews University, 1951. Typescript. 4to. Pp [2], 80, [2]. Bibliography.   DUL

HAY, WILLIAM *Report on the various Mortifications for Charitable and Educational Purposes in Dundee*, December, 1873. Dundee: Printed by D R Clark, nd [1873]. 8vo. Pp 28.   BM

LEWIS, GEORGE *The School Bill of Dundee*, and how little can be made of it. Dundee: W Middleton, 1841. 8vo. Pp 16.

Report on the Fund for Education in Dundee, bequeathed by the late James Webster, Esq., by a Committee of the Dundee Guildry. Dundee: Printed by R S Rintoul, 1821. 8vo. Pp 31.   GUL

T D 'Dundee Schools and Teachers of Old Times'; *Dundee Year Book, 1901* (Dundee: John Lang & Co, 1902), 219-220.

THOMSON, JAMES 'Educational Institutions'; *History of Dundee* from the Earliest to the Present Time, new and enlarged edition, edited by James MacLaren (Dundee: John Durham & Son, 1874), 295-313.
The first edition was published in 1847.

Dundee High School

'Acts made by the Magistrates in relation to the Grammar School to be observed in all time coming. February 19, 1674'; in WARDEN, ALEX J *Burgh Laws of Dundee* (London: Longmans, Green, & Co, 1872), 61-2.

An Address to the Inhabitants of Dundee on the unfinished state of the New Buildings, and on the System of Education in the Public Seminaries. From the Directors. Dundee: Printed at the *Chronicle* Office, 1834. 8vo. Pp 48.

'The Burgh Schools, and their Incorporation with the Public Seminaries, 1829'; *Charters, Writs, and Public Documents of the Royal Burgh of Dundee, 1292-1880*, ed HAY, WILLIAM (Dundee, 1880), 195-204.

A Critical Review of the Letter by Parens to Messieurs Craik and Millar, of the Grammar School, Dundee. Dundee: Printed by R S Rintoul, 1810. 8vo. Pp 16.   DPL

'Deposition of Mr Patrick Lyon, Master of the Grammar School of Dundie, for teaching his scholars a Catechism not authorised by the Church, and for having joined the preachers who prayed for the Pretender under the title of King James ye Eight. 1st May, 1716'; *Charters, Writs, and Public Documents of the Royal Burgh of Dundee, 1292-1880*, ed HAY, WILLIAM (Dundee, 1880), 140-1.

DUNCAN, THOMAS *Address to the Inhabitants of Dundee, on the Necessity of a New Building for the Academy.* Dundee: Printed by R S Rintoul, nd [c 1825]. 8vo. Pp 27.

DUNDEE PUBLIC SEMINARIES *Constitution of the Public Seminaries of Dundee*, under the joint Patronage of the Provost, Magistrates, and Town Council, and of the Subscribers. Dundee: Printed by James Chalmers, 1829. 8vo. Pp 14, 3.
GUL

H

—*Constitution of Dundee Public Seminaries.* (As amended 16th May 1853). Dundee: Printed at the *Northern Warder* Office, 1853. 8vo. Pp 19.   Mit

—*Address by the Directors.* Dundee, 1851. 4to. Pp 2.   Mit

—*Report to the Directors of the Public Seminaries,* by the Committee appointed in reference to obtaining a Site for the Buildings. Dundee: Printed by D Hill, at the *Courier* Office, 1829. 8vo. Pp 16. DPL

— —. Dundee: Printed by D Hill, at the *Courier* Office, 1830. 8vo. Pp 15. DPL

DUNDEE TOWN COUNCIL *Memorial for the Provost, Magistrates, and Town Council* in regard to the Action for Declarator against them at the instance of the Presbytery of Dundee. Edinburgh: Printed by Alex Laurie & Co, 1857. 8vo. Pp 36.   GUL

—*Report on the Dundee Seminaries.* By a Committee of the Town Council. September 1827. Dundee: Printed by D Hill, at the *Courier* Office, 1827. 8vo. Pp 24, 54.

—*Reports by a Committee appointed by the Town Council, for considering the State of Education in Dundee,* and the Means of Improving the Public Schools. 1st, Report on Sessional Schools. 2d, Report on the Dundee Seminaries. Dundee: Printed by D Hill, at the *Courier* Office, 1827. 8vo. Pp 19, 24, 54.   DPL

ENDOWED SCHOOLS AND HOSPITALS (SCOTLAND) COMMISSION 'Dundee High School'; *Second Report* (1874), 425-36; *Appendix to Third Report* (1875), **1**, 382-420.

HARVEY, THOMAS, and SELLAR, ALEX C 'Dundee High School'; *Report on the State of Education in the Burgh and Middle-Class Schools in Scotland* (1868), **2**, 44-62.

[IVORY, THOMAS] *Reply, by Parens, to the Animadversions of 'A Sincere Friend to Children',* the Defence by *'A.B',* and the *Fastidious Criticism of 'C.D'.* Dundee: Printed by R S Rintoul, 1810. 8vo. Pp 27.   BM

MAXWELL, ALEXANDER 'The Grammar School'; *History of Old Dundee, narrated out of the Town Council Register* (Edin-

burgh: David Douglas; Dundee: William Kidd, 1884), 86-93, 328-36.

MILLAR, A H 'The High School of Dundee. Historical Notes'; *Handbook of the Congress of the Educational Institute of Scotland, Dundee, 1907,* 40-55.

Royal Warrant in favour of Incorporation of the High School of Dundee. Dundee: Printed by Park, Sinclair, & Co, 1859. 8vo. Pp 14, 14.   GUL

THOMSON, JAMES 'The High School'; *History of Dundee,* new and enlarged edition, edited by James MacLaren (Dundee: John Durham & Son, 1874), 288-91.

Dundee Industrial School

CHAMBERS, WILLIAM 'Two Days in Dundee'; *Chambers's Edinburgh J,* new series, 13 Mar 1847, **7**, 161-4.

Dundee Infant Schools
Dundee New Infant School Society

The Reference Department of the Dundee Central Library has a number of Annual Reports of these two Institutions covering various years between 1830 and 1843. That for 1834 of the first of them is entitled, *Report of the Hawkhill and Wallace Feus Infant Schools.*

Dundee Music School

MAXWELL, ALEXANDER 'The Music School'; *History of Dundee, narrated out of the Town Council Register* (Edinburgh: David Douglas; Dundee: William Kidd, 1884), 336-40.

Dundee Royal Orphan Institution

Byelaws. Dundee: Printed by J Chalmers, 1831. 8vo. Pp 8.   DPL

Report by the Directors. Dundee: Printed by J Chalmers, 1831. 8vo. Pp 4. DPL

Report on the Progress and Prospects, by a Committee of Directors; with the Rules of the Management, and an Abstract of the Funds. Dundee: Printed for the Institution by James Chalmers, 1823. 8vo. Pp 9.   DPL

Dundee Sessional Schools

See *Dundee High School*. Dundee Town Council: Reports by a Committee, 1827.

GORDON, JOHN 'Report on the Sessional Schools of Edinburgh, Glasgow, Aberdeen, Dundee and Perth'; *Minutes of the Committee of Council on Education, 1848-49-50* (1850), **2**, 570-605.

Greenfield and Wallace Feus Infant School Society

Statement by the Committee. Dundee: Printed at the *Chronicle* Office, 1840. 8vo. Pp 3.   DPL

Maxwelltown Infant School

Report of the Committee for 1839. Dundee: Printed at the *Chronicle* Office, 1840. 8vo. Pp 3.   DPL

Morgan Hospital

ENDOWED SCHOOLS AND HOSPITALS (SCOTLAND) COMMISSION 'Morgan Hospital, Dundee'; *First Report* (1873), 693-701; *Appendix to Third Report* (1875), **1**, 78-81.

THOMS, PATRICK HUNTER *An Account of the Morgan Hospital*, with a Sketch of the Morgans of Dundee, the Scheme for the Erection and Endowment of the Hospital, and the Regulations for its Government. Dundee: Printed by James P Mathew & Co, 1870. 8vo. Pp [6], 65. Frontispiece.

THOMSON, JAMES 'The Morgan Hospital'; *History of Dundee*, new and enlarged edition, edited by James MacLaren (Dundee: John Durham & Son, 1874), 291-3.

Watt Institution

Constitution and Regulations, as agreed on at a General Meeting held 10th November 1824: and amended at a General Meeting held 4th July 1836. Dundee: Printed at the *Advertiser* Office, 1837. 8vo. Pp 6.   DPL

Constitution and Regulations, as agreed on at a General Meeting held 10th November 1824: amended at a General Meeting held 4th July 1836, and 6th July 1842.

Dundee: Printed at the *Warder* Office, 1843. 8vo. Pp 7.   DPL

Records of the Dundee Watt Institution. *Reports of the First Twenty Years: also Minutes of the Origin and Formation of the Institution*. 1825-1845. Dundee: Printed by J & J Taylor, 1845. 8vo. Pp [212].   DPL

Report of Committee on the History of the late Watt Institution: with Details as to similar Institutions, and Suggestions as to a New Scientific and Literary Institution for Dundee. Dundee: Printed at the *Northern Warder* Office, 1853. 8vo. Pp 19.   DPL

THOMSON, JAMES 'Watt Institute'; *History of Dundee from the Earliest to the Present Time* (Dundee: Published for the Proprietors by Robert Walker, 1846), 202-7.

EDINBURGH

ARNOT, HUGO 'Seminaries of Learning' and 'Charitable Foundations'; *History of Edinburgh* (Edinburgh: Printed for W Creech; and J Murray, London, 1779), 420-7, 561-9. 4to.

The High School. The Academy for Drawing. The Academy for the Deaf and Dumb. The Society for Propagating Christian Knowledge. The Orphan Hospital. The Merchants Maiden Hospital. The Trades Maiden Hospital. Heriot's Hospital. Watson's Hospital. The text remained unaltered in all subsequent editions, ie, the second of 1788, the third of 1816, and the fourth of 1818. The third and fourth editions have the title, *The History of Edinburgh, from the Earliest Accounts, to the Year 1780*, and are in octavo; the page references for them are 323-8, 434-41.

Articles of Agreement betwixt the Professors and Teachers, or who have been such, of the Liberal Arts and Sciences, and Branches and Parts thereof, within the City of Edinburgh, Liberties, Suburbs, and Dependencies thereof; 2d February, 1737. Edinburgh: Printed by Tho and Wal Ruddimans, 1739. 8vo. Pp 23.   EUL

BACHE, ALEXANDER D 'Education Hospitals for Boys, at Edinburgh'; *Report on Education in Europe* (1839), 12-48.   EUL

Orphan Hospital. Heriot's Hospital. George Watson's Hospital. John Watson's Institution. Cauvin's Hospital.

FAIRLEY, JOHN A 'Extracts from the Reports of the Old Tolbooth'; *Book of the Old Edinburgh Club*, **8** (1915), 108; **11** (1922), 73.
Entries referring to schoolmasters who had been 'warded' for keeping unlicensed schools.

FOX, JOSEPH 'View of the Process [*sic*] of the Lancastrian System of Education, and of its Present State in Edinburgh and Glasgow'; *Scots Mag*, Apr 1814, **76**, 259-66.

GIBSON, JOHN 'Report on certain of the chief schools inspected in the Presbytery of Edinburgh'; *Minutes of the Committee of Council on Education, 1843* (1844), 220-40.
Heriot's Hospital Schools. Dr Bell's Schools. Monitorial Schools.

GRANT, SIR ALEXANDER 'The Endowed "Hospitals" of Scotland'; *Recess Studies*, ed GRANT, SIR ALEXANDER (Edinburgh: Edmonston and Douglas, 1870), 117-50.
Merchant Maidens' Hospital. Trades' Maidens' Hospital. Orphan Hospital. George Watson's Hospital. John Watson's Hospital. James Schaw's Hospital [Prestonpans, East Lothian]. Daniel Stewart's Hospital. George Stiell's Hospital [Tranent, East Lothian]. James Donaldson's Hospital. Louis Cauvin's Hospital.

LAUDER, SIR JOHN, OF FOUNTAINHALL *Historical Notices of Scotish Affairs* (Edinburgh: Bannatyne Club, 1848), 274-94.
References to 'outed' schoolmasters who were forbidden to keep Latin schools.

LAW, ALEXANDER *Education in Edinburgh in the Eighteenth Century*. Scottish Council for Research in Education, publication 52. London: University of London Press Ltd, 1965. 8vo. Pp 239. Appendices. Bibliography. Index of Names. Index of Topics.

— 'Teachers in Edinburgh in the Eighteenth Century'; *Book of the Old Edinburgh Club*, **32** (1966), 108-57.

[LIDDLE, JOSEPH] 'Parochial Schools'; *Statements relative to the City of Edinburgh* (Edinburgh: William Tait, 1833), 45-50.

MAITLAND, WILLIAM 'Seminaries of Learning' and 'Charitable Foundations'; *History of Edinburgh from its Foundation to the Present Time* (Edinburgh: Printed by Hamilton, Balfour, and Neill, for the author, 1753), 420-2, 430-84. Fol.
French School. High School. Charity Work-house. Heriot's Hospital. Merchants Maiden Hospital. Trades Maiden Hospital. Orphans Hospital. Society for Propagating Christian Knowledge. Watsons Hospital.

MARWICK, WILLIAM H 'Early Adult Education in Edinburgh'; *J of Adult Education*, Apr 1932, **5**, 389-404.

Memorial of the Teachers of Edinburgh, unto the Honourable the Commissioners of Police for the City of Edinburgh. [*c* 1850]. 4to. Pp 2.   EPL

P 'Remarks on the Present State of Science in Edinburgh'; *Edinburgh Mag and Literary Miscellany*, Dec 1817, **1**, 417-23.

PARKER, WILLIAM M 'Edinburgh's Famous Schools'; *Scots Mag*, new series, Feb-Mar 1954, **60**, 352-8, 471-7.
Royal High School. George Heriot's School. Edinburgh Academy. Merchiston Castle School. Daniel Stewart's College. Fettes College. George Watson's College.

Proposal for the Establishment of a School in the Southern Districts of Edinburgh, for teaching English, Writing, Arithmetic, and Geography. Edinburgh: Printed by J Pillans & Sons, 1826. Fol. Pp 3.
                                                        EPL

Prospectus of an Educational Institution, on Christian Principles, proposed to be established in Edinburgh. Edinburgh: Printed by Anderson & Bryce, 1824. 8vo. Pp 49.   EPL

ROBERTSON, DAVID 'Education in the Middle of Last Century'; *The Princes Street Proprietors*, and other Chapters in the History of the Royal Burgh of Edinburgh (Edinburgh: Oliver and Boyd, 1935), 308-18.
Evening Schools in 1845. The Original Ragged Schools.

ROBERTSON, JOHN *A View of the System of Education pursued in the Public Schools and University of Edinburgh*: with remarks on the present state of learning in Scotland. London: printed for J W Warren by R Clay, 1818. 8vo. Pp 35. BM Reprinted in enlarged form from the *Monthly Magazine* for Apr 1818.

ROBERTSON, WILLIAM 'Educational Establishments'; *New Statistical Account of Scotland*, 1 (1845), 683-6.
High School. Edinburgh Academy. Scottish Naval and Military Academy. Other educational establishments. Heriot Schools. Sunday Schools. School of Arts.

SIMPSON, JAMES 'Education'; *Report from the Select Committee on Education in England and Wales* (1835), 121-206.

THORBURN, THOMAS 'Various Particulars in regard to the Education of the Young'; *Statistical Analysis of the Census of the City of Edinburgh, 1851* (Edinburgh: Adam and Charles Black, 1851), 60-3.

Aird House School

ANDERSON, JOHN 'Aird House School, Merchiston'; *Illustrations*, Apr 1889, **4**, 209-11.

Association for Promoting Education amongst Workmen, Apprentices, &c

Pleas for Education; being Addresses delivered to the pupils of the Apprentice Schools of Edinburgh, at a Meeting held in the Music Hall, Edinburgh, February 7, 1849. Revised by the Speakers. Edinburgh: Sutherland & Knox, 1849. 8vo. Pp 28.

Third Annual Report. Edinburgh: Printed by Anderson and Bryce, 1848. 8vo. Pp 22.

Catholic Schools of Edinburgh

Report of Proceedings at the Annual General Meeting of the Subscribers and Friends, held on 29th December, 1851. [Edinburgh], nd [?1852]. Lei

Circus Place School

BACHE, ALEXANDER D 'Notice of the Circus Place School of Edinburgh'; *Report on Education in Europe* (1839), 196-8. EUL

'Circus Place School'; *Quarterly J of Education*, Oct 1834, **8**, 378.

Extracts relating to Circus-Place School. Edinburgh: Robert Hamilton, 1826. 12mo. Pp 11. EPL

Plan of the Circus-Place School, opened 3d January 1826. Edinburgh, 1834. 8vo. Pp 3. EUL

Proposal for the Establishment of a School in the New Town of Edinburgh. Edinburgh: Printed by Anderson & Bryce, 1825. 4to. Pp 3. EUL

Deaf and Dumb Academy

GREEN, FRANCIS 'A Particular Account of the Academy of Messrs Braidwood of Edinburgh'; *Vox Oculis Subjecta* (London, 1783), 135-67, 195-219.

Deaf and Dumb Day-School

The Deaf and Dumb Day-School, 18 St John Street. *Third Annual Report, 1840.* Edinburgh: Printed by Thomas Allan & Co, 1841. 8vo. Pp 11. EUL

Donaldson's Hospital

BALSILLIE, DAVID *Report as to the best Mode of admitting children into Donaldson's Hospital, and of dismissing them when their time has expired.* Edinburgh, 1872. 8vo. Pp 8.

COWE, GEORGE 'Donaldson's School for the Deaf'; *SEJ*, 14 July 1950, **33**, 471-2.

Documents relating to Donaldson's Hospital. 1851. Edinburgh: Printed by Neill and Company, 1851. 8vo. Pp xvii, 74.

ENDOWED SCHOOLS AND HOSPITALS (SCOTLAND) COMMISSION 'Donaldson's Hospital'; *First Report* (1873), 605-36; *Third Report* (1875), 59-65; *Appendix to Third Report* (1875), **1**, 39-47.

NISSEN, HARTVIG 'Donaldson's Hospital'; *Beskrivelse over Skotlands Almueskolevaesen* (1854), 121-3.

SKINNER, ROBERT T 'Donaldson's Hospital—Centenary of Founder's Death'; *Figures and Figure-heads* (Edinburgh: Printed privately by T and A Constable Ltd, 1931), 50-6.

Edinburgh Academical Institution

[SCOTT, WILLIAM] *Milton's Plan of Education, in his Letter to Hartlib, with the Plan of the Edinburgh Academical Institution founded thereon.* Edinburgh: Printed for William Laing and Messrs Fairbairn and Anderson, and for Longman and Co, London, 1819. 8vo. Pp [2], 47.
BM

Edinburgh Academy

ANGLO-SCOTUS 'The new High School'; *Edinburgh Mag and Literary Miscellany,* Apr 1823, **12**, 471-5.

BACHE, ALEXANDER D 'The Academy of Edinburgh'; *Report on Education in Europe* (1839), 368-74.   EUL

EDINBURGH ACADEMY *Plan for the Establishment of a seventh class in the Edinburgh Academy.* Edinburgh, 1826. 4to. Pp 3.
EUL

—*Draft proposed Charter in favour of the Proprietors of the Edinburgh Academy.* 27th June 1823. [Edinburgh, 1823]. Fol. Pp 4.   EUL

—*Report by the Committee of Contributors to the Edinburgh Academy.* April 1823. Edinburgh: Printed by J & C Muirhead, 1823. 8vo. Pp 33.

—*Report by the Committee to the General Meeting of Contributors to the Edinburgh Academy.* [Edinburgh], 1822. 8vo. Pp 4.   BM

—*Report by the Directors to the Proprietors of the Academy.* Edinburgh: Printed by J & C Muirhead, 1825. 8vo. Pp 44.

—*Report by the Directors to the Proprietors of the Edinburgh Academy on a Plan for the Extension of the Academy.* Edinburgh: Printed by Thomas Constable, 1855. 8vo. Pp 13.   EPL

—*Report by the Directors to the Proprietors on the Pronunciation of Latin.* Edinburgh: Printed by J & C Muirhead, 1827. 8vo. Pp 32.   EUL

—*Scheme for the Establishment of a School in the New Town of Edinburgh,* on a Plan similar to that of the High School. [Edinburgh], nd [?1822]. 4to. Pp 13.
BM

—*Second Report of the Third Committee on the Plan of Education, 11th December, 1823.* [Edinburgh], 1823. 8vo. Pp 20.
BM

—*Statement by the Directors,* explanatory of the Scheme of that Institution. December, 1823. Edinburgh: Printed by John Hutchison, 1824. 8vo. Pp 41. Plate and 2 plans.

—*Third Report of the Third Committee on the Plan of Education.* 16th December, 1823. [Edinburgh], 1823. 8vo. Pp 16, 3.   BM

'The Edinburgh Academy'; *Edinburgh Mag and Literary Miscellany,* Jan 1824, **14**, 17-22.

FEARON, DANIEL R 'Edinburgh Academy'; *Schools Inquiry Commission Report* (1868), **6**, pt 5, 191-203.

FERGUSSON, ALEXANDER *Chronicles of the Cumming Club and Memories of Old Academy Days, MDCCCXLI-MDCCCXLVI.* Edinburgh: Printed for the Cumming Club by T & A Constable, 1887. 4to. Pp xx, 229. Frontispiece. Index.

GRAY, WILLIAM FORBES 'A Great Public School (Edinburgh Academy)'; *An Edinburgh Miscellany* (Edinburgh: Robert Grant and Son, 1925), 216-25.

HARVEY, THOMAS, and SELLAR, ALEX C 'The Edinburgh Academy'; *Report on the State of Education in the Burgh and Middle-Class Schools in Scotland* (1868), **2**, 193-202.

HENDERSON, THOMAS, and HAMILTON-GRIERSON, PHILIP F 'Introduction'; *The Edinburgh Academy Register* (Edinburgh: Printed by T and A Constable for the Edinburgh Academical Club, 1914), xi-xxvii.

'High School: New Academy of Edinburgh'; *Edinburgh Mag and Literary Miscellany,* May 1824, **14**, 525-8*.

MILLAR, JOHN HEPBURN 'The Edinburgh Academy'; *Public School Mag,* Jan 1901, **7**, 1-10.

'Plan of the Edinburgh Academy'; *Edinburgh Mag and Literary Miscellany,* Oct 1825, **17**, 459-60.

SCOTTISH UNIVERSITIES COMMISSION 'Plan of the Edinburgh Academy, October, 1827'; *Evidence* (1837), **1**, Appendix, 238-9.

THOMPSON, D'ARCY WENTWORTH *Day Dreams of a Schoolmaster.* Edinburgh: Edmonston and Douglas, 1864. 8vo. Pp viii, 328.

— —. New edition. London: Isbister & Company Limited, 1898. 8vo. Pp viii, 328.

— —. Another edition. The Harrap Library. London: George G Harrap & Co, 1912. 8vo. Pp 254. Frontispiece.

—'A Teacher's Experiences'; *Wayside Thoughts* (1868), 112-47.

Edinburgh Asylum for the Blind

THE ROYAL BLIND ASYLUM AND SCHOOL, EDINBURGH *A History and an Appeal.* Edinburgh: Printed by Pillans and Wilson, 1925. 12mo. Pp 12.   EPL

Edinburgh Collegiate School

'The Edinburgh Collegiate School'; *Illustrations*, Sept 1889, **4**, 370-2.

The Edinburgh Drawing Institution

'The Edinburgh Drawing Institution'; *Edinburgh Mag and Literary Miscellany*, Feb 1826, **18**, 190-3.

Prospectus of a Drawing Academy in Edinburgh. [Edinburgh], nd [?1824]. 8vo. Pp 14.   EUL

Prospectus of a Drawing Academy in Edinburgh. Edinburgh: Printed at the *Caledonian Mercury* Press, 1825. 8vo. Pp 17.   New Coll

Statement by the Directors of the Edinburgh Drawing Institution, explanatory of the Object and General System of Instruction to be pursued in that Establishment. December 1825. Edinburgh: Archibald Constable & Co, and Charles Smith & Co, 1825. 8vo. Pp 40.   EUL

Edinburgh Education Society

Report of the Committee of Directors to the General Meeting of the Society, held on November 28, 1814. Edinburgh: Printed by Alex Lawrie & Co, 1814. 8vo. Pp 32.   EUL

Edinburgh Gratis Sabbath School Society

EDINBURGH GRATIS SABBATH SCHOOL SOCIETY *The Instruction of the Rising Generation in the Principles of the Christian Religion, recommended.* To which is added, An Account of the Edinburgh Gratis Sabbath School Society, containing the Object, Plan, and Rules, of that Institution. Edinburgh: Printed by J Ritchie for the Society, 1812. 8vo. Pp 36.

Edinburgh Infant School Society

BACHE, ALEXANDER D 'School of the Edinburgh Infant School Society'; *Report on Education in Europe* (1839), 166-7.   EUL

EDINBURGH INFANT SCHOOL SOCIETY *First Report.* Edinburgh, 1824. 8vo. Pp 24.

LLOYD, R B 'An Edinburgh Infant School a Hundred Years Ago'; *SEJ*, 27 May 1932, **15**, 658.

WILDERSPIN, SAMUEL *Extracts on Edinburgh Infant Schools.* Bury: Crompton, [1835]. 8vo. Pp 8.   EIS

Edinburgh Institution (now Melville College)

BACHE, ALEXANDER D 'Edinburgh Institution for Languages, Mathematics, etc. Hill Street'; *Report on Education in Europe* (1839), 382-90.   EUL

EDINBURGH INSTITUTION CENTENARY *A Short Outline of the School's History and Future.* Edinburgh: Privately printed for the Edinburgh Institution, 1933. 4to. Pp 14. 2 plates.   EPL

EDINBURGH INSTITUTION FOR CLASSICAL, MATHEMATICAL, AND COMMERCIAL EDUCATION *Prospectus for Session 1853-54.* Edinburgh, 1853. 8vo. Pp 8.   EIS

HARVEY, THOMAS, and SELLAR, ALEX C 'Edinburgh Institution'; *Report on the State of Education in the Burgh and Middle-Class Schools in Scotland* (1868), **2**, 315-18.

YOUNG, JAMES R S *Edinburgh Institution, 1832-1932.* Edinburgh: Printed for the Centenary Committee by George Waterston & Sons Ltd, 1933. 4to. Pp xix, 443. Frontispiece and 17 plates.

*Edinburgh Institution for the Education
of Deaf and Dumb Children*

*Buildings erecting for the Edinburgh Deaf
& Dumb Institution, in Cannonmills Park,
north of the New Town.* Edinburgh, 1823.
8vo. Pp 3.   EUL

EDINBURGH DEAF AND DUMB INSTITUTION
*An Historical Sketch of the Rise, Progress,
and Present State;* with a State of the
Funds, etc. for 1834. Established June
1810, and incorporated by Seal of Cause
from the Magistrates of Edinburgh.
Edinburgh: Printed for the Institution
by Shaw and Company, 1835. 8vo.
Pp 28.   EUL

—*Report, with an Appendix, containing
Account of the Formation of an Auxiliary
Society in Glasgow;* the Names of the
Children in the Institution; A few
Specimens of their Composition, etc.
Edinburgh: Printed by J Ritchie, 1815.
8vo. Pp 33.

—*A Short Account of the Institution for the
Education of the Deaf and Dumb Children
of the Poor. Established in Edinburgh on
the 25th June 1810.* Under the care and
tuition of Mr John Braidwood. Edinburgh: Thomas Allan & Company,
1811. 8vo. Pp 18.   EUL

—*A Short Account of the Institution for the
Education of the Deaf and Dumb Children
of the Poor, established on the 25th June
1810.* Under the care and tuition of Mr
Robert Kinniburgh. Edinburgh: Printed
by A & J Aikman, 1814. 8vo. Pp 15.
                                             EUL

Edinburgh Lancastrian School Society[1]

EDINBURGH LANCASTRIAN SCHOOL SOCIETY
*Report of the Ordinary Directors to the
General Meeting of the Society,* held on
Monday the 11th Day of May 1812. To
which is subjoined, An Address to the
Public, &c. &c. Edinburgh: Printed by
Alex Lawrie & Co, 1813. 8vo. Pp 38.
                                             EUL

—*Reports of the Ordinary Directors to the
General Meetings of the Society,* held on
July 2, and November 15, 1813. Edin-

1. The name was changed in 1814 to 'The Edinburgh
Education Society'.

burgh: Printed by Alex Lawrie & Co,
1813. 8vo. Pp 49.   EUL

MONCRIEFF, SIR HENRY WELLWOOD, BART
'Account of the Foundation and Present
State of the Edinburgh Lancastrian
School'; *Scots Mag,* June 1812, **74,** 441-
444.

*Observations upon the Propriety of Estab-
lishing a Lancastrian School in Edinburgh.*
Edinburgh: Printed by Alex Lawrie &
Co, 1811. 8vo. Pp 23.   EUL

Edinburgh Merchant Company

BOYD, THOMAS J *Educational Hospital
Reform:* The Scheme of the Edinburgh
Merchant Company. Edinburgh: Oliver
and Boyd, 1871. 8vo. Pp 22.

HARRISON, JOHN *The Company of Merchants
of the City of Edinburgh and its Schools,
1694-1920.* Edinburgh: The Merchants'
Hall, 1920. 4to. Pp 48. Frontispiece
and 4 plates.

HERON, ALEXANDER *The Rise and Progress
of the Company of Merchants of the
City of Edinburgh, 1681-1902.* Edinburgh: T & T Clark, 1903. 4to. Pp xv,
400. Index.

LAURIE, SIMON SOMERVILLE *Reports on the
Hospitals under the Administration of the
Merchant Company, Edinburgh, and
General Remarks on Hospital Training.*
July 1868. Edinburgh: Printed for the
Governors of the Hospitals by Edward
Ravenscroft, 1868. 8vo. Pp 131.
                                             EUL

*On the Scholastic Position and Results of
the Merchant Company's Schools.* By
Sit Jus. Edinburgh: Seton and Mackenzie, 1870. 8vo. Pp 18.   EUL

STEVENSON, THOMAS GEORGE *Edinburgh
Merchant Company Hospitals:* Their
Origin and Purposes. With an Appendix
of Illustrative Documents. Edinburgh:
Seton and Mackenzie, 1874. 8vo. Pp
18.

*To the Master and Members of the Merchant
Company of Edinburgh.* Edinburgh:
Printed by Thornton & Collie, 1841,
4to. Pp 3.   EPL

A letter signed 'A Member of the Merchant Company of Edinburgh'.

Edinburgh Merchant Company Schools

(a) Daniel Stewart's Hospital

23 and 24 Vict, c 2. Act to incorporate the Governors of the Hospital in Edinburgh founded by Daniel Stewart, and to amend and explain his Trust Settlement. (Private Act, 1860.)

28 and 29 Vict, c cxxxviii. The Edinburgh Merchant Company Act, 1865. An Act . . . to amend the Act relating to Daniel Stewart's Hospital. (Local Act.)

ANDERSON, JOHN 'Daniel Stewart's College'; *Illustrations*, Feb 1889, **4**, 151-2.

EDINBURGH MERCHANT COMPANY *Report by the Master, Assistants, and Treasurer, in reference to the Company accepting of the Management of the late Mr Daniel Stewart's Hospital.* 19th April, 1859. Edinburgh: Printed by W Burness, 1859. 8vo. Pp 14.

Endowed Institutions (Scotland) Act. 1. Petition by the Governors of Daniel Stewart's Hospital, Edinburgh, for powers under the Act. April, 1870. 2. Provisional Order or Scheme for the future Administration of Daniel Stewart's Hospital, Edinburgh. April, 1870. 3. Provisional Order for Daniel Stewart's Hospital, Edinburgh. 1870. Fol. Pp 17, 12, 13.

ENDOWED SCHOOLS AND HOSPITALS (SCOTLAND) COMMISSION 'Daniel Stewart's Hospital'; *First Report* (1873), 543-55; *Appendix to Third Report* (1875), **1**, 26-28.

THOMPSON, JOHN *A History of Daniel Stewart's College, 1855-1955.* Edinburgh: Daniel Stewart's College, 1955. 8vo. Pp 119. Frontispiece and 15 plates. EUL

(b) George Watson's Hospital

15 and 16 Vict, c 7. An Act to explain and amend the Powers of the Governors of the Hospital founded in Edinburgh by George Watson, Merchant Burgess of Edinburgh. (Private Act, 1852.)

BALLANTYNE, JAMES *To the Members of the Merchant Company of Edinburgh, on the Proposal to sell George Watson's Hospital.* [Edinburgh], 1869. 4to. Pp 3. EPL

EDINBURGH MERCHANT COMPANY *Memorial by the Governors of George Watson's Hospital*; submitted to the Consideration of the Company of Merchants of the City of Edinburgh, and the other reverend and honourable Persons to whom are committed the Review and Alteration of the Statutes of George Watson's Hospital. Edinburgh: Printed by James Walker, 1831. 8vo. Pp 16.
EPL

—*Report of the Committee appointed to consider the Memorial from the Governors of George Watson's Hospital* in reference to a new edition of the Statutes of that Institution. Edinburgh, 1841. 4to. P 1.
EPL

Endowed Institutions (Scotland) Act, 1869. 1. Petition by the Governors of George Watson's Hospital and the Edinburgh Merchant Company for Powers under the Act. April, 1870. 2. Provisional Order or Scheme for the future Administration of George Watson's Hospital, Edinburgh. April, 1870. 3. Provisional Order for George Watson's Hospital, Edinburgh. London, 1870. Fol. Pp 23, 12, 13.

ENDOWED SCHOOLS AND HOSPITALS (SCOTLAND) COMMISSION 'George Watson's Hospital'; *First Report* (1873), 524-42; *Appendix to Third Report* (1875), **1**, 22-5.

GALLAWAY, WILLIAM *Letter to the Master and Members of the Merchant Company of Edinburgh, relative to George Watson's College.* Edinburgh: Printed by Thornton & Collie, 1841. 8vo. Pp 15.
EPL

GEORGE WATSON'S HOSPITAL *Regulations for George Watson's Hospital.* Compiled from the Statutes and Minutes of the Governors, and approved of at a General Meeting of the Governors, held on the 12th Day of February 1828. Edinburgh: Printed by Order of the Governors, by James Walker, 1831. 8vo. Pp 31.

—*Regulations for George Watson's Hospital.* Compiled from the Statutes and Minutes of the Governors, and approved of at a General Meeting of the Governors, held on the 11th Day of August 1842. Edinburgh: Printed by Order of the Governors, by W Burness, 1842. 8vo. Pp 28.

—*Report by the Committee of the Governors, with reference to the Meal Hours and Diet of the Boys*, and the Allotment of Time for their Study and Recreation. Edinburgh, 1844. 8vo. Pp 7.   EPL

—*The Rules and Statutes of George Watson's Hospital*. Edinburgh: Printed by William Brown and John Mosman, 1724. 12mo. Pp xvii, 56.

—*The Statutes and Rules of George Watson's Hospital*. Edinburgh: Printed by W Sands, A Brymer, A Murray & J Cochran, 1740. 12mo. Pp xxiii, 40.

— —. Revised, amended and improven, by his Trustees, conform to the Powers reserved to them at compiling the Statutes *anno* 1724, and at revising the same *anno* 1740. Edinburgh: Printed by Hamilton, Balfour and Neill, 1755. 12mo. Pp xxiii, 47.

— —. —. Edinburgh: Printed by D Schaw, 1810. 12mo. Pp xxiii, 49.

— —. — 1740, and by the Company of Merchants of the City of Edinburgh afterwards, conform to the powers vested in them. Edinburgh: Reprinted by William Burness, 1842. 8vo. Pp xlv, 30.

SKINNER, ROBERT T *George Ogilvie, LL.D. and George Watson's College, Edinburgh*. Printed for private circulation. Edinburgh, 1899. 8vo. Pp 72. Portrait.

(c) *James Gillespie's Hospital*

'Account of James Gillespie's Hospital and Free School'; *Edinburgh Mag and Literary Miscellany*, new series, June 1803, **21**, 407-8.

Endowed Institutions (Scotland) Act, 1869. 1. Petition by the Governors of James Gillespie's Hospital and Free School, for powers under the Act. April, 1870. 2. Provisional Order or Scheme for the future Administration of James Gillespie's Hospital and Free School, Edinburgh. April, 1870. 3. Provisional Order for James Gillespie's Hospital and Free School, Edinburgh. London, 1870. Fol. Pp 16, 9, 10.

ENDOWED SCHOOLS AND HOSPITALS (SCOTLAND) COMMISSION 'James Gillespie's Hospital'; *First Report* (1873), 556-68; *Appendix to Third Report* (1875), **1**, 184-6.

'Gillespie's Hospital'; *Scots Mag*, Apr 1809, **71**, 260.

JAMES GILLESPIE'S HOSPITAL *Rules and Regulations* of James Gillespie's Hospital; approved of by the Governors at a General Meeting, held the 20th October 1829. Edinburgh: Printed (Gratis) at the *Caledonian Mercury* Press, 1829. 8vo. Pp 16.

—*The Statutes and Rules of James Gillespie's Hospital and Free School*. Edinburgh: Printed by D Willison, 1802. 8to. Pp 37.   EUL

— —. Edinburgh: Printed by John Pillans, 1822. 8vo. Pp 32.

(d) *Merchant Maiden Hospital (now The Mary Erskine School for Girls)*

'1707. 25th March, cap. 95. Act in favours of the Maiden Hospitall founded by the Company of Merchants of Edinburgh & Mary Erskine'; *Acts of the Parliaments of Scotland*, **11**, 1702-7 (1824), 487.

ANDERSON, JOHN 'Edinburgh Ladies College'; *Illustrations*, Dec 1888, **4**, 85-7.

'Description of the new Building erecting for the Merchant Maiden Hospital'; *Scots Mag*, Oct 1816, **78**, 723-4.

Endowed Institutions (Scotland) Act, 1869. 1. Petition for the Governors of the Merchant Maiden Hospital, Edinburgh, for powers under the Act. April, 1870. 2. Provisional Order or Scheme for the future Administration of the Merchant Maiden Hospital, Edinburgh. April, 1870. 3. Provisional Order for the Merchant Maiden Hospital, Edinburgh. London, 1870. Fol. Pp 20, 11, 12.

ENDOWED SCHOOLS AND HOSPITALS (SCOTLAND) COMMISSION 'Merchant Maiden Hospital'; *First Report* (1873), 569-90; *Appendix to Third Report* (1875), **1**, 29-34.

GRISCOM, JOHN 'Merchant Maiden Hospital'; *A Year in Europe* (1823), **2**, 345.   BM

MERCHANT MAIDEN HOSPITAL *The Rules and Constitutions*, for governing and managing the Maiden-Hospital. With a List of the Subscrivers and Donators, or Contributers thereto, preceeding [*sic*] the 1st of July, 1702. Edinburgh: Printed by Order of the Contributors and Allowance of the Magistrates, by George Mosman, 1702. Pp [8], 32.

—*The Rules and Constitutions* for governing and managing the Maiden-Hospital, founded by the Company of Merchants, and *Mary Erskine*, in *anno* 1695. Allowed and confirmed by an Act of Parliament of her Majesty Queen Anne, dated the 25th March 1707. Amended and approven in a General Meeting of the Contributors, upon the 9th February 1708. Ratified by the Lord Provost, Baillies and Town Council, upon the 19th March the said year. Edinburgh: Printed by the Heirs and Successors of Andrew Anderson, 1708. 8vo. Pp [18], 59.[1]   EUL

—*The Rules and Constitutions . . .* the said year, except in so far as the same have been altered by an Act of the Contributors, dated 10th February 1718. Edinburgh: Printed by Robert Fleming and Company, 1731. 12mo. Pp ix, [6], 46.

—*Rules for the Government and Order of the Merchant Maiden Hospital, Edinburgh.* Edinburgh: Printed by Balfour and Smellie, 1776. 12mo. Pp 38.

— —. Edinburgh, 1785. 8vo. Pp 32.
                                        EPL

—*Statutes of the Maiden Hospital,* founded by the Company of Merchants of Edinburgh, and Mary Erskine. Edinburgh: Printed by William Smellie, 1783. 8vo. Pp 38.   EPL

— —. Edinburgh: Printed by Geo Reid & Co, 1804. 8vo. Pp 38.   EUL

— —. Edinburgh: Printed by William Burness, 1840. 8vo. Pp 30.   EPL

PRYDE, DAVID ['Edinburgh Ladies College']; *Pleasant Memories of a Busy Life.* (Edinburgh and London: William Blackwood and Sons, 1893), 128-60.

TOWILL, EDWIN S 'The Minutes of the Merchant Maiden Hospital'; *Book of the Old Edinburgh Club,* **29** (1956), 1-92.

---

1. Actually 60, since two pages are numbered 44.

Edinburgh Northern District School

COMMITTEE OF COUNCIL ON EDUCATION 'Return of the Application for Aid to the Edinburgh Northern District School, and the Correspondence and Communications relative to that Application between the Educational Committee of the Privy Council, or their Secretary, and the Committee of the Association for the Erection of the said School, or their Secretary'; *Schools (Scotland)* (1844), 12-19.

EDINBURGH NORTHERN DISTRICT SCHOOL *Letter to Joseph Mainzer, Esq., from the Directors,* being an Exposure of the Misrepresentations contained in a Letter addressed by him to the Rev. A. W. Brown, printed and privately circulated. Edinburgh: W P Kennedy; Glasgow: D Bryce; Ayr: D Guthrie; Dundee: W Middleton; Aberdeen: C Panton, 1847. 8vo. Pp 11, 7.

MAINZER, JOSEPH *Letter to the Rev. A. W. Brown.* Printed in the *Letter to Joseph Mainzer,* issued by the Edinburgh Northern District School.

—*Second Letter to the Rev. A. W. Brown and the Directors of the Northern District School.* Edinburgh: Fraser and Company, 1847. 8vo. Pp 30.

Edinburgh Original Ragged School

ASSOCIATION FOR THE ESTABLISHMENT OF RAGGED INDUSTRIAL SCHOOLS FOR DESTITUTE CHILDREN IN EDINBURGH 'Constitution and Rules'; in GUTHRIE, THOMAS, *Seed-time and Harvest of Ragged Schools* (1860), 187-8.

Reprinted in GUTHRIE, THOMAS *The City, its Sins and Sorrows* (1877), 262-3.

—*Report of a Meeting held in the Music Hall, Edinburgh, on Friday the 14th April 1848*; with the First Annual Report of the Committee of Management, &c. Edinburgh: John Elder; William Collins, Glasgow; and James Nisbet & Co, London, 1848. 8vo. Pp 58.   EPL

—*Edinburgh Ragged Schools. Eight months' experience.* Edinburgh: John Elder, 1848. Fol. 8vo. Pp 27.

—*Speeches delivered at the Second Annual Meeting.* Edinburgh: John Elder, 1849. 8vo. Pp 24.

—*Eight Months Experience of the Edinburgh Original Ragged or Industrial Schools, Castlehill and Ramsay Lane;* conducted on the Principles advocated by the Rev. Thomas Guthrie. Reprinted by the Committee of Management. Edinburgh: John Elder, 1848.   Hull

—*An Industrial Brigade as an Adjunct to the Ragged Schools in Edinburgh.* Edinburgh: Printed by Murray and Gibb, 1867. 8vo. Pp 28.   EPL

—*Statement as to the Working and the Results of the Edinburgh Industrial Brigade,* for the six months since its Commencement. June 1st, 1868. Edinburgh: Printed by Murray and Gibb, 1868. 8vo. Pp 14.   EPL

GUTHRIE, THOMAS 'The Edinburgh Original Ragged School: How it was got up, and what it has done'; *Good Words for 1861,* 3-8.

Reprinted in GUTHRIE, THOMAS *Out of Harness* (London: Alexander Strahan, 1867), 1-21.

—*A Plea for Ragged Schools; or, Prevention better than Cure.* Edinburgh: John Elder; Glasgow: William Collins; London: James Nisbet and Co, 1847. 8vo. Pp 48.

Another eleven editions of this pamphlet followed within the first twelve months after its first publication.

— —. Another edition. Edinburgh: John Elder, 1849. 8vo. Pp 15.

—'Ragged Schools'; *Autobiography of Thomas Guthrie, D.D., and Memoir by his Sons* (London: Daldy, Isbister, & Co, 1875), **2,** 109-77.

—*Supplement to 'A Plea for Ragged Schools'.* Edinburgh: John Elder; Wm Collins, Glasgow; and James Nisbet & Co, London, 1847. 8vo. Pp 16.

— —. Second edition. Edinburgh: John Elder, 1847. 8vo. Pp 16.   BM

Reprinted in GUTHRIE, THOMAS *Seed-time and Harvest of Ragged Schools* (1860), 179-87; *The City, its Sins and Sorrows* (1877), 256-62.

—*A Second Plea for Ragged Schools; or, Prevention better than Cure.* With illustrations by W Douglas. Edinburgh: John Elder; William Collins, Glasgow; and James Nisbet & Co, London, 1849. 8vo. Pp 58.

At least five editions had been published by 1851.

—*Seed-time & Harvest of Ragged Schools; or, A Third Plea,* with new editions of the First & Second Pleas. Edinburgh: Adam and Charles Black, 1860. 8vo. Pp [vii], 206. Frontispiece.

—'*Seed-time and Harvest; or Pleas for Ragged Schools*'; *The City, its Sins and Sorrows* (London: Daldy, Isbister & Co, 1877), 115-255.

—*A Short Plea for the Free and Full Use of the Bible in Ragged Schools.* Published by the original Ragged School Committee. Edinburgh: John Maclaren, 1852. 8vo. Pp 8.

The Centenary Celebrations of Dr Guthrie's Schools for Boys and Girls. Founded 9th April 1847. Edinburgh: Printed by Geo Stewart & Co, Ltd, 1947. 8vo. Pp 24. 4 plates.   EPL

Public Education: The Original Ragged School and the United Industrial School of Edinburgh; being a Comparative View of their recorded Results. Edinburgh: Sutherland & Knox; London: Simpkin, Marshall, & Co, 1855. 8vo. Pp 16.

Reprinted, with alteration and additions, from the *Scotsman,* 21st March 1855.

Report of a Discussion regarding Ragged Schools, held in the Music Hall, Edinburgh, on Friday, July 2, 1847. Edinburgh: John Elder; William Collins, Glasgow; and James Nisbet & Co, London, 1847. 8vo. Pp ix, 46.

Report of the Speeches delivered at a Great Public Meeting, to promote the Establishment of an Industrial Farm in connection with the Edinburgh Original Ragged School. Edinburgh: J Maclaren, 1853. 8vo. Pp 30.   New Coll

'Schools of Industry in Edinburgh'; *Chambers's Edinburgh J,* new series, 31 Jan 1846, **5,** 75-6.

'Visit to Dr Guthrie's Edinburgh Ragged Schools'; *Leisure Hours,* 18 Apr 1861 **10,** 247-51.

Edinburgh Orphan Hospital

An Account of the Hospital at Edinburgh, from its Establishment in 1733. Printed in WALKER, ROBERT *We have nothing which we did not receive* (Edinburgh: Printed by A Murray and J Cochran, 1776), 29-44.   EUL

An Account of the Progress and Present Situation of the Institution. Printed in BENNET, WILLIAM *The Care of Orphans stated* (Edinburgh: Printed by C Stewart & Co, 1801), 37-46; and in DICKSON, DAVID *On the Education of the Lower Orders of Society* (Edinburgh: Printed by Walker and Greig, 1806), 55-63.

An Account of the Rise, Progress, and Present State of the Institution. Printed in MAKELLAR, ANGUS *Sermon preached in St Andrews Church, Edinburgh, on Tuesday, July 16, 1816* (Edinburgh: Printed by J Ritchie, 1817), 39-48.

ENDOWED SCHOOLS AND HOSPITALS (SCOTLAND) COMMISSION 'Orphan Hospital'; *First Report* (1873), 661-72; *Appendix to Third Report* (1875), **1**, 61-5.

EDINBURGH ORPHAN HOSPITAL *An Abstract of the Regulations and Statutes of the Charity-School, Orphan-Hospital and Work-house at Edinburgh.* Edinburgh: Printed by Tho Lumisden and Jo Robertson, 1736. 8vo. Pp 16.   EPL

—A Brief Account of the Rise, Progress, Management and State of the Orphan-School, Hospital and Work-house at Edinburgh, as on the 1st January 1735. Edinburgh: Printed by Thomas Lumisden and John Robertson, 1735. 8vo. Pp 20.   EUL

—A Further Account of the State of the Orphan-School, Hospital, and Workhouse at Edinburgh. Edinburgh: Printed by Tho Lumisden and Jo Robertson, 1736. 8vo. Pp 12.   EPL

—An Historical Account of the Orphan Hospital of Edinburgh. Drawn up and printed by desire of the Managers. Edinburgh: Printed by J and C Muirhead, 1833. 8vo. Pp 69. Frontispiece. Plans.

—Letters Patent in favours of the Orphan Hospital. [Edinburgh], nd [1742]. 4to. Pp 8.   BM

—Regulations appointed by the Managers of the Orphan Hospital to be punctually adhered to by those who apply to have their Children admitted to the Hospital. [Edinburgh], 1803. 4to. P 1.   EUL

—Regulations for the Orphan Hospital. Prepared by the Managers, and approved by the Corporation, 11th August, 1834. Edinburgh: Printed by Order of the Managers, by James Walker, 1834. 8vo. Pp 21.   EUL

—Regulations or By-Laws of the Corporation of the Orphan Hospital and Work-House at Edinburgh: Approven of by a General Meeting of the Corporation on Monday the 21st of November 1743. With a Preface, shewing the Rise and Progress of the same. Edinburgh: Printed by Tho Lumisden and Jo Robertson, 1745. 8vo. Pp viii, 37.

—Rules for the Government and Order of the Orphan Hospital. Edinburgh: Printed by J Ritchie, 1823. 8vo. Pp 11.   EUL

—Statement relative to the Orphan Hospital. Edinburgh, May 1838. [Edinburgh, 1838.] 8vo. Pp 4.   EPL

—Statutes of the Corporation of the Orphan Hospital and Workhouse at Edinburgh. To which is prefixed an Account of the said Hospital from its Establishment in 1733. Edinburgh: Printed by James Donaldson, 1777. 8to. Pp 46.   EUL

—Statutes of the Corporation of the Orphan Hospital and Workhouse at Edinburgh. To which are prefixed, An Account of the Hospital, and Letters Patent in its favour. [Edinburgh]: Printed by J Ritchie, nd [?1822]. 8vo. Pp 31.   EUL

GAIRDNER, ANDREW *An Historical Account of the Old People's Hospital, commonly called, the Trinity Hospital, in Edinburgh; also, Proposals how to raise a Fond for the Maintenance of Widows and Orphans, under the Title of a Charity-Bank.* Edinburgh, 1728. 8vo. Pp viii, 56.

—An Historical Account of the Old People's Hospital, commonly called, The Trinity Hospital, in Edinburgh; to which is subjoined, Page 34, Proposals to raise a Fund for the Maintenance of Orphans, educating them in Religion, and bringing them up to virtuous Employments, accord-

*ing to their different Capacities, under the
Title of a Charity-Bank*. Edinburgh,
1728. 8vo. Pp viii, 56.

JOHNSTON, DAVID 'Statement respecting the
Orphan Hospital, 14th August 1809';
Scots Mag, Oct 1809, **71**, 649-51.

'Orphan Hospital'; *Scots Mag*, Apr 1809,
71, 259.

'Short Account of the Orphan Hospital of
Edinburgh'; Printed in MUIR, WILLIAM
*The Duty of 'Doing all to the Glory of
God'* (Edinburgh: Printed by J Ritchie,
1825), 41-56.

TOD, THOMAS *An Account of the Rise,
Progress, Present State, and Intended
Enlargements, of the Orphan Hospital.*
Edinburgh: Printed by James Donaldson,
1785. 4to. Pp 44. Frontispiece.

Edinburgh Philosophical Association

See *Edinburgh Philosophical Institution*.

Edinburgh Philosophical Institution

COMBE, GEORGE 'Account of the Edinburgh
Association for procuring Instruction in
useful and entertaining Sciences'; *Lectures
on Popular Education* (1835), 62-76.
EUL

— '—'; now named the Philosophical
Institution'; *Lectures on Popular Education*, second edition, corrected and enlarged (1837), 92-111, 117-20.

— '—'; *Lectures on Popular Education*,
third edition, corrected and enlarged
(1848), 61-74.

EDINBURGH ASSOCIATION FOR PROCURING
INSTRUCTION IN USEFUL AND ENTERTAIN-
ING SCIENCES Reports of the Directors.
Edinburgh: Printed by Neill & Co. 8vo.
Oct 1832—pp 8   Jan 1834—pp 8
Mar 1833—pp 8   Mar 1835—pp 6
July 1833—pp 4

—*Answer of the Directors to the Protest of
Mr William Fraser.* Edinburgh: Peter
Brown, 1836. 8vo. Pp 16.

EDINBURGH   PHILOSOPHICAL   INSTITUTION
*Prospectus of the Philosophical Institution,
to be established in Edinburgh*, consisting
of a Library and Reading-Room, a
News-Room, &c; and in which Courses

of Popular Lectures on the more inter-
esting Branches of Science, Arts, and
Literature, will be regularly delivered.
Edinburgh: Printed by Robert Hardie &
Co, 1846. 8vo. Pp 15.   EIS

—*Report of the Speeches delivered at the
Public Entertainment in Celebration of the
Opening of the Philosophical Institution,*
Edinburgh, 4th November 1846. Edin-
burgh: Printed for the Institution, 1847.
8vo. Pp 36.

—*Report to the Ordinary Directors*, by the
Sub-Committee to whom it was remitted
'to consider and report on a proposal
that the privileges of the Philosophical
Institution shall be extended to members
of the proposed Glasgow Athenaeum,
when they shall have occasion to visit
Edinburgh—and *vice versa*'. Edinburgh,
1847. 8vo. Pp 7.   EIS

—''Tis Fifty Years Since'; *Jubilee Book of
the Philosophical Institution* (Edinburgh:
Institution Rooms, 1897), 11-33.

FRASER, WILLIAM *Reasons of Protest against
the Laws of the Edinburgh Philosophical
Association.* Edinburgh: Printed by
Neill & Co, 1836. 8vo. Pp 20.

MILLER, W ADDIS *The 'Philosophical'*: A
Short History of the Edinburgh Philosophical Institution, 1846-1948. Edinburgh: C J Cousland and Sons Ltd, 1949.
8vo. Pp 96. Frontispiece and 6 plates.
Index.

Edinburgh School for Blind Children, Gayfield Square (founded 1836)

Report by the Directors, with Laws and
Regulations. March, 1874. [Edinburgh],
nd [?1874]. 12mo. Pp 4, 8.

Edinburgh School of Arts

EDINBURGH SCHOOL OF ARTS FOR THE BETTER
EDUCATION OF THE MECHANICS OF EDIN-
BURGH *Regulations*, etc. 1821. 8vo. Pp
12.

HUDSON, JAMES WILLIAM 'The Edinburgh
School of Arts'; *History of Adult
Education* (1851), 39-41, 75-9.

LAWSON, WILLIAM R 'The Heriot-Watt
College, Edinburgh'; *John Bull & his
Schools* (1908), 106-15.

PRYDE, DAVID 'School of Arts'; *Pleasant Memories of a Busy Life* (1893), 83-98.

'School of Arts'; *Edinburgh Rev*, Oct 1824, **41**, 109-14.

Edinburgh School of Design

DEPARTMENT OF SCIENCE AND ART 'Report upon the School of Art, Edinburgh'; *Sixth Report* (1859), 195-8.

LAING, DAVID *The Edinburgh School of Design in 1784*. From the Proceedings of the Society of Antiquaries of Scotland, January 11, 1869. [Edinburgh], 1869. 8vo. Pp 8.

MASON, JOHN 'The Edinburgh School of Design'; *Book of the Old Edinburgh Club*, **27** (1949), 67-96.

Edinburgh Sessional School

BACHE, ALEXANDER D 'The Sessional School of Edinburgh'; *Report on Education in Europe* (1839), 189-94.

'Edinburgh Sessional School'; *Blackwood's Edinburgh Mag*, Jan 1829, **25**, 106-34.

—; *Quarterly J of Education*, Jan 1831, **1**, 78-83.

GORDON, JOHN 'Report on the Sessional Schools of Edinburgh, Glasgow, Aberdeen, Dundee, and Perth'; *Minutes of the Committee of Council on Education, 1848-49-50* (1850), **2**, 570-605.

[NORVALL, JAMES] 'Edinburgh Sessional School'; *Letter addressed to the Parochial Schoolmasters of Scotland* (1829), 9-19. EUL

'Notice of the Edinburgh Sessional School, and of a School to be established in the New Town of Edinburgh, upon improved Principles'; *Edinburgh Mag and Literary Miscellany*, Sept 1825, **17**, 643-7.

PILLANS, JAMES 'Edinburgh Sessional School'; *Principles of Elementary Teaching* (1828), 111-30.

R, D 'The Edinburgh Sessional School'; *SEJ*, 7 July 1933, **16**, 821-2.

SHAND, A W 'Edinburgh Sessional School— Its Origin and Progress'; *Edinburgh Mag and Literary Miscellany*, Feb 1826, **18**, 129-43.

WOOD, JOHN *Account of the Edinburgh Sessional School*, and the other Parochial Institutions for Education established in that City in the year 1812; with strictures on Education in general. Edinburgh: Printed for John Wardlaw; W Collins, and Wardlaw & Co, Glasgow; Howell & Stewart, London; and James M Leckie, Dublin, 1828. 12mo. Pp xii, 262.

— —. Second edition. Edinburgh: Printed for John Wardlaw; W Collins, & Wardlaw & Co, Glasgow; A Brown & Co, Aberdeen; James Duncan, London; and James M Leckie, Dublin, 1829. 12mo. Pp xii, 273.

— —. Third edition. Edinburgh: Printed for John Wardlaw; W Collins, and Wardlaw & Co, Glasgow; A Brown and Co, Aberdeen; James Duncan, and Whittaker, Treacher and Arnot, London; and James M Leckie, Dublin, 1830. 12mo. Pp xii, 300. BM

— —. Fourth edition, with additions. Edinburgh: Printed for John Wardlaw; W Collins, Glasgow; A Brown & Co, Aberdeen; Bancks and Co, Manchester; James Duncan, and Whittaker, Treacher, and Arnot, London; and W Curry, Jun and Co, Dublin, 1833. 12mo. Pp xii, 314.

— —. To which is now added an Appendix, containing Observations on Normal Schools, Bible Education, &c. Fifth edition. Edinburgh: Oliver & Boyd; and Simpkin, Marshall, & Co, London, 1840. 12mo. Pp 328. BM

— —. Sixth edition. Edinburgh: Oliver & Boyd; Simpkin, Marshall, & Co, London, 1854. 12mo. Pp 328.

—*Account of the Proceedings connected with the Testimonial presented to John Wood, Esquire*, on 23rd December, 1837; And a Preface containing an Account of the Edinburgh Sessional School, and of Mr Wood's connection with that Institution. Edinburgh: William Whyte and Company, 1838. 8vo. Pp 40. EUL

—*Answer to a Letter of Thanks from the Members of the Society enjoying the benefits of the Edinburgh Evening Sessional School Library*. Edinburgh: Printed by A Balfour and Co, 1831. 8vo. Pp 12. EUI

—*Letter to the Rev. George M. Musgrove, containing Strictures on a Protest and a Pamphlet termed a Justification of the Protest against the First and Second Books of the Edinburgh Sessional School* being admitted into the Workhouse of the Docking Union, by the Rev. Kirby Trimmer, Stanhoe, Norfolk. Edinburgh, 1838. 8vo. Pp 40.

Edinburgh Society of Teachers

Rules: 1836. With Amendments certified in 1842 and 1851. Edinburgh: Printed for the Society by W Burness, 1851. 8vo. Pp 28.   EIS

Edinburgh Southern Academy

EDINBURGH SOUTHERN ACADEMY *System of Education.* Edinburgh: Printed by J Hutchison, 1829. 8vo. Pp 11.   EPL

Edinburgh Village Sabbath School Society

Tenth Report, 1831. Edinburgh: Printed for the Society by Andrew Jack & Co, 1831. 8vo. Pp 16.   EUL

Episcopal Free School

EPISCOPAL FREE SCHOOL *Constitution and Regulations.* np, nd. 8vo. Pp 6.   EPL

Esdaile School

Esdaile, 1863-1963: A Short History of the School. np, [1963]. 4to. Pp 20. Illustrated.

Fettes College

ENDOWED SCHOOLS AND HOSPITALS (SCOTLAND) COMMISSION 'Fettes College'; *First Report* (1873), 637-50; *Appendix to Third Report* (1875), **1**, 48-56.

The Fettes Endowment. Edinburgh: Printed by William Blackwood & Sons, 1863. 4to. Pp 13.

—. Another edition. Edinburgh: Printed by William Blackwood and Sons, 1868. 4to. Pp 20.

HARVEY, THOMAS, and SELLAR, ALEX C 'Fettes College'; *Report on the State of Education in the Burgh and Middle-Class Schools in Scotland* (1868), **2**, 326-30.

Gayfield Square School

COMBE, GEORGE 'Gayfield Square School, Edinburgh'; *Lectures on Popular Education,* second edition (1837), 220-2.

George Heriot's Hospital

Acta Parliamenti, 1695, 449. Recommendation in favours of George Heriot's Hospital.

Reprinted in CONSTABLE, A *Memoirs of George Heriot* (1822), 157-9; STEVEN, WILLIAM *Memoir of George Heriot* (1845), Appendix xiv; *History of George Heriot's Hospital* (1859), 333-4; (1872), 389-90.

6 and 7 Will 4, c 25 An Act to explain and extend the power of the Governors of the Hospital in Edinburgh, founded by George Heriot, Jeweller to King James the Sixth. (Private Act, 1836.)

An Address to the Citizens of Edinburgh, relative to the Management of George Heriot's Hospital. By a Free Burgess of Edinburgh. [Edinburgh], 1773. 8vo. Pp 19.

Answer for the Magistrates, Ministers, and Council of the City of Edinburgh, Governors of George Heriot's Hospital, Edinburgh, Defenders: to the Petition of the Merchant-Company and Trades of Edinburgh, Pursuers. November 19, 1765. [Edinburgh], 1765. 4to. Pp 12.   EUL

BAILLIE, JAMIESON *Walter Crighton:* or, Reminiscences of George Heriot's Hospital. Illustrated with wash drawings and portraits by J R Abercromby. Edinburgh: E & S Livingstone, 1898. 8vo. Pp xxiv, 286. Glossary of School Slang.   BM

NOTE The second and third editions, issued by the same publishers in 1901 and 1906, are identical with that of 1898.

BALCANQUHALL, WALTER *Last Will and Testament, and Codicil thereto, of George Heriot: and the Original Statutes of the Hospital.* Edinburgh: Printed by Neill & Company, 1835. 8vo. Pp 90.

NOTE The *Statutes* are printed in MAIT-LAND, WILLIAM *History of Edinburgh* (1753), 441-50; CONSTABLE, A *Memoirs of George Heriot* (1822), 105-54; STEVEN, WILLIAM *Memoir of George Heriot* (1845), Appendix vii; *History of George Heriot's Hospital* (1859), 273-90; (1872), 328-51.

BEDFORD, SIR CHARLES H 'Memoir of F. W. Bedford, D.C.L., LL.D., &c., the last House Governor. With portrait'; in GUNN, CLEMENT B *George Heriot's Hospital* (1902), 177-211.

[BROWN, MALCOLM] *Memorial by a considerable Number of the Burgesses of the City of Edinburgh, relative to the Management of Mr George Heriot's Hospital.* [Edinburgh], 1763. 4to. Pp 8.

BRUTUS, LUCIUS JUNIUS (*pseudonym*) *Considerations on the Management of George Heriot's Hospital.* Dedicated to the most impudent man alive. Edinburgh: Printed for C Elliott; and Cadell, Dodsley, and Murray, London, 1774. 4to. Pp vi, 20. BM

NOTE The dedicatee is named in an old hand on the title-page as Gilbert Laurie.

CRAWFORD, DAVID 'A Description of Heriot's Hospital'; *Poems, chiefly in the Scottish Dialect, on various Subjects* (Edinburgh: Printed for the Author, by J Pillans & Sons, 1798), 6-9.

D, M *An Account of the Arraignment, Tryal, Escape, and Condemnation of the Dog of Heriot's Hospital in Scotland, that was supposed to have been hang'd, but did at last slip the Halter.* London: Printed for the Author, 1682. Fol. Pp 2.

DAVIDSON, — *The Herioter no Monk*, or Strictures on the Sermon delivered to the Parents, Children, and Governors, on the late Anniversary of George Heriot's Day, by the Rev. Dr R. Lee, one of the Governors, and on his proposed Alterations on the Constitution of the Hospital. By an 'Auld Callant'. Edinburgh: Bell and Bradfute, 1846. 8vo. Pp 29. EPL

Δ 'Lines on the Portrait of George Heriot'; in THOMSON, THOMAS *Historical & Descriptive Account of George Heriot's Hospital, including a Memoir of the Founder* (1827), 30-2.

I

DEWAR, WILLIAM MCL *George Heriot's School, Edinburgh.* Edinburgh: Printed by McLagan and Cumming, Ltd, 1950. 8vo. Pp 17. Frontispiece and 14 photographs. EPL

Dialogue between a Son and his Governor, and the Views of Cousin John on the Motion to be considered by the Governors of George Heriot's Hospital, on Thursday, 2nd June, 1859, 'That the Boys in the Hospital be allowed a glass of weak wine on Heriot's Day as formerly'; Edinburgh: John Dickson, [1859]. 8vo. Pp 15. EPL

ENDOWED SCHOOLS AND HOSPITALS (SCOTLAND) COMMISSION 'George Heriot's Hospital'; *First Report* (1873), 517-23; *Third Report* (1875), 43-55; *Appendix to Third Report* (1875), **1**, 3-18.

FAIRBAIRN, JAMES *Observations on Report of Special Committee of Conveners of Committees, relative to the Duties of House-Governor, or House-Master, of George Heriot's Hospital*, August 10, 1844. [Edinburgh, 1844]. 8vo. Pp 8. GUL

FEARON, DANIEL R 'Heriot's Hospital'; *School Inquiry Commission Report* (1868), **6**, pt 5, 179-83.

FRANCE, LEWIS DE 'Application to the Magistrates of Edinburgh, as Governors of Heriot's Hospital, to be allowed to teach the boys there Church Music; 8th September 1684'; in MAIDMENT, JAMES *Analecta Scotica*, second series (Edinburgh: Thomas G Stevenson, 1837), 263-4.

GEORGE HERIOT'S HOSPITAL *Case for the Feofees of Trust and Governors of George Heriot his Hospital*, for Opinion of Counsel; with Answers to Queries. Edinburgh: Printed by William Neill and Company, 1847. 8vo. Pp 24. EPL

—*Information for the Magistrates, Ministers and Council of the City of Edinburgh,* Governors of George Heriot's Hospital, and others, Defenders; against Alexander Brown and others, Pursuers, Nov. 7, 1764. [Edinburgh, 1764]. 4to. Pp 32. EPL

—*Inventory of Original Documents in the Archives of George Heriot's Hospital,* ed

LAING, DAVID. Edinburgh: Printed for the Governors, 1857. 8vo. Pp [8], 52. Frontispiece.

—*Memorial for the Magistrates, Ministers, and Council of the City of Edinburgh,* Governors of George Heriot's Hospital, and others, Defenders; against Alexander Brown, and others, Pursuers, July 23, 1765. [Edinburgh, 1765]. 4to. Pp 31.
EPL

—*Memorial humbly presented to His Grace his Majesties Commissioner, and the Right Honourable the Estates of Parliament.* By the Administrators of Heriot's Hospital in behalf of the Poor thereof. [Edinburgh, 1695]. 4to. P 1.   BM

—*Minutes and Report on the Number of Boys which the present Dormitories can adequately, and with comfort and consideration for their health, contain.* [Edinburgh], 1853. 8vo. Pp 15.   EPL

—*Petition of the Boys of the said Hospital to the Governors of Heriot's Hospital.* Oct. 10. 1775. [Edinburgh, 1775]. 4to. Pp 2.

—*Regulations* enacted by the Governors of George Heriot's Hospital, upon the 13th Day of October 1834, as to the Superintendence to be exercised over the Boys at their leaving the Institution, and afterwards. [Edinburgh, 1834]. 8vo. Pp 8.

—*Regulations for George Heriot's Hospital.* Edinburgh: Printed by Order of the Governors, 1795. 12mo. Pp 35.   BM

— —. Edinburgh: Printed by Order of the Governors, by Peter Hill, 1809. 8vo. Pp 35.   EPL

—*Regulations for the Internal Management of George Heriot's Hospital.* Enacted by the Governors, 1st November, 1833. Edinburgh: Printed by Neill & Company, 1833. 8vo. Pp 32.

— —. Enacted by the Governors, 1849. Edinburgh: Printed by Neill and Company, 1849. 16mo. Pp 51.   BM

—*Regulations for the Internal Management, and for the Offices of Treasurer and Superintendent of Works, of George Heriot's Hospital.* Edinburgh: Printed by Neill and Company, 1855. 8vo. Pp 68.   EPL

—'*Regulations in regard to the Bursars of*

George Heriot's Hospital. Approved by the Governors, 12th December, 1844'; STEVEN, WILLIAM *Memoir of George Heriot* (1845), Appendix xi; *History of George Heriot's Hospital* (1859), 320-4; (1872), 372-4.

—*Report by Committee on Schools.* [Edinburgh], 1836. 8vo. Pp 7.

—*Report by Sub-Committee on proposed Modification of the System of Tuition and Discipline in George Heriot's Hospital.* [Edinburgh], 1855. 8vo. Pp 24.   EPL

—*Report of the Sub-Committee of the Education and House Committees upon the Office of House-Governor of George Heriot's Hospital.* [Edinburgh, 1838]. 8vo. Pp 8.   EIS

—*Reports of the Committee of Conveners of Committees, relative to the Duties of House-Governor or Headmaster of George Heriot's Hospital,* February 10, 1844. [Edinburgh, 1844]. 8vo. Pp 4.   GUL

—*Report of the Committee of Conveners of Committees and of the Education Committee of Heriot's Hospital, on the Observations of the House-Governor on their Report* of date 10th February 1844. September 2, 1844. [Edinburgh, 1844]. 8vo. Pp 3.   GUL

—*Reports and Deliverance of Governors on the Duties of House-Governor or Headmaster of George Heriot's Hospital.* 1844. 8vo. Pp 16.   EPL

—*Resolution to be submitted to the Governors of George Heriot's Hospital.* 1844. 8vo. Pp 4.   GUL

—*The Statutes of George Heriot's Hospital.* Edinburgh: Printed by Order of the Magistrats, Ministers, and Council of George Heriot's Hospital, 1696. 12mo. Pp 56.

— —. Edinburgh: Reprinted by Order of the Governors of the Hospital, 1734. 12mo. Pp 64.

— —. Edinburgh: Printed by Order of the Governors, by William Creech, 1789. 12mo. Pp 8, 86.

— —. Edinburgh: Printed by Order of the Governors, by Peter Hill, 1811. 12mo. Pp 8, 88.   EUL

— —. Edinburgh: Printed by Order of the Governors, 1818. 12mo. Pp vii, 88.

—'System of Education pursued in George Heriot's Hospital'; STEVEN, WILLIAM *Memoir of George Heriot* (1845), 235-47; *History of George Heriot's Hospital* (1859), 188-99; (1872), 216-27.

—*The Tercentenary of the Laying of the Foundation Stone of George Heriot's School.* Edinburgh, 1928. 8vo. Pp 64. 10 plates. Bibliography. EPL

GLOVER, THOMAS MILLER *A Few Remarks (by an Old Citizen) on a Pamphlet, entitled 'Substance of a Speech, delivered at a Meeting of the* Governors of George Heriot's Hospital, by John Macfarlane, Esq.' Edinburgh: Printed by F Gilchrist, 1834. 8vo. Pp 25. EPL

—*Observations in regard to the Description of Boys who appear agreeably to the Statutes, entitled to be admitted into George Heriot's Hospital.* By an Old Governor. Edinburgh: Printed by J and C Muirhead, 1827. 8vo. Pp 18.

GOLDICUTT, JOHN *Heriot's Hospital.* [London, 1826]. Fol. Pp 2. 5 plates and plan. EUL

GRANT, JAMES 'George Heriot's Hospital'; *Cassell's Old and New Edinburgh* (1882), 2, 363-71.

GRISCOM, JOHN 'Heriot's Hospital'; *A Year in Europe* (1823), 2, 367. BM
Reprinted in KNIGHT, EDGAR W *Reports on European Education* (New York, 1930), 88-9.

Guide to George Heriot's Hospital. Edinburgh: Bell & Bradfute, 1872. 8vo. Pp 48. Frontispiece and 2 plates.

GUNN, CLEMENT B *George Heriot's Hospital.* Memories of a Modern Monk; being Reminiscences of Life in the Hospital. Illustrated by copper engravings, portraits, and sketches. Edinburgh: E & S Livingstone, [1902]. Portfolio. Pp 8, 146.

HERIOT, GEORGE Disposition and Assignment of his Property to the Town of Edinburgh, dated 3rd September, 1623: registered, 2nd January, 1624.
Printed in STEVEN, WILLIAM *Memoir of George Heriot* (1845), Appendix V; *History of George Heriot's Hospital* (1859), 238-51; (1872), 291-307.

—Last Will and Testament. December 10, 1623.
Printed in MAITLAND, WILLIAM *History of Edinburgh* (1753), 431-9; CONSTABLE, ARCHIBALD *Memoirs of George Heriot* (1822), 67-102; STEVEN, WILLIAM *Memoir of George Heriot* (1845), Appendix VI; *History of George Heriot's Hospital* (1859), 252-70; (1872), 307-28.

'Heriot's Hospital'; *Scots Mag*, Apr 1809, 71, 259-60.

[LEE, JOHN] *Facts for the Consideration of the Governors of George Heriot's Hospital*, in connection with the questions relating to the Status, Duties, Salaries, and Terms of the Appointment of the Master and other Officers. Edinburgh: Printed by Order of the House and Education Committees, 1836. 8vo. Pp 56.

MACKENZIE, GEORGE *Letter on Heriot's Hospital.* [Edinburgh, ?1711]. 4to. Pp 16. EPL

MCLAREN, DUNCAN *Heriot's Hospital Trust and its Proper Administration.* An Address. (From the *Daily Review*—revised.) Edinburgh: William Oliphant & Co, 1872. 8vo. Pp 32.

— —. (From the *Daily Review*—revised, with additional notes.) Second edition. Edinburgh: William Oliphant & Co, 1873. 8vo. Pp 32. EUL

NISSEN, HARTVIG 'George Heriot's Hospital og Skoler'; *Beskrivelse over Skotlands Almueskolevaesen* (1854), 115-21.

PRYDE, DAVID *Heriot's Hospital.* A Short History. Edinburgh: Lindsay & Company Limited, 1938. 8vo. Pp 22. 2 plates.

A Remonstrance humbly offered to the Reverend and Honourable the Governors of Mr George Heriot's Hospital, by the United Committees of the Merchant Company, the Incorporations of Goldsmiths, &c., the Societies of Barbers, and Candlemakers, and a Friendly Meeting of Persons bred up in Heriot's Hospital, all Freemen Burgesses of Edinburgh. [Edinburgh, 1763]. 4to. Pp 8.

RHIND, WILLIAM *Tributary Lay*, so justly due to the Memory of George Heriot, the Founder of Heriot's Hospital. Edinburgh: Printed by J Hay and Co, 1813. 8vo. Pp 4.   BM

THOMSON, THOMAS *Historical and Descriptive Account of George Heriot's Hospital,* including a Memoir of the Founder. Edinburgh: J Cunningham and J and J Johnston, 1827. Pp [4], 44. Portrait and 8 engravings.

NOTE There are sometimes said to be two editions of this work, one a quarto and the other an octavo, but what are taken to be two separate editions are in fact only two issues of the same edition, one of these issues being a large paper one. In every respect save width of margin the two issues are identical, though it seems largely a matter of chance whether the text or the engravings come first.

WOODFORD, EDWARD 'Special Report on Heriot's Hospital, and the Heriot Hospital Schools'; *Minutes of the Committee of Council on Education, 1855-56* (1856), 556-60.

BILLINGS, ROBERT W 'Heriot's Hospital'; *Baronial and Ecclesiastical Antiquities of Scotland* (Edinburgh and London: Published for the Author by William Blackwood and Sons), 3 (1852), 4. 5 plates.

— —, ed WISTON-GLYNN, A W (Edinburgh & London: T N Foulis), 3 (1909), 260-6. 5 plates.

BLANC, HIPPOLYTE J 'George Heriot's Hospital'; *Book of the Old Edinburgh Club,* 4 (1911), Report of Fourth Annual Meeting, 4-10.

—'Heriot's Hospital & Contemporary Work'; *Transactions of the Edinburgh Architectural Association,* 2 (1892), 3-11. 6 plates.
Reprinted in *The Architect,* 2 Dec 1892, 48, 361-3.

—'The Hospital described from an architectural standpoint. Illustrated with measured drawings, and by a complete collection of the Masons' Marks on the Building'; in GUNN, CLEMENT B *George Heriot's Hospital* (1902), 149-74.

LAING, DAVID 'Who was the Architect of Heriot's Hospital?'; *Transactions of the Architectural Institute of Scotland,* 2 (1852), 13-40.

MACGIBBON, DAVID, and ROSS, THOMAS 'George Heriot's Hospital, Edinburgh'; *Castellated and Domestic Architecture of Scotland,* 4 (1892), 138-55. Plans and drawings.

RHIND, DAVID 'On the respective claims of Inigo Jones; Dr Balancanquhall, Dean of Rochester; and William Wallace,— to have been the Designer of Heriot's Hospital'; *Transactions of the Architectural Institute of Scotland,* 2 (1852), 173-186.

RITCHIE, ROBERT *Additional Report as to who was Architect of Heriot's Hospital.* Edinburgh: Printed by Neill and Company, 1856. 8vo. Pp 32.

—*Report as to who was the Architect of Heriot's Hospital.* With 3 plates. Edinburgh: Bell and Bradfute, 1855. 8vo. Pp 32.

— —. Another edition. Edinburgh: Printed by Neill and Company, 1854. 8vo. Pp 27.   EPL

SIMPSON, W DOUGLAS 'George Heriot's Hospital'; *Book of the Old Edinburgh Club,* 31 (1962), 33-42.

Grange House School

Annual Report with Outlines of the Course of Study, etc., Session 1859-60. Edinburgh: Printed by Thomas Constable, 1860. 8vo. Pp 41.   EIS

Heriot Foundation Schools

An Act to explain and extend the Powers of the Governors of the Hospital in Edinburgh, founded by George Heriot. Edinburgh: Printed by Sir D Hunter Blair and M T Bruce, 1836. 8vo. Pp 23.
Printed in STEVEN, WILLIAM *Memoir of George Heriot* (1845), Appendix xv; *History of George Heriot's Hospital* (1859), 334-41; (1872), 391-9.

ENDOWED SCHOOLS AND HOSPITALS (SCOTLAND) COMMISSION 'The Heriot Free Schools'; *Third Report* (1875), 53-5.

MACKIE, JOHN B 'Establishment of Heriot Free Schools'; *Life and Work of Duncan McLaren* (Edinburgh: Thomas Nelson and Sons, 1888), 1, 133-47.

—'Overthrow of the Heriot Free School System'; *Life and Work of Duncan McLaren* (1888), **2**, 184-214.

MCLAREN, DUNCAN *Suggestions for the Consideration of Heriot's Hospital*, in support of the Motion of Bailie McLaren, 'To consider and report as to the Propriety of applying any part of the surplus Revenue of the Hospital to the erection of one or more Schools for the education of such Burgesses' Sons as cannot be admitted into the Hospital'. [Edinburgh], 1835. 8vo. Pp 15.   EPL

STEVEN, WILLIAM 'Account of the Heriot Foundation Schools'; *Memoir of George Heriot* (1845), 249-82, and Appendix xvii; *History of George Heriot's Hospital* (1859), 207-28; (1872), 253-80.

WOODFORD, EDWARD 'Heriot Hospital Schools'; *Report of the Committee of Council on Education, 1855-56* (1856), 556-60.

High School of Edinburgh

'Academical Intelligence: The Royal High School of Edinburgh'; *New Scots Mag*, Apr 1829, **1**, 327-33.   EUL

'Address relative to the High School'; *Scots Mag*, Mar 1775, **37**, 164-5.

[BROWN W] *Letter to the Right Hon. the Lord Provost of the City of Edinburgh, regarding the System of Education pursued at the High School*. Edinburgh: Adam Black; and Longman, and Co, London, 1829. 8vo. Pp 30.

CHALMERS, GEORGE 'Various Proceedings with regard to the Use of Ruddiman's *Rudiments* and *Grammar* in the High School of Edinburgh'; *Life of Thomas Ruddiman* (1794), 88-95, 390-403.

COLSTON, JAMES The *High School Fees*: What the Patrons ought to do regarding them. A Letter to the Hon. the Lord Provost, and the Hon. the Magistrates and Town Council of the City of Edinburgh. Edinburgh: Andrew Elliot, 1863. 8vo. Pp 32.   EPL

—*History of Dr Boyd's Fourth High School Class* with Biographical Sketch of Dr Boyd. Portrait by George Aikman, Junr.

Edinburgh: Printed for private circulation by Colston & Son, 1862. 8vo. Pp xvi, 129.

— —; and Reminiscences of High School Days. Second edition. Edinburgh: Printed for private circulation, by Colston & Son, 1873. 4to. Pp xii, 162. Frontispiece and portrait.

—*Report on the Present and Future Arrangements of the Royal High School*. Submitted to the Education Committee [of Edinburgh Town Council] by Councillor Colston. June 1866. [Edinburgh, 1866]. 8vo. Pp 18.   EPL

COMBE, GEORGE 'Observations on Education, submitted to a Committee of the Town Council of —, appointed to collect information preparatory to the erection of a new Academy'; *Phrenological J*, **4** (1827), 407-20.

Considerations on the Proposals for building a new Grammar School, in the City of Edinburgh; setting forth the Inutility of such a Scheme, and the Prejudice that may result therefrom to Education. With a Proposal for the Increase of Latin-Schools, and some Observations on the present Mode of Teaching. Edinburgh: Printed for Charles Elliot, 1775. 8vo. Pp 27.   EPL

COWAN, WILLIAM 'The Site of the Blackfriars Monastery'; *Book of the Old Edinburgh Club*, **5** (1912), 67-93.

'Criticism of the Inscription on the new High School of Edinburgh'; *Scots Mag*, Aug 1777, **39**, 443-5.

DALGLEISH, WALTER SCOTT *The High School of Edinburgh*: An Inquiry, with Suggestions. Edinburgh: Edmonston & Douglas, 1866. 8vo. Pp 32.   EPL

—*Memorials of the High School of Edinburgh*; containing a Historical Sketch, and Biographical Notices. Edinburgh: Maclachlan and Stewart; London: Simpkin, Marshall, & Co, 1857. Large 4to. Pp [4], ii, 50. Frontispiece and 5 portraits.

DONALDSON, SIR JAMES 'On the Organisation of the High School, Edinburgh, and cognate Institutions'; *Transactions of the National Association for the Promotion of Social Science, 1863* (1864), 361-2.

DUNCAN, ANDREW *A Letter to John Waugh, Esq. Preses of a Committee of the Town-Council, respecting a new High School at Edinburgh.* [Edinburgh, 1823]. 8vo. Pp 14.

EDINBURGH TOWN COUNCIL *Address from the Town Council of Edinburgh, on the Subject of the new buildings for the High School,* of which the Foundation was laid on 28th July 1825. [Edinburgh, 1825]. 8vo. Pp 8. Frontispiece.
Reprinted in the *Edinburgh Mag and Literary Miscellany,* Nov 1825, **17,** 513-519.

—*Inquiry into the State of Education in the High School.* Edinburgh: Printed by Neill & Co, 1834. 8vo. Pp 3.   BM

—*Minutes of the Education Committee relative to the High School of Edinburgh,* 12th and 13th June 1866. [Edinburgh], 1866. 8vo. Pp 8.   EPL

—*Minutes of the Town Council, and Report of the Committee, respecting the proposed new High School.* (Ordered to be printed 16th April 1823.) [Edinburgh, 1823]. 8vo. Pp 26.

—*Notes as to the Position and Emoluments of the Rector of the High School of Edinburgh.* [Edinburgh], 1864. 8vo. Pp 8.   EPL

—*Report by the Education Committee in regard to the existing arrangements in the High School.* [Edinburgh], 1870. 8vo. Pp 17.   EPL

—*Report by the Education Committee on Letter from the Rector and Classical Masters of the High School,* as to certain Modifications on the present System of the School.* [Edinburgh], 1863. Pp [2], 4.   EPL

—*Report by the Education Committee under the various Remits to them regarding the Financial Arrangements connected with the High School.* Edinburgh: Printed by H & J Pillans, 1867. 8vo. Pp 6.   EPL

—*Report of the College Committee of the Town Council of Edinburgh, regarding the teaching of Elementary Science in the High School.* July 1851. Edinburgh: Printed by Neill and Company, 1851. 8vo. Pp 7.   EPL

—*Report of the Sub-Committee of the Education Committee appointed to con-*sider and report on the existing Arrangements of the High School,* and what changes should be made with a view to increase its Usefulness and Prosperity. [Edinburgh], 1866. 8vo. Pp 4.   EPL

—*Tabular Statement with reference to Bailie Skinner's Report regarding the High School.* [Edinburgh], 1866. 8vo. Pp 8.   EPL

ENDOWED SCHOOLS AND HOSPITALS (SCOTLAND) COMMISSION 'Edinburgh High School'; *Second Report* (1874), 437-48.

'Estimate of "Classical Learning", with a view towards a new arrangement of the Grammar Schools, and of education therein'; *Edinburgh Mag and Literary Miscellany,* Sept 1824, **15,** 336-9; Oct 1824, **15,** 398-9.

FEARON, DANIEL R 'Edinburgh High School'; *Schools Inquiry Commission Report* (1868), **6,** pt 5, 97-118.

FLEMING, DAVID HAY 'The High School of Edinburgh and its situation before 1555'; *SHR,* Jan 1923, **20,** 170-1.

GRANT, JAMES 'High School of Edinburgh'; *Cassell's Old and New Edinburgh* (1882), **2,** 110-14, 287-96.

GRISCOM, JOHN 'High School of Edinburgh'; *A Year in Europe* (1823), **2,** 334-6, 365-6.
Reprinted in KNIGHT, EDGAR W *Reports on European Education* (New York, 1930), 84-8.

GUNN, WILLIAM M 'System of Education pursued in the Junior Classes of the High School of Edinburgh'; in STEVEN, WILLIAM *History of the High School of Edinburgh* (1849), 273-90.

HARVEY, THOMAS, and SELLAR, ALEX C 'Edinburgh High School'; *Report on the State of Education in the Burgh and Middle-Class Schools in Scotland* (1868), **2,** 203-224.

HIGH SCHOOL OF EDINBURGH *Ex Tentaminibus Metricis Puerorum* in Schola Regia Edinensi Provectiorum electa, anno MDCCCXII. Edinburgh: William Blackwood; London: J Murray, and R Baldwin, 1812. 8vo. Pp xiv, 116.

—*The Inauguration of the Bust of His Royal Highness the Prince of Wales in the High School of Edinburgh.* Edinburgh: Printed for private circulation by Colston

& Son, 1863. 8vo. Pp [8], 102. Frontispiece.

—*Memorial addressed by the Rector and Masters of the High School, to the Right Honourable the Lord Provost, the Magistrates, and Town Council of Edinburgh.* [Edinburgh], 1850. 8vo. Pp 7.   GUL

—*Memorial for the Rector and Masters of the High-School of Edinburgh, humbly offer'd to the Right Honourable the Lord Provost, Magistrates and Council of this City.* June 14 1749. [Edinburgh], 1749. 4to. Pp 8.   EPL

—*Memorial respectfully addressed by a majority of the Masters of the High School to the Right Honourable the Lord Provost, Magistrates & Town Council of Edinburgh.* Edinburgh, 1851. 8vo. Pp 11.

—*Memorial respectfully addressed by the Rector and Masters of the High School of Edinburgh, to the Right Honourable the Lord Provost, the Magistrates, and Town Council of that City, in reference to the appointment of a College Tutor, and the continued Teaching of the Elements of the Greek Language in the Metropolitan University.* Edinburgh, 1852. Fol. P 1.   GUL

—*Order of Procession to be observed at Laying the Foundation Stone of the Royal High School,* on Thursday, July 28. 1825. [Edinburgh, 1825]. Fol. P 1.

—'Ordo Scholae Grammaticae Edinensis; exhibiting a View of the Course of Study prescribed for the High School of Edinburgh, in 1640'; printed in CHALMERS, GEORGE *Life of Thomas Ruddiman* (1794), 88-95; HENDERSON, A *Life and Character of Dr Adam* (1810), Appendix no 1.

—*Regulations for the External Discipline of the High School of Edinburgh.* [Edinburgh], nd. 8vo. Pp 4.
Printed in STEVEN, WILLIAM *History of the High School of Edinburgh* (1849), 297-301; TROTTER, J J *The Royal High School, Edinburgh* (1911), 128-35; and ROSS, W C A *The Royal High School* (1934), 126-32, who says that they were drafted by Drs Boyd and Gunn and approved by the Rector and Masters in 1846.

A Letter to the Lord Provost, on the Mischievous Tendency of a Scheme for abolishing the High School of Edinburgh. Edinburgh: Printed for Bell & Bradfute, and David Brown, 1822. 8vo. Pp 27.   EUL
Signed 'Scotus'. A note in Henry Cockburn's hand on the title-page of the British Museum copy says, 'By a High School Master'.

MACKAY, BENJAMIN 'Plan of Education practised in the High School, by Benjamin Mackay, M.A., and, in Substance, recommended by him to the Patrons of the Institution in the year 1834'; in STEVEN, WILLIAM *History of the High School of Edinburgh* (1849), 166-203.

[MUIRHEAD, CLAUDE] 'On the proposed new High School in Edinburgh'; *Blackwood's Edinburgh Mag,* Dec 1822, **12**, 756-9.

—'Remarks on the new High School'; *Blackwood's Edinburgh Mag,* June 1823, **13**, 709-15.
Both articles are signed 'Avus Edinensis', and are dated from 21 Heriot Row, Edinburgh. The earlier letter was published as a pamphlet of 24 pages by Oliver and Boyd in 1823, but without an author's name on the title-page.

'Musae Edinenses'; *Edinburgh Rev,* Nov 1812, **20**, 387-405.

New High School at Edinburgh. [Edinburgh], 1777. 8vo. Pp 2. Plate.   EPL

'Opening of the New High School'; *New Scots Mag,* June 1829, **1**, 483-93.   EUL

PATTERSON, JOHN BROWN 'Recollections of the High School'; in STEVEN, WILLIAM *History of the High School of Edinburgh* (1849), 195-201.
The writer was dux of the school in 1820.

PILLANS, JAMES *Course of Study in the Rector's Class,* High School, Edinburgh, during the session ending August, 1823. [Edinburgh, 1823]. 8vo. Pp 15.

—*The Rationale of Discipline* as exemplified in the High School of Edinburgh. Edinburgh: Maclachlan & Stewart; London: Taylor, Walton, and Maberly, and Simpkin, Marshall, and Co, 1852. 8vo. Pp xvi, 199, 67.

'Recollections of the High School of Edinburgh'; *Leisure Hours,* 28 Mar 1863, **12**, 197-9.

REID, PETER *A Letter to the Patrons of the High School, and the Inhabitants of*

Edinburgh, on the abuse of Classical Learning, and on the formation of a national school, adapted to the spirit of the age, the wants of Scotsmen, and the fair claims of other branches of education. Edinburgh: Published by Peter Brown, 1821. 8vo. Pp 34.   EUL

Remarks on the proposed new High School. See MUIRHEAD, CLAUDE.

ROSS, WILLIAM C A *The Royal High School.* Edinburgh and London: Oliver and Boyd, 1934. 8vo. Pp viii, 148. 8 plates.

SCHMITZ, LEONHARD *Report by the Rector concerning certain reforms to be introduced in the High School of Edinburgh.* Edinburgh, 1855. 8vo. Pp 8.   EUL

—'System of Education pursued in the Rector's Class'; in STEVEN, WILLIAM *History of the High School of Edinburgh* (1849), 291-6.

SCOTT, A *The Case of the Inhabitants of Edinburgh, relative to the Classical Education of their Sons.* Edinburgh: Printed for Adam Black, 1823. 8vo. Pp 66.

SCOTTISH UNIVERSITIES COMMISSION 'Outline of Course of Study at the High School of Edinburgh, with the principal class-books. October 1, 1827'; *Evidence*, 1 (1837), Appendix, 238.

SKINNER, WILLIAM *Report on the Present Position and Future Arrangements of the High School of Edinburgh.* Submitted to the Education Committee [of Edinburgh Town Council], by the Convener, Bailie Skinner. June, 1866. [Edinburgh, 1866]. 8vo. Pp 16.   EPL

SOUTHEY, ROBERT 'Electa Tentamina—Scholâ Regiâ Edinensi'; *Quarterly Rev*, Dec 1812, 8, 395-406.

'State of Education in Scotland'; *New Scots Mag*, Aug 1829, 2, 113-28.

STEVEN, WILLIAM *The History of the High School of Edinburgh.* Edinburgh: Maclachlan & Stewart, 1849. 8vo. Pp xx, 367, 220. Frontispiece, 10 illustrations, and 2 facsimiles.

TROTTER, FRANK J 'High School Education —Past and Present'; *SEJ*, 30 Dec 1932, 15, 1588-9.

TROTTER, JAMES J *The Royal High School, Edinburgh.* London: Sir Isaac Pitman

& Sons, Ltd, 1911. 8vo. Pp xii, 195. Frontispiece and 32 plates.

John Watson's Institution

ENDOWED SCHOOLS AND HOSPITALS (SCOTLAND) COMMISSION 'John Watson's Institution'; *First Report* (1783), 591-604; *Third Report* (1875), 56-9; *Appendix to Third Report* (1875), 1, 35-8.

JOHN WATSON'S INSTITUTION *Papers relating to John Watson's Institution for Destitute Children.* I. Act of Parliament. II. Regulations for Management. III. Regulations for Master and Matron. Edinburgh, 1827. 8vo. Pp 7, 7, 16.

—*Papers relating to John Watson's Institution for Destitute Children.* 1. Deed of Settlement. 2. Deed of Destination of the Funds. 3. Act of Parliament. 4. Regulations for Management. 5. Regulations for Master and Matron. Edinburgh, 1830. 8vo. Pp 8, 7, 7, 21.

—*Report of the Majority of the Committee appointed by the Directors of John Watson's Institution, on 15th December 1854, in relation to introducing lessons on Physiology*, and its application to Health, into the Institution. [Edinburgh], 1855. 8vo. Pp 25.

THOMSON, D M *The History of John Watson's School, 1828-1938.* Edinburgh: Printed at the Darien Press, 1938. 8vo. Pp 15. Frontispiece and 2 plates.   EPL

Lady Glenorchy's School

1 and 2 Vict, c 22. An Act to explain and extend the powers of the Trustees of Lady Glenorchy's Chapel and School in Edinburgh.   (Private Act, 1838)

Local Sabbath Schools

COMMITTEE FOR PROMOTING THE ESTABLISHMENT OF LOCAL SABBATH SCHOOLS, IN EDINBURGH AND ITS VICINITY *Report.* June 2, 1824. Edinburgh: Printed for the Committee by William Aitchison, 1824. 8vo. Pp iv, 56.   EUL

GALL, JAMES *Letter to the Secretary of the Committee for establishing Local Sabbath Schools in Edinburgh.* Edinburgh:

Printed by Hay, Gall, & Co, 1822. 8vo.
Pp 63.

System of Local Sabbath Evening Schools.
Edinburgh: Printed by Hay, Gall, & Co,
1821. 4to. Pp 3.   EUL

Local System of Sabbath Schools. Edinburgh: Printed by Hay, Gall, & Co, nd.
8vo. Pp 3.   EUL

Melville College

See *Edinburgh Institution.*

Merchiston Castle School

HARVEY, THOMAS, and SELLAR, ALEX C
'Merchiston Castle'; *Report on the
State of Education in the Burgh and
Middle-Class Schools in Scotland* (1868),
2, 331-3.

*The Jubilee Commemoration of Merchiston
Castle School.* (Reprinted from *The
Merchistonian,* August 1883.) Edin-
burgh: H & J Pillans, 1883. 8vo. Pp 53.

MURRAY, DAVID *Merchiston Castle School,
1855-58.* Glasgow: James Maclehose
and Sons, 1915. 8vo. Pp x, 195.
Frontispiece, 4 plates and 1 illustration.

Military Academy

*An Address to the Noblemen and Gentlemen
of Scotland; with the Rules of the
Military Academy, Edinburgh*: Instituted
November 1787, under the superintendence of Major D'Asti. Edinburgh, 1787.
8vo. Pp 25.   EPL

Monitorial Schools

See GIBSON, JOHN *Report on certain of
the Chief Schools inspected in the Presbytery of Edinburgh.*

Moray House Training College

GUNN, JOHN 'Moray House'; *Maurice
Paterson. A Memorial Biography* (1921),
112-39.

MALCOLM, CHARLES A, and HUNTER, J
NORMAN W *Moray House. A Brief
Sketch of its History.* Edinburgh:
Printed by the Darien Press Ltd, 1948.
4to. Pp 31. 2 plates.

Newington Academy

Selections from Exercises by the Pupils:
with Outline of Course of Study. Twenty-
fourth and twenty-fifth sessions. Edinburgh: Newington Academy, 1857-8.
8vo.   EPL
  1857—pp [4], 76.   1858—pp 72.
Prospectus, 1863-64, and *Examination Report,* 1863. [Edinburgh, 1864]. 8vo.
Prospectus, pp 4. *Examination Report,*
pp 5.

St Cuthbert's Parish

ST CUTHBERT'S PAROCHIAL BOARD *Report by
the Acting Committee of that Board, in
regard to the best Mode of Maintaining
and Training Children on the Poor's Roll
of the Parish.* Edinburgh: Printed by
Murray and Gibb, 1852. 8vo. Pp 20.
                                     GUL

St George's Parish School

'Letter on the New System of Education—
St George's Parish School, Edinburgh';
Edinburgh Mag and Literary Miscellany,
Mar 1826, **18**, 338-43.

St James's Episcopal School

ENDOWED SCHOOLS AND HOSPITALS (SCOT-
LAND) COMMISSION 'St James's Episcopal
School, Edinburgh'; *Appendix to Third
Report* (1875), **2**, 285-6.

St John's Episcopal School

BLAMIRE, JOHN 'The Record of an Educational Venture'; *SEJ,* 22 Aug 1952, **35**,
506-8.

Scottish Institution for the Education
of Young Ladies

COMBE, GEORGE 'Scottish Institution for the
Education of Young Ladies'; *Lectures on
Popular Education,* second edition (1837),
122-4.

'The Scottish Institution (Edinburgh) for the
Education of Young Ladies'; *Chambers's
Edinburgh J,* 7 Nov 1840, **9**, 334.

SCOTTISH INSTITUTION FOR THE EDUCATION OF YOUNG LADIES *Report*; with an Appendix, containing separate Reports, by the different Teachers, of the Course of Instruction, and the System pursued, in their respective Classes. Edinburgh: Oliver & Boyd, 1835. 8vo. Pp 32.

—*Second Report*. Edinburgh: Oliver & Boyd, 1837. 8vo. Pp 32.

—*Report*. Edinburgh: Printed by Murray & Gibb, 1850. 8vo. Pp 32.

Scottish Naval and Military Academy

DOWNES, CHARLES *A Letter to the Subscribers of the Scottish Naval and Military Academy, on the management of that institution*. Edinburgh: Printed by Peter Brown for William Tait, 1832. 8vo. Pp 22.   EUL

'Scottish Military Education. (Mr Geo. Scott's Scottish Military Academy)'; *Edinburgh Mag and Literary Miscellany*, Aug 1824, **15**, 214-18.

SCOTTISH NAVAL AND MILITARY ACADEMY *Report by the Directors to the Subscribers*: occasioned by a printed letter addressed to them by Major Downes. Edinburgh: Printed by Thomas Allan, Jun & Co, 1832. 8vo. Pp 36.   EUL

—*Report of the Directors*. Edinburgh: Printed by M Anderson, 1826. 8vo. Pp 11.   EUL

—*Reports of the Ordinary Directors, 1829-30*. Edinburgh: Printed by M Anderson. 8vo.
1829—pp 16.   1830—pp 16.

—Rules and Regulations. Edinburgh: Printed by Oliver & Boyd, 1834. 8vo. Pp 24.   EUL

—*View of the System of Education and of the various Branches of Study pursued*. Instituted 1825. Edinburgh: Printed by Oliver & Boyd, 1835. 8vo. Pp 24.
                                          EUL

Trades Maiden Hospital

1707, 25 Mar, c 79. Act in favours of the Incorporations of Edinburgh, for erecting a Maiden Hospital. In *Acts of the Parliaments of Scotland, 1702-1707* (1824), 478-9.

Also printed as a folio sheet without place or date; a copy in this form is in the National Library of Scotland.

ENDOWED SCHOOLS AND HOSPITALS (SCOTLAND) COMMISSION 'The Trades Maiden Hospital'; *First Report* (1873), 651-60; *Appendix to Third Report* (1875), **1**, 57-60.

TRADES MAIDEN HOSPITAL *Rules and Constitutions of the Maiden Hospital*, founded by the Crafts-men of Edinburgh, and Mary Erskine. Edinburgh: Printed by the Heirs and Successors of Andrew Anderson, 1707. 8vo. Pp [17], 46.
                                          EUL

— —. Edinburgh: Printed by R Fleming and Company, 1734. 8vo. Pp [15], 58.

— —. Edinburgh: Printed by J Ruthven, 1788. 8vo. Pp xii, 56.   EPL

— —. Edinburgh: Printed by J Hay and Co, 1814. 8vo. Pp xv, 91.   EUL

— —. Edinburgh: Printed by W Burness, 1859. 8vo. Pp 50.

—*Rules for the Government and Order of the Maiden Hospital*, founded by the Crafts-men of Edinburgh and Mary Erskine. Edinburgh: Printed by Alex Smellie, 1798. 8vo. Pp 43.   EPL

— —. Edinburgh: Printed by Alex Smellie, 1825. 8vo. Pp 40.   EPL

— —. Edinburgh: Printed by W Burness, 1859. 8vo. Pp 21.

TOWILL, EDWIN S 'The Minutes of the Trades Maiden Hospital'; *Book of the Old Edinburgh Club*, **28** (1953), 1-43.

United Industrial School

UNITED INDUSTRIAL SCHOOL *Constitution and Rules*. Edinburgh: Printed by Andrew Aikman & Co, 1847. 8vo. Pp 8.
                                          EPL

—*Explanations regarding the Establishment of the United Industrial Schools*. With an Appendix of Documents, showing the Reasons why the Promoters dissent from the System of Management of the Original Ragged Schools. Edinburgh: William Blackwood and Sons, 1847. 8vo. Pp 56.   EPL

—*The United Industrial School of Edinburgh*; A Sketch of its Origin, Progress, and

Practical Influence. Edinburgh: Adam & Charles Black, 1851. 8vo. Pp 43, 8. Frontispiece and 1 plate.   EPL

FINDLAY, J R 'On the United Industrial School, Edinburgh'; *Transactions of the National Association for the Promotion of Social Science, 1863* (1864), 349-51.

Vennel School, Grassmarket

New Greyfriar's School, Vennel, Grassmarket, Edinburgh. *Report for 1859.* Edinburgh, 1859. 4to. Pp 3.

The Williams Secular School

COMMITTEE OF COUNCIL ON EDUCATION 'Memorial praying that Aid from the Parliamentary Grant may be extended to "Williams's Secular School" in Edinburgh, with Reply to the same'; *Minutes,* 1853/4, **I**, 43-5.

—'Correspondence between the Promoters of the Secular Schools, St Andrews' Square, Glasgow, and the Committee of Council on Education; and between the Promoters of Williams' Secular School, Edinburgh, and the same Committee.' P 6. *PP*, 1854, lix, 227.

JOLLY, WILLIAM 'The Secular School in Edinburgh'; *Education. Its Principles and Practice as developed by George Combe* (1879), 201-18.

NISSEN, HARTVIG 'Om Williams Secular School'; *Beskrivelse over Skotlands Almueskolevaesen* (1854), 199-231.

THE WILLIAMS SECULAR SCHOOL *Prospectus of a School for the Secular Education of Boys.* Edinburgh, 1848. 8vo. Pp 4.
                                                EUL

—*Prospectus.* np [Edinburgh], nd [?1854]. 8vo. Pp 7.   EUL

—*Annual Reports.* Edinburgh: Maclachlan and Stewart; London: Simpkin, Marshall, and Co, 1850-5. 8vo.   EUL

1850—pp 20	1853—pp 36
1851—pp 38	1854—pp 18
1852—pp 36	1855—pp 4

—*Report of the Annual Examination.* Edinburgh: Maclachlan and Stewart; London: Simpkin, Marshall, and Co, 1851. 8vo. Pp 15.   EIS

Canongate

ANDERSON, HELEN MAUD 'The Grammar School of the Canongate'; *Book of the Old Edinburgh Club,* **20** (1935), 1-25. Plan.

Colinton

SHANKIE, DAVID 'Schools and Schoolmasters'; *The Parish of Colinton* (Edinburgh: Printed by John Wilson, 1902), 116-36.

Cramond

CROWTHER, JOAN *The 'Old Schoolhouse' of Cramond, Edinburgh, and Education in Cramond, 1653-1875.* Moray House Publications, no 1. Edinburgh: Moray House College of Education, 1965. 8vo. Pp 49. Plate, maps and plans.

Dreghorn

DREGHORN COLLEGE *Reports and Prize-list for 1866-67.* Edinburgh: Printed by Thomas Constable, 1867. 8vo. Pp 40.
                                                BM

Duddingston

1827. 7 and 8 Geo 4, c 11. An Act to explain and modify the Trust Settlement of the late Louis Cauvin, for the Endowment and Maintenance of an Hospital for the Support and Education of Boys. (Private Act)

1842. 5 and 6 Vict, c 39. An Act to amend and explain the Act passed in the seventh and eighth years of his late Majesty George the Fourth, chapter 11, intituled, *An Act to explain and modify the Trust Settlement of the late* Louis Cauvin, *for the Endowment and Maintenance of an Hospital for the Support and Education for Boys*; and further to explain and modify the said Trust Settlement. (1842). Fol. Pp 7. (Private Act)

CAUVIN'S HOSPITAL *Hints for the Constitution of Cauvin's Hospital,* as far as regards the Subject of Education, submitted to the Governors for their Remarks and Suggestions. [Edinburgh], 1833. 8vo. Pp 7.   GUL

ENDOWED SCHOOLS AND HOSPITALS (SCOT-
LAND) COMMISSION 'Cauvin's Hospital';
First Report (1873), 673-8; *Appendix to
Third Report* (1875), **1**, 66-9.

*Hillhousefield, Bonnington, and
Newhaven Education Society*

Director's Report. Leith, 1825. 4to. Pp 2.
EUL

Holyrood House

Royal College at Holy-Rood-House. *Rules
of the Schools.* Holyrood-House: Printed
by Mr P B, Enginneer [*sic*] and Printer to
the King's Most Excellent Majesty, 1688.
Fol. P 1.

Leith

ADAM, MARGARET 'The Story of "Dr Bell's"
of Leith'; *Edinburgh Tatler*, Apr 1965,
6, 20-1.

*The History of South Leith Sabbath Evening
School*; intended as a Practical Illustration of the Utility and Advantages of
similar Institutions. Edinburgh: Printed
for James Taylor Smith & Co, nd [1827].
12mo. Pp [8], 122. Frontispiece and 2
plates.

INSH, GEORGE PRATT 'An Old School
Account [Mr Forrester's School, Leith,
1719-1720]'; *SEJ*, 12 Sept 1930, **13**, 948.

JOLLY, WILLIAM 'The Secular Schools in
Leith'; *Education. Its Principles and
Practice as developed by George Combe*
(1879), 218-19.

LEITH LOCAL SABBATH SCHOOL SOCIETY
Report for 1823. With an Appendix,
containing the Regulations of the Society,
&c. Leith: Printed by Archibald
Allardice, 1823. 8vo. Pp 24.

TIMON 'Account of a Charity School established in Leith, with a Sketch of Lancaster's System of Education'; *Scots Mag*,
Feb 1809, **71**, 89-94.

ENDOWED SCHOOLS AND HOSPITALS (SCOT-
LAND) COMMISSION 'High School of
Leith'; *Second Report* (1874), 516-20.

HARVEY, THOMAS, and SELLAR, ALEX C
'Leith High School'; *Report on the State
of Education in the Burgh and Middle-
Class Schools in Scotland* (1868), **2**, 122-6.

MCARA, CHARLES *Leith Academy, 1560-1960.*
With illustrations by Richard Lovell.
Edinburgh and London: Oliver & Boyd
Ltd, 1960. 8vo. Pp viii, 30.   EUL

MACKAY, ALEXANDER *A Sketch of the
History of Leith Academy.* Leith:
Printed by William R Duff & Co, 1934.
8vo. Pp 36. Frontispiece and 2 plates.

Leith Walk

*Address to the Ladies of Leith Walk,
Greenside, and Broughton.* [Edinburgh],
1819. 4to. Pp 3.   EUL

FEMALE EDUCATION SOCIETY FOR LEITH WALK,
GREENSIDE, AND BROUGHTON *State of the
School*, List of Subscribers, and Abstract
of Accounts from July 1819, to July 1820.
Edinburgh, 1820. 8vo. Pp 16.   EUL

Newhaven

NEWHAVEN EDUCATION SOCIETY *Report,
1828.* Edinburgh, 1828. Fol. Pp 3.
EPL

Pilrig

COMMITTEE OF COUNCIL ON EDUCATION
'Correspondence and Reports respecting
Grants to certain Schools in Scotland';
Minutes, 1845, 443-4.

GLASGOW

B See THOM, WILLIAM.

BROWNLIE, W M 'Early French Teaching in
Glasgow'; *SEJ*, 18 Sept 1936, **19**, 1128-9.

CLELAND, JAMES 'Education'; *Annals of
Glasgow* (Glasgow: Printed by James
Hedderwick, 1816), **2**, 412-21.

—'Educational Institutions'; *Annals of
Glasgow* (1816), **1**, 218-68.
Hutchison's School. Tennent's Morti-
fication. Wilson's Charity School.
Millar's Charity. Highland Society.
Sunday School Society. Anderston and
Calton Sabbath-Day School Society.
Lancastrian School Society. Auxiliary
Society for the Support of Gaelic
Schools. Society for the Instruction of
Deaf and Dumb Children. Sabbath
Evening-School Society. Fleshers' Free
School.

DORSEY, ALEXANDER J D 'State of Education in Glasgow'; *Report from the Select Committee on Education in England and Wales* (1835), 37-46.

EDUCATION COMMISSION (SCOTLAND) *Report on the State of Education in Glasgow*, by James Greig and Thomas Harvey. Edinburgh: HMSO, 1866. Fol. Pp iv, 159. Map.

'Education in the West—Infant Schools—Glasgow'; *The Scotsman*, 29 Aug 1829.

ENDOWED SCHOOLS AND HOSPITALS (SCOTLAND) COMMISSION 'Glasgow Educational Mortifications'; *Appendix to Third Report* (1875), 1, 245-89.
Alexander's Charity. MacMillan's Mortification. The Buchanan Mortification. Millar's Charity. Wilson's Charity School. Glen's School. Logan and Johnston School. M'Farlane's School. Muir's Bequest. Murdoch's Trust. Gorbals Youths' School. Gorbals Mission School.

—'Glasgow Endowed Schools'; *Appendix to Third Report* (1875), 1, 290-326.
The Buchanan Institution. Glen's School. Hutcheson's School. Millar's School. 'Wilson's Charity' School. M'Farlane's School. Gardner's Free School. Murdoch's Schools. Springburn School. Alexander's Charity School. Gorbals Youths' School. M'Lachlan's Free School. Logan and Johnston's School. Peddie and Tennant's School. Graham's Free School.

EYRE-TODD, GEORGE 'The Song Schools and Grammar School'; *History of Glasgow* (Glasgow: Jackson, Wylie & Co), 2 (1931), 100-10.

GIBSON, JOHN 'Report on Schools'; *Minutes of the Committee of Council on Education, 1843-44* (1845), 154-67.
Woodside School. Highland Society of Glasgow Schools. Hutchesons' Hospital Schools. Trades School. Maclachlan's Free School. Gardner's Charity School. Macfarlane Free School. St Enoch's School.

GIBSON, JOHN (1) 'Of the Expence of Education'; *History of Glasgow*, from the Earliest Accounts to the Present Time (Glasgow: Printed by Rob Chapman

and Alex Duncan, for the Author, 1777), 191-5.

GLASGOW TOWN COUNCIL *Extract of Minutes of Council*, relative to Dr Bell's Bequest, and an Extract of that Bequest. With a Copy of the Settlement made with the Kirk Sessions of Glasgow, relative thereto, &c. Glasgow: Printed by Bell and Bain, 1835. 8vo. Pp 20.

GRIFFIN, JOHN 'Evening Classes in Glasgow 90 Years Ago'; *SEJ*, 8 Mar 1957, 40, 132.

M'COLL, DUGALD *Among the Masses*; or, Work in the Wynds. London, Edinburgh, and New York: T Nelson and Sons, 1867. 8vo. Pp 383.

MACGILL, STEVENSON 'Appendix on the Schools of Glasgow'; *The Qualifications of the Teachers of Youth* (Glasgow: Printed by James Hedderwick, 1814), 47-55.
Hutchesons' School. Wilson's School. The Trades House School. Miller's School. Hospital School. Highland Society Schools. Six Sessional Schools. Lennox School. Highland Society Day-School. Fleshers' School. Peddie's School. Sabbath Schools. Grammar School. Private Schools.

MARWICK, WILLIAM H 'Adult Education in Glasgow Eighty Years Ago'; *Proceedings of the Royal Philosophical Society of Glasgow*, 1930-1, 59, 86-97.

RELIGIOUS INSTRUCTION (SCOTLAND) COMMISSION 'Presbytery of Glasgow'; *Second Report*, with Appendices (1838), 1-808.
PP, 1837/38, xxxiii, 109

Report of the Proceedings at a Meeting of the Citizens of Glasgow for the Formation of a Society to be called the Glasgow Public School Association, held in the City Hall, on the 18th March, 1851. (From the *North British Mail*.) Manchester: A Ireland and Co, 1851. 4to. Pp 8.

SKINNIDER, SISTER MARTHA 'Catholic Elementary Education in Glasgow, 1818-1918'; in *Studies in the History of Scottish Education, 1872-1939*, ed BONE, T R (Scottish Council for Research in Education, Publication 54. 1967), 13-70.

SOMERS, ROBERT *Results of an Inquiry into the State of Schools and Education in*

Glasgow. London and Glasgow: Richard Griffin and Company, 1857. 8vo. Pp 32.

STRANG, JOHN *Bursaries, Schools, Mortifications, and Bequests, for which the Magistrates and Council of the City of Glasgow act*, either in whole or in part, as Trustees, Patrons, or Administrators. Glasgow: Printed at the University Press by George Richardson, 1861. 8vo. Pp vi, 126.
                                                        Mit

THOM, WILLIAM *The Defects of an University Education, and its Unsuitableness to a Commercial People*: with the Expediency and Necessity of Erecting at Glasgow, an Academy, for the Instruction of Youth. In a Letter to J. M. Esq; From a Society interested in the Success of this Public-spirited Proposal. London: Printed for E Dilly, 1762. 8vo. Pp 53.

Reprinted in *The Works of William Thom* (Glasgow: Printed for James Dymock, 1799), 263-301.

—*Remarks upon a Pamphlet concerning the Necessity of erecting an Academy at Glasgow*. In a Letter to the Authors. Glasgow: Printed for James Duncan, Junior, 1762. 8vo. Pp 38.

Signed 'B'. Reprinted in *The Works of William Thom* (1799), 302-23.

—*The Scheme for erecting an Academy at Glasgow, set forth in its own proper Colours*. In a Letter from a Society of the Inhabitants of the City, who are not yet tainted with a Taste for Literature; to their Brethren of the same Principles at Paisley. Glasgow: Printed for James Duncan, 1762. 8vo. Pp 44.   GUL

Reprinted in *The Works of William Thom* (1799), 324-50.

'Weir against St George's Session, Glasgow'; *The Museum*, new series, 1 Mar 1867, **3**, 450-4; 1 Apr 1867, **4**, 25-7; 1 July 1867, 4, 140-3.

Allan Glen's School

RAE, JOSEPH *The History of Allan Glen's School, 1853-1953*. Glasgow: Printed by Aird & Coghill, Limited, 1953. 8vo. Pp 178. 16 plates.   GUL

SEXTON, ALEXANDER H 'Allan Glen's School, 1853-1894'; *The First Technical College* (1894), 139-53.

Anderson's University

Account of the Andersonian Museum, Glasgow [with Memoir of Professor Anderson]. Glasgow: Printed at the University Press for John Smith & Son; Oliver and Boyd, Edinburgh; and Longman, Rees & Co, London, 1831. 8vo. Pp 31. Frontispiece.   GUL

CLELAND, JAMES 'Anderson's University'; *Enumeration of the Inhabitants of the City of Glasgow and County of Lanark. For the Government Census of MDCCCXXXI*, second edition. (Glasgow: John Smith & Son; Edinburgh: Adam Black, 1832), 64-5.

Extracts from the Latter Will and Codicil of Professor John Anderson. Glasgow: Printed by W Lang, 1837. 8vo. Pp 26.

FLYNN, JAMES A *The Origin of the Andersonian and the Growth of Technical Education in Glasgow*. Unpublished MEd thesis, Glasgow University, 1967. Typescript. 4to. Pp 200. Bibliography.   GUL

GARNETT, THOMAS 'Anderson's University'; *Observations on a Tour through the Highlands of Scotland* (London: T Cadell, Junior, & W Davies, 1800), **2**, 193-202.

HUDSON, JAMES WILLIAM 'Anderson's Institution' and 'Anderson's University'; *History of Adult Education* (1851), 31-9.

Latter Will and Codicil of Professor John Anderson, the Founder of the University. Glasgow: Printed by Bell and Bain, [1796]. 8vo. Pp 12.   Mit

MCVAIL, SIR DAVID C *Anderson's College; Its Founder and its Medical School*. (Reprinted from the *Glasgow Medical Journal*, February 1879.) Glasgow: Printed by Alex Macdougall, 1879. 8vo. Pp 20.

MUIR, JAMES *John Anderson. Pioneer of Technical Education and the College he founded*. Glasgow: John Smith & Son (Glasgow) Ltd, 1950. 8vo. Pp xi, 162. Frontispiece and 6 plates.

Report by the Managers to the Trustees, as the Property, Affairs, and increased Means of Instruction of Anderson's University of Glasgow. Glasgow: Printed in the *Chronicle* Office, nd [1832]. Pp 6, 18, 8.   Mit

SEXTON, ALEXANDER H *The Andersonian: A Centenary Sketch.* Glasgow, 1897. 8vo. Pp 11.   GUL
An offprint from *Proceedings of the Royal Philosophical Society of Glasgow*, **28**, 1896-7 (1897), 161-72.

—*The First Technical College.* A Sketch of the History of 'The Andersonian', and the Institutions descended from it, 1796-1894. With portraits and illustrations. London: Chapman and Hall, Ld, 1894. 8vo. Pp xviii, 188. Index.

Statement of the Affairs of Anderson's University. At 1st January, 1832. np, nd [1832]. 8vo. Pp 8.   GUL

View of the Constitution and History of Anderson's Institution. np, nd [1825]. 8vo. Pp 16.   Mit

Buchanan Institution

GILLESPIE, ANDREW 'The Buchanan Institution'; *Sir Michael Connal and his Young Men's Institute. A Story of Fifty Years* (Glasgow: Morison Brothers, 1898), 169-71.   Jor

LEGGATT, WILLIAM *An Account of the Ten Years' Educational Experiment among Destitute Boys conducted in the Buchanan Institution, Glasgow.* Glasgow: Printed by Leggatt Brothers, 1871. 8vo. Pp 34.
                                       GUL

—'The Buchanan Institution and the Education of Destitute Boys'; *Educ News*, 6 May 1876, **1**, 245; 13 May 1876, **1**, 252-3.
                                       EIS

Free St John's School of Industry

Statement submitted to the Kirk Session of Free St. John's, by the Ladies' Committee of the Free St. John's School of Industry. Glasgow: Printed by Bell and Bain, 1870. 8vo. Pp 11.   New Coll

Glasgow Academy

FEARON, DANIEL R 'Glasgow Academy'; *Schools Inquiry Commission Report* (1868), **6**, pt 5, 187-91.

The Glasgow Academy. The First Hundred Years. Glasgow: Printed and published for the Glasgow Academy by Blackie &

Son Ltd, 1946. 8vo. Pp xvi, 277. 37 plates.   GUL

PHILIP, GEORGE ERNEST 'At the Glasgow Academy'; *A Scots Boy's World Sixty Years Ago* (Edinburgh and Glasgow: William Hodge and Company, Limited, 1922), 58-94.

R, J G 'Glasgow Academy'; *Scottish Field*, Oct 1934, **64**, 247-50.

Glasgow and West of Scotland Technical College

BUTT, JOHN 'The Royal College of Science and Technology, Glasgow, Past and Present'; *SEJ*, 19 Jan 1962, **45**, 49-50.

DYER, HENRY 'The Glasgow and West of Scotland Technical College'; *Educ News*, 20 Oct 1888, **13**, 736-7.

FULTON, T CRICHTON 'The Glasgow and West of Scotland Technical College'; *Cassier's Mag*, Sept 1893, **4**, 355-62.

LAWSON, WILLIAM R 'The Glasgow and West of Scotland Technical College'; *John Bull & his Schools* (Edinburgh and London: William Blackwood and Sons, 1908), 98-106.   EUL

STOCKDALE, H F 'The Royal Technical College'; *Educational Institute of Scotland Congress Handbook*, 1925, 55-62.

Glasgow Association for the Education of Roman Catholics, particularly Children

Report of the Third Annual Meeting. Glasgow: Printed by Andrew & John M Duncan, 1822. 8vo. Pp 15.   New Coll

Report of the Sixth Annual Meeting. Glasgow: Printed in the Free Press Office, 1825. 8vo. Pp 15.   New Coll

Glasgow Athenaeum

HUDSON, JAMES W 'The Glasgow Athenaeum'; *History of Adult Education* (1851), 82-4.

LAUDER, JAMES *The Glasgow Athenaeum. A Sketch of Fifty Years' Work* (1847-1897). Glasgow: At the St Mungo Press, Limited, 1897. 4to. Pp [14], 203. Frontispiece, portraits, and plates. Index.

*Glasgow Auxiliary Society for the
Support of Gaelic Schools*

COMMITTEE OF MANAGEMENT First, Seventh,
and Fourteenth Annual Reports. Glasgow: Printed by S Hunter & Co, *Herald*
Office, 1813, 1819, and 1826. 8vo.
1813—pp 20. 1819—pp 33. 1826—pp
38.

Glasgow Collegiate School

HITCHEN, ISAAC *Address delivered at the
Opening of the Glasgow Collegiate School*,
14th February, 1842. Glasgow: John
Smith and Son; Edinburgh: William
Blackwood and Sons; London: Long-
man, Brown, & Co, 1842. 8vo. Pp 44.
                                                    EIS

Glasgow Commercial College

*Constitution of the Glasgow Commercial
College*. Instituted 3d December, 1845.
Glasgow: Printed by W J Paterson, 1846.
8vo. Pp 7.   Mit

GRAHAM, JOHN *One Hundred and Twenty-
five Years*. The Evolution of Commercial Education in Glasgow. Glasgow:
Scottish College of Commerce, 1964.
8vo. Pp 88. 8 plates.

YOUNG, THOMAS PETTIGREW 'A Bit of Glasgow History. The Commercial College
and the Athenaeum'; *Glasgow Herald*,
11 Apr 1925.

Glasgow Deaf and Dumb Institution

*A Brief Historical Sketch of the Origin and
Progress of the Glasgow Deaf and Dumb
Institution*. Founded, January 1819, and
incorporated by seal of Cause from the
Magistrates of Glasgow. Glasgow:
Printed for the Institution at the *Guardian*
Office, and published by John Smith &
Son, 1835. 8vo. Pp 35.   GUL

Glasgow Educational Association

GLASGOW EDUCATIONAL ASSOCIATION Prospectus, 1864. Reprinted in LAUDER,
JAMES *The Glasgow Athenaeum* (1897),
169-71.   Ba

Glasgow Educational Society

*Appeal on behalf of the Glasgow Normal
Seminary*. Glasgow: William Collins,
1836. 8vo. Pp 16.   GUL

BACHE, ALEXANDER D 'Juvenile Training
School of the Glasgow Education
Society'; *Report on Education in Europe*
(1839), 178-89.   EUL

—'Model Infant School of the Glasgow
Education Society'; *Report on Education
in Europe* (1839), 159-66.   EUL

BUCHANAN, ROBERT (2) 'Speech delivered at
a Meeting of the Glasgow Educational
Society'; *Church of Scotland Mag*, Dec
1834, **1**, 375-81.

GLASGOW EDUCATIONAL SOCIETY *Hints towards the Formation of a Normal Seminary
in Glasgow*, for the professional training
of schoolmasters. Glasgow: Printed in
the *Scottish Guardian* Office, 1835. 8vo.
Pp 16.   GUL

LEADBETTER, J 'On the Normal School of
Glasgow'; *British Association, Glasgow
Meeting, 1840—Notices and Abstracts of
Communications* (1841), 170-1.

MCNEILL, HUGH *Speech at the Public Meeting
of the Glasgow Educational Society*, held
on Wednesday, October, 12, 1836. Also
*Appeal on behalf of the Glasgow Normal
Seminary*. Glasgow: William Collins,
1836. 8vo. Pp 16.   GUL

Glasgow Industrial Schools

GLASGOW INDUSTRIAL SCHOOL SOCIETY *Report from 1st May, 1850, to 31st December
1851*. Glasgow: Printed by W G
Blackie & Co, 1852. 8vo. Pp 22.
                                                   GUL

—Twenty-second and Twenty-fifth Annual
Reports. Glasgow: Thomas Murray
and Son, 1869 and 1873. 8vo.   GUL
     1869—pp 36.   1873—pp 40.

Report on Industrial Schools, to the Committees, from the Parochial Boards of
Glasgow, Barony, Gorbals, Govan, etc.
1846. Glasgow: Printed in the *Scottish
Guardian* Office. 1846. 8vo. Pp 7.
                                                   GUL

Glasgow Lancastrian Society School

Proceedings at a Meeting held on the 31st January, 1814, with Illustrations and Remarks by Joseph Fox. Edinburgh: Archibald Constable and Company, 1814. 8vo. Pp 78. GUL

NOTE Part of Fox's speech was printed in the *Scots Mag*, Apr 1814, **76**, 259-66, with the title, *View of the Process [sic] of the Lancastrian System, and of the Present State in Edinburgh and Glasgow.*

Glasgow Secular School Society

GLASGOW SECULAR SCHOOL SOCIETY *Reports of the Directors and Teachers.* Glasgow: Printed by William Rankin, 1856, 1857, and 1860. 8vo. EIS
1856—pp 19. 1857—pp 19. 1860—pp 24.

JOLLY, WILLIAM 'The Secular Associations and Schools in Glasgow'; *Education: Its Principles and Practice as developed by George Combe* (1879), 219-24.

CONTENTS The Secular Sunday Schools. The St Andrew Square Secular School. The Carlton Place Secular School.

MAYER, JOHN 'The Glasgow Secular School'; *The Museum*, new series, 1 Jan 1867, **3**, 363-7.

Glasgow Sessional Schools

GORDON, JOHN 'Report on the Sessional Schools of Edinburgh, Glasgow, Aberdeen, Dundee, and Perth'; *Minutes of the Committee of Council on Education, 1848-49-50* (1850), **2**, 570-605.

Glasgow Society of Teachers

Laws and Regulations of the Glasgow Society of Teachers. Glasgow: Printed by James Hedderwick, 1815. 8vo. Pp 16. GUL

Glasgow Trades' House Free School

Articles and Regulations for conducting the Trades' House Free School of Glasgow. Glasgow: Printed in the *Herald* Office, 1827. 8vo. Pp 10. GUL

INCORPORATION OF WEAVERS *Minutes embodying Report on the Trades' School.* Glasgow: Printed by Robert Muir & Co, 1863. 8vo. Pp 11. GUL

Report by the Committee appointed by the Trades' House, the Delegates appointed by the Incorporations, and the Directors of the School, to consider and Report upon a Scheme for continuing the Trades' School after 1st October, 1864. Glasgow: Printed by Robert Muir & Co, 1864. 8vo. Pp 7. GUL

Report by the Directors of the Trades' School, to the Trades' House of Glasgow. Glasgow: Printed by Robert Muir & Co, 1862. 8vo. Pp 11. GUL

Glasgow Western Academy

GREIG, GEORGE 'Progress of Liberal Education—The Glasgow Western Academy'; *Phrenological J*, **16** (1843), 19-27. EUL

NELSON, ROBERT J 'Prospectus: The Glasgow Western Academy'; *Outlines of the Theory and Practice of Education* (1842), 1-8.

Glasgow Youths' Auxiliary Society for the Support of Gaelic Schools in the Highlands and Islands of Scotland

Fourth Annual Report. Glasgow: Printed by Starke, 1821. 8vo. Pp 15. GUL

Sixth Annual Report. Glasgow: Printed by James Young, 1823. 8vo. Pp 15. GUL

High School of Glasgow

ANDERSON, JAMES *Letter to the Members of the Grammar School Committee.* Glasgow: Printed by James Hedderwick & Son, 1827. 8vo. Pp 14. GUL

BACHE, ALEXANDER D 'Notice of the Glasgow High School'; *Report on Education in Europe* (1839), 374-9. EUL

BELL, JAMES, and MACLEAN, J DALZIEL *The High School of Glasgow and the Endowed Schools Commission Report.* Extract from the *N B Daily Mail*, 3rd December 1875. Glasgow, 1875. Fol. P 1. GUL

BURNS, JAMES CLELAND *The History of the High School of Glasgow*: containing the

K

Historical Account of the Grammar School; by James Cleland, LL.D. And a Sketch of the History from 1825 to 1877; by Thomas Muir, M.A., F.R.S.E. Edited, with a Memoir of Dr Cleland, by James Cleland Burns. Glasgow: David Bryce & Son, and James Lumsden, Son, & Co, 1878. 4to. Pp xxiii, 76.

CLARK, P W 'High School or College for Merchants'; *British Educator*, July 1856, 225-31. BM

CLELAND, JAMES 'Grammar School'; *Annals of Glasgow* (1816), 2, 156-74.

—'Grammar School'; *Enumeration of the Inhabitants of the City of Glasgow and County of Lanark. For the Government Census of MDCCCXXXI*, second edition (1832), 69-70.

—*Historical Account of the Grammar School of Glasgow*, with a List of the Duxes, from 1782 till 1825. Glasgow: Printed by Khull, Blackie, and Co, 1825. 8vo. Pp 56. 2 plates.

—'Public Grammar School'; *Rise and Progress of the City of Glasgow* (1820), 26-8.

CUTHBERTSON, DONALD *Addresses delivered at the Annual Distribution of Prizes*, to the Pupils of the Glasgow Grammar School, from 1828 to 1833, inclusive. Glasgow: Printed at the University Press, by Edward Khull, 1833. 12mo. Pp [6], 111.

ENDOWED SCHOOLS AND HOSPITALS (SCOTLAND) COMMISSION 'High School of Glasgow'; *Second Report* (1874), 471-6; *Appendix to Third Report* (1875), 1, 327-361.

FEARON, DANIEL R 'The High School, Glasgow'; *Schools Inquiry Commission Report* (1868), 6, pt 5, 118-32.

GLASGOW TOWN COUNCIL *Report by the Committee of the Town Council on High School and Education, on the present Position of the High School.* Glasgow, nd [?1865]. 8vo. Pp 7. GUL

—*Report by the Committee on the High School as to the Future Constitution of the School.* np, nd. 8vo. Pp 12. GUL

—'Report of the Committee, on the Grammar School, recommending an

Extension of the System of Education pursued in that Seminary'; *Report of Proceedings at the Annual Presentation of Prizes*, October 1834 (Glasgow: Printed by William Collins & Co, 1834), 20-4.
GUL

HARVEY, THOMAS, and SELLAR, ALEX C 'Glasgow High School'; *Report on the State of Education in the Burgh and Middle-Class Schools in Scotland* (1868), 2, 304-12.

MCURE (*alias* CAMPBELL), JOHN 'Grammar School'; *Glasghu Facies: A View of the City of Glasgow*, ed GORDON, J S (Glasgow: John Tweed, 1872), 662-8.

MUIR, THOMAS. See BURNS, JAMES CLELAND.

REID, ROBERT 'The Glasgow Grammar School of Olden Time'; *Autobiography of the late Robert Reid* (Glasgow: David Robertson, 1865), 14-31.

Hutchesons' Hospital

Abstract of the Rules & Regulations by which Hutchesons' Hospital is governed, in conformity to the original Mortifications, or the Bye Laws, or established Usage of the Patrons. To which is added, The History of said Hospital; and an Appendix containing the principal Papers relative thereto. Glasgow: Printed in the *Courier* Office by W Reid & Co, 1800. 8vo. Pp 77, xciii. GUL

The Constitution, Rules, and History of the Royal Incorporation of Hutchesons' Hospital, founded, 1639—chartered 1821. Glasgow: Printed by Francis Orr & Sons, 1850. 8vo. Pp 176, xci. 2 maps.
GUL

ENDOWED SCHOOLS AND HOSPITALS (SCOTLAND) COMMISSION 'Hutchesons' Hospital'; *Third Report* (1875), 148-54; *Appendix to Third Report* (1875), 1, 149-171.

HILL, LAURENCE *Hutchesoniana*, giving the Story of Partick Castle; and an Account of the Founders of Hutchesons' Hospital, their Parentage, Family, & Times. In Letters to David Mackinlay, Preceptor of the Hospital. Printed for private circulation. Edinburgh: T Constable, 1855. 8vo. Pp 48. Frontispiece and 3 plates.

HILL, WILLIAM HENRY *An Account of Hutchesons' School in Glasgow*, since the date of its Foundation in 1641 to the present time, submitted for the Information of the Patrons, and especially with reference to a Proposal to establish a School for Girls in connection with the Institution. Glasgow: Printed by Bell & Bain, 1867. 8vo. Pp 112.   GUL

'Hutchesons' Hospital founded, upheld, and administered by Churchmen'; *Church of Scotland Mag*, Dec 1834, **1**, 381-5.

HUTCHINSON, JOHN M 'Three Centuries of Hutchesons'. New Home for an Old School'; *The Glasgow Herald*, 11 May 1960.

LAURIE, DAVID *Memorial to the Hon. the Preceptor and Patrons of Hutchesons' Hospital*. Glasgow: Printed by Bell & Bain, 1834. 8vo. Pp 18.   GUL

MCFARLANE, JAMES *Hutchesons' Hospital and its Founders*: A Chapter in the Life of Glasgow. Glasgow: Printed by Robert Anderson, 1914. 8vo. Pp 52.   GUL

MEIKLEJOHN, JOHN M D *Secondary Education in Glasgow*. A Letter to Archibald Gray Macdonald, Esq., Preceptor of the Royal Incorporation of Hutchesons' Hospital in the City of Glasgow. Glasgow: James Maclehose, 1875. 8vo. Pp 32. Map.   GUL

MENZIES, THOMAS 'Hutchesons' Hospital'; *Transactions of the National Association for the Promotion of Social Science, 1874* (1875), 473-8.

NEIL, ROBERT W *Hutchesons' Boys' Grammar School, 1641-1960*. Illustrated. Glasgow: Printed by George Outram & Co, Ltd, 1960. 4to. Pp 28.   Mit

RITCHIE, W TOD 'Three Hundred Years of Hutchesons' Boys' Grammar School'; *SEJ*, 2 June 1950, **33**, 370-1.

Maclachlan's Free School

Exemplification of the Letters of Administration, with Will annexed, of John Maclachlan, Esq. late of Calcutta. Glasgow: Printed by John Niven, 1823. 8vo. Pp 14.   Mit

Notes as to the Incorporation of the Maclachlan Free School. Glasgow: Printed by Robert Anderson, 1875. 8vo. Pp 23.   GUL

Regulations of the Maclachlan Free School. Glasgow: Printed by E Khull & Son, 1829. 8vo. Pp 11.   Mit

Royal Warrant and Charter of Incorporation in favour of the Trustees of the School founded by John Maclachlan, Esq. of Calcutta. Dated 29th December, 1841. Edinburgh: Printed by the University Press, 1842. 8vo. Pp 16.   GUL

Mechanics' Institution

CLELAND, JAMES 'Glasgow Mechanics' Institution'; *Enumeration of the Inhabitants of the City of Glasgow and County of Lanark. For the Government Census of MDCCCXXXI*, second edition (1832), 65-8.

HEYDON, R J *Origin and Development of the Glasgow Mechanics' Institution*. Unpublished MEd thesis, Glasgow University, 1968. 4to. Typescript.   GUL

HUDSON, JAMES WILLIAM 'The Glasgow Mechanics' Institute'; *History of Adult Education* (1851), 42-3, 84-8.

MUIR, JAMES 'The First Mechanics' Institution'; *John Anderson. Pioneer of Technical Education* (1950), 123-8.

SEXTON, ALEXANDER H 'The Mechanics' Institution and the College of Science and Arts, 1823-1887'; *The First Technical College* (1894), 69-89.

Millar's School for Girls

Abstract of the Rules of Mr Archibald Millar's Charity School for Girls, in Glasgow, as established by the Deed of Mortification, and the different Minutes of the Governors. Glasgow: Printed by D Prentice & Co, *Chronicle* Office, 1812. 8vo. Pp 15.   GUL

Abstract of the Rules as established by the Deed of Mortification, and the Different Minutes of the Governors. Glasgow: Printed by John Graham, 1830. 8vo. Pp 30, 2.   GUL

Murdoch's Boys' School

MARWICK, SIR JAMES D *Notes as to the Incorporation of Murdoch's Boys' School.* Glasgow: Printed by Robert Anderson, 1874. 8vo. Pp 27.   Mit

New Vennel School Society

Report for 1849-50. Glasgow: Printed by Harrower & Brown, 1850. 8vo. Pp 12.
                                            GUL

Sabbath Evening-School Society

Fourth and Fifth Annual Reports by the Committee of Management. Glasgow: Printed by Andrew Duncan, 1813-14. 8vo.   GUL
      1813—pp 12.   1814—pp 18.

St Mungo's Academy

HANDLEY, JAMES EDMUND *The History of St Mungo's Academy, 1858-1958.* Paisley: Printed by John Aitken & Sons, nd [?1960]. 8vo. Pp [4], 233. 23 plates.
                                            Mit

Society for Managing the Sunday Schools in Glasgow

Fourth Annual Report. Glasgow: Printed by A Duncan and R Chapman, 1791. 8vo. Pp 12.

Eighth Annual Report. Glasgow: Printed by James and Andrew Duncan, 1795. 8vo. Pp 13.

United Sabbath Day Schools oʃ Glasgow and its Vicinity

Report. Glasgow: Printed by R Chapman, 1814. 8vo. Pp 16.   GUL

Wilson's Charity School

Copy of Mr George Wilson's Will, with the Rules for the Government of the Charity and a List of the Governors. Glasgow: Printed in the *Courier* Office, by William Reid, 1795. 8vo. Pp 24.   GUL

WILSON, GEORGE *Loose Hints or General Outlines of a Plan, for a Charity School.* Glasgow, 1779. 8vo. Pp 24.   GUL

Anderston

First Report of their Proceedings by the Directors of the Burgh of Anderston Parochial Schools. Glasgow: Printed by John Malcolm, 1839. 8vo. Pp 11.
                                            Mit

ANDERSTON AND CALTON SABBATH-DAY SCHOOL SOCIETY *Report by the Committee.* Glasgow: Printed by Edward Khull & Co, 1812. 8vo. Pp 16.   GUL

Gorbals

Analysis of a New System of General Education; in which Lancastrian Principles are discussed and enlarged, in a Project for the Erection of a Grand Public Academy at Glasgow, to be supported by Public Markets in the Suburbs of that City, but applicable to every large Town. Addressed to the Heritors of the Barony of Gorbals. London: Printed for Gale & Curtis, 1811. 8vo. Pp ccviii, 272. 2 plans.   GUL

LAURIE, DAVID *A Project for erecting Public Markets, and a Grand Academy, on improved Principles in the Gorbals;* . . . contained in an Address to the Heritors. With a general Introduction, illustrating the Advantages of instituting a Royal Academical Society, in the City of Glasgow. Glasgow: Printed by R Chapman, 1810. 8vo. Pp ccviii, 272. Map and plan.

ORD, JOHN 'Schools'; *The Story of the Barony of Gorbals* (Paisley: Alexander Gardner, 1919), 112-15.

Maryhill

THOMSON, ALEXANDER 'Schools and Schoolmasters'; *Maryhill from 1750 till 1894* (Glasgow: Kerr & Richardson, 1895), 83-94.   Mit

Partick

GREENHORNE, WILLIAM 'Early Education in Partick'; *History of Partick* (Glasgow: John Tomlinson Limited, 1928), 61-90.

—*Old Partick: Its Schools and Schoolmasters.* Glasgow: John Tomlinson

Ltd, 1914. 12mo. Pp 63. Frontispiece, maps, portraits, and other illustrations.
GUL

NAPIER, JAMES 'Schools'; *Notes and Reminiscences relating to Partick* (Glasgow: Hugh Hopkins, 1873), 84-95.

Ruchazie

MILLER, JOHN F *Ruchazie, a District and a School in the Provan*. Printed for private circulation. Glasgow: Maclehose, Jackson & Co, 1920. 8vo. Pp 57. 4 plates.

St Rollox

DOW, HUGH AITKEN *History of St Rollox School Glasgow*, together with Memorabilia of same, and a poetical Sketch of the Old School and its Notabilities. Edinburgh: Printed for private circulation by Murray and Gibb, 1876. 8vo. Pp 192. Frontispiece and 2 plates.

Counties
ABERDEENSHIRE

ALLARDYCE, JOHN 'Schoolmasters and Education'; *Byegone Days in Aberdeenshire* (Aberdeen: Central Press, 1913), 125-53.

COMMITTEE OF THE COMMISSIONERS OF SUPPLY FOR THE COUNTY OF ABERDEEN *Report on the Proposals of the Committee of the General Assembly of the Church of Scotland, and otherwise, regarding the Parochial School Establishment of Scotland*. Aberdeen: Printed by D Chalmers and Company, 1852. 12mo. Pp 15.   EIS

KEMP, DANIEL W 'Old Teachers of Aberdeenshire, 1771-1853'; *Scottish Notes and Queries*, second series, Apr 1900, **1**, 152-153; May 1900, **1**, 166-7.

NOTE These were teachers in SSPCK Schools.

MIDDLETON, DAVID *General Report on the Schools connected with the Established Church and other Schools inspected in the North-East Division of Scotland. During the year 1858*. Edinburgh: Thomas Constable and Co; London: Hamilton, Adams and Co, 1859. 12mo. Pp 19.

MIDDLETON, DAVID, and KERR, JOHN *General Reports on Schools in the North-East of Scotland, for the years 1859, 1860, 1861*. Aberdeen: John Smith, 1862. 8vo. Pp 40.   AUL

PAUL, WILLIAM 'State of Education about Half a Century Ago and its Present Improvements'; *Past and Present of Aberdeenshire, or Reminiscences of Seventy Years*, second edition. (Aberdeen: Lewis Smith & Son, 1881), 80-90.

SIMPSON, IAN J *Education in Aberdeenshire before 1872*. Scottish Council for Research in Education, publication no 25. London: University of London Press, Ltd, 1947. 8vo. Pp xi, 229. Map. 4 plates. Glossary. Bibliography. Index.

Dick Bequest

Another Communication to the Presbyteries within the Counties of Aberdeen, Banff, and Moray; being Observations on that made by the Trustees of the Dick Bequest regarding the case of Kemnay, &c. &c. Aberdeen: A Brown & Co; Edinburgh: A & C Black, 1853. 8vo. Pp 47.   APL

DICK BEQUEST TRUSTEES *Communication to the Presbyteries within the Counties of Aberdeen, Banff, and Moray, by the Trustees of the Dick Bequest, regarding the case of Kemnay, &c.* Edinburgh: Printed by T Constable, 1853. 8vo. Pp iii, 48.   EUL

—*Correspondence to the Presbyteries within the Counties of Aberdeen, Banff, and Moray, by the Trustees of the Dick Bequest, regarding the case of Kemnay, &c.* Edinburgh: Printed by T Constable, nd [1853]. 8vo. Pp 53.   APL

—*Opinions received by the Trustees of Mr Dick's Bequest, as to Parochial Schoolmasters holding permanent Appointments as Preaching Assistants*. np [Edinburgh], nd [1839]. 8vo. Pp 19.   EUL

—*Opinions received by the Trustees of Mr Dick's Bequest, as to Parochial Schoolmasters holding permanent Engagements to preach statedly, with relative Minutes*. Edinburgh, 1841. 8vo. Pp 28.   EUL

ENDOWED SCHOOLS AND HOSPITALS (SCOTLAND) COMMISSION 'Dick Bequest'; *Third*

Report (1875), 121-4; *Appendix to Third Report* (1875), **1**, 113-18.

CRUICKSHANK, MARJORIE 'The Dick Bequest: The Effect of a Famous Nineteenth-Century Endowment on Parish Schools of North East Scotland'; *History of Education Q*, Sept 1965, **5**, 153-65.   Jor

LAURIE, SIMON SOMERVILLE *Report on Education in the Parochial Schools of the Counties of Aberdeen, Banff and Moray.* Addressed to the Trustees of the Dick Bequest. Edinburgh: Printed by Thomas Constable, 1865. 8vo. Pp xv, 401.

MENZIES, ALLAN *Report of Twenty-one Years' Experience of the Dick Bequest* for elevating the Character and Position of the Parochial Schools and School-masters in the Counties of Aberdeen, Banff, and Moray, embracing an Exposition of the Design and Operation of the Parish School. Edinburgh: William Blackwood and Sons; and A Brown and Co, Aberdeen, 1854. 8vo. Pp xvi, 478. Index.

—*Report to the Trustees of the Bequest of the late James Dick, Esq. for the Benefit of the Country Parochial Schoolmasters in the Counties of Aberdeen, Banff, and Moray.* Edinburgh: Printed by Thomas Constable, 1835. 8vo. Pp xi, 163.

——. Second edition. Edinburgh: Oliver and Boyd, 1836. 8vo. Pp xii, 100. EUL

—*Report to the Trustees of the Dick Bequest for the Benefit of the Parochial Schoolmasters and Schools in the Counties of Aberdeen, Banff, and Moray, after Ten Years' Experience of its Application.* With an Appendix, containing Papers used in the Examination of Teachers. Edinburgh and London: William Blackwood and Sons, 1844. 8vo. Pp xvi, 324, cii.

NISSEN, HARTVIG 'Dicks Legat'; *Beskrivelse over Skotlands Almueskolevaesen* (Christiania, 1854), 123-30.

Observations on the Administration of the Dick Bequest. Reprinted from the *Aberdeen Journal*, of 21 July 1852. Aberdeen: Printed by D Chalmers and Company, 1852. 8vo. Pp 20.   EUL

RUSTICUS 'Education in Aberdeenshire and the North-East: The Dick Bequest'; *Educ News*, 17 May 1912, **37**, 432.

Milne Bequest

CRUIKSHANK, JOHN *Report to the Trustees of the late Dr John Milne, respecting the Schools admitted, or eligible, to the Benefit of the Bequest;* for the year ending with the Harvest Vacation of 1852. Aberdeen: Printed by W Bennett, 1852. 8vo. Pp 23. APL

ENDOWED SCHOOLS AND HOSPITALS (SCOTLAND) COMMISSION 'Milne Bequest'; *Third Report* (1875), 124-7; *Appendix to Third Report* (1875), **1**, 119-24.

MILNE BEQUEST TRUSTEES *Settlements of Dr John Milne,* late President of the Medical Board on the Bombay Establishment, with Decree of Declarator thereto. np, nd. 8vo. Pp 16.   APL

—*Settlements of Dr John Milne,* late President of the Medical Board on the Bombay Establishment. np, nd. 8vo. Pp 19. APL

—*Settlements of Dr John Milne,* late President of the Medical Board on the Bombay Establishment. np, 1845. 8vo. Pp 20.   APL

—*Rules and Regulations established by the Trustees of the late Dr John Milne of Bombay for the due Regulation and Conducting of his Bequest for the Promotion of Education in Aberdeenshire and the Parish of Banchory-Devenick.* Aberdeen: Printed by D Chalmers and Company, 1845. 8vo. Pp 17.   APL

NISSEN, HARTVIG 'Milnes Legat'; *Beskrivelse over Skotlands Almueskolevaesen* (Christiania, 1854), 130-1.

Buchan

WILL, JAMES 'Educational Developments in Buchan'; *Book of Buchan*, ed TOCHER, J F (Peterhead: The Buchan Club, 1910), 388-406.

Cairnie

PIRIE, JAMES 'Education (Schools and Schoolmasters)'; *The Parish of Cairnie* (Banff: Printed at the *Banffshire Journal* Office, 1906), 106-22.

Deeside

HENDERSON, JOHN A 'Schoolmasters'; *Annals of Lower Deeside* (Aberdeen: D Wyllie & Son, 1892), 131-5.

Ellon

GODSMAN, JAMES 'Schools of the Parish'; *History of the Burgh and Parish of Ellon, Aberdeenshire* (Aberdeen: W & W Lindsay, 1958), 291, 296-8.

ROBERTSON, JAMES 'Education'; *New Statistical Account of Scotland* (1845), **12**, 926-40.

Fraserburgh

ANDERSON, PETER J 'The University of Fraserburgh'; *Book of Buchan*, ed TOCHER, J F (Peterhead: The Buchan Club, 1910), 336-9.

—'Universities at Fraserburgh and Peterhead'; *Scottish Notes and Queries*, Oct 1891, **5** (1892), 77; Jan 1892, **5**, 114.

CRANNA, JOHN 'Fraserburgh Schools and Schoolmasters'; *Fraserburgh: Past and Present* (Aberdeen: The Rosemount Press, 1914), 202-35.

ENDOWED SCHOOLS AND HOSPITALS (SCOTLAND) COMMISSION 'Fraserburgh Academy'; *Second Report* (1874), 469-70.

PRATT, JOHN BURNETT 'Fraserburgh University'; *Buchan*, fourth edition, revised by Robert Anderson (Aberdeen: Lewis Smith & Son, 1901), 269-72.

THOMSON, WILLIAM 'The Aberdeen University at Fraserburgh and Peterhead'; *Scottish Notes and Queries*, Sept 1891, **5**, 57-8; Dec 1891, **5**, 108.

Garioch

DICK BEQUEST TRUSTEES *Extract from Minutes of the Trustees of the Dick Bequest, April 22, 1842*. np, [Edinburgh], nd [1842]. 8vo. Pp 13.   EUL

—*Minutes of the Trustees of the Dick Bequest, November 26, 1841*. np, [Edinburgh], 1841. 8vo. Pp 16.   EUL

PRESBYTERY OF GARIOCH *Correspondence between a Committee of the Presbytery of Garioch and the Trustees of the Dick*

Bequest respecting the Parish School of Kemnay, Aberdeenshire, N.B. With a relative Statement; also, Observations on the Constitution and Administration of the Dick Bequest, and on the Supervision of Parochial Education. Aberdeen: Lewis Smith; Oliver & Boyd, Edinburgh, 1852. 8vo. Pp 82.   EUL

Inverallochy

WILSON, ROBERT *George MacPherson, M.A., Schoolmaster of Inverallochy. A Memoir.* Aberdeen: Taylor and Henderson, 1911. 8vo. Pp 103.   BM

Kemnay

'The Parish School of Kemnay'; *Chambers's Edinburgh J*, 16 Jan 1841, **9**, 412-13.

King Edward

GODSMAN, JAMES 'Schools of the Parish'; *King Edward, Aberdeenshire. The Story of a Parish* (Banff: Printed by the *Banffshire Journal* Limited, 1952), 330-49.

Old Deer

ENDOWED SCHOOLS AND HOSPITALS (SCOTLAND) COMMISSION 'Smith's Prize Fund'; Appendix to the Third Report (1875), **2**, 260-1.

Peterculter

CORMACK, ALEXANDER A *Education in the Eighteenth Century. Parish of Peterculter, Aberdeenshire.* Banff: Printed by the *Banffshire Journal* for the Author, 1965. 8vo. Pp 71. Frontispiece.   Jor

Peterhead

BUCHAN, PETER 'Education and the State of Learning: Character of the Teachers'; *Annals of Peterhead* (Peterhead: Printed at the Auchmedden Press, 1819), 77-80.

ENDOWED SCHOOLS AND HOSPITALS (SCOTLAND) COMMISSION 'Peterhead Academy'; *Second Report* (1874), 569-73.

FINDLAY, JAMES THOMAS 'Education in Peterhead, from 1597'; *A History of*

Peterhead (Peterhead: P Scrogie Ltd; Aberdeen: D Wyllie & Son, 1933), 182-192.   Mit

Rhynie

SMITH, ROBERT HARVEY *An Aberdeenshire Village Propaganda Forty Years Ago.* Edinburgh: David Douglas, 1889. 8vo. Pp xviii, 175. Frontispiece.

St Fergus

WHYTE, ALEXANDER *The Heritors & Schoolmaster of St Fergus on the Parochial School Buildings.* Peterhead: Printed at the *Sentinel* Office, 1869. 8vo. Pp 32.
                                                  Mit

Tullyduke

DON, JOHN 'Tullyduke School in the Middle of last century'; *Aberdeen University Rev*, Mar 1920, 7, 152-3.   EUL

Turriff

OGILVIE, JOSEPH *Memories of Turiff Parish School in the Fifties.* By an Old Master. Reprinted from the Turiff School Magazine of January and April. Aberdeen: Printed by W Jolly & Sons, Albany Press, 1911. 8vo. Pp 11.   AUL

ANGUS

JESSOP, J C *Education in Angus.* An Historical Survey of Education up to the Act of 1872, from original and contemporary sources. Scottish Council for Research in Education, publication no 2. London: University of London Press, Ltd, 1931. 8vo. Pp vii, 328. Bibliography. Indexes.

ROBERTSON, WILLIAM *Report of the Schools in the Glens and Braes of Angus.* Dundee: Printed by William Brown for the Author, 1836. 8vo. Pp 32.   BM

Arbroath

COWIE, J *Education in Arbroath.* Unpublished EdB thesis, St Andrews, 1956. Typescript. Fcp. Pp viii, 265. Bibliography.   StAUL

ENDOWED SCHOOLS AND HOSPITALS (SCOTLAND) COMMISSION 'Arbroath High School'; *Second Report* (1874), 347-52.

HARVEY, THOMAS, and SELLAR, ALEX C 'Arbroath Parochial or Burgh School' and 'Arbroath High School'; *Report on the State of Education in the Burgh and Middle-Class Schools in Scotland* (1868), 2, 38-43.

HAY, GEORGE 'Schools and Schoolmasters'; *History of Arbroath to the Present Time* (Arbroath: Thomas Buncle, 1876), 259-271.   EUL

— —, second edition (Arbroath: Thomas Buncle & Co, 1899), 278-89.

MCBAIN, JAMES M 'Educational'; *Arbroath: Past & Present* (Arbroath: Brodie & Salmond, 1887), 253-84.

Memorial unto the Right Honourable, the Honourable, and others, the Directors of the Public Schools of Arbroath. To be submitted to the Adoption of the Public Meeting of the Inhabitants of Arbroath, called for the Evening of Wednesday, the 24th of July [1844]. np, nd. 8vo. Pp 6.
                                              New Coll

Observations on the Constitution of the Arbroath Academy; occasioned by an anonymous Letter, published in the *Dundee, Perth, and Cupar Advertiser,* May 16, 1822. Dundee: Printed by R S Rintoul, 1822. 8vo. Pp 20, 4.   Mit

SALMOND, DAVID S 'Arbroath Educational Institution'; *Reminiscences of Arbroath and St Andrews* (Arbroath: Brodie and Salmond, 1905), 65-71.

Statement regarding certain late Proceedings of the Directors of Arbroath Academy, and of Reasons for forming a New Educational Institution. By a Committee of Subscribers to the Institution. Arbroath: James Adam, 1845. 8vo. Pp 20.   New Coll

Auchterhouse

CAMERON, J KIRKLAND and VALENTINE, M OLIPHANT 'Our School'; *Auchterhouse Old and New. An Historical and Social Record* (Dundee: David Winter & Son, 1932), 53-9.

ROBERTSON, JOHN *Education: with Notices of the Schools and Schoolmasters of Auchterhouse for the last Two Hundred Years.* Montrose: Printed at the *Standard* Office, nd [1887]. 8vo. Pp 47. Frontispiece.

Brechin

ENDOWED SCHOOLS AND HOSPITALS (SCOTLAND) COMMISSION 'Brechin Grammar School'; *Second Report* (1874), 366-8.

HARVEY, THOMAS, and SELLAR, ALEX C 'Brechin Burgh School'; *Report on the State of Education in the Burgh and Middle-Class Schools in Scotland* (1868), **2**, 34-7.

THOMS, DAVID BOATH 'Church and School in Brechin'; *Book of the Society of Friends of Brechin Cathedral*, no 9 (1956), 10-36.

—'The College of Brechin'; *Book of the Society of Friends of Brechin Cathedral*, no 3 (1950), 6-12.

Forfar

ENDOWED SCHOOLS AND HOSPITALS (SCOTLAND) COMMISSION 'Forfar Academy'; *Second Report* (1874), 460-4.

HARVEY, THOMAS, and SELLAR, ALEX C 'Forfar Burgh School'; *Report on the State of Education in the Burgh and Middle-Class Schools in Scotland* (1868), **2**, 31-3.

REID, ALAN 'Schools'; *The Royal Burgh of Forfar* (Paisley: J & R Parlane; Houliston & Sons, London; John Menzies & Co, Edinburgh and Glasgow; G S Nicolson, *Herald* Office, Forfar, 1902), 147-55.

Glenesk

'An Educational Record of last century'; *SEJ*, 21 Dec 1945, **28**, 640-1.

Kirriemuir

EASTON, THOMAS *Hints on the Resources for Education in the Parish of Kirriemuir, and the best mode of distributing them; addressed to the heritors of the parish.* Glasgow: Printed by William Collins & Co, 1837. 8vo. Pp vi, 24.

ENDOWED SCHOOLS AND HOSPITALS (SCOTLAND) COMMISSION 'Webster's Seminary'; *Second Report* (1874), 507-13.

REID, ALAN 'Educational'; *The Regality of Kirriemuir* (Edinburgh: John Grant, 1909), 167-83.

Lunanhead

MILNE, WILLIAM J 'Schools and Schoolmasters'; *Reminiscences of an Old Boy: Being Autobiographic Sketches of Scottish Rural Life from 1832 to 1856.* (Forfar: Printed by John Macdonald, *Review* Office, 1901), 34-41.

Monifieth

MALCOLM, JOHN 'Schools and Teachers'; *The Parish of Monifieth in Ancient and Modern Times* (Edinburgh and London: William Green & Sons, 1910), 170-87.

New Coll

Montrose

ENDOWED SCHOOLS AND HOSPITALS (SCOTLAND) COMMISSION 'Montrose Grammar School'; *Second Report* (1874), 529-31.

FRASER, WILLIAM R 'Schools and Schoolmasters'; *St Mary's of Old Montrose* (Edinburgh and London: William Blackwood and Sons, 1896), 204-11.

HARVEY, THOMAS, and SELLAR, ALEX C 'Montrose Academy'; *Report on the State of Education in the Burgh and Middle-Class Schools in Scotland* (1868), **2**, 27-30.

JOHNS, TREVOR W 'The Library of the Grammar School of Montrose'; *The School Librarian*, July 1961, **10**, 396-403.

INSH, GEORGE PRATT 'A Sixteenth Century Schoolboy (From the Diary of Mr James Melville)'; *School Life in Old Scotland from Contemporary Sources*, (1925), 3-7.

MACFARLAND, HENRY S N 'The Education of James Melville (1556-1614)'; *Aberdeen University Rev*, Autumn 1956, **36**, 362-70.

EUL

MITCHELL, DAVID 'Education in Montrose'; *History of Montrose* (Montrose: George Walker, 1866), 41-51.

—'Trades' School, now Dorward's Seminary'; *History of Montrose* (Montrose: George Walker, 1866), 58-68.

SMITH, VALERIE GRAEME *Montrose Schools, 1750-1820.* Unpublished BEd thesis, Edinburgh University, 1960. Typescript. 4to. Pp [4], vi, 158, [4].   EUL

ARGYLL

MACKINNON, DONALD 'Education in Argyll and the Isles (1638-1709)'; *Records of the Scottish Church History Society*, **6** (1938), 46-54.

Appin

CAMPBELL, MAIRI M 'The Old Dominie, Barcaldine School'; *SEJ*, 26 Oct 1934, **17**, 1333.

Kintyre

ENDOWED SCHOOLS AND HOSPITALS (SCOTLAND) COMMISSION 'Dalintober (Miss Campbell's) Schools, Campbeltown'; *Appendix to Third Report* (1875), **2**, 362-363.

HARVEY, THOMAS and SELLAR, ALEX C 'Campbeltown Burgh and Parochial School'; *Report on the State of Education in the Burgh and Middle-Class Schools in Scotland* (1868), **2**, 156.

MCKERRAL, ANDREW 'Education'; *Kintyre in the Seventeenth Century* (Edinburgh and London: Oliver and Boyd, 1948), 148-60.

Lochgoilhead

EDUCATION COMMISSION (SCOTLAND) 'Lochgoilhead'; *First Report* (1865), 403-4.

Lorne

SMITH, A L 'Notes on Education in Lorne'; *SEJ*, 17 May 1935, **18**, 632.

Mull

SMITH, A L 'Notes on Education in Mull, Morvern, Tiree, and Coll'; *SEJ*, 2 Apr 1937, **20**, 420-1.

AYRSHIRE

AYRSHIRE EDUCATIONAL ASSOCIATION *First Report.* 1841. Ayr: Printed by J Watson, 1841. 8vo. Pp 20. New Coll

BOYD, WILLIAM *Education in Ayrshire through Seven Centuries.* Scottish Council for Research in Education, publication no 45. London: University of London Press Ltd, 1961. 8vo. Pp xv, 233. 2 maps. Bibliography. Indexes.

EDGAR, ANDREW 'Provision for Education in Olden Times'; *Old Church Life in Scotland* (Paisley and London: Alexander Gardner, 1886) 63-133.

FOWLER, JAMES J 'The Presbytery of Ayr: Its Schools and Schoolmasters, 1642-1746'; *Ayrshire Archaeological and Natural History Society Collections*, second series, **6**, [1958-60], 81-174.

GORDON, JOHN 'Report on the State of Education in the County of Ayr'; *Minutes of the Committee of Council on Education, 1846*, 387-403.

Ardrossan

GUTHRIE, ARTHUR 'Educational'; *A Sketch, Descriptive and Historical, of Ardrossan & Saltcoats*, second edition (Ardrossan: Herald Office: Printed by Arthur Guthrie, 1879), 44-50, 75-8.

— '—'; *Ardrossan, Saltcoats and Neighbourhood* (Ardrossan: Arthur Guthrie, [1883]), 85-92, 134-6.

Ayr

CAIRNS, J DOUGLAS 'Education in Ayr, 1233-1952'; *SEJ*, 13 June 1952, **35**, 374-6.

MCCLELLAND, JAMES 'Schools'; *The Royal Burgh of Ayr*, ed DUNLOP, ANNIE I (Edinburgh and London: Oliver and Boyd, 1953), 212-35.

MCGLOIN, JAMES 'Catholic Education in Ayr, 1823-1918: Part One'; *Innes Rev*, **13** (1962), 77-103.

Charter erecting the Managers and Directors of the Academy of Air, into one Body Politic and Corporate. 1798. Ayr: Printed by Wilson & Paul, 1812. 8vo. Pp 8.

ENDOWED SCHOOLS AND HOSPITALS (SCOT-
LAND) COMMISSION 'Ayr Academy'; *Second Report* (1874), 353-9.

FEARON, DANIEL R 'Ayr Academy'; *Schools
Inquiry Commission Report* (1868), 6, pt 5,
83-96.

HARVEY, THOMAS, and SELLAR, ALEX C
'Ayr Academy'; *Report on the State of
Education in the Burgh and Middle-Class
Schools in Scotland* (1868), 2, 262-70.

PATRICK, DAVID *Air Academy and Burgh
Schule, 1233-1895.* (Compiled for the
Academy Bazaar, 1895). Ayr: Printed
by the *Ayrshire Post,* 1895. 8vo. Pp 163.
15 plates. GUL

Report on the Funds of the Academy. Ayr:
Printed at the *Courier* Office, 1822. 8vo.
Pp 19.

RUSK, ROBERT R 'Ayr Academy Sept-
Centenary'; *SEJ,* 23 June 1933, 16, 764-
765.

—'Rector and Assistant: Ayr Academy
100 Years Ago'; *SEJ,* 11 July 1952, 28,
434-6.

TAYLOR, A L 'The Grammar School of Ayr,
1746-1796'; *Ayrshire Archaeological and
Natural History Collections,* second
series, 7 (1961-6), 58-89.

Beith

ENDOWED SCHOOLS AND HOSPITALS (SCOT-
LAND) COMMISSION 'Spiers' Trust, Beith';
Appendix to Third Report (1875), 2, 264-9.

MITCHELL, JOHN 'Education'; *Memories of
Ayrshire about 1780,* ed DICKSON, W K, in
Miscellany of the Scottish History Society,
6 (1939), 272-6.

Colmonell

See BIOGRAPHY, SNELL, JOHN.

Cumnock

WARRICK, JOHN 'Education in Olden Times';
History of Old Cumnock (Paisley and
London: Alexander Gardner, 1899), 263-
273.

Cunningham

W, J 'In Cunningham 120 Years Ago';
SEJ, 6 Aug 1937, 32, 1012.

Dundonald

'Discipline of a Parish School in 1640';
Edinburgh Mag, Mar 1819, 4, 231-3.

Irvine

ENDOWED SCHOOLS AND HOSPITALS (SCOT-
LAND) COMMISSION 'Royal Academy of
Irvine'; *Second Report* (1874), 503-4.

HARVEY, THOMAS, and SELLAR, ALEX C
'Irvine Academy'; *Report on the State
of Education in the Burgh and Middle-
Class Schools in Scotland* (1868), 2, 271-3.

MCJANNET, ARNOLD F '[Schools]'; *Royal
Burgh of Irvine* (Glasgow: Civic Press,
Limited, 1938), 212-44.

Kilmarnock

ENDOWED SCHOOLS AND HOSPITALS (SCOT-
LAND) COMMISSION 'Wilson's Charity
School, Kilmarnock'; *Appendix to Third
Report* (1875), 1, 270-1.

HARVEY, THOMAS, and SELLAR, ALEX C
'Kilmarnock Academy'; *Report on the
State of Education in the Burgh and
Middle-Class Schools in Scotland* (1868),
2, 143-5.

MACKAY, ARCHIBALD 'Early Schools and
Schoolmasters'; *History of Kilmarnock,*
fourth edition, revised and enlarged
(Kilmarnock: Archibald Mackay, 1880),
153-70.

Kilmaurs

M'NAUGHT, DUNCAN 'Schools and Schoolmasters'; *Kilmaurs Parish and Burgh*
(Paisley: Alexander Gardner, 1912), 197-
222. GUL

Kilwinning

ENDOWED SCHOOLS AND HOSPITALS (SCOT-
LAND) COMMISSION 'Mrs Smith's Mortification, in the Parishes of Kilwinning
and Stevenston'; *Appendix to Third
Report* (1875), 2, 272-3.

HAY, JOHN 'The Parish School'; *Short
History of Kilwinning Parish* (Kilmarnock: Geo Outram & Co Ltd, 1967), 31-
42.

KER, WILLIAM LEE '[Educational]'; *Kilwinning* (Kilwinning: A W Cross, nd [1900]), 108-16.

BANFFSHIRE

BARCLAY, WILLIAM *The Schools and Schoolmasters of Banffshire*. Banff: Published by the *Banffshire Journal*, Ltd, for the Banffshire Branch of the Educational Institute of Scotland, 1925. 8vo. Pp xv, 308.

CRAMOND, WILLIAM 'Extracts bearing on Education from Presbytery and Kirk Session Records'; *Educ News*, 29 Nov 1890, **15**, 811-13; 13 Dec 1890, **15**, 843-4.

R, W 'Education and the Kirk in Banffshire, 1560-1872'; *SEJ*, 11 Aug 1961, **44**, 587-8.

Banff

ENDOWED SCHOOLS AND HOSPITALS (SCOTLAND) COMMISSION 'Mortifications in the Burgh of Banff'; *Appendix to Third Report* (1875), **1**, 194-214.

—'Wilson's Institution and Banff Grammar School'; *Second Report* (1874), 360-1.

HARVEY, THOMAS, and SELLAR, ALEX C 'Banff Academy'; *Report on the State of Education in the Burgh and Middle-Class Schools in Scotland* (1868), **2**, 16-23.

IMLACH, JAMES 'Educational Establishments and Banff Academy'; *History of Banff* (Banff: Published by Robert Leask, 1868), 59-60.

'The School, Banff'; *Annals of Banff*, ed CRAMOND, WILLIAM (Aberdeen: New Spalding Club, publication no 10, 1893), **2**, 165-208.

Fordyce

CORMACK, ALEXANDER A *An Historical Outline of the George Smith Bounty (Fordyce Academy)*. Reprinted from the *Banffshire Journal*, Dec. 4, 1951-Jan. 15, 1952. Banff: Printed by the *Banffshire Journal* Ltd, 1952. 8vo. Pp 30.

—*More about Founder of Fordyce Academy*. Reprinted from the *Banffshire Journal*; January- February, 1957. Banff: Printed by the *Banffshire Journal* Limited, nd [1957]. 8vo. Pp 49. 8 illustrations.

ENDOWED SCHOOLS AND HOSPITALS (SCOTLAND) COMMISSION 'Redhyth Mortification, Parish of Fordyce'; *Appendix to Third Report* (1875), **2**, 274-6.

HARVEY, THOMAS, and SELLAR, ALEX C 'Fordyce'; *Report on the State of Education in the Burgh and Middle-Class Schools in Scotland* (1868), **2**, 324-5.

MACLEAN, DOUGLAS G *The History of Fordyce Academy*. Life at a Banffshire School, 1592-1935. Banff: The *Banffshire Journal* Limited, 1936. 8vo. Pp xv, 250. Frontispiece and 12 plates.

'The Schools within the Presbytery of Fordyce Forty-five Years Ago'; *Educ News*, 29 Jan 1887, **12**, 86-7.

Glenrinnes

BARCLAY, WILLIAM 'An old-time dominie: Alexander Lautitt'; *Banffshire Field Club Transactions*, 1934, 143-68.

Grange

'My Scotch School'; *Cornhill Mag*, Aug 1861, **4**, 220-8.

Keith

LAWRENCE, JAMES *An Historical Account of the Schools and Schoolmasters in the Parish of Keith from 1631 to the Present Time*. Reprinted from the *Banffshire Herald*. Keith: John Mitchell & Son, 1907. 8vo. Pp 106.

BERWICKSHIRE

FRASER, H D 'Two Centuries of Dominies'; *SEJ*, 11 Jan 1935, **18**, 36.

GIBSON, JOHN 'Report on Schools Inspected in the Presbyteries of Chirnside, Dunse, and Lauder'; *Minutes of the Committee of Council on Education, 1842-43*, 202-19.

LESLIE, DAVID S 'Educational Interests'; *Notes on Hutton Parish* (Berwick-upon-Tweed: Martin's Printing Works, Limited, 1934), 124-30.

THOMSON, ANDREW 'Schools and Schoolmasters'; *Lauder and Lauderdale* (Galashiels: Craighead Brothers, 1902), 237-245.

BUTE
Cumbrae

ENDOWED SCHOOLS AND HOSPITALS (SCOT-
LAND) COMMISSION 'Maclean Bequest';
Third Report (1875), 141-2; *Appendix to
Third Report* (1875), **1**, 143-4.

Kingarth

ALLISON, MENA 'School Life in an Old Bute
Parish'; *SEJ*, 11 Mar 1932, **15**, 330.

THOMSON, A D 'School Life in an Old Bute
Parish'; *SEJ*, 13 May 1932, **15**, 603.

Rothesay

HARVEY, THOMAS, and SELLAR, ALEX C
'Rothesay Parochial School'; *Report on
the State of Education in the Burgh and
Middle-Class Schools in Scotland* (1868),
2, 153.

ORR, ALEXANDER M *Rothesay Public School.
A Brief Sketch of its History, 1655 till
1955.* Rothesay: Printed by Robt C
Ross, 1955. 8vo. Pp 48. Illustrations.

CAITHNESS

GUNN, ROBERT 'Rise and Spread of Education'; *The County of Caithness*, ed
HORNE, JOHN (Wick: W Rae, 1907), 181-
204.

MALCOLM, CHARLES A 'Edinburgh Caithness
Association Bursaries'; *Short History of
the Edinburgh Caithness Association*
(Edinburgh: The John o' Groat Bene-
volent, &c Association, 1924), 6-16.

Bower

STEPHEN, DAVID 'Some Bower Schoolmasters'; *Gleanings in the North* (Haddington: William Sinclair, 1891), 5-9.

Thurso

ENDOWED SCHOOLS AND HOSPITALS (SCOT-
LAND) COMMISSION 'Miller Institution';
Second Report (1874), 604-7.

Wick

ENDOWED SCHOOLS AND HOSPITALS (SCOT-
LAND) COMMISSION 'Rhind's Trust, Wick';
Appendix to Third Report (1875), **2**,
277-9.

HORNE, JOHN 'Schools of Other Days'; *Ye
Towne of Wick in ye Oldene Tymes*
(Wick: W Rae, 1895), 63-71.

CLACKMANNAN

HUTCHISON, HENRY *Education in Clackman-
nanshire from the earliest times to the
Education Act of 1872.* Unpublished
PhD thesis, Glasgow University, 1966.
4to. Typescript. Pp [4], iv, 206.
Bibliography.   GUL

Alloa

'Narrative of Certain Tyrannical Proceed-
ings, relative to the Management of a
Charity School in Alloa'; *Voluntary
Church Mag*, Sept 1836, **4**, 396-400.

Dollar

10 & 11 Vict, c 16. An Act to increase the
Number of Trustees for the Management
of the Dollar Institution, or John
M'Nabb's School, and to incorporate
the Trustees.   (Private Act, 1847)

DOLLAR ACADEMY *Statutes and Rules for the
Dollar Institution, or John MacNab's
School,* founded in 1828. np, 1828.
8vo. Pp 53.   EIS

DOUGALL, CHARLES S 'Dollar Institution';
*Educational Institute of Scotland Congress
Handbook, 1908,* 98-105.

ENDOWED SCHOOLS AND HOSPITALS (SCOT-
LAND) COMMISSION 'Dollar Institution';
Second Report (1874), 405-17.

FEARON, DANIEL R 'Dollar Institution';
Schools Inquiry Commission Report
(1868), **6**, pt 5, 203-5.

GIBSON, WILLIAM 'Dollar Academy'; *Reminiscences of Dollar,* second edition
(Edinburgh: Andrew Elliot, 1883), 57-70,
85-105.

GORDON, JOHN 'Report on the Dollar
Academy'; *Minutes of the Committee of
Council on Education, 1845,* 425-36.

HARVEY, THOMAS, and SELLAR, ALEX C
'Dollar Institution'; *Report on the State
of Education in the Burgh and Middle-
Class Schools in Scotland* (1868), **2**, 99-
111.

PORTEOUS, PETER *The Civil Campaigns of an Old Grey*; or, The Annals of the Parish of Dollar: exposing the conduct of the Rev. Dr Mylne and his elders, in the management of the Academy. Edinburgh: Printed by H & J Pillans, 1831. 8vo. Pp 151.

R, J G 'Dollar Academy'; *Scottish Field*, July 1934, **64**, 17-21.

WILSON, J S M *A History of Dollar Academy*. Illustrated. Dollar: Alex Muckersie, [1937]. 8vo. Pp 16.   Mit

Tillicoultry

'The School Days of Dr John Eadie'; *Educ News*, 11 May 1878, **3**, 233-4; 18 May 1878, **3**, 245-6.

Specimens read at the Autumn Examination of Tillicoultry Academy, taught by the Rev. Archibald Browning, 1828. Edinburgh: Printed by H & J Pillans, 1828. 8vo. Pp 58.   GUL

DUNBARTONSHIRE

MACPHAIL, IAN M M 'Education'; *Short History of Dumbartonshire* (Dumbarton: Bennett & Thomson, 1962), 100-2.

Cardross

MURRAY, EUNICE G *The Old School of Cardross*. A Chapter in Village Life. Glasgow: Jackson, Son & Company, 1949. 8vo. Pp [10], 113. Frontispiece and 3 plates.

Dumbarton

ENDOWED SCHOOLS AND HOSPITALS (SCOTLAND) COMMISSION 'Dumbarton Burgh Academy'; *Second Report* (1874), 418-21.

HARVEY, THOMAS, and SELLAR, ALEX C 'Dumbarton Academy'; *Report on the State of Education in the Burgh and Middle-Class Schools in Scotland* (1868), **2**, 127-9.

IRVING, JOHN *Early Burgh Schools in Dumbarton*. Dumbarton: Bennett & Thomson, 1918. 8vo. Pp 30.   New Coll

ROBERTS, FERGUS *The Grammar School of Dumbarton*. Reprinted from the *Lennox*

Herald, August, 1948. Dumbarton, 1948. 8vo. Pp 20.

Kirkintilloch

STEWART, ANDREW 'Schools and Schoolmasters'; *Kirkintilloch*, ed HORNE, JOHN (Kirkintilloch: D Macleod, Limited, *Herald* Office, 1910), 137-66.

WATSON, THOMAS 'Educational'; *Kirkintilloch: Town and Parish* (Glasgow: John Smith and Son, 1894), 295-9.

DUMFRIESSHIRE
Annan

ENDOWED SCHOOLS AND HOSPITALS (SCOTLAND) COMMISSION 'Annan Academy'; *Second Report* (1874), 344-6.

Statement regarding the Academy of Annan. Dumfries: Printed at the *Journal and Advertiser* Office by W Carson, 1828. 8vo. Pp 10.
Not seen. Listed in MILLER, FRANK *A Bibliography of the Parish of Annan*, Dumfries, 1925.

Caerlaverock

'Correspondence and Report on Caerlaverock Mortification'; *Minutes of the Committee of Council on Education, 1845*, 444-54.

ENDOWED SCHOOLS AND HOSPITALS (SCOTLAND) COMMISSION 'Hutton Hall Academy, Caerlaverock'; *Second Report* (1874), 373-4.

—'Hutton Bequest'; *Third Report* (1875), 145-7; *Appendix to Third Report* (1875), **1**, 234-41.

Closeburn

ENDOWED SCHOOLS AND HOSPITALS (SCOTLAND) COMMISSION 'Closeburn School, or Wallace Academy, Closeburn, Dumfries'; *Second Report* (1874), 375-8; *Appendix to Third Report* (1875), **1**, 215-222.

WALLACE, ROBERT *Observations on the Past and Present Conditions of Wallace-Hall Free School*, in the County of Dumfries; with suggestions to the patrons and trustees in regard to its future management. With an appendix containing the documents referred to. Glasgow: Atkinson & Co; and R B Lusk, Greenock; M'Kinnell & M'Kie, Dumfries; J Wardlaw, Edinburgh, 1831. 8vo. Pp 37.

GUL

Dumfries

SCOTTISH UNIVERSITIES COMMISSION 'Proposed College at Dumfries'; *Evidence, Oral and Documentary*, 1 (1837), Appendix, 239-43.

CRITCHLEY, JOHN W 'Dumfries Academy: Retrospective'; *Educational Institute of Scotland Congress Handbook*, 1907, 43-9.

EIS

ENDOWED SCHOOLS AND HOSPITALS (SCOTLAND) COMMISSION 'Dumfries Academy, Greyfriars, Dumfries'; *Second Report* (1874), 422-4.

FEARON, DANIEL R 'Dumfries Academy'; *Schools Inquiry Commission Report* (1868), 6, pt 5, 157-63.

HARVEY, THOMAS, and SELLAR, ALEX C 'Dumfries Academy'; *Report on the State of Education in the Burgh and Middle-Class Schools in Scotland* (1868), 2, 187-92.

MCDOWALL, WILLIAM *History of the Burgh of Dumfries*. Edinburgh: Adam and Charles Black, 1867. 8vo.
The Schools of the Burgh, 594-600. Erection of an Academy, 735-7. Ragged Schools, 869-70.

— —, second edition. Edinburgh: Adam and Charles Black, 1873. 8vo.
The Schools of the Burgh, 502-6. Erection of an Academy, 619-22. Ragged Schools, 735-6.

— —. Third edition. Dumfries: Thomas Hunter & Co, 1906. 8vo.
Schools of the Burgh, 548-53. Erection of an Academy, 677-80. RC Schools, 754, note (a). Episcopal Schools, 757, note (a). Ragged Schools, 817-18.

NICOL, W BERNARD DE BEAR 'The Dumfries and Maxwelltown Mechanics' Institute, 1825-1900'; *Transactions of the Dumfriesshire and Galloway Natural History & Antiquarian Society*, third series, 28 (Dumfries, 1951), 64-74.

RUSSELL, JAMES A 'Old Masters of the Academy'; *SEJ*, 7 June 1963, 46, 469.

SUTHERLAND, DAVID J S 'A History of Dumfries Academy'; *SEJ*, 14 July 1939, 22, 858-9; 21 July 1939, 22, 869-71.

ENDOWED SCHOOLS AND HOSPITALS (SCOTLAND) COMMISSION 'Muirhead's Hospital, Dumfries'; *First Report* (1873), 770-1.

Glencairn

CORRIE, JOHN 'Education'; *Glencairn (Dumfriesshire). The Annals of an Inland Parish* (Dumfries: Thos Hunter & Co, 1910), 83-91.

Langholm

HYSLOP, JOHN, and HYSLOP, ROBERT 'Schools and Schoolmasters'; *Langholm as it was* (Sunderland: Hills and Company; Robert Scott, Langholm; Simpkin, Marshall, Hamilton, Kent and Co, London; John Menzies and Co, Ltd, Edinburgh and Glasgow, 1912), 714-19.

Lochmaben

HENDERSON, JAMES *Petition for Mr James Henderson School-master at Lochmaben*, against the Viscount of Stormount. np, nd [?1701]. Fol. P 1.

—*Answers for Mr James Henderson School-master of Lochmaben* to the Petition given in by David Viscount of Stormount. np, nd [?1701]. Fol. Pp 2.

Middlebie

GORDON, JOHN 'Report on Middlebie'; *Minutes of the Committee of Council on Education, 1845*, 440-2.

Moffat

ENDOWED SCHOOLS AND HOSPITALS (SCOTLAND) COMMISSION 'The Grammar School, Moffat'; *Second Report* (1874), 526-8; 'Moffat Academy (Grammar and Parochial Schools)'; *Appendix to Third Report* (1875), 2, 280-4.

Sanquhar

BROWN, JAMES 'Education'; *History of Sanquhar* (Dumfries: J Anderson & Son, 1891), 396-407.   New Coll

Troqueer

PEACOCK, JOHN 'Education'; *An East Galloway Parish: or Troqueer, Past and Present* (Dumfries: Printed at the Standard Office, 1896), 19-21.
New Coll

Wamphray

PATERSON, JOHN 'The Parish School'; *Wamphray* (Lockerbie: Printed for the Author by James Halliday, 1906), 133-57.
New Coll

FIFE

BEALE, J M *A History of the Burgh and Parochial Schools of Fife, from the Reformation to 1872.* Unpublished PhD thesis, Edinburgh University, 1953. Typescript. 4to. Pp ii, 393, 67. Bibliography.   EUL

GORDON, JOHN 'Report on the Madras College St Andrews and the Madras or Bell's School Cupar-Fife'; *Minutes of the Committee of Council on Education, 1855-56*, 560-4.

Anstruther

ENDOWED SCHOOLS AND HOSPITALS (SCOTLAND) COMMISSION 'Waid's Orphan Naval Academy, Anstruther-Easter, Fife'; *Appendix to Third Report* (1875), 2, 291-3.

Burntisland

BLYTH, JOHN J 'Schools and Schoolmasters'; *Burntisland: Early History and People* (Kirkcaldy: Fifeshire Advertiser Ltd, 1948), 177-81.   Fi

ENDOWED SCHOOLS AND HOSPITALS (SCOTLAND) COMMISSION 'Burntisland Grammar School'; *Second Report* (1874), 369-72.

ERSKINE, WILLIAM 'Education'; *Glimpses of Modern Burntisland* (Kirkcaldy: Fife

Free Press Office, nd [c 1930]), 112-15, 160-2.   Fi

HARVEY, THOMAS, and SELLAR, ALEX C 'Burntisland Burgh School'; *Report on the State of Education in the Burgh and Middle-Class Schools in Scotland* (1868), 2, 95-6.

YOUNG, ANDREW 'Education'; *History of Burntisland* (Kirkcaldy: Printed by the Fifeshire Advertiser Limited, 1913), 64-7.

NOTE A second edition, published in 1924, is no more than a reprint of this one.

Carnock

WEBSTER, J M 'The School'; *History of Carnock* (Edinburgh and London: William Blackwood and Sons, 1938), 155-79.
Fi

Cupar-Fife

ENDOWED SCHOOLS AND HOSPITALS (SCOTLAND) COMMISSION 'Baxter Institution, Cupar-Fife'; *Second Report* (1874), 389-391.

Madras Academy. A Present and Prospective View of the Pecuniary Affairs of the Trust, showing that the Carrying on of the Schools, on their present Footing, is incompatible with the Reduction and total liquidation of the existing Debt, at latest by Martinmas, 1847. Cupar-Fife: Printed in the *Fifeshire Journal* Office, 1840. 8vo. Pp 4.   Fi

—*Memorial for the Parents & Guardians of Children attending the Madras Academy, Cupar.* Cupar: Printed in the *Fifeshire Journal* Office, 1840. 8vo. Pp 15.   Fi

—*Particulars regarding the Foundation and Establishment of the Madras Academy of Cupar.* Cupar: Printed at the St Andrews University Press, 1832. 8vo. Pp 11.   Fi

ENDOWED SCHOOLS AND HOSPITALS (SCOTLAND) COMMISSION 'Cupar Madras Academy, Fife'; *Second Report* (1874), 392-404.

HARVEY, THOMAS, and SELLAR, ALEX C 'Cupar-Fife Madras Academy'; *Report on the State of Education in the Burgh and Middle-Class Schools in Scotland* (1868), 2, 85-90.

Dunfermline

CHALMERS, PETER 'Education'; *Historical and Statistical Account of Dunfermline* (Edinburgh and London: William Blackwood and Sons), **1** (1844), 437-47; **2** (1859), 370-1, 417-19.

'The Memorial and Petition of the Magistrates and Town Council of the Royal Burgh of Dunfermline'; *Inspectors of Schools (Scotland), 1841.* (Parliamentary Papers), 30-6.

DUNFERMLINE EDUCATION SOCIETY *Report.* np, 1842. 4to. Pp 4.   Df

GORRIE, D *The High School of Dunfermline.* Dunfermline: Printed by W Clark & Son, 1902. 8vo. Pp 36.   Ki

HARVEY, THOMAS, and SELLAR, ALEX C 'Dunfermline Burgh or Grammar School'; *Report on the State of Education in the Burgh and Middle-Class Schools in Scotland* (1868), **2**, 97-8.

Information for Mr George Brown, Schoolmaster at Dunfermline, pursuer, against the Heritors of the said Parish of Dunfermline, defenders. np, 1768. 4to. Pp 10.   Df

Information for the Earl of Elgin, and other Heritors of the Parish of Dunfermline; against George Brown, Master of the Grammar School of the Burgh of Dunfermline. np, 1768. 4to. Pp 10.   Df

JOHNSON, NORMAN M 'The Dunfermline Song School'; *SEJ*, 16 Jan 1942, **25**, 36.

WEBSTER, J M *The Song School in Dunfermline.* Typescript, [c 1953]. 4to. Pp 13.   Df

FEMALE INDUSTRIAL SCHOOL *Report.* np, 1863. 4to. Pp 3.   Df

Dysart

RICHMOND, JAMES *Lecture on Self-Improvement*, delivered on Saturday evening, 26th September 1840, in the Large Hall of the Dysart New School, for the Benefit of that Institution. Kirkcaldy: Printed for the Author by J Jeffers Wilson, 1840. 8vo. Pp 15.

L

Inverkeithing

STEPHEN, WILLIAM 'Education'; *History of Inverkeithing and Rosyth* (Aberdeen: G & W Fraser, 1921), 389-408.

Kinghorn

DAVIDSON, JOHN *Distribution of Classes and of Time, in Kinghorn School, February, 1835.* Kirkcaldy: Printed by J Birrell, 1835. Large folio. Pp 2.   Ki

Kirkcaldy

ENDOWED SCHOOLS AND HOSPITALS (SCOTLAND) COMMISSION 'Philp Bequest'; *Third Report* (1875), 127-31; *Appendix to Third Report* (1875), **1**, 128-37.

HARVEY, THOMAS, and SELLAR, ALEX C 'Kirkcaldy Burgh School'; *Report on the State of Education in the Burgh and Middle-Class Schools in Scotland* (1868), **2**, 91-4.

INNES, JOHN LOCKHART 'The High School of Kirkcaldy. An Historical Sketch'; *Educational Institute of Scotland Congress Handbook, 1909*, 29-46.   EIS

PHILP BEQUEST *Memorial and Queries, for the District Managers of Philp's Bequest.* Kirkcaldy: J Birrell, 1839. 8vo. Pp 8.   Fi

—*Trust-Disposition and Settlement.* Robert Philp, Esquire, of Edenhead, in favour of Trustees for the Purpose therein specified, dated 15th May, 1820. Recorded 23rd May, 1828. Edinburgh: M Anderson, nd. 8vo. Pp 23.   Fi

Leuchars

FORSYTH, WILLIAM S 'An Obstinate Dominie [Alexander Anderson, 1706-1732]'; *SEJ*, 4 Aug 1950, **33**, 507-8.

Newburn

ENDOWED SCHOOLS AND HOSPITALS (SCOTLAND) COMMISSION 'Wood's School, Newburn, by Largo, Fife'; *First Report* (1873), 762-6; *Appendix to Third Report* (1875), **2**, 294-5.

St Andrews

BACHE, ALEXANDER D 'Elementary Department of the Madras College at St Andrews'; *Report on Education in Europe* (1839), 194-6, and Appendix V.   EUL

ENDOWED SCHOOLS AND HOSPITALS (SCOTLAND) COMMISSION 'The Madras College of St. Andrews, St. Andrews, Fife'; *Second Report* (1874), 577-94.

HARVEY, THOMAS, and SELLAR, ALEX C 'Madras College, St Andrews'; *Report on the State of Education in the Burgh and Middle-Class Schools in Scotland* (1868), **2**, 63-84.

LYONS, CHARLES J 'Madras School'; *History of St Andrews, Episcopal, Monastic, Academic, and Civil* (Edinburgh: William Tait; Simpkin, Marshall, & Co, London; and John Cumming, Dublin, 1843), **2**, 213-20.

SALMOND, DAVID S 'The Madras College in 1855-7'; *Reminiscences of Arbroath and St Andrews* (Arbroath: Brodie and Salmond, 1905), 146-8.

SOUTH STREET ACADEMY *Prospectus*, 1863. Cupar-Fife: Printed at the *Fife Herald* Office, [1863]. 8vo. Pp 9.

WOODFORD, EDWARD 'Special Report on the Madras College and the Madras or Bell's Schools'; *Minutes of the Committee of Council on Education, 1855-56* (1856), 560-4.

Wemyss

GRUB, JOHN *Orations on various subjects*, by Mr John Grub, late Schoolmaster of the Parish of Wemyss, in Fifeshire, as performed by his scholars after the usual Examination on Harvest Vacation Days, and on Shrove Tuesdays, in place of Cockfighting. These Orations for the use of Grammar-Schools on the above days, are published by Mr Robert Wilson of Sylvania, near Dunfermline. Edinburgh: Printed for the Editor, 1794. 12mo. Pp 287.

THE HIGHLANDS AND ISLANDS

ANDERSON, JOHN 'Education'; *On the State of Society and Knowledge in the High-lands of Scotland, particularly in the Northern Counties, at the period of the Rebellion in 1745, and of their Progress up to 1825* (Edinburgh: Printed for William Tait; and Charles Tait, London, 1827), 106-18.

ARKLEY, PATRICK *Letter to the Reverend Alexander Beith, Stirling*, one of the Secretaries of the Gaelic School Society, on the Recent Decision of the Committee of that Society. Edinburgh: Thomas Paton; Smith & Son, Glasgow; A Brown & Co, Aberdeen; J Dewar, Perth; W Peddie, Stirling; Smith & Co, Montrose, 1846. 8vo. Pp 31.

BEATON, ANGUS JOHN 'Education'; *Social and Economic Condition of the Highlands of Scotland since 1800* (Stirling: Eneas Mackay, 1906), 42-5.

BEITH, ALEXANDER *Letter to Patrick Arkley, Esq., Advocate*, in reply to a Letter addressed to him to Rev. Alexander Beith, Stirling, one of the Secretaries of the Gaelic School Society, on the recent Decision of the Committee of that Society. Edinburgh: W P Kennedy; Glasgow: D Bryce; Stirling: J Shearer; Ayr: D Guthrie; Dundee: W Middleton; Perth: J Dewar & Son; Aberdeen: C Panton, 1846. 8vo. Pp 14.   EUL

BOYD, JOHN 'Historical Notes on Education in the Highlands'; *Transactions of the Gaelic Society of Glasgow*, **1**, 1887-1889 (Glasgow, 1892), 120-6.

CELTIC SOCIETY *Objects and Regulations*, with Copies of several of the Reports of the Distribution of the Society's Prizes for 1832-3-4. Edinburgh: Printed at the University Press, 1834. 8vo. Pp 43.
    EUL

CHURCH OF SCOTLAND *Extracts from Reports of the Ministers of Parishes in some Synods of Scotland, made in 1818 and 1819, as to Parochial Schools*. Edinburgh, 1824. 8vo. Pp viii, 36, 6.   EUL

—*Statement as to the Want of Schools and Catechists in the Highlands and Islands*. By a Committee of the General Assembly of the Church of Scotland. Edinburgh: Printed by Duncan Stevenson, 1825. 8vo. Pp 7.   EUL

—EDUCATION COMMITTEE OF THE GENERAL ASSEMBLY 'Correspondence relative to

certain Articles in the Revised Code';
Report, 1863, 26-8. New Coll

— —, 'General Observations on the Present
Means of Education, and of Religious
Instruction in the Western Islands';
Abstract of Report, 1828, 35-9.
New Coll

COUCHERON, P J B *Beretning om Almueskole-
vaesenets Ordining in Skottlands Sprog-
distrikter.* [Report on the Organisation
of the Elementary School System in the
Bilingual Districts of Scotland.] Kristi-
ania, 1866. Not seen

DUNDEE AUXILIARY GAELIC SCHOOL SOCIETY
Third and Fourth Annual Reports. Dun-
dee: Printed by Colville, 1820-1. 8vo.
DPL
Third Report—pp 7 *Fourth Report*—pp 8
—*Sixth, seventh, eighth, and eleventh
Annual Reports.* Dundee: James Chal-
mers, 1823-5, 1828. 8vo. Each pp 8.
DPL

EDUCATION COMMISSION (SCOTLAND) 'The
Hebrides and Western Highlands'; *Sec-
ond Report* (1867), lxiii-lxxxvi.
PP, 1867, xxv, [3845]

'Education in the Highlands and Islands of
Scotland'; *Quarterly J of Education*,
July-Oct 1831, **2**, 227-42.

EWART, HUGH J 'Education in the Highlands
during the Eighteenth Century'; *SEJ*,
23 July 1937, **20**, 958-9; 30 July 1937, **20**,
986-7; 6 Aug 1937, **20**, 1006-7; 13 Aug
1937, **20**, 1026-7.

FULLARTON, ALLAN, and BAIRD, CHARLES R
'Increased Means of Education'; *Re-
marks on the Evils at present affecting the
Highlands and Islands of Scotland; with
some Suggestions as to their Remedies*
(Glasgow: William Collins; Oliver &
Boyd, W Whyte & Co, and W Oliphant
& Son, Edinburgh; William Curry, Jun
& Co, Dublin; James Nisbet & Co and
Hamilton, Adams, & Co, London, 1838),
71-6.

GAELIC SCHOOL SOCIETY *Appeal for Funds.*
np, nd [1871]. 8vo. Pp 3.

'Highland Schools Two Hundred Years
Ago'; *SHR*, Oct 1918, **16** (1919), 88.

INVERNESS SOCIETY FOR THE EDUCATION OF
THE POOR IN THE HIGHLANDS *Moral
Statistics of the Highlands and Islands of*
Scotland: to which is prefixed, a Report,
on the Past and Present State of Educa-
tion in these Districts. Inverness: Printed
for the Education Society, 1826. 8vo.
Pp 73, xlviii.

KENNEDY, JOHN 'Schools and Schoolmasters'; *Old Highland Days. The
Reminiscences of Dr John Kennedy*
(London: The Religious Tract Society,
1901), 27-31.

LADIES' ASSOCIATION IN SUPPORT OF GAELIC
SCHOOLS IN CONNECTION WITH THE
CHURCH OF SCOTLAND. Instituted in
1846. *First Report.* 1847. Edinburgh:
Printed by Stark and Company, 1847.
8vo. Pp 28. New Coll

MACDONALD, KENNETH 'Education'; *Social
and Religious Life in the Highlands*
(Edinburgh: R W Hunter, 1902), 186-96.

MACINNES, JOHN 'Highland Schools and
Schoolmasters: Their Achievement and
its Significance, 1688-1800'; *The Evan-
gelical Movement in the Highlands of
Scotland, 1688-1800* (Aberdeen: The
University Press, 1951), 221-61.

MACKAY, WILLIAM *Education in the Highlands in the Olden Times.* Inverness:
Printed at the *Northern Chronicle* Office,
1921. 12mo. Pp 44.
Reprinted with additions from the *Celtic
Mag*, June 1888, **13**, 360-7, and July 1888,
13, 402-12. It had originally appeared in
the *Educ News*, 2 June 1883, **8**, 351-2, and
9 June 1883, **8**, 371-2. It was also printed
in MACKAY, WILLIAM *Sidelights on Highland History* (Inverness, 1925), 109-39.

—'Old Highland Schools and Schoolmasters'; *Educ News*, 30 June 1888, **13**,
448.

—*Records of the Presbyteries of Inverness
and Dingwall, 1643-1688.* Publications of
the Scottish History Society, **24** (1896).
For references to schools and schoolmasters, and to the education of 'Irish'
boys, see Index.

MACKENZIE, SIR KENNETH S, Bart 'Education
in the Highlands'; *Educ News*, 3 Dec
1887, **12**, 847-8.

MACKENZIE, WILLIAM C 'Education'; *History
of the Outer Hebrides* (Paisley: Alexander
Gardner, 1903), 529-33.

MACKINNON, DONALD 'The Church and Education in Argyll and the Isles, 1560-1709'; *SSTA Mag*, Feb 1954, **8**, 42-3; June 1854, **8**, 12-14.

MACLEAN, MAGNUS 'The Historical Development of the Different Systems of Education in the Highlands'; *Proceedings of the Royal Philosophical Society of Glasgow*, **xxxv**, 1903-1904 (1904), 63-81.

Reprinted in *The Old Highlands, being Papers read before the Gaelic Society of Glasgow, 1895-1906* (Glasgow: Alexander Sinclair, 1908), 169-99.

M'NISH, NEIL *The True Method of Preserving the Gaelic Language*. Glasgow: Printed by D McLure and Co for George A Douglass, Edinburgh, 1828. 8vo. Pp 72.

MACRAE, DONALD 'Gaelic Teaching in Highland Schools'; *Transactions of the Gaelic Society of Inverness*, **3** and **4**, 1873-4 and 1874-5 (1875), 136-8.

—'The State of Education in the Western Highlands'; *Transactions of the Gaelic Society of Inverness*, **3** and **4**, 1873-4 and 1874-5 (1875), 61-6.

MASSON, DAVID 'The Church and Education in the Highlands'; *Transactions of the Gaelic Society of Inverness*, **16**, 1889-90 (1891), 8-26.

MILLAR, A H *Scottish Forfeited Estate Papers, 1715; 1745*. Edinburgh: Publications of the Scottish History Society, **57** (1909).

The estates covered are those of Simon, Lord Fraser of Lovat, and Alexander Robertson of Struan.

MITCHELL, ALEXANDER F *General Assembly Commission Records, 1648 and 1649*. Edinburgh: Publications of the Scottish History Society, **25** (1896).

There are several references to the education of 'Irish' boys.

NICOLSON, ALEXANDER *Report on the State of Education in the Hebrides*. Edinburgh: HMSO, 1866. Fol. Pp 200. *PP*, 1867, xxv, [3485-IV].

Proposal for Civilising the Highlands, by erecting of Schools there; and providing of Ministers to be sent thither: with some Reasons perswading thereunto. np, nd [?1695]. Fol. Pp 2.

R, D 'Thoughts on the Beneficial Effects of Gaelic Schools, and on the Present State of Religion in the Isle of Skye'; *Edinburgh Christian Instructor*, May 1817, **14**, 281-7.

RAMSAY, JOHN *A Letter to the Right Honourable the Lord Advocate for Scotland, on the State of Education in the Outer Hebrides in 1862*. Glasgow: Printed by William Gilchrist, 1863. 8vo. Pp 17.

RELIGIOUS INSTRUCTION (SCOTLAND) COMMISSION 'Digest of the Evidence taken regarding each of those Parishes in the following Presbyteries, in which a Deficiency in the Opportunities of Public Religious Worship, and the Means of Religious Instruction and Pastoral Superintendence, is alleged to exist:—The presbyteries of Islay and Jura, Lorn, Mull, Skye, Uist, Lewis, Lochcarron, Dornoch, Tongue, Caithness, Tain, and Dingwall'. *Fourth Report*, Appendix I, 1-313.   *PP*, 1837/38, xxxiii, 122

School Endowment Scheme—Proposed Reenactment of the Test Acts against Dissenters. np, nd [?1838]. 12mo. Pp 8.   New Coll

SCHOOLS (SCOTLAND) Proceedings taken by the Lords of the Treasury for carrying into effect an Act of the 1st & 2d Victoria, c. 87. 'For facilitating the Foundation and Endowment of Additional Schools in Scotland', showing the Schools endowed, and the money invested, for the purpose of carrying the Provisions of the Act into effect. Fol. Pp 14.

PP, 1840, xl, 382

—*An Account of Schools in the Highlands and Islands of Scotland, endowed under the Provisions of the Act 1 & 2 Victoria, cap. 87*. Fol. P 1.

PP, 1842, xxxiii, 543

SMITH, JOHN 'A Forgotten Chapter in Scottish Education'; *Broken Links in Scottish Education* (1913), 1-29.

SOCIETY FOR THE SUPPORT OF GAELIC SCHOOLS IN THE HIGHLANDS AND ISLANDS OF SCOTLAND *First Annual Report*. With an Appendix respecting the Present State of the Highlands and Islands of Scotland, &c. Edinburgh: Printed for the Society by A Balfour, 1811. 8vo. Pp viii, 52.

— —. The Second edition. To which are prefixed, The Proceedings of the Society from its Commencement. Edinburgh:

Printed for the Society by A Balfour, 1812. 8vo. Pp 72.   EUL

Annual Report—Third to Sixth. Edinburgh: Printed for the Society by A Balfour, 1813-1816. 8vo.

1813—pp viii, 55   1815—pp viii, 62
1814—pp viii, 79   1816—pp viii, 114

—*Seventh to Tenth.* Edinburgh: Printed for the Society by Balfour and Clarke, 1818-21. 8vo.

1818—pp viii, 56   1820—pp viii, 79
1819—pp viii, 70   1821—pp xii, 84
                    Map

—*Eleventh Annual Report.* Edinburgh: Printed for the Society by Abernethy & Walker, 1822. 8vo. Pp x, 71.

—*Twelfth Annual Report.* Edinburgh: Printed for the Society by Anderson & Bryce, 1823. 8vo. Pp 80.

—*Thirteenth Annual Report.* Edinburgh: Printed for the Society by T Colquhoun, 1824. 8vo. Pp 70.

—*Fourteenth, Fifteenth, Seventeenth to Nineteenth, Twenty-third to Thirtieth, and Thirty-second Annual Reports.* Edinburgh: Printed for the Society by James Walker, 1825, 1826, 1828-30, 1834-41, 1843. 8vo.

1825—pp x, 74   1836—pp 52
1826—pp viii, 68   1837—pp 82
1828—pp 85   1838—pp 54
1829—pp 82   1839—pp 50
1830—pp 82   1840—pp 55
1834—pp 68   1841—pp 43
1835—pp 72   1843—pp 60

—*Twentieth and Twenty-first Annual Reports.* Edinburgh: Printed for the Society by James Colston, 1831-2. 8vo.

1831—pp 80   1831—pp 72

—*Twenty-second Annual Report.* Edinburgh: Printed for the Society by Anderson & Bryce, 1833. 8vo. Pp 60.

—*Thirty-first Annual Report.* Edinburgh: Printed for the Society by Balfour and Jack, 1842. 8vo. Pp 56.

—*Thirty-third Annual Report.* Edinburgh: Printed for the Society by Murray and Gibb, 1844. 8vo. Pp 59.

—*The Teacher's Guide in Conducting the Gaelic Circulating Schools, particularly recommended to his constant Attention,* by the Committee of Management. Edinburgh: Printed for the Society by A Balfour, 1815. 8vo. Pp [4], 35.

—*A Report on the Objects of the Society,* and the Results obtained by its Schools, compiled by Henry Crawford. Edinburgh, 1817. 8vo. Pp 15.

U, C F 'Education in the Eighteenth Century'; *SEJ*, 14 Aug 1936, **19**, 1010.

WALLACE, THOMAS 'Education in the Highlands'; *Educ News*, 2 Jan 1904, **29**, 16-18.

INVERNESS-SHIRE

CHURCH OF SCOTLAND: EDUCATION COMMITTEE 'Statement as to the Schools at present on the Committee's Scheme, and which were taken over from the Inverness Education Committee'; *Report, 1847,* 21-5.   New Coll

Inverness

ANDERSON, PETER J *The Grammar School and Royal Academy of Inverness.* Inverness: Printed by Robt Carruthers & Sons, 1907. 8vo. Pp 30. Frontispiece and 3 plates.

BARRON, EVAN M 'An Old Inverness School'; *Transactions of the Inverness Scientific Society and Field Club, 1918-25,* **9**, 257-302.

—'Ewen MacLachlan and Inverness Royal Academy. A Famous Highland Controversy'; *Transactions of the Inverness Scientific Society and Field Club, 1906-1912,* **7**, 131-56.

ENDOWED SCHOOLS AND HOSPITALS (SCOTLAND) COMMISSION 'Inverness Royal Academy'; *Second Report* (1874), 495-502.

FEARON, DANIEL R 'The Royal Academy, Inverness'; *Schools Inquiry Commission Report* (1868), **6**, pt 5, 144-56.

GARNETT, THOMAS 'Inverness Academy'; *Observations on a Tour through the Highlands of Scotland* (London: T Cadell, Junior, & W Davies, 1800), **2**, 2-7.

HARVEY, THOMAS, and SELLAR, ALEX 'Inverness Academy'; *Report on the State of Education in the Burgh and Middle-Class Schools in Scotland* (1868), **2**, 291-9.

'Inverness Royal Academy'; *SSTA Mag,* June 1949, **3**, 19-25.

NICOL, JOHN INGLIS *Royal Academy. Report of a Committee.* Inverness: R Carruthers, 1834. 8vo. Pp 62.   Inv

Dr Bell's Educational Endowment to Inverness, with Trust Deed of Dr Andrew Bell. [Inverness], 1838. Fol. Pp 2.

Inv

FEARON, DANIEL R 'The High School, Inverness'; *Schools Inquiry Commission Report* (1868), **6**, pt 5, 205-8.

JOHNSTON, — *Announcement of the Opening of a new Private Academy.* Inverness, 1819. 4to. P 1.

Project to obtain Government Consent to a Charter, with Collegiate privileges for Inverness. May 22nd, 1848. Inverness, 1848.   Inv

Resolutions of a Committee, appointed by the County and Town of Inverness, for considering the present state of education in the Northern Counties. Inverness, 1787. 4to. P 1.

Appeal for Subscriptions towards the Establishment of a new Academy. Inverness, 1787. Fol. P 1.

Kiltarlity and Convinth

MACDONALD, ARCHIBALD 'Kiltarlity and Convinth; Church and Education'; *Proceedings of the Gaelic Society of Inverness, 1912-1914,* **28** (1918), 130-48.

Urquhart and Glenmoriston

MACKAY, WILLIAM 'Education and Culture in the Parish'; *Urquhart and Glenmoriston. Olden Times in a Highland Parish* (Inverness: Northern Counties Newspaper and Printing and Publishing Company, Limited, 1893), 393-416.
The second edition of 1914 is identical with this.

KINCARDINE
Banchory

PAUL, WILLIAM 'State of Education about Half a Century Ago, and its Present Improvements'; *Past and Present of Aberdeenshire, or, Reminiscences of Seventy Years* (Aberdeen: Lewis Smith & Son, 1881), 66-75.

— —. Second edition (Aberdeen: Lewis Smith & Son, 1881), 80-90.

Glenbervie

KINNEAR, GEORGE H 'Schools and Schoolmasters'; *History of Glenbervie,* second and improved edition (Laurencekirk: *Kincardineshire Observer* Office; Edinburgh and Glasgow: John Menzies and Co, Ltd, 1910), 97-108.
The first edition had been published at Montrose in 1895.

Laurencekirk

FRASER, WILLIAM R 'Schoolmasters' and 'Village Teachers'; *History of the Parish and Burgh of Laurencekirk* (Edinburgh and London: William Blackwood and Sons, 1880), 268-84.

KIRKCUDBRIGHT

RUSSELL, JAMES A *History of Education in the Stewartry of Kirkcudbright from Original and Contemporary Sources.* Newton-Stewart: The *Galloway Gazette* Press, 1951. 8vo. Pp [7], 182, 3 illustrations. Bibliography. Index.

Borgue

MCMASTER, MAXWELL 'The Academy, Borgue, Stewartry of Kirkcudbright'; *Scottish Educational and Literary J,* Jan 1854, **2**, 151-6.

Kelton

RUSSELL, JAMES A 'Earlier Education in the Parish of Kelton, Castle-Douglas'; *SEJ,* 2 Feb 1951, **34**, 70-2.

Kirkcudbright

ENDOWED SCHOOLS AND HOSPITALS (SCOTLAND) COMMISSION 'Kirkcudbright Academy'; *Second Report* (1874), 505-6.

HARVEY, THOMAS, and SELLAR, ALEX C 'Kirkcudbright Academy'; *Report on the State of Education in the Burgh and Middle-Class Schools in Scotland* (1868), **2**, 177-80.

ROBISON, J 'Kirkcudbright Schoolmasters in the late Sixteenth Century'; *SEJ*, 17 Apr 1942, **25**, 236.

RUSSELL, JAMES A 'Crisis in the Academy'; *SEJ*, 20 June 1958, **41**, 412.

Kirkpatrick-Durham

ENDOWED SCHOOLS AND HOSPITALS (SCOTLAND) COMMISSION 'Brooklands Institution'; *First Report* (1873), 758-61; *Appendix to Third Report* (1875), **1**, 108-9.

LANARKSHIRE

CLELAND, JAMES 'Salaries of the Parochial Schoolmasters in the Landward Parishes of Lanarkshire in 1831'; *Enumeration of the Inhabitants of the City of Glasgow and County of Lanark. For the Government Census of MDCCCXXXI* (Glasgow: John Smith & Son; Adam Black, Edinburgh; and Longman, Rees, Orme, Brown, Green, & Longman, London, 1832), 83.

GORDON, JOHN 'On the State of Education among the Mining Population of Lanarkshire'; *Transactions of the National Association for the Promotion of Social Science, 1860* (1861), 370-9.

Airdrie

GORDON, JOHN 'Report on Airdrie'; *Minutes of the Committee of Council on Education, 1845*, 437-40.

HARVEY, THOMAS, and SELLAR, ALEX C 'Airdrie Academy'; *Report on the State of Education in the Burgh and Middle-Class Schools in Scotland* (1868), **2**, 163-165.

KNOX, SIR JAMES 'Schools and Schoolmasters of the "Old Town" '; *Airdrie: A Historical Sketch* (Airdrie: Baird & Hamilton, 1921), 45-9.

—'Schools of last Century prior to 1872'; *Airdrie: A Historical Sketch* (1921), 112-116.

Blantyre

WRIGHT, STEWART 'Education'; *Annals of Blantyre* (Glasgow: Wilson & McCormick, 1885), 114-17.

Bothwell

BOTHWELL PARISH SCHOOL *Petitions and Memorials relating to the Bothwell Parish School Case*, presented to the Court of Session. Edinburgh, 1792-3. 8vo. Pp 221. GUL

Carluke

'Schools and Schoolmasters'; *Notices, Historical, Statistical and Biographical, relating to the Parish of Carluke, from 1288 to 1874* (Glasgow: William Rankin, 1874), 112-20. GUL

Coatbridge

MILLER, ANDREW 'Education'; *The Rise and Progress of Coatbridge* (Glasgow: David Robertson; London: Longman & Co, 1864), 43-7.

—'Mechanics' Institute'; *The Rise and Progress of Coatbridge* (1864), 80-1.

Dolphinton

ENDOWED SCHOOLS AND HOSPITALS (SCOTLAND) COMMISSION 'Dolphinton Parish Mortifications'; *Appendix to Third Report* (1875), **2**, 296-8.

Hamilton

ENDOWED SCHOOLS AND HOSPITALS (SCOTLAND) COMMISSION 'Hamilton Academy'; *Second Report* (1874), 491-4.

FEARON, DANIEL R 'The Academy, Hamilton'; *Schools Inquiry Commission Report* (1868), **6**, pt 5, 133-44.

HARVEY, THOMAS, and SELLAR, ALEX C 'Hamilton Academy'; *Report on the State of Education in the Burgh and Middle-Class Schools in Scotland* (1868), **2**, 254-61.

Lanark

COWAN, W A 'Schools'; *History of Lanark* (Lanark: Robert Wood, 1867), 52-60.

ENDOWED SCHOOLS AND HOSPITALS (SCOTLAND) COMMISSION 'Lanark Burgh School'; *Second Report* (1874), 514-15.

—'Lanark School Bursaries'; *Appendix to Third Report* (1875), **1**, 191-3.

HARVEY, THOMAS, and SELLAR, ALEX C 'Lanark Burgh School'; *Report on the State of Education in the Burgh and Middle-Class Schools in Scotland* (1868), **2**, 112-14.

R, A D 'Trouble in the Old School'; *SSTA Mag*, June 1955, **9**, 42-3.

Lesmahagow

GREENSHIELDS, JOHN B 'Educational Societies'; *Annals of the Parish of Lesmahagow* (Edinburgh: The Caledonian Press, 1864), 196-9.

Nemphlar

ROBINSON, JOHN 'The Biography of John Bell, Teacher, Nemphlar'; *Educ News*, 5 Feb 1876, **1**, 75-6; 4 Mar 1876, **1**, 125-6; 11 Mar 1876, **1**, 145.   EIS

New Lanark

CHURCH OF SCOTLAND: GENERAL ASSEMBLY 'Abstract Report of the Committee on the Examination of Schools. 1823. June 2. Act 9'; Pitcairn, *Acts of the General Assembly of the Church of Scotland, 1637-1842* (1842), 987-8.

COLE, MARGARET 'Principles of Education' and 'The Schools in Practice'; *Robert Owen of New Lanark* (1953), 71-90.

GRISCOM, JOHN 'New Lanark'; *A Year in Europe* (1823), 375-8.   BM
Reprinted in *Reports on European Education*, ed KNIGHT, EDGAR W (New York and London: McGraw-Hill Book Company, Inc, 1930), 90-3.

MACNAB, HENRY GREY *The New Views of Mr Owen of Lanark impartially examined: also Observations on the New Lanark School*. London: Printed for J Hatchard and Son, 1819. 8vo. Pp iv, 234.

OWEN, ROBERT *A New View of Society*: Essay Third. London: Printed for Cadell and Davies, 1813. 8vo. Pp 61.
EUL
Reprinted in OWEN, ROBERT *A New View of Society & Other Writings*, ed COLE, G D H (Everyman's Library, 1927), 39-62.

OWEN, ROBERT DALE *An Outline of the System of Education at New Lanark*. Glasgow: Printed at the University Press, for Wardlaw & Cunninghame, Glasgow: Bell & Bradfute, Edinburgh; and Longman, Hurst, Rees, Orme, Brown, & Green, London, 1824. 8vo. Pp 103.

R Owen at New Lanark. By One formerly a Teacher at New Lanark. Manchester: Printed by Cave and Sever, 1839. 8vo. Pp 16.   BM

Rutherglen

GRAY, GEORGE *The Burgh School of Rutherglen*. Printed for private circulation. [Rutherglen], 1891. 8vo. Pp vi, 107.

Shotts

ENDOWED SCHOOLS AND HOSPITALS (SCOTLAND) COMMISSION 'Wilson's Endowed Schools in the Parishes of Shotts and Cambusnethan'; *Appendix to Third Report* (1875), **2**, 299.

GROSSART, WILLIAM 'Schools and Schoolmasters'; *Historic Notices and Domestic History of the Parish of Shotts* (Glasgow: Printed by Aird & Coghill, 1880), 192-9.

Stonehouse

NAISMITH, ROBERT 'Education'; *Stonehouse: Historical and Traditional* (Glasgow: Robert Forrester, 1885), 82-4.

EAST LOTHIAN

GIBSON, JOHN 'Report on the State of Elementary Education in the Presbyteries of Haddington and Dunbar'; *Minutes of the Committee of Council on Education, 1841-42*, 93-100.

WITHRINGTON, D J 'Schools in the Presbytery of Haddington in the 17th Century'; *East Lothian Antiquarian and Field Naturalists' Society Transactions*, **9** (1963), 90-111.

Dunbar

1736. Geo II, c 4. An Act for confirming an Act passed in the Fifth Year of his late Majesty King George the First, intituled, An Act for Laying a Duty of Two Pennies Scots, or one sixth of a Penny Sterling, upon every Pint of Ale or Beer that shall be vended or sold within the Town of Dunbar, for . . . Building a School . . . there.

MILLER, JAMES 'The Schools'; *The History of Dunbar* (Dunbar: William Miller, 1830), 210-15; (Dunbar: James Downie, 1859), 220-6.

HARVEY, THOMAS, and SELLAR, ALEX C 'Dunbar Burgh School'; *Report on the State of Education in the Burgh and Middle-Class Schools in Scotland* (1868), 2, 157-9.

Haddington

BROWN, SAMUEL (*Amended*) *Statement laid before the Committee of the Council, appointed to report on the future Arrangements of Haddington Schools.* np [?Haddington], nd [?1837]. 8vo. Pp 8.

ENDOWED SCHOOLS AND HOSPITALS (SCOTLAND) COMMISSION 'Haddington Burgh Schools'; *Second Report* (1874), 490.

GRAY, WILLIAM FORBES, and JAMIESON, JAMES H 'Schools and Schoolmasters'; *A Short History of Haddington* (Edinburgh: Printed for the East Lothian Antiquarian and Field Naturalists' Society by Neill and Company, Limited, 1944), 128-38.

HARVEY, THOMAS, and SELLAR, ALEX C 'Haddington Burgh School'; *Report on the State of Education in the Burgh and Middle-Class Schools in Scotland* (1868), 2, 138-42.

MARTINE, JOHN 'Haddington Burgh Schools'; *Reminiscences of the Royal Burgh of Haddington* (Edinburgh and Glasgow: John Menzies & Co, 1883), 181-91.

MILLER, JAMES 'Early Scholars and Schoolmasters'; *The Lamp of Lothian; or, The History of Haddington from the Earliest Records to the Present Period* (Haddington: James Allan, 1844), 443-460.

— —, new edition (Haddington: William Sinclair, 1900), 193-8.

Suggestions for Organising the Haddington Burgh Schools. np [?Haddington], nd [?1838]. 8vo. Pp 8.

MARTINE, JOHN 'Haddington Old Sunday School'; *Reminiscences of the Royal Burgh of Haddington* (1883), 206-13.

Morham

LOUDEN, DAVID 'Morham School—Personal'; *History of Morham* (Haddington: Wm Sinclair; Edinburgh: J Menzies & Co, 1889), 15-23.

North Berwick

HARVEY, THOMAS, and SELLAR, ALEX C 'North Berwick School'; *Report on the State of Education in the Burgh and Middle-Class Schools in Scotland* (1868), 2, 151-2.

Prestonpans

ARBUCKLE, SIR WILLIAM F 'School Exercises of the 17th Century from Prestonpans'; *East Lothian Antiquarian and Field Naturalists' Society—Transactions,* 10 (1967), 1-17.

MCCRIE, THOMAS 'Grammar School of Prestonpans'; *Life of Andrew Melville* (Edinburgh: William Blackwood; and T Cadell and W D Davies, London, 1819). 2, 503-5.

— —, the second edition (Edinburgh: William Blackwood; and T Cadell, London, 1824), 2, 509-11.

Copies of Deeds relative to the institution of an Hospital for the Maintenance and Education, &c. &c. of Poor Boys. Endowed by the deceased James Schaw, Esq. of Preston. np; Printed by Order of his Trustees, nd [?1788]. 4to. Pp 30.
EUL

ENDOWED SCHOOLS AND HOSPITALS (SCOTLAND) COMMISSION 'James Schaw's Hospital, Parish of Prestonpans'; *First Report* (1873), 688-92; *Appendix to Third Report* (1875), 1, 73-7.

Saltoun

ENDOWED SCHOOLS AND HOSPITALS (SCOTLAND) COMMISSION 'Burnett Bequest'; *Appendix to Third Report* (1875), 1, 226-233.

Tranent

ENDOWED SCHOOLS AND HOSPITALS (SCOT-
LAND) COMMISSION 'Stiell's Hospital';
First Report (1873), 679-87; *Appendix to
Third Report* (1875), **1**, 70-2.

MCNEILL, PETER 'Educational'; *Tranent and
its Surroundings* (Edinburgh & Glasgow:
John Menzies & Co; Tranent: Peter
McNeill, 1883), 81-5.

—— ——, second edition (1884), 99-102.

SANDS, JOHN 'Stiell's Charity School';
Sketches of Tranent in the Olden Time
(Edinburgh: Printed for the Author by
James Hogg, 1881), 91-102.

MIDLOTHIAN
Cranstoun

DICKSON, JOHN 'Educational'; *Cranstoun:
A Parish History* (Anstruther: Privately
printed for the Author by C S Russell,
1907), 110-26.

Crichton

DICKSON, JOHN 'The Educational Story';
*Crichtoun: Past and Present. The Story
of the Parish* (Edinburgh: Andrew Elliot,
1911), 87-97.

Currie and Glencorse

ENDOWED SCHOOLS AND HOSPITALS (SCOT-
LAND) COMMISSION 'Charles Smith's Mortification'; *Appendix to Third Report*
(1875), **1**, 223-5.

Lasswade

MARTIN, HUGH Village Lecture on Scientific
Education. Delivered at the Opening of
the Lasswade and District Science School
on 19th October, 1871. Edinburgh:
John Maclaren, 1871. 8vo. Pp 19.
EUL

Mid-Calder

MCCALL, HARDY BERTRAM 'The Grammar
School'; *History and Antiquities of the
Parish of Mid-Calder* (Edinburgh:
Richard Cameron, 1894), 34-6.

PAUL, SIR JAMES BALFOUR 'Thomas Mudie
and his Mortifications'; *SHR*, July 1917,
14, 310-20.

Musselburgh

HARVEY, THOMAS, and SELLAR, ALEX C
'Musselburgh Grammar School'; *Report
on the State of Education in the Burgh and
Middle-Class Schools in Scotland* (1868),
2, 130-4.

PATERSON, JAMES 'Schools and Education';
History of the Regality of Musselburgh
(Musselburgh: James Gordon, 1857),
71-8.

Loretto's Hundred Years, 1827-1927. London: Thomas de la Rue & Co, Ltd, 1928.
4to. Pp xi, 186. Frontispiece and 14
plates.

TRISTRAM, HENRY B *Loretto School: Past and
Present*. With twelve illustrations. London: T Fisher Unwin, 1911. 8vo. Pp
320. Index.

Newbattle

CARRICK, JOHN CHARLES 'The Schools of
Newbattle'; *The Abbey of St Mary,
Newbattle*, second edition (Selkirk:
George Lewis; Edinburgh: John Men-
zies & Co, 1908), 342-4.

NOTE A third edition, identical with this,
was published in the same year. The
section on the schools does not appear in
the first edition.

Newton

ENDOWED SCHOOLS AND HOSPITALS (SCOT-
LAND) COMMISSION 'Parish of Newton
Mortifications'; *Appendix to Third Re-
port* (1875), **2**, 287-8.

MACBETH, JOHN *The Story of a Scottish
Country School*. An Outline of Reader-
Precentor and Schoolmaster (for three
centuries) in the Parish of Newton,
Dalkeith. Dalkeith: Printed by P & D
Lyle, 1915. 8vo. Pp 41. 5 plates.

Penicuik

WILSON, JOHN JAMES 'Education'; *The
Annals of Penicuik* (Edinburgh: Pri-

vately printed by T & A Constable, 1891), 54-60.

WEST LOTHIAN
Abercorn

WHYTE, DONALD 'Schoolmasters of Abercorn Parish, 1646-1872'; *Scottish Genealogist*, Mar 1968, **15**, 7-14.

Bathgate

DAVIDSON, THOMAS *Bathgate Academy, 1833-1933*. Bathgate: The West Lothian Printing and Publishing Company, Ltd, 1933. 8vo. Pp 95. 17 illustrations.

STAUL

ENDOWED SCHOOLS AND HOSPITALS (SCOTLAND) COMMISSION 'Bathgate Academy'; *Second Report* (1874), 362-5.

GRAHAM, DAVID 'The Academy'; *John Newland: An Account of the Founder of Bathgate Academy* (Arbroath: Brodie & Salmond, 1901), 87-100.

Bo'ness

SALMON, THOMAS J 'Educational'; *Borrowstounness and District* (Edinburgh and London: William Hodge & Company, 1913), 412-18.

Linlithgow

ENDOWED SCHOOLS AND HOSPITALS (SCOTLAND) COMMISSION 'Linlithgow Grammar School'; *Second Report* (1874), 524-5.

HARVEY, THOMAS, and SELLAR, ALEX C 'Linlithgow Burgh School'; *Report on the State of Education in the Burgh and Middle-Class Schools in Scotland* (1868), **2**, 115-18.

KIRKWOOD, JAMES (1) See pp 70, 182.

South Queensferry

ENDOWED SCHOOLS AND HOSPITALS (SCOTLAND) COMMISSION 'The Wilson Trust'; *Appendix to Third Report* (1875), **2**, 300.

Whitburn

ENDOWED SCHOOLS AND HOSPITALS (SCOTLAND) COMMISSION 'Wilson's Endowed Schools in the Parish of Whitburn (Linlithgow) and Shotts and Cambusnethan (Lanarkshire)'; *Appendix to Third Report* (1875), **2**, 299.

MORAY

DICK BEQUEST See ABERDEENSHIRE.

MURRAY, (MISS) A S *Education in the Province of Moray in Former Days*. Reprinted from the Elgin *Courant and Courier*, 8th, 15th and 22nd November, 1929. np [?Elgin], nd [?1929]. 8vo. Pp 23.

Elgin

'Contracts between the Town Council and Masters of the Grammar School, 1566-1785'; *The Records of Elgin, 1234-1800* (Aberdeen: Printed for the New Spalding Club), **2** (1908), 395-403.

CRAMOND, WILLIAM 'The School, 1652-1795'; *Records of Elgin, 1234-1800*, **2** (1908), 404-50.

ELGIN INSTITUTION *Statutes and Regulations of the Elgin Institution*, for Support of Old Age, and the Education of Youth. Elgin: Printed by A C Brander, 1834. 8vo. Pp 23.   AUL

—*Statutes and Regulations of the Elgin Institution for the Support of Old Age and the Education of Youth*, founded under the Trust Disposition and Settlement, dated 23rd November, 1815, of Major-General Andrew Anderson, H.E.I.C.S. Elgin: Printed at the *Courant* Office, 1865. 8vo. Pp 30.   AUL

ENDOWED SCHOOLS AND HOSPITALS (SCOTLAND) COMMISSION 'Elgin Academy'; *Second Report* (1874), 449-52.

—'The Elgin Institution'; *First Report* (1873), 742-50; *Appendix to Third Report* (1875), **1**, 98-105.

HARVEY, THOMAS, and SELLAR, ALEX C 'Elgin Academy'; *Report on the State of Education in the Burgh and Middle-Class Schools in Scotland* (1868), **2**, 8-12.

Fochabers

6 & 7 Vict, c lxxxvii. An Act to incorporate the Directors of Milne's Free School

in the Town of Fochabers, and for the better Government thereof.
(Local Act, 1843)

ENDOWED SCHOOLS AND HOSPITALS (SCOTLAND) COMMISSION 'Milne's Free School, Bellie, Morayshire'; *Second Report* (1874), 453-9.

GORDON, JOHN 'Report on Milne's Free School, Fochabers'; *Minutes of the Committee of Council on Education, 1848-49-50* (1850), **2**, 566-70.

HARVEY, THOMAS, and SELLAR, ALEX C 'Milne's Institution, Fochabers'; *Report on the State of Education in the Burgh and Middle-Class Schools in Scotland* (1868), **2**, 13-15.

OGILVIE, JOSEPH *Fochabers revisited, and some Recollections of Milne's Institute.* By an Old Boy. Reprinted from *Milne's Institute Mag*, Jan 1912, **1**, no 1. np, [1912]. 8vo. Pp 7.   AUL

SUTHERLAND, DAVID J S 'The History of Milne's Institution, Fochabers'; *SEJ*, 23 Aug 1946, **29**, 464-5; 30 Aug 1946, **29**, 480-1; 6 Sept 1946, **29**, 492-3.

Forres

ENDOWED SCHOOLS AND HOSPITALS (SCOTLAND) COMMISSION 'Forres Academy'; *Second Report* (1874), 465-8.

—'Burgh of Forres Mortifications'; *Appendix to Third Report* (1875), **2**, 289-90.

HARVEY, THOMAS, and SELLAR, ALEX C 'Forres Academy'; *Report on the State of Education in the Burgh and Middle-Class Schools in Scotland* (1868), **2**, 5-7.

RITCHIE, JAMES B *Forres: Its Schools and Schoolmasters,* A Record of Three Hundred Years. np, 1926. 8vo. Pp 117.
EIS

Grantown-on-Spey

ENDOWED SCHOOLS AND HOSPITALS (SCOTLAND) COMMISSION 'Speyside Charity School (or Hospital)'; *First Report* (1873), 767-9; *Appendix to Third Report* (1875), **1**, 110.

NAIRN

ENDOWED SCHOOLS AND HOSPITALS (SCOTLAND) COMMISSION 'Rose's Academical Institution, Nairn'; *Second Report* (1874), 532-4.

'Secondary Schools in Nairn'; *Educational Institute of Scotland Congress Handbook, 1933*, 101-8.

Invera'an

DUNNETT, HAMILTON 'Education in Invera'an'; *Invera'an, A Strathspey Parish* (Paisley: Alexander Gardner, 1919), 83-94.

ORKNEY

CHURCH OF SCOTLAND: EDUCATION COMMITTEE 'Report on the State of Education in Orkney'; *Report, 1853*, 36-54.
New Coll

LAMB, G A W *Education in Orkney before 1800.* EdB thesis, Aberdeen, 1962. Typescript. 4to. Pp [5], 94.   AUL
Printed in *The Orcadian* (Kirkwall), 26 Apr; 3, 17, and 31 May; 14, 21, and 28 June; 19 July; 2 and 9 Aug, and 13 Sept, 1962.

RAMSAY, GEORGE G 'Report on the Local Educational Circumstances of Orkney and Shetland'; *First Annual Report of the Board of Education for Scotland, 1874*, 94-105.

WOODFORD, EDWARD 'Operation of Privy Council Minutes in Certain Districts'; *Minutes of the Committee of Council on Education, 1856-57* (1857), 621-5.

Cairston

POGUE, VICTOR C 'Schools in the Cairston Presbytery in the Eighteenth Century'; *Orkney Miscellany, being Orkney Record and Antiquarian Society Papers* (Kirkwall, 1956), 47-67.   Mo

Kirkwall

HARVEY, THOMAS, and SELLAR, ALEX C 'Kirkwall Grammar School'; *Report on The State of Education in the Burgh and Middle-Class Schools in Scotland* (1868), **2**, 300-3.

HOSSACK, B H 'The Grammar School'; *Kirkwall in the Orkneys* (Kirkwall: William Peace & Son, 1900), 261-78.

MOONEY, JOHN 'Old Grammar School'; *The Cathedral and Royal Burgh of Kirkwall* (Kirkwall: W R Mackintosh, 1943), 137-40.
The 1947 reprint of this work is an exact copy of this edition.

PEEBLESSHIRE
Broughton

BAIRD, ANDREW 'Schools and Schoolmasters'; *The Annals of a Tweeddale Parish* (Glasgow: John Smith & Son (Glasgow) Ltd, 1924), 167-72.

Peebles

ENDOWED SCHOOLS AND HOSPITALS (SCOTLAND) COMMISSION 'Burgh Grammar School, Peebles'; *Second Report* (1874), 560-1.

HARVEY, THOMAS, and SELLAR, ALEX C 'Peebles Grammar and English School'; *Report on the State of Education in the Burgh and Middle-Class Schools in Scotland* (1868), **2**, 146-50.

PENDLE, GEORGE 'A Peebles Schoolmaster of the Seventeenth Century'; *Scottish Notes and Queries*, third series, Aug 1928, **6**, 152-3.

'Schoolmasters in the Olden Times'; *Educ News*, 3 June 1876, **1**, 289-90; 29 July 1876, **1**, 384-5; 26 Aug 1876, **1**, 437; 19 May 1877, **2**, 241; 2 June 1877, **2**, 265.
EIS

PERTHSHIRE
Breadalbane

GILLIES, WILLIAM A 'Schools and Schoolmasters'; *In Famed Breadalbane* (Perth: The Munro Press Ltd, 1938), 324-35.

Callander

CUMMING, ALEXANDER D *A History of Education in the Parish of Callander for Four Centuries*. Callander: D Ferguson, 1908. 8vo. Pp 24. EUL

Crieff

ENDOWED SCHOOLS AND HOSPITALS (SCOTLAND) COMMISSION 'Morrison's Academy'; *Second Report* (1874), 379-88.

PORTEOUS, ALEXANDER 'Schools and Schoolmasters'; *History of Crieff from the Earliest Times to the Dawn of the Twentieth Century* (Edinburgh and London: Oliphant, Anderson & Ferrier, 1912), 191-204.

Dunkeld

STEWART, ELIZABETH 'Schools and Education'; *Dunkeld: An Ancient City* (Perth: The Munro Press, Limited, 1926), 60-8. Pe

ENDOWED SCHOOLS AND HOSPITALS (SCOTLAND) COMMISSION 'Bishopric Rents of Dunkeld'; *Appendix to Third Report* (1875), **2**, 301-3.

Fortingall

STEWART, ALEXANDER 'Schools and Schoolmasters'; *A Highland Parish, or, The History of Fortingall* (Glasgow: Alex MacLaren & Sons, 1928), 252-68.

Glenalmond

ANDERSON, JOHN 'Trinity College, Glenalmond'; *Illustrations*, Oct 1888, **4**, 19-21.

Deed of Constitution of the Council of Trinity College, Glenalmond, Perthshire. Edinburgh: Printed by John Goldie and Co, 1845. 8vo. Pp 16. GUL

Jubilee of Trinity College, Glenalmond. Reprinted from *Perthshire Advertiser.* Perth: Printed by Cowan and Co, Limited, 1891. 8vo. Pp 15. Pe

LYTTEL, E S *Trinity College, Glenalmond.* Illustrated by E S Lyttel. Richmond: Morgan & Kidd, 1903. 8vo. Pp [4], 16. Frontispiece and 42 photographs. Pe

'Trinity College, Glenalmond'; *Public School Mag*, Apr 1901, **7**, 241-50.

HARVEY, THOMAS, and SELLAR, ALEX C 'Trinity College, Glenalmond'; *Report on the State of Education in the Burgh and Middle-Class Schools in Scotland* (1868), **2**, 241-53.

WRIGHT-HENDERSON, PATRICK A 'A Highland School Sixty Years Ago'; *Glasgow & Balliol and other Essays* (London: Humphrey Milford, 1926), 125-45.

Perth

CALDERWOOD, ALAN H R *Education in Perth.* A Study of the Development of Educational Facilities in the City and Royal Burgh of Perth. Unpublished EdB thesis, St Andrews University, 1955. Typescript. 4to. Pp [2], iii, 164, [8]. Bibliography. 2 maps.   DUL

ENDOWED SCHOOLS AND HOSPITALS (SCOTLAND) COMMISSION 'King James VI Hospital, Perth'; *Appendix to Third Report* (1875), **1**, 187-8.

—'The "Seymour Munro Free School", Perth'; *Appendix to Third Report* (1875), **2**, 312-13.

FEARON, DANIEL R 'The Sharp Institution, Perth'; *Schools Inquiry Commission Report* (1868), **6**, pt 5, 208-10.

GORDON, JOHN 'Report on Sessional Schools in Edinburgh, Glasgow, Aberdeen, Dundee and Perth'; *Minutes of the Committee of Council on Education, 1848-49-50* (1850), **2**, 570-605.

'Objections to Inspection of Schools'; *Inspectors of Schools (Scotland), 1841* (1841), 36-9.

PEACOCK, DAVID 'Educational Institutions'; *Perth: Its Annals and its Archives* (Perth: Thomas Richardson, 1849), 524-8.

PERTH RAGGED SCHOOL FARM *First Report.* Perth: Printed by James Dewar and Son, 1850. 8vo. Pp 11.   Pe

PERTH MECHANICS' INSTITUTION *Second Report.* Perth: Printed for the Institution by J Taylor. 12mo. Pp 36.   Pe

SMART, EDWARD 'Music—The Sang School'; *History of Perth Academy* (1932), 131-5.

—'Sharp's Institution, 1860-1915'; *History of Perth Academy* (1932), 204-26.

Report of Speeches delivered at the Formation of the Perth Anderson Institution, at a Public Meeting of the Inhabitants, held on Wednesday, 17th February, 1847. Perth: Printed for the Directors by J & W Bayne, 1847. 8vo. Pp 36.   Pe

Perth Academy

A, A 'On the Perth Academy'; in RUSSELL, MICHAEL *View of the System of Education at Present pursued in the Schools and Universities of Scotland* (1813), Appendix, xliv-xlix.

ENDOWED SCHOOLS AND HOSPITALS (SCOTLAND) COMMISSION 'Perth Academy and Grammar School'; *Second Report* (1874), 562-8.

FEARON, DANIEL R 'Perth Academy and Grammar School'; *Schools Inquiry Commission Report* (1868), **6**, pt 5, 163-9.

GARNETT, THOMAS 'Perth Grammar School' and 'Perth Academy'; *Observations on a Tour through the Highlands of Scotland* (London: T Cadell, Junior, & W Davies, 1800), **2**, 100-3.

HARVEY, THOMAS, and SELLAR, ALEX C 'Perth Academy'; *Report on the State of Education in the Burgh and Middle-Class Schools in Scotland* (1868), **2**, 233-40.

LORIMER, JAMES 'The Burgh Schools of Scotland half a century ago'; *The Museum*, new series, 1 Oct 1864, **1**, 258-9.

MILLER, THOMAS 'Scotch Burgh Schools'; *The Museum*, new series, 1 Nov 1864, **1**, 298.

SMART, EDWARD *History of Perth Academy.* Perth: Milne, Tannahill, & Methven, 1932. 8vo. Pp viii, 271. Index. 2 plates.

STEELE, WILLIAM D 'Perth Academy'; *The Museum*, new series, 1 Nov 1864, **1**, 299.

SUTHERLAND, DAVID J S 'Some Old School Notebooks written a century ago'; *SEJ*, 13 Jan 1939, **22**, 42-3.

Pitlochry

SUTHERLAND, DAVID J S 'The History of Education in Pitlochry District'; *SEJ*, 20 Aug 1948, **31**, 468-70.

RENFREWSHIRE
Eastwood

REED, WILLIAM *A Short Account of the Domestic Treatment of the Pupils, and of the Plan of Education, at the Academy at Eastwood,* near Glasgow. Glasgow: Printed by J Scrymgeour, at the University Press, 1806. 8vo. Pp 15.   GUL

Greenock

DENNISTON, ARCHIBALD *Remarks on Education in Greenock*, contained in Letters to the Editor of the *Greenock Advertiser*. By Civilis. Greenock: Andrew Laing, 1847. 8vo. Pp 28.   New Coll

ENDOWED SCHOOLS AND HOSPITALS (SCOTLAND) COMMISSION 'Scott Institution or Town of Greenock Hospital'; *First Report* (1873), 738-41; *Appendix to Third Report* (1875), **1**, 97.

—'Greenock Academy'; *Second Report* (1874), 482-9.

GREENOCK CHARITY SCHOOL *Report for the Year ending 6th July, 1836*. Greenock: Printed by J Hislop, 1836. 8vo. Pp 8.
                                                            GUL

HARVEY, THOMAS, and SELLAR, ALEX C 'Greenock Academy'; *Report on the State of Education in the Burgh and Middle-Class Schools in Scotland* (1868), **2**, 171-6.

SMITH, ROBERT MURRAY *A Page of Local History: being a Record of the Origin and Progress of Greenock Mechanics' Library and Scientific Institution*. Greenock: Printed by John Mitchell Pollock, 1904. 8vo. Pp 128. Frontispiece. Index.

WILLIAMSON, GEORGE 'Educational History of Old Greenock'; *Old Greenock*, second series (Paisley and London: Alexander Gardner, 1888), 143-255.

Inchinnan

MCCLELLAND, ROBERT 'Schools and Schoolmasters'; *The Church and Parish of Inchinnan* (Paisley: Alexander Gardner, 1905), 131-9.

Paisley

METCALFE, WILLIAM M 'Educational'; *A History of Paisley, 600-1908* (Paisley: Alexander Gardner, 1909), 388-99.

BROWN, ROBERT *The History of the Paisley Grammar School*, from its foundation in 1576; of the Paisley Grammar School and Academy, and of the other Town's schools. Paisley: Alex Gardner, 1875.

8vo. Pp xiv, 609. Frontispiece, 48 plates and other illustrations. Index.

ENDOWED SCHOOLS AND HOSPITALS (SCOTLAND) COMMISSION 'King James' Grammar School, Paisley'; *Second Report* (1874), 546-50.

HARVEY, THOMAS, and SELLAR, ALEX C 'Paisley Grammar School and Academy'; *Report on the State of Education in the Burgh and Middle-Class Schools in Scotland* (1868), **2**, 166-70.

METCALFE, WILLIAM M 'The Grammar School'; *A History of Paisley, 600-1908* (1909), 168-73.

BROWN, ROBERT 'Neilson Educational Institution'; *History of Paisley* (Paisley: J & J Cook, 1886), **2**, 324-8.

ENDOWED SCHOOLS AND HOSPITALS (SCOTLAND) COMMISSION 'The John Neilson Educational Institution, Paisley'; *Second Report* (1874), 551-9.

'The John Neilson Educational Institution, Oakshaw-head, Paisley'; *Scottish Educational and Literary J*, Feb 1854, **2**, 215-219.

The John Neilson Institution, 1852-1952. Paisley: John Neilson Centenary Committee, 1952. Portfolio. Pp 64. Illustrations.   GUL

METCALFE, WILLIAM M *The John Neilson Institution: Its first Fifty Years*. With illustrations. Paisley: Alexander Gardner, 1902. 8vo. Pp 141.

BROWN, ROBERT 'Paisley Ragged School'; *History of Paisley* (1886), **2**, 319-24.

FERRIER, W *Two Discourses: . . . The Second*, preached in the High Church of Paisley before the Friends of the Sabbath Schools. To these is added, A Short Authentic Account of the Rise, Progress, and Present State of the Sabbath Schools in Paisley. Paisley: Printed by Neilson & Weir, 1798. 8vo. Pp 176.   EUL

PAISLEY SABBATH AND WEEK DAY EVENING SCHOOLS *Report on their Present State*. Paisley: Printed by J Neilson, 1814. 12mo. Pp 26.   GUL

MORE, WILLIAM S *A Review of the Adult Education Provision in the Town of Paisley in the 19th Century*. Unpublished

MEd thesis, Glasgow University, 1967.
Typescript. 4to. Pp 212.   GUL

Port Glasgow

BARR, JAMES *Statement of the Rev. Dr Barr, with regard to the Erection of the New Parochial School in the Town of Port Glasgow.* Greenock: John Mennons & Co, 1842. 8vo. Pp 16.   GUL

HARVEY, THOMAS, and SELLAR, ALEX C 'Port-Glasgow Burgh School'; *Report on the State of Education in the Burgh and Middle-Class Schools in Scotland* (1868), 2, 135-7.

Renfrew

ENDOWED SCHOOLS AND HOSPITALS (SCOTLAND) COMMISSION 'Renfrew Grammar School'; *Second Report* (1874), 574-6.

HARVEY, THOMAS, and SELLAR, ALEX C 'Renfrew Burgh and Grammar School'; *Report on the State of Education in the Burgh and Middle-Class Schools in Scotland* (1868), 2, 119-21.

ROSS AND CROMARTY
Cromarty

MILLER, HUGH 'The Story of a Parish School'; *The Witness*, 27 Mar 1850.

Fortrose

MACDOWALL, CHARLES GEORGE 'Early Schools and Schoolmasters'; *The Chanonry of Ross* (Fortrose: Printed and published for the Author by Highland Printers Ltd, Inverness, 1963), 159-68.

Lewis

MACKENZIE, WILLIAM C 'Education'; *The Book of the Lews: The Story of a Hebridean Isle* (Paisley: Alexander Gardner, 1919), 179-85.

Tain

ENDOWED SCHOOLS AND HOSPITALS (SCOTLAND) COMMISSION 'Royal Academy, Tain'; *Second Report* (1874), 600-3.

HARVEY, THOMAS, and SELLAR, ALEX C 'Tain Academy'; *Report on the State of Education in the Burgh and Middle-Class Schools in Scotland* (1868), 2, 1-4.

Royal Charter, List of Subscribers, State of Funds, &c. &c. of the Tain Academy. London: Printed by T Sabine, 1810. 8vo. Pp 35. Frontispiece.

ROXBURGH
Hawick

MICHIE, ALEXANDER 'Memories of Local Schools and School Life Seventy Years Ago'; *Transactions of the Hawick Archaeological Society, Season 1908*, 73-9.

VERNON, JOSHUA JOHN 'Old Schools and Schoolmasters of Hawick and Wilton'; *Transactions of the Hawick Archaeological Society for 1902*, 51-9.

WATTERS, ALEXANDER M 'History of the Orrok Educational Bequest, and Two Hundred Years of Secondary Education in Hawick'; *Transactions of the Hawick Archaeological Society, Session 1927*, 40-53.

WILSON, ROBERT 'Schools and Education'; *History of Hawick*, second edition, corrected and considerably enlarged (Hawick: Robert Armstrong, 1841), 94-108.

Jedburgh

Board & Education at Jedburgh. Jedburgh, 1811. 12mo. Pp 4.

MABON, WELLS 'Religious Education in an Old Parish School'; *Transactions of the Hawick Archaeological Society, 1936*, 60-2.

WATSON, GEORGE *The History of Jedburgh Grammar School.* Reprinted from *Jedburgh Gazette*—1909. np [Jedburgh], nd [1909]. 4to. Pp 18.

Kelso

SMITH, JAMES *History of Kelso Grammar School.* Kelso: Printed by John Smith for the Tweedside Physical and Antiquarian Society; and published by J & J H Rutherford, 1909. 8vo. Pp xv, 151. Frontispiece and 3 plates.

SELKIRKSHIRE

Galashiels

EDUCATION COMMISSION (SCOTLAND) 'Gala Subscription School'; *Appendix to First Report* (1867), 117-19.

HALL, ROBERT 'Educational'; *History of Galashiels* (Galashiels: Alexander Walker & Son, 1898), 449-78.

—*Schools and Schoolboy Life in Galashiels Forty Years Ago.* Galashiels: Printed by John McQueen, 1893. 8vo. Pp 46.

RITCHIE, WILLIAM D 'Burgh School, Galashiels'; *SEJ*, 21 Sept 1934, **17**, 1197-8.

Lilliesleaf

SYM, ARTHUR POLLOCK 'The Schools and Schoolmasters of Lilliesleaf'; *The Parish of Lilliesleaf* (Selkirk: James Lewis, 1913), 133-42.

Selkirk

ENDOWED SCHOOLS AND HOSPITALS (SCOTLAND) COMMISSION 'The "Scott or Campbell" and "Oliver" Trusts, Selkirk'; *Appendix to Third Report* (1875), **2**, 314-316.

HARVEY, THOMAS, and SELLAR, ALEX C 'Selkirk Burgh School'; *Report on the State of Education in the Burgh and Middle-Class Schools in Scotland* (1868), **2**, 154-5.

SHARPE, JOHN 'The School'; *Selkirk: Its Church, Its School, and Its Presbytery* (Selkirk: James Lewis, nd [1914]), 68-92.

SHETLAND

ENDOWED SCHOOLS AND HOSPITALS (SCOTLAND) COMMISSION 'Anderson Educational Institution, Lerwick'; *Second Report* (1874), 521-3.

KEMP, DANIEL W 'Old Teachers of Shetland, 1771-1852'; *Scottish Notes and Queries*, second series, June 1900, **1**, 180-1; July 1900, **2**, 7-9.

RAMSAY, GEORGE G See ORKNEY.

M

STIRLINGSHIRE

BAIN, ANDREW *Education in Stirlingshire from the Reformation to the Act of 1872.* Scottish Council for Research in Education, publication no 51. London: University of London Press Ltd, 1965. 8vo. Pp 297. Glossary. Bibliography. Indexes. 4 plates.

Falkirk

FALKIRK SCHOOL OF ARTS *Correspondence between the Committee and the Rev. Mr Rutherford.* Falkirk: Printed by Archibald Johnston, [1839]. 8vo. Pp 18.
                                                    EUL

—*Vindication of the Falkirk School of Arts,* from the Aspersions of the Rev. Mr Rutherford and his Friends, by the Committee. With an Appendix, containing a Correspondence with the Rev. Messrs Steel and Welsh, &c. &c. Falkirk: Printed by Archibald Johnston, [1839]. 8vo. Pp 24.   EUL

HARVEY, THOMAS, and SELLAR, ALEX C 'Falkirk Grammar and Parochial School'; *Report on the State of Education in the Burgh and Middle-Class Schools in Scotland* (1868), **2**, 160-2.

J, G *Strictures on the Correspondence between the Committee of the Falkirk School of Arts, and the Reverend Mr Rutherford.* Falkirk: Charles Jeffrey, 1839. 8vo. Pp 12.   EUL

LOVE, JAMES *The Schools and Schoolmasters of Falkirk, from the Earliest Times.* Reprinted from the *Falkirk Herald.* Falkirk: Printed by F Johnston and Co, *Herald* Office, 1898. 8vo. Pp 250. Index.

RUTHERFORD, ALEXANDER C *Reply to the Vindication of the Falkirk School of Arts.* With an Appendix of Letters. Falkirk: Charles Jeffrey, 1839. 8vo. Pp 36.
                                                    EUL

Larbert

EDUCATION COMMISSION (SCOTLAND) 'Larbert Free Church Schools'; *Appendix to First Report* (1867), 113-17.

Plean

BAIN, DAVID 'Peeps into the Minutes of Plean Subscription School'; *SEJ*, 30 Sept 1949, **32**, 620-2.

Polmont

ANDERSON, JOHN 'Blairlodge School, Polmont'; *Illustrations*, Nov 1888, **4**, 52-4.

GUNN, JOHN 'Blair Lodge'; *Maurice Paterson. A Memorial Biography* (1921), 38-53.

LOWER, H 'Blairlodge School'; *Public School Mag*, Mar 1902, **9**, 224-30.

Stirling

ENDOWED INSTITUTIONS (SCOTLAND) COMMISSION 'Stirling Hospitals Inquiry'; Stirling: James Hogg, Alex Miller, R S Shearer, and J F Crawford, 1871. 8vo. Pp 15.   GUL

Extracts from the Records of the Royal Burgh of Stirling, A.D. 1667-1752. Scottish Burgh Record Society, publication no 30. Glasgow, 1889. 8vo. Index. See Index under: Grammar School; Music School; Schoolmaster; Schoolmistress; School(s).

ENDOWED SCHOOLS AND HOSPITALS (SCOTLAND) COMMISSION 'Stirling Hospitals—Allan's and Cunningham's Mortifications'; *Appendix to Third Report* (1875), **1**, 178-83.

Stirling High School

ENDOWED SCHOOLS AND HOSPITALS (SCOTLAND) COMMISSION 'High School of Stirling'; *Second Report* (1874), 595-9.

FEARON, DANIEL R 'Stirling High School'; *Schools Inquiry Commission Report*(1868), **6**, pt 5, 169-74.

GRAHAM, JAMES LASCELLES (ed) *'Old Boys' and their Stories of the High School of Stirling*. Stirling: Aeneas Mackay, 1900. Portfolio. Pp 241. Frontispiece, 30 portraits, and 7 other illustrations.

HARVEY, THOMAS, and SELLAR, ALEX C 'Stirling High School'; *Report on the State of Education in the Burgh and Middle-Class Schools in Scotland* (1868), **2**, 225-32.

HUTCHISON, ANDREW F *History of the High School of Stirling*. With Notices of Schools and Education in the Burgh generally. Stirling: Aeneas Mackay, 1904. 8vo. Pp xvi, 326. Frontispiece, 36 plates, and numerous facsimiles of signatures of old masters. Index.

NOTE Mitchell and Cash, *A Contribution to the Bibliography of Scottish Topography* (1917), attribute to the same author a volume entitled *Eight Centuries of a Scottish School*, which, they say, was published at Stirling in 1902. No trace of such a work has been found, and the entry is almost certainly a faulty reference to Hutchison's volume of 1904.

STIRLING TOWN COUNCIL *Appeal for Subscriptions towards the cost of the New High School of Stirling*, with an engraving of the proposed undertaking. Stirling, 1853. 4to. Pp 3.

SUTHERLAND

'At a Highland School Seventy Years Ago. Our Village Schoolmaster'; *SEJ*, 25 Nov 1932, **15**, 1418-19.

BEATON, DAVID 'The Establishment of Parish Schools in Sutherland and Caithness at the Beginning of the 18th Century'; *Old Lore Miscellany of Orkney, Shetland, Caithness, and Sutherland* (London: Printed for the Viking Club Society for Northern Research, King's College, University of London, 1912), July 1912, **5**, 98-100.

Dornoch

SAGE, DONALD 'School-boy Days at Dornoch'; *Memorabilia Domestica* (Wick: W Rae; Edinburgh: John Menzies and Co, 1889), 143-71; second edition (1899), 112-19.

Durness

ENDOWED SCHOOLS AND HOSPITALS (SCOTLAND) COMMISSION 'Campbell's Bequest, Parish of Durness, Sutherlandshire'; *Appendix to Third Report* (1875), **2**, 317-318.

WIGTOWNSHIRE
Newton Stewart

ENDOWED SCHOOLS AND HOSPITALS (SCOT-
LAND) COMMISSION 'Samuel Douglas Free
School'; *First Report* (1873), 751-7;
Appendix to Third Report (1875), **1**, 196-7.

—'Endowed Schools of Newton-Stewart';
Appendix to Third Report (1875), **1**, 424-5.

—'The Ewart Institute High School,
Newton-Stewart'; *Second Report* (1874),
535-45.

HARVEY, THOMAS, and SELLAR, ALEX C
'Ewart Institute'; *Report on the State of
Education in the Burgh and Middle-Class
Schools in Scotland* (1868), **2**, 181-6.

Miscellaneous

ADAM, JAMES *The Knowledge Qualification.*
A Plea for the Reciprocal Extension of
Education and the Franchise. Edinburgh: W Tait; Aberdeen: L Smith,
1837. 8vo. Pp 23.   Mit

ANDERSON, ALEXANDER *Gymnasia: or Intermediate Institutions.* To which are prefixed Five Letters on Free Church University Education, with special reference to
Aberdeen and the North of Scotland,
originally addressed to the Editor of the
Aberdeen "Banner". Edinburgh: John
Johnstone, 1846. 8vo. Pp 44.   EUL

ANDERSON, GEORGE *Letter to Leonard
Horner, Esq., Inspector of Factories, in
Reply to his Strictures on the Educational
Test Scheme,* in the Factory Report for
June, 1857. Glasgow: Thomas Murray
and Son, 1857. 8vo. Pp 12.

ANTIQUARIES, SOCIETY OF *Letter to the
Schoolmasters of Scotland.* Edinburgh:
Printed by Neill and Company, 1860.
8vo. Pp 13.   Mit
Asks for support in promoting an
interest in Scottish antiquities.

'A Tale of Certificates'; *Scottish Educational and Literary J*, Oct 1852, **1**, 13-19.

BACHE, ALEXANDER DALLAS *Report on Education in Europe.* Philadelphia: Printed by
Lydia R Bailey, 1839. 8vo.   EUL
Education Hospitals for Boys, at Edinburgh, 12-48. Primary Schools, 159-67,
178-98. Secondary Education, 365-74,
382-90.

BEATTIE, JAMES *Scoticisms, arranged in
Alphabetical Order,* designed to correct

Improprieties of Speech and Writing.
Edinburgh: Printed for William Creech;
and T Cadell, London, 1787. 8vo. Pp
[4], 121.

BEGG, JAMES *The Ecclesiastical and Social
Evils of Scotland,* and how to remedy
them. Edinburgh: Johnstone, Hunter,
& Co, 1871. 8vo. Pp 35.   New Coll

BELL, ALEXANDER MELVILLE *The Art of
Delivery,* and the Influence of School
Discipline on Public Oratory. Edin-
burgh: W F Kennedy; London: Ham-
ilton, Adams, & Co, nd [1854]. 8vo.
Pp 22.

BLACK, ARCHIBALD MUIR *The Educational
Work of Robert Owen.* Unpublished
PhD thesis, St Andrews University, 1950.

BLACK, GEORGE F *The Beginning of the Study
of Hebrew in Scotland.* New York, 1929.
8vo. Pp 18. Plate.
An offprint from the A S Freidus
Memorial Volume, 463-80.

BLACK, JOHN *Hints on the Origin and
Significance of certain educational terms.*
Aberdeen: A Brown & Co, 1870. 12mo.
Pp 31.

BONE, THOMAS R *School Inspection in Scotland, 1840-1966.* Scottish Council for
Research in Education, publication no
57. London: University of London
Press Ltd, 1968. 8vo. Pp 276. Frontispiece and 4 plates. Bibliography. Index.

BROWN, JOHN (Biggar) *Remarks on the
Plans and Publications of Robert Owen,
Esq. of New Lanark.* Edinburgh:

Printed by and for Ogle, Allardice, and Thomson; and for David Brown, Edinburgh; M Ogle, Glasgow; and Ogle, Duncan, and Cochran, and J Hatchard, London, 1817. 8vo. Pp 60.
New Coll

BRYCE, ARCHIBALD HAMILTON 'A Grammar School Bill for Scotland—The Necessary Complement of the Universities' Act'; *Transactions of the National Association for the Promotion of Social Science, 1863* (1864), 287-92.

BRYCE, JAMES *Address at the Annual Meeting of the Educational Institute of Scotland, September 17, 1853*. Edinburgh: Printed by Murray and Gibb, 1853. 8vo. Pp 15.
EUL
Reprinted from the *Scottish Educational and Literary J*, Dec 1853, **2**, 93-105.

CHADWIN, SIR EDWIN *Communication on the Half-Time School System.* London: HMSO, 1861. 8vo.   GUL
Evidence on Scottish conditions was given by David Donaldson, 9-13, and by T A Morrison, 124-8.

CHALMERS, THOMAS *On the Use and Abuse of Literary and Ecclesiastical Endowments.* Glasgow: Printed for William Collins; William Whyte & Co, and Wm Oliphant, Edinburgh; R M Tims, and Wm Curry, Jun & Co, Dublin; and G B Whittaker, London, 1827. 8vo. Pp 194.
Reprinted in CHALMERS, T *Church and College Establishments* (Edinburgh: Printed for Thomas Constable by Sutherland and Knox, 1848), 21-184; *Works of Thomas Chalmers* (Glasgow: William Collins, nd), **17**, 21-184; *Select Works*, ed HANNA, WILLIAM (Edinburgh: Thomas Constable & Co), **11** (1857), 11-116.

CHRISTISON, ALEXANDER *The General Diffusion of Knowledge one great cause of the prosperity of North Britain.* With an Appendix: containing a proposal for improving the present mode of teaching the Greek language. Edinburgh: Peter Hill, 1802. 8vo. Pp 35.

[COOK, JOHN (Haddington)] *An Examination of the Census Report and Tables of Religious Worship and Education for Scotland, 1851.* By Censor. Reprinted from the *Edinburgh Evening Courant* of

15th and 20th July 1854. (Revised and corrected.) Edinburgh, 1854. 12mo. Pp 24.   New Coll

CURRIE, JAMES 'On School Punishments'; *The Museum*, Apr 1861, **1**, 59-66.

'David Stow, 1793-1864: Moral Teaching and the First Teachers' College'; *TES*, 6 Nov 1964, 806.

The Dominie's Disaster, and other Poems. By a Member of the Musomanik Society of Anstruther. Cupar: Printed by R Tullis, for Henry Colburn, London; A Mackay, Edinburgh; and W Cockburn, Anstruther, 1816. 12mo. Pp 24.

DUNCAN, HENRY 'The Cottage Fireside'; *The Scotch Cheap Repository of Tracts*: containing Moral Tales, for the Instruction of the Young. By a Society of Clergymen in Dumfries-shire. Corrected and greatly enlarged (Edinburgh: Printed for Oliphant, Waugh, & Innes, 1815), 207-408.
BM
'A very considerable addition has been made to the longest tale in the collection —*The Cottage Fireside*. This tale is also republished separately in its enlarged state,' from the Preface.

—*The Cottage Fireside*; or, The Parish Schoolmaster: A Moral Tale, intended chiefly to convey, in an alluring Form, an Important Practical Lesson to Parents, in the Education of their Children; and to Young Persons, in the Duty of Obedience, and the Happiness of Good Conduct. Second edition, greatly enlarged. Edinburgh: Printed for Oliphant, Waugh & Innes, 1815. 8vo. Pp [8], 202.   BM
The first separate publication.

— —. Third edition. Edinburgh: Printed for Oliphant, Waugh, & Innes, 1816. 12mo. Pp vii, 255.   BM

— —. Fourth edition. Edinburgh: Printed for Waugh & Innes; and T Hamilton, Ogle, Duncan, & Co, and W Baynes & Son, London, 1821. 12mo. Pp 254.
New Coll

—*The Cottage Fireside*, or, The Parish Schoolmaster. Sixth edition. Edinburgh: William Oliphant and Co; London: Hamilton, Adams, and Co, nd [1862]. 8vo. Pp 251. Frontispiece.

DUNDAS, ROBERT 'Heritors' Assessments for Parish Schools'; *Edinburgh Evening Courant*, 14 Mar 1872.

EDINBURGH PHONETIC SOCIETY *Orthographic Reform the only Means of securing General Education*. Edinburgh: David Hay; and Paton and Ritchie; London: Fred Pitman, 1850. 8vo. Pp 16.

'The Educational Forces of Society'; *Scottish Rev*, Jan 1857, **5**, 38-51.

'Education Deliverance and Debate in the late Commission'; *The Watchword*, 1 Apr 1872, **7**, 7-15.   New Coll

The Educational Lever: or, A Mode by which the chief Difficulties in Education may be removed. By a Sabbath-School Teacher. Glasgow: George Gallie; London: Fred Pitman; Edinburgh: C Ziegler, 1850. 8vo. Pp 16.

EVERETT, JOSEPH D *The Philosophy of Teaching*, or Psychology in its relation to Intellectual Culture. London and Glasgow: Richard Griffin and Company, 1858. 8vo. Pp 32.

'Examination Day'; *Scottish Educational and Literary J*, Apr 1853, **1**, 289-93.

FRASER, WILLIAM 'Compulsory Education'; *Transactions of the National Association for the Promotion of Social Science, 1858* (1859), 278-82.

FURLONG, (MRS) LEIGH *New Movement in Education. What is it!* 'Oral' Education on the 'Scottish' System. London: Thomas Hatchard, and William Gurner, 1855. 8vo. Pp 16.

GIBSON, GEORGE A 'Napier and the Invention of Logarithms'; Glasgow Royal Philosophical Society, 1914. 8vo. Pp 24. Reprint from *Proceedings*, **xlv** (1913-19), 35-56.   GUL

GRAHAM, GILBERT *Address to the Free Church Teachers' Association*. np, nd [1868]. 8vo. Pp 8.   New Coll

GRUB, JOHN *Orations on various select Subjects* by Mr John Grub, late Schoolmaster of the Parish of Wemyss, in Fifeshire, as performed by his Scholars after the usual Examination on Harvest Vacation Days, and on Shrove Tuesdays in place of Cockfighting. These Orations, for the use of Grammar-Schools on the above Days, are published by Robert Wilson of Sylvania, near Dunfermline. Edinburgh: Printed for the Editor, 1794. 12mo. Pp 287.

HAMILTON, ELIZABETH 'Hints concerning the Duties of a Schoolmaster'; *The Cottagers of Glenburnie* (Edinburgh: Printed by James Ballantyne and Co, for Manners & Miller, and S Cheyne, Edinburgh; T Cadell and W Davies, and William Miller, London, 1808), 364-92.

This is the eighteenth and final chapter of a once popular novel. Three editions appeared in 1808, others followed in 1810, 1815, 1822, 1837, 1843, 1850, 1859, 1872, 1881, 1885, and 1891, and there was also an undated one about 1850.

HAMILTON, SIR WILLIAM, Bart *Discussions on Philosophy and Literature, Education and University Reform*. Chiefly from the *Edinburgh Review;* corrected, vindicated, enlarged, in Notes and Appendices. London: Longman, Brown, Green, and Longmans: Edinburgh: Maclachlan and Stewart, 1852. 8vo. Pp x, 758. Index.

— —. Second edition, enlarged. London: Longman, Brown, Green, and Longmans; Edinburgh: Maclachlan and Stewart, 1853. 8vo. Pp xii, 852. Index.   EUL

— —. Third edition. Edinburgh and London: William Blackwood and Sons, 1866. 8vo. Pp xiv, 846. Index.

HOPE, JOHN *The British League Evening Classes*; or, Water *versus* Whisky & Tobacco: An Answer to the Right Honourable Fox Maule, His Grace the Duke of Argyll, and the Rev. Thomas Guthrie, D.D. in regard to certain Statements made by them at Meeting in the Music Hall, 31st December, 1850. Edinburgh: Published for the Author, by William Blackwood & Sons, 1851. 8vo. Pp 31.

JAMIESON, GEORGE *The Education-Question, philosophically and practically considered*, in its bearing upon individual Development and Social Improvement. Aberdeen: John Smith; London: George Bell; Edinburgh: T & T Clark; Glasgow: Griffin & Co, 1854. 8vo. Pp vi, 43.

KIRKWOOD, JAMES (1) *The History of the Twenty Seven Gods of Linlithgow*; being an exact and true Account of a Famous Plea betwixt the Town-Council of the said Burgh, and Mr *Kirkwood*, schoolmaster there. Edinburgh, 1711. 4to. Pp viii, 79.

—*Mr Kirkwoods Plea before the Kirk, and Civil Judicatures of Scotland*. Divided into Five Parts. London: Printed by D E for the Author, 1698. 8vo. Pp 144.

—*A Short Information of the Plea betwixt the Town Council of Linlithgow, and Mr James Kirkwood Schoolmaster there*, whereof a more full Account may perhaps come out hereafter. np, nd [1690]. 4to. Pp 20.

KIRKWOOD, JAMES (2) *A Copy of a Letter anent A Project, for erecting a Library in every Presbytery, or at least County, in the Highlands*: From a reverend Minister of the *Scots* Nation now in England, to a Minister of Edinburgh. With reasons for it, and a Schem for erecting and preserving these Libraries. Edinburgh: Printed by George Mosman, in the year, 1702. 4to. Pp 11.

—*An Overture for Founding & Maintaining of Bibliothecks in every Paroch throughout this Kingdom*: Humbly offered to the consideration of this present Assembly. np, printed in the year 1699. 4to. Pp 15.

— —: Humbly offered to the consideration of the General-Assembly. np, printed in the year 1701. 4to. Pp 17.

—*Proposals made by the Rev. James Kirkwood (Minister of Minto) in 1699 to found Public Libraries in Scotland*. Reprinted verbatim et literatim from the rare copy in the Free Public Library, Wigan. With introductory remarks by William Blades. London: privately printed, 1889. 4to. Pp 9, 15.   BM

KNOX, THOMAS *Temperance in School-Books*. London: William Tweedie; Edinburgh: D Mathers, 1857. 8vo. Pp 16.   GUL

L, W 'Stow's Training System'; *Scottish Educational and Literary J*, Aug 1853, **1**, 521-4.

LANCASTER, JOSEPH 'Plan for the Introduction of Mr Lancaster's system of education into Scotland'; *Scots Mag*, Feb 1810, **72**, 112-14.

LAURIE, SIMON SOMERVILLE 'General Remarks on Hospital Training'; *Report on the Hospitals under the Administration of the Merchant Company, Edinburgh* (Edinburgh, 1868), 113-30.   EUL

LELLO, A J E 'Robert Owen's Pioneer Work in Education'; *SEJ*, 7 Nov 1958, **41**, 693.

'Letter of a Schoolmaster to a Clergyman'; *Scots Mag*, Nov 1802, **64**, 904.

LONG, JAMES *History and Principles of Stow's Training System*; with a Brief Review of the prevailing State of Education in the Colleges and Higher Schools of the Kingdom. Glasgow: W Hamilton, 1852. 8vo. Pp 157, [2].   GUL

MCCRIE, JAMES *Autopaedia*: or, Instructions on Personal Education. Designed for Young Men. Aberdeen: John Smith, 1866. 8vo. Pp viii, 383. Frontispiece.   EUL

— —. Second edition—greatly enlarged. London: S W Partridge & Co; Edinburgh & Glasgow: J Menzies & Co; Aberdeen: A & R Milne, 1871. 8vo. Pp xvi, 628. Index.

MACFARLAND, HENRY S N 'The Education of James Melville (1556-1614)'; *Aberdeen University Rev*, Autumn 1956, **36**, 362-70.   EUL

MACLEOD, NORMAN *The Home School or Hints on Home Education*. Edinburgh: Paton and Ritchie; London: Hamilton, Adams, and Co; Glasgow: T Murray and Son, 1856. 8vo. Pp xiv, 175.   BM
'Made up chiefly of papers contributed at different periods to the Edinburgh Christian Magazine', Preface, vii. Other three identical editions appeared in 1856 and another in 1857.

—'The Schoolmaster'; *Reminiscences of a Highland Parish* (London: Alexander Strahan, 1867), 275-95.
Reprinted from *Good Words*, 1863, 725-9. The parish was Morvern in Argyllshire, and the time the early part of the nineteenth century.

— — (London: Charles Burnet & Co, (1891 ?)), 61-5.

— —. With six illustrations (London: S W Partridge & Co, Ltd, 1911), 204-20.

MACTAGGART, DAVID *The Teacher's Office.* Its Nature, Duties and Responsibilities. A Sermon. Aberdeen: George & Robert King; Edinburgh: Paton & Ritchie, 1853. 8vo. Pp 20.   AUL

MANN, HORACE 'Education in Scotland'; *Census of Great Britain, 1851; Education in Great Britain* (London: George Routledge and Co, 1854), 153-72.

MASSON, DAVID *The State of Learning in Scotland.* A Lecture. Edinburgh: Edmonston and Douglas, 1866. 8vo. Pp 28.

MEIKLE, HENRY W 'The Learning of the Scots in the Eighteenth Century'; *SHR*, Apr 1910, 7, 289-93.

Memorial about a Commission for visiting Schools, Colleges, and Universities. np, 1704. 4to. Pp 4.

'Middle-Class Education in Scotland'; *The Museum*, new series, 1 Feb 1867, 3, 401-3.

MILLER, HUGH *My Schools and Schoolmasters, or, The Story of my Education.* Edinburgh: Thomas Constable, 1858. 8vo.

'Education' is here used in its widest sense, and only chapters 3 and 7 deal with the author's formal schooling. The book was frequently reprinted.

MITCHELL, HUGH *Scotticisms, Vulgar Anglicisms, and Grammatical Improprieties corrected*, with Reasons for the Corrections; being a Collection upon a new plan: Alphabetically arranged, and adapted to the Use of Academies, Men of Business, and Private Families. Glasgow: Printed by Falconer & Willison, for the Author, 1799. 8vo. Pp 96.

MOCKET, RICHARD *God and the King*: or, A Dialogue, shewing, That our Sovereign Lord the King, being immediate under God within his Dominions, doth rightly claim whatsoever is required by the Oath of Allegiance; As also the Duty and Allegiance of the Subject. With a Preface to this Edition, wherein some further Arguments for the Oath of Allegiance are fully prosecuted, and Objections answered. As also an Appendix, containing some Papers, copied out of the publick Records, referred to in the said Preface. The Third edition. Edinburgh:

Printed by Charles Dallas, 1725. 8vo. Pp lxxv, 163.

This was in fact the fourth edition of this work, the first having been printed at London in 1615 and the second and third also there in 1616 and 1633 respectively. See the *Register of the Privy Council of Scotland*, May–June, 1616.

MONCRIEFF, JAMES, Lord Moncrieff. *Address on his Installation as Lord Rector of the University of Edinburgh* on the 18th of January 1869. Edinburgh: Edmonston and Douglas, 1869. 8vo. Pp 41.

New Coll

MORE, JOHN S 'Opinion concerning the Right of Private Teachers to teach Schools without being liable to Presbyteries, &c. [Edinburgh], 15th March, 1824'; *Records of the Scottish Church History Society*, 3 (1929), 79-80.

'Mr George Combe on Education'; *The Free Church Mag*, Feb 1848, 5, 33-6.

MUIR, WILLIAM *A Letter to the Members of the late General Assembly of the Church of Scotland, on his having resigned the Convenership of the Education Committee*; and on other Topics relative to recent Proceedings on the Subject of Education. With Appendix. Edinburgh: Paton and Ritchie; Glasgow: T Smith and Son; and T Murray, 1849. 8vo. Pp [3], 55.

MURRAY, DAVID *Some early Grammars and other School books in use in Scotland*, more particularly those printed at or relating to Glasgow. Glasgow: Printed for the Royal Philosophical Society of Glasgow, 1905-6. 8vo. First Part, pp 34. Second Part, pp 52.

Reprinted from *Proceedings of the Royal Philosophical Society of Glasgow*, 36 (1904-5), 266-97; 37 (1905-6), 142-91.

—'Some Teachers of Bookkeeping and Accounts in Glasgow, Edinburgh, and other Scotch Towns'; *Chapters in the History of Bookkeeping, Accountancy, and Commercial Arithmetic* (Glasgow: Jackson, Wylie & Co, 1930), 32-51.

—'Some Writers on Bookkeeping: Scotland'; *Chapters in the History of Bookkeeping, Accountancy, and Commercial Arithmetic* (Glasgow: Jackson, Wylie & Co, 1930), 308-49.

'My First School; or, 'Tis Fifty Years Since'; *Scottish Educational and Literary J*, Jan 1853, **1**, 148-52.

'On Robert Owen's System of Education'. A Letter to the editor of the *Caledonian Mercury* by a member of the Co-operative and Economical Society of Edinburgh. Edinburgh, 1822. 4to. Pp 4.   GUL

On the Best Means of promoting Scientific Education. A report presented to the General Committee of the British Association for the Advancement of Science, at Dundee, 1867. London: John Murray, 1868. 8vo. Pp 40.

'On the Fees payable by the Pupils in our Schools and Universities, and those recommended by the Royal Commissioners'; *Aberdeen University Mag*, 21 June 1836, **1**, 213-15; 6 July 1836, **1**, 217-26.

'Our Hospital Establishments'; *The Museum*, new series, 1 Mar 1867, **3**, 445-8; 1 Feb 1868, **4**, 401-4.

'Our School Vacation—When?'; *Scottish Educational and Literary J*, Aug 1853, **1**, 506-8.

OWEN, ROBERT *An Address delivered to the Inhabitants of New Lanark* on the First of January, 1816, at the Opening of the Institution established for the Formation of Character. London: J Hatchard, 1816. 8vo. Pp 48.

—*A New View of Society*. London: T Cadell and W Davies, 1813. 8vo. Pp 64.   GUL

—*A Statement regarding the New Lanark Establishment*. Edinburgh: John Moir, 1812. 8vo. Pp 23.   GUL

PARKINSON, T B *Education in itself and in its relation to Present Wants*. A Lecture delivered in St Andrew's School, Glasgow, June 12, 1863. London: Burns & Lambert; Glasgow: H Margey; Preston: E Buller, nd [1863]. 12mo. Pp 42.

PARISH SCHOOLMASTER, A 'Remarks on Catechical Instruction, as pursued in the Parochial Schools in Scotland, with Hints for its Improvement'; *Edinburgh Christian Instructor*, Apr 1817, **14**, 219-22.

PAROCHIAL SCHOOLMASTER, A 'Superfluous Schools'; *The Museum*, new series, 1 July 1867, **4**, 139-40.

PILLANS, JAMES *Contributions to the Cause of Education*. London: Longman, Brown, Green, & Longman, 1856. 8vo. Pp xii, 591.

CONTENTS Principles of Elementary Teaching. Seminaries for Teachers. Minutes of Evidence taken before a Select Committee of the House of Commons on Education, 1834. Three Lectures on the relative Importance of Classical Training in the Education of Youth. Rationale of Discipline. A Word for the Universities of Scotland.

—*Educational Papers*. Edinburgh: James Gordon; London: Hamilton, Adams, & Co, 1862. 8vo. Pp vii, 81.

CONTENTS A Glance at the Present Aspect of the Educational Question in the three great Divisions of the British Empire. On some prevailing Errors in the Educational Training of the Working Classes, and the Means of Cure. On the Nature and Extent of the Duties incumbent on Domestic Tutors. Hints for Improving the Preliminary Stages of a Classical Education.

—*The Rationale of Discipline* as exemplified in the High School of Edinburgh. Edinburgh: Maclachlan & Stewart; London: Taylor, Walton, and Maberly, and Simpkin, Marshall, and Co, 1852. 8vo. Pp xvi, 199.

Reprinted in PILLANS, JAMES *Contributions to the Cause of Education* (1856), 308-420. It was originally written in 1823.

'The Position of the Free Church Schools in Britain'; *The Watchword*, 1 Oct 1866, **1**, 210-11.   New Coll

'Progress of Social Disorganisation. No. 1 — The Schoolmaster'; *Blackwood's Edinburgh Mag*, Feb 1834, **13**, 228-48.

RAINY, ALEXANDER *Self-Education*. Aberdeen: D Wyllie & Son; Edinburgh: William Blackwood & Sons, 1858. 8vo. Pp 20.

Report of the Proceedings of a Public Meeting held in Edinburgh, on the evening of Tuesday, May 2, to adopt Measures for opposing the Education Clauses in Sir James Graham's Factory Bill: containing the Principal Clauses objected to, and Sir J. Graham's proposed Modifications.

Edinburgh: Adam and Charles Black, John Johnstone, Charles Ziegler, and W P Kennedy, 1843. 8vo. Pp 30. EIS

Results of the Census of 1851, with respect to the religious and educational establishments of Scotland. Edinburgh: Adam & Charles Black, nd [1854]. 12mo. Pp 30. New Coll

ROBERTSON, JOHN *A View of the System of Education pursued in the Public Schools and Universities of Edinburgh*: with remarks on the present state of learning in Scotland. London: Printed for J W Warren, 1818. 8vo. Pp 35. BM

RUSK, ROBERT R 'Voluntary Schools and Government Building Grants'; *SEJ*, 8 June 1928, 11, 660-1; 15 June 1928, 11, 691-2.

RUSSELL, MICHAEL *Remarks and Explanations connected with the 'View of the System of Education at present pursued in the Schools and Universities of Scotland'.* Edinburgh: Bell & Bradfute, Doig & Stirling, and David Brown; A & J M Duncan, Glasgow; Wm Reid, Leith; F C & J Rivington, London; Deighton, Cambridge; and Bliss, Oxford, 1815. 8vo. Pp 100.

—*View of the System of Education at present pursued in the Schools and Universities of Scotland.* With an Appendix, containing communications relative to the University of Cambridge, School of Westminster, the Perth Academy; together with a more detailed Account of the University of St Andrews. Edinburgh: Printed by John Moir, 1813. 8vo. Pp vii, 168, lv.

SAUNDERS, WILLIAM 'Mr Robert Bruce, Schoolmaster in Edinburgh, and the Common Tunes'; *SEJ*, 4 Apr 1941, 24, 220-1; 11 Apr 1941, 24, 240-1.

School Endowment Scheme—Proposed reenactment of the Test Act against Dissenters. np, nd [1838]. 12mo. Pp 8. New Coll

'Scottish Grammar Schools'; *Scottish Educational and Literary J*, Sept 1854, 2, 651-9.

SHUTTLEWORTH, SIR JAMES KAY *The School in its relations to the State, the Church, and the Congregation,* being an explana-

tion of the Minutes of the Committee of Council on Education in August and December, 1846. London: John Murray, 1847. 8vo. Pp 71.

—'The Minutes of 1846. With additional Appendices'; *Four periods of Public Education* (London: Longman, Green, Longman, and Roberts, 1867), 433-551.

STOW, DAVID *Infant Training.* A Dialogue, explanatory of the system adopted at the Infant Model School, Glasgow. By a Director. Glasgow: Printed for William Collins, 1833. 16mo. Pp 144.
The first separate printing of *Granny and Leezy*; it had originally appeared in the *Glasgow Infant School Mag.*

—*Granny and Leezy.* A Scottish Dialogue. Grandmother's Visit to the first Infant Training School. Sixth edition. London: Longman, Green, Longman, & Roberts, 1860. 8vo. Pp 81. Frontispiece and 5 plates.

SUTHERLAND, DAVID J S 'Some Old School Notebooks written a century ago'; *SEJ*, 13 Jan 1939, 22, 42-3.

TROWER, WALTER JOHN *On the Principle involved in the Inspection of Schools on Secular Subjects only.* Edinburgh: R Grant and Son, 1850. 8vo. Pp 22.

WALLIS, P J 'The National Register, 1852-1855'; *British J of Educational Studies*, Nov 1964, 13, 50-5, 68-9.

WARDLAW, RALPH *An Essay on Mr Joseph Lancaster's Improvements in Education*: including an abridged view of his Plan of Teaching; with a few remarks on some of its peculiar advantages. Glasgow: Printed by R Chapman, 1810. 8vo. Pp 68.

WEBB, R K 'Literacy among the Working Classes in Nineteenth Century Scotland'; *SHR*, Oct 1954, 33, 100-14.

WILSON, JOHN *Popular Reflections on the Legislative Support of Parish Teachers and Parish Ministers.* Edinburgh: William Whyte and Company, 1831. 8vo. Pp xi, 97. New Coll

'A Word in favour of our future Prospects; or, an Answer to the Question, What are the probable Effects of increasing Knowledge on the Condition of Society?'; *Edinburgh Mag and Literary Miscellany*, Jan 1819, 4, 22-7.

YOUNG, DAVID *Self-Culture*. Edinburgh: Q Dalrymple; Glasgow: George Gallie, and William Collins; Aberdeen: George King, and Lewis Smith; Berwick: William Thompson; Paisley: Alex Gardner and J Wotherspoon; Dundee: J Chalmers; Ayr: S Irvine, 1842. 12mo. Pp 24.   New Coll

—*Self-Education*. Perth: Perth Printing Company, 1842. 8vo. Pp 23.   Pe

Periodicals

Aberdeen University Magazine. Sixteen Parts. Aberdeen: P Gray, 1836. 8vo.

The British Educator Magazine. Seven Parts. Glasgow: Thomas Murray & Son, 1856. 8vo.   Mit

The Educational Journal of the Free Church of Scotland. Fourteen Parts. np, Edinburgh, 1849-50. 8vo.   EUL

The Free Church Educational Journal, Mar 1848-Apr 1850. Edinburgh: Printed by Miller & Fairly. 8vo.   EUL

Glasgow and West of Scotland Educational Guide; comprising the Prospectuses of various Public and Private Educational Institutions, Boarding Establishments, Academies, Seminaries and Schools. 2 vols. Glasgow: David Bryce & Son, 1870-1.   BM

NOTE Contains also a section on Edinburgh and Country Schools.

The Museum. A Quarterly Magazine of Education, Literature, and Science. 3 vols. Edinburgh: James Gordon, and London: Edward Stanford and Simpkin, Marshall, & Co, 1862-4. 8vo.

The Museum: and English Journal of Education. New series. 4 vols. London: Thomas Nelson and Sons, 1865-8. 8vo.

The Quarterly Journal of Education. 10 vols. London: Charles Knight, 1831-5. 8vo.

The Schoolmaster, and *Edinburgh Weekly Magazine*. Edited by John Johnstone. Edinburgh: John Anderson, Jun; Glasgow: John MacLeod, and Atkinson & Co, 1832-3. 2 vols. 4to.

The Scottish Educational and Literary Journal. Issued under the sanction of the Educational Institute of Scotland. 3 vols. Edinburgh: Sutherland and Knox, 1853-5. 8vo.

The Scottish Educational Journal, Mar 1856-Feb 1857. London and Glasgow: Richard Griffin and Company; Edinburgh: Sutherland and Knox, 1857. Vol 1.   EIS
No more published.

Whitaker's Educational Register, 1854. *Whitaker's Educational Register and Family Almanack*, 1855. 4 vols.

Schools

Parochial

B, J S 'The Parochial Schools of Scotland'; *Tait's Edinburgh Mag*, Aug 1844, **11**, 515-21; Sept 1844, **11**, 565-71.   EUL

BIOT, JEAN BAPTISTE 'Sur le mode d'éducation du peuple en Ecosse, et particulièrement sur un genre d'éducation très-influent appelé écoles paroissiales. (Extrait du *Journal des Savants*, Mars, 1822)'; Mélanges Scientifiques et Littéraires (Paris: Michel Levy Frères, 1858), tome troisième, 225-45.

— M. Biot on the Parochial Schools of Scotland. Translated by the Right Hon. Lord Brougham, with Notes and an Appendix. London: James Ridgway, 1859. 8vo. Pp 52.

BRYCE, JAMES *Public Education in its relation to Scotland and its Parish Schools. A Letter to the Right Hon. the Earl of Aberdeen, K.T. &c. &c. &c.* Edinburgh and London: William Blackwood and Sons, 1854. 8vo. Pp 39.

CANDLISH, ROBERT S *A Letter to the Most Noble the Marquess of Lansdowne, on the Reform and Extension of the Parish School System in Scotland.* Edinburgh and London: Johnstone & Hunter, 1850. 8vo. Pp 20.

CHALMERS, THOMAS *Considerations on the System of Parochial Schools in Scotland,* and on the Advantage of establishing them in Large Towns. Glasgow: Printed by James Hedderwick, 1819. 8vo. Pp 32.   EUL
Reprinted in CHALMERS, THOMAS *Works* (Glasgow: William Collins, nd), **xii**, 191-219; CHALMERS, THOMAS *Select Works,* ed HANNA, WILLIAM (Edinburgh: Thomas Constable & Co, 1856), **ix**, 517-36.

CHAMBERS, WILLIAM 'The Scottish Parish Schools'; *Chambers's Edinburgh J*, 28 Aug 1847, **8**, 136-9.

CHURCH OF SCOTLAND: PRESBYTERY OF CUPAR-FIFE *Memorial to the Right Honourable Lord John Russell, on the State of the Parish Schools of Scotland.* Edinburgh: Myles Macphail, 1848. 8vo. Pp 12, 11.   New Coll

COOK, JOHN (Haddington) *A Letter to a Member of Parliament on the Parochial Schools of Scotland.* Edinburgh and London: William Blackwood and Sons, 1854. 8vo. Pp 18.

COOK, JOHN (St Andrews) *Statement of Facts regarding the Parochial Schools of Scotland.* London: Printed by Harrison and Sons, 1855. 8vo. Pp 16.   BM

D, R 'Parochial Schools'; *Edinburgh Christian Instructor,* Feb 1828, **27**, 115-21; Mar 1828, **27**, 184-90; Aug 1828, **27**, 517-27.

An Examination of the Effects likely to result from the Interference of the Pres- bytery, in the Management of Parochial Schools. Glasgow: Printed in the *Scotsman* Office, 1812. 8vo. Pp 14.   GUL

[FLEMING, JOHN] *The Necessity of a Reform in the Parochial School System of Scotland*: By one who has long witnessed its existing defects. In a letter to the Right Honourable Andrew Rutherford, M.P., Her Majesty's Lord Advocate. Edinburgh: Adam and Charles Black; London: Longman, Brown, Green, and Longmans, 1848. 8vo. Pp 47.   New Coll

FREE CHURCH TEACHER, A 'The Parochial School; How far it meets the Wants of Rural Parishes'; *The Museum,* new series, 1 June 1867, **4**, 107-8.

'The Increased Endowment of the Parish Schools. What should be done? A Minister of the Free Church'; *Free Church Mag,* Sept 1847, **4**, 288-9.

'Influence of the Parish Schools on the Purity of the Dissenting Churches of Scotland'; *Voluntary Church Mag,* Aug 1835, **3**, 355-62.

INGLIS, SIR ROBERT HARRY, Bart *Parochial Schools of Scotland.* Substance of a Speech delivered in the House of Commons, on Wednesday, the 4th June, 1851. London: T Hatchard; Edinburgh: William Blackwood and Sons, 1851. 8vo. Pp 16.

LEE, WILLIAM *Parish School Statistics.* Means of Education in Scotland carefully revised. Reprinted from the *Church of Scotland Magazine and Review* for February, 1854. Edinburgh: Alexander C Moodie, 1854. 8vo. Pp 16.   New Coll

A Letter to the Right Honble Viscount Drumlanrig on the Parish Schools. Edinburgh: Alexander C Moodie, 1854. 8vo. Pp 16.
Reprinted from the *Church of Scotland Mag and Rev,* Jan 1854.

[MACKAY, ALEXANDER *A Plea for the Parish Schools.* By a Parish Schoolmaster. Edinburgh and London: William Blackwood and Sons, 1867. 8vo. Pp 36.   GUL

'Method of Conducting Parochial Schools in Scotland'; *Literary and Statistical Mag for Scotland*, Nov 1819, **3**, 392-405.

OBSERVER 'The Parish Schools'; *Edinburgh Evening Courant*, 9 June 1855.

On the Parochial Schools of Scotland: Their Past and Present State. In a letter to the Right Honourable Lord John Russell. By a Practical Educator. London: Wertheim & Macintosh; Edinburgh: Thomas C Jack, 1854. 8vo. Pp 20.   BM

'Our Parish Schools and their Assailants'; *Church of Scotland Mag and Rev*, Jan 1854, **2**, 36-44.
Reprinted in *A Letter to the Right Honble Viscount of Drumlanrig* (1854), 8-16.

The Parish Schools of Scotland. [*Religious*] *Tests for Teachers* and Superintendence of Schools. Edinburgh: Paton and Ritchie, 1860. 8vo. Pp 19.

'The Parochial Education of Scotland'; *Voluntary Church Mag*, Apr 1834, **2**, 122-30.

The Parochial Schools and the Established Church: with remarks upon kindred subjects, respectfully addressed to all whom they may concern. By a Country Presbyter. Edinburgh: William P Kennedy; Glasgow: D Bryce; London: Hamilton & Co, 1856. 8vo. Pp 24.

PAROCHIAL SCHOOLMASTER, A 'The Parochial School—How far it meets the Wants of Rural Parishes'; *The Museum*, new series, 1 May 1867, **4**, 63-6.

—'Fees in Parish Schools'; *The Museum*, new series, 1 Aug 1866, **3**, 182-3.

PATER 'On the Defects of the Law with respect to Parochial Schools'; *Literary and Statistical Mag for Scotland*, May 1818, **2**, 117-20.

RAMAGE, CRAUFURD TAIT *Defence of the Parochial Schools of Scotland*, in a series of letters to Viscount Drumlanrig, M.P., the landowners, the tenantry, and the Free Church clergy of Scotland. Edinburgh: Paton and Ritchie; Dumfries: John Sinclair, 1854. 8vo. Pp 64.

'Scottish Parochial Schools'; *Edinburgh Rev*, June 1827, **46**, 107-32.

SCOTUS 'On Parochial Schools in Scotland'; *Literary and Statistical Mag for Scotland*, Feb 1817, **1**, 1-8; May 1817, **1**, 113-21.

SCOTUS, VERUS 'Parochial School System'; *Church of Scotland Mag*, July 1834, **1**, 180-4.

SKINNER, JOHN 'On Parochial Revenues and a Parochial System of Education'; *Voluntary Church Mag*, May 1834, **2**, 158-62.

THOMSON, PETER D 'The Parish School and Schoolmaster'; *Parish and Parish Church. Their Place and Influence in History* (London and Edinburgh: Thomas Nelson and Sons Ltd, 1948), 202-11.

'What should be done with the Parish Schools?'; *Voluntary Church Mag*, Sept 1835, **3**, 398-407.

WILSON, JOHN 'The Old Parish School System'; *Educ News*, 1 Nov 1912, **37**, 1017-18.

Ragged, Reformatory, and Industrial

BEGG, JAMES 'A Visit to the Perth Juvenile Industrial Farm; and a Plan for National Education by which Country Schools may to a large extent become self-contained'; *The Witness*, 2 Nov 1850, **11**, 7.

BONE, ROBERT RAMSAY *The History of the Scottish Approved Schools*. Unpublished EdB thesis, Glasgow University, 1966. Typescript. 4to. Pp [3], 184. Bibliography.   GUL

COMMITTEE OF COUNCIL ON EDUCATION 'Industrial Schools'; *Minutes, 1850-51* (1851), xxi-xxviii.

EDUCATION COMMISSION (SCOTLAND) 'Industrial Ragged Schools'; *Third Report*, 1868, **1**, xxxvi-lii.

HILL, ALFRED *Train up a Child in the Way he should go*: A Paper on the Industrial Schools of Scotland, and the Working of Dunlop's Act. London: Cash; Bristol: I Arrowsmith, [1856]. 8vo. Pp 20.

HILL, MATTHEW D 'Aberdeen Feeding Schools'; *Suggestions for the Repression of Crime* (1857), 360-2.

LIDDELL, ANDREW *Letter on Industrial Schools*, addressed to the Conveners of Committees on Schools of Industry.

Glasgow: Printed by James Hedderwick & Son, 1846. 8vo. Pp 16.   New Coll

M J 'A Ragged School of a Hundred Years Ago'; *SEJ*, 21 Dec 1951, **34**, 743.

MCHARDY, ARCHIE *The Origins and Development of the Scottish Approved School System.* Unpublished EdB thesis, St Andrews University, 1966. Typescript. 4to. Pp [3], 84. Index.   StAUL

'Dean Ramsay and the Original Ragged Schools'; *The Museum*, new series, 1 Feb 1867, **3**, 419-21.

RATCLIFF, CHARLES *Ragged Schools in relation to the Government Grants for Education.* London: Longman, Green, Longman, & Roberts, 1861. 8vo. Pp xviii, 87.

Report of a Discussion regarding Ragged Schools; held in the Music Hall, Edinburgh, on Friday, July 2, 1847. Edinburgh: John Elder; William Collins, Glasgow; and James Nisbet & Co, London, 1847. 8vo. Pp 46.

Report of the Proceedings of a Conference on the Subject of Preventive and Reformatory Schools held at Birmingham, on the 9th and 10th December, 1851. London:

Longman, Brown, Green, and Longman, 1851. 8vo. Pp vi, 102.

THOMSON, ALEXANDER *Industrial Schools; Their Origin, Rise, and Progress, in Aberdeen.* Aberdeen: George Davidson; London: Nisbet & Co; Edinburgh: Johnstone; Glasgow: Collins; Dundee: Middleton, 1847. 8vo. Pp 42.

WATSON, WILLIAM 'Industrial Schools'; *Pauperism, Vagrancy, Crime, and Industrial Education in Aberdeenshire, 1840-1875* (Edinburgh and London: William Blackwood and Sons; Aberdeen: John R Smith, 1877), 43-9.

—*The Juvenile Vagrant and the Industrial School*; or 'Prevention better than Cure'. Aberdeen: George Davidson; London: Nisbet & Co; Edinburgh: Johnstone and Hunter; Glasgow: David Bryce, 1851. 8vo. Pp 36.

—*Chapters on Ragged and Industrial Schools.* Edinburgh and London: William Blackwood and Sons, 1872. 8vo. Pp 31.

WOODFORD, EDWARD 'Report on Industrial Schools'; *Minutes of the Committee of Council on Education, 1850-51* (1851), **2**, 731-4.

Schoolmasters and Teachers

Parochial and Burgh

ANDERSON, CHARLES *A statement of the Experience of Scotland, with regard to the Education of the People*; with Remarks on the intended Application of the Schoolmasters to Parliament. Dumfries: Printed for Arch Constable & Co, Edinburgh, by J McDiarmid & Co, 1825. 8vo. Pp 37.

The British Museum copy of this pamphlet, press-mark 8364.b.23(6), is contained in a bound volume of pamphlets which originally belonged to Henry, Lord Cockburn, who has added Anderson's name to the title page. Anderson

was at this time minister of Closeburn, Dumfries.

BARTY, JAMES STRACHAN *Remarks on the Parochial and Burgh Schoolmasters Act, 1861*, giving some Digest of the Chief Provisions of the Statute. With an Appendix containing the Regulations respecting the Examination of Schoolmasters-elect, issued by the University Examiners. Edinburgh and London: William Blackwood and Sons, 1862. 8vo. Pp 48.   New Coll

D 'Parochial Schoolmasters of Scotland'; *Edinburgh Mag & Literary Miscellany*, Jan 1826, **18**, 81-90.

Remarks on a Pamphlet entitled 'Statement and Representation respecting the Parochial Schoolmasters of Scotland'. Edinburgh: Printed for Alexander McCredie, 1825. 8vo. Pp 18.   BM

'Remarks on the Measures about to be proposed in Parliament, for the relief of Burgh and Parochial Schoolmasters'; *Edinburgh Mag and Literary Miscellany*, Mar 1826, **18**, 280-4.

ROBERTSON, STEWART A 'Old Parochials'; *SEJ*, 2 May 1919, **2**, 304-5.   EIS

'A Word in Defence of the Scotch Teacher'; *Scottish Educational and Literary J*, May 1853, **1**, 337-40.

Salaries and Status

'An Augmentation to the Living of Scots Schoolmasters pleaded for in preference to the Clergy'; *Scots Mag*, June 1750, **12**, 289-92.

BURGH AND PAROCHIAL SCHOOLMASTERS, PRESBYTERY OF IRVINE *Heads of a Bill to amend an Act made in the Forty-third Year of the Reign of his late Majesty George III, for making better Provision for the Parochial Schoolmasters, and for making further Regulations for the better Government of the Parish Schools in Scotland.* Kilmarnock: Printed by James Crawford, 1824. 8vo. Pp 12.   BM

CANDIDUS 'Hints for Increasing Schoolmasters Incomes'; *Scots Mag*, Apr 1765, **27**, 169-75.

CANDLISH, ROBERT S *Speech on the Sustentation of Schoolmasters.* Edinburgh: Printed at the *Witness* Office by Miller and Fairly, 1846. 8vo. Pp 15.   GUL

CHRISTISON, ALEXANDER *The General Diffusion of Knowledge one great Cause of the Prosperity of North Britain* (1802), 15-25.

COCKBURN, HENRY (Lord Cockburn) 'Answers to Memorial and Queries, for the Meeting of Schoolmasters'; *Report of the Committee of the General Purpose Fund* (1821), 20-4.   BM

CRAIGIE, JAMES 'The Campaign for better Salaries Two Hundred Years ago'; *SEJ*, 13 Dec 1963, **46**, 911-12.

—'Once upon a Time Salaries. . . .'; *SEJ*, 20 July 1951, **34**, 447-9.

CREECH, WILLIAM 'Letters [on Modern Education]'; *Edinburgh Evening Courant*, 18 Feb, 11, 18, and 26 Mar, 1, 8, and 17 Apr, and 15 May, 1786. Signed 'Belzebub'.

These eight letters were reprinted in CREECH, WILLIAM *Edinburgh Fugitive Pieces* (1791), 206-52; (1815), 247-99. A ninth letter, promised in that of 15 May 1786, first appeared in the 1791 volume.

—'A Letter respecting the Situation of the Schoolmasters of Scotland'; *Edinburgh Evening Courant*, 22 Mar 1784. Signed 'Cato'.

Reprinted in CREECH, WILLIAM *Edinburgh Fugitive Pieces* (1791), 168-71; (1815), 209-12.

DONALDSON, SIR JAMES 'On Teaching as a Profession'; *The Museum*, new series, 1 June 1867, **4**, 86-95.

DOUGLAS, ROBERT K *Letter to the Lord Advocate, on the Claims of the Parochial Schoolmasters.* np, 1825. 8vo. Pp 14.   BM

DUNCAN, HENRY *Statement and Representation respecting the ParochialSchoolmasters of Scotland*; with a view to the Bill about to be brought into Parliament for the Amelioration of their Condition. By a Dumfriesshire Clergyman. Dumfries: Printed at the *Courier* Office, by J McDiarmid & Co, 1825. 8vo. Pp 20.

'Emoluments of Old Parochials [in Kincardineshire]'; *SEJ*, 12 Apr 1935, **18**, 478.

FRASER, LUKE *Memorial for the Parochial Schoolmasters in Scotland, 1782.* Printed in CHAPMAN, GEORGE *Supplement to the Fifth Edition of Dr Chapman's Treatise on Education* (1796), 34-44; in CHAPMAN, GEORGE *Hints on the Education of the Lower Ranks of the People* (1801), 24-33; and in SINCLAIR, SIR JOHN *Statistical Account of Scotland*, **xxi** (1799), 336-41.

FREE CHURCH OF SCOTLAND *Education Scheme—Sustentation of Schoolmasters.* np, nd [?1847]. 8vo. Pp 4.   New Coll

—Acting Education Committee. *Explanatory Minute*. Edinburgh: Printed by T Constable, nd [1850]. 8vo. Pp 16.
New Coll

'Funds proposed for the Augmentation of Teachers Salaries'; *Scots Mag*, Oct 1748, **10**, 501.

GENERAL PURPOSE FUND *The Memorial of the Schoolmasters of Scotland*. np, nd [1824]. 4to. Pp 2. BM

—*Report of the Committee on the State of the Schoolmasters of Scotland under the Act 1803*. Edinburgh, 1821. 8vo. Pp 28.

JAFFRAY, THOMAS *An Essay for illustrating the Roman Poets* (1705), 3-4.

K, N 'Letter to Sir John Sinclair, Bart. on the State of National Education in Scotland'; *Statistical Account of Scotland*, **xxi** (1799), 301-36.

'A Letter from a Country Schoolmaster'; *The Bee, or, Literary Weekly Intelligencer*, ed ANDERSON, JAMES, 30 May 1792, **9**, 134-6.

MCGLASHAN, A 'The Position and Prospects of Scottish Schoolmasters Associations'; *The Museum*, new series, 1 Feb 1867, **3**, 411-19.

'Memorial for the Parish Schoolmasters in Scotland'; *Scots Mag*, Jan 1784, **46**, 1-4.
Reprinted in the *Edinburgh Evening Courant*, 17 May 1784.

PAROCHIAL SCHOOLMASTER, A 'Hindrances to the Attainment of a Proper Social Position by the Schoolmaster'; *The Museum*, new series, 1 Jan 1867, **3**, 379-381.

'Position and Character of our Future Teachers'; *Scottish Educational and Literary J*, July 1853, **1**, 433-7.

'The Position of the Teacher as affected by the "Minutes of Council" '; *Scottish Educational and Literary J*, Feb 1854, **2**, 203-7.

Q, V 'The Profession. Its Position and Prospects'; *Scottish Educational and Literary J*, Feb 1855, **3**, 105-9.

Reasons for Augmenting the Salaries and other Incomes of the Established Schoolmasters in Scotland, humbly proposed to the Consideration of the Publick. Edinburgh: Printed by Gideon Crawfurd, 1748. 8vo. Pp 8. BM
Reprinted in the *Scots Mag*, Sept 1748, **10**, 442-3, as part of an article signed 'D', and having as its title, *The Reasons for Augmenting the Salaries and other Incomes of the established Schoolmasters in Scotland, published by Order of the Meeting of Sept. 1*; and in MORREN, NATHANIEL *Annals of the General Assembly of the Church of Scotland* (Edinburgh, 1838), 376-83, in a brief account of the agitation for better salaries in 1748, under the title of *Proposal to Augment the Salaries of Schoolmasters*.

'Remarks on the Petition to Parliament, by the Schoolmasters in Scotland, for an Augmentation of their Salaries anno 1784'; *The Bee, or, Literary Weekly Intelligencer*, ed ANDERSON, JAMES, June 1792, **9**, 252-63.

SCHOOLMASTER, A 'A Plan for increasing the Salaries of Schoolmasters'; *Scots Mag*, Mar 1765, **27**, 114-16.

SCHOOLMASTERS' WIDOWS' FUND *Heads of a Bill for altering, &c. the Act 43 George III, cap. liv.* np, nd [?1824]. 8vo. Pp 16.
BM

SCOTICUS 'Reasons for Augmenting the Schoolmasters Salaries'; *Scots Mag*, June 1748, **10**, 282-3.

SIMPSON, JAMES 'On the Expediency and the Means of elevating the Profession of the Educator in Public Esteem'; in *Educator Prize Essays* (London: Printed for Taylor and Walton, 1839), 351-431. EUL

SMITH, WILLIAM 'Some Reflections on Education, with a modest Scheme for augmenting Schoolmasters Livings'; *Scots Mag*, Oct 1750, **12**, 488-92.

TAYLOR, GEORGE 'The Dignity and Importance of the Teacher's Office'; *Scottish Educational and Literary J*, Jan 1853, **1**, 173-80.

CRAIGIE, JAMES 'Teachers' Widows' Pensions in the Past'; *SEJ*, 2 Mar 1962, **45**, 171-2.

'Fund for Schoolmasters Widows'; *Scots Mag*, May 1762, **24**, 275-6.

Proposal to establish a Benefit Society for Governesses and Female Teachers. Edinburgh, 1830. 4to. Pp 3.   EUL

SCOTTISH FRIENDLY SOCIETY OF GOVERNESSES AND FEMALE TEACHERS Instituted 10th January 1831. *Rules.* Edinburgh: Printed at the *Caledonian Mercury* Press, for the Society. 8vo. Pp 32.

Teacher Training

BARNARD, HENRY 'Normal Schools in Edinburgh and Glasgow'; *Normal Schools, and other Institutions, Agencies, and Means designed for the Professional Education of Teachers* (Hartford, USA: Case, Tiffany, and Company, 1851), pt II, 427-35.

'The Certification of Teachers'; *Scottish Educational and Literary J*, Feb 1853, **1**, 193-5.

CHURCH OF SCOTLAND: EDUCATION COMMITTEE 'Correspondence relative to proposed Change in the Mode of Aid from the Committee of Council on Education to the General Assembly's Normal Schools'; *Report, 1852*, 31-40.

—'Correspondence [with the Committee of Council on Education] respecting the Establishment and Maintenance of Normal and Model Schools in Edinburgh and Glasgow'; *Report of the Committee for Increasing the Means of Education and Religious Instruction in Scotland, 1848*, 31-95.

—'Edinburgh Normal School'; *Report on the Returns from Presbyteries on the State of Schools in the Year 1841*, 93-100; *Report, 1844*, 26-9.

—'Glasgow Normal School'; *Report, 1844*, 29-32.

—*Historical Statement* having reference to the Letter of their Lordships of the Committee of Privy Council on Education, dated 23d February 1863 . . . requiring the Dismissal of 92 Queen's Scholars from the Edinburgh and Glasgow Normal Schools. Edinburgh, 1863. 8vo. Pp 23.   EUL

—*Minutes of the Education Committee, and relative Documents, in reference to the Minutes of Privy Council on Education.*

Edinburgh: Printed by Paton and Ritchie, 1849. 8vo. Pp 28, 8.

New Coll

—*Opening of the Normal Institution, Castlehill*, [Edinburgh]. May, 1845. Edinburgh: Stevenson and Co, 1845. 12mo. Pp 23. Frontispiece.   EUL

—'Regulations as to the Admission of Students to the Normal Institution in Edinburgh'; *Report of the Committee for increasing the Means of Education and Religious Instruction in Scotland, 1845*, 43-4.

—*Statement in regard to the Glasgow Normal Seminary*, np, 1848. 8vo. Pp 6.

New Coll

—'Supplementary Minute relating to Queen's Scholars, Apprentices, and Certificated Teachers'; *Report, 1855*, 48-70.

CRAIG, A R *The Philosophy of Training*; with suggestions on the necessity of Normal Schools for Teachers to the wealthier classes, and Strictures on the prevailing mode of teaching languages. London: D and A Macmillan, 1843. 8vo. Pp iv, 92.   BM

—*The Philosophy of Training*; or, The principles and art of a Normal Education; with a brief review of its origin and history. Also, Remarks on the practice of corporal punishment in schools; and strictures on the prevailing mode of teaching languages. Second edition. London: Simpkin & Marshall, 1847. 8vo. Pp xx, 377.

CURRIE, JAMES 'Memorandum on the Training of Elementary School Teachers, with special reference to the working of the Edinburgh Church of Scotland Training College'; *Education Commission (Scotland): Appendix to the First Report* (1867), 130-9.

DEMOGEOT, J, and MONTUCCI, H 'Écoles Normales; *De l'Enseignement Secondaire en Angleterre et en Écosse* (Paris, 1868), 429-37.

DICK, THOMAS 'On the Qualifications of Teachers, and Seminaries for their Instruction'; *On the Mental Illumination and Moral Improvement of Man* (1835), 489-501.

DICKSON, WILLIAM P 'Memorandum on the working of the Pupil-Teacher System'; *University of Glasgow: Report of the Committee of Senate on Elementary Schools in their relation to the Universities* (Glasgow, 1868), 19-24.   EUL

—National Education—A Memorandum on the Working of the Pupil-Teacher System. Glasgow, 1868. 8vo. Pp 8.
GUL

EDUCATION COMMISSION (SCOTLAND) 'Plan for combining University with Normal School Training'; *Third Report* (1868), 1, xxix.

EDUCATIONAL INSTITUTE OF SCOTLAND 'Memorial to Lord Granville'; *Scottish Educational and Literary J*, May 1855, 3, 184-6.

The Educational Register and Family Almanack (London: Whitaker, 1854-5), 206-7.   BM
Identical with the *Family Almanack and Educational Register*.

The Family Almanack and Educational Register (London: Whitaker, 1852-3), 184-5.   BM
Church of Scotland Training College, Edinburgh. Dundas Vale Normal Seminary, Glasgow. Episcopal Training Institution, Edinburgh. General Assembly's Normal Institution, Glasgow. Moray House, Edinburgh.

FEARON, DANIEL R 'Qualifications of Scottish Teachers'; *Report on Certain Burgh Schools and other Schools of Secondary Education in Scotland* (1868), 41-7.

FRASER, WILLIAM *The Educational Equipment of the Trained Teacher*. Edinburgh: James Gordon, 1861. 8vo. Pp 31.

Free Church Normal Training School (for Male and Female Teachers), Moray House, Edinburgh. *Plan, with descriptive Text*. 4to. P 1.

GLASGOW EDUCATIONAL SOCIETY *Hints towards the Formation of a Normal Seminary in Glasgow*, for the Professional Training of Schoolmasters. Glasgow, 1835. 8vo. Pp 16, 4.

'Government Certificates of Merit'; *Scottish Educational and Literary J*, Jan 1854, 2, 163-6.

N

K 'On the Training of Teachers'; *The Museum*, new series, 1 Sept 1866, 3, 208-211.

[LAURIE, SIMON SOMERVILLE] 'Training Schools in Scotland'; *The Museum*, July 1862, 2, 199-202.
Signed 'An Edinburgh Graduate'.

MACGILL, STEVENSON *The Qualifications of the Teachers of Youth*, considered in a Discourse delivered on the Anniversary of Wilson's Charity, at Glasgow, 1812. Glasgow: Printed by James Hedderwick & Co, 1814. 8vo. Pp iv, 55.

MCNEILL, HUGH *Speech at the Public Meeting of the Glasgow Educational Society, October, 1836*, also an Appeal on behalf of the Glasgow Normal Seminary. Glasgow: Printed by William Collins, 1836. 8vo. Pp 16.   GUL

MORGAN, ALEXANDER 'History of the Training of Primary & Secondary Teachers in Scotland'; *Educ News*, 4 Mar 1905, 30, 166-8; 18 Mar 1905, 30, 199-202.

NISSEN, HARTVIG 'Laererseminarier'; *Beskrivelse over Skotlands Almueskolevaesen* (1854), 131-55.

PATERSON, MAURICE 'Statement regarding the Edinburgh Free Church Normal School'; *Education Commission (Scotland); Appendix to the Third Report* (1867), 124-30.

—Parochial Schools (Scotland) Bill. Training and Examination of Teachers. np, 1869. 8vo. Pp 8.   New Coll

PILLANS, JAMES 'Seminaries for Teachers'; *Edinburgh Rev*, July 1834, 59, 486-502.

RUSK, ROBERT R *The Training of Teachers in Scotland*; An Historical Review. Edinburgh: Educational Institute of Scotland, 1928. 8vo. Pp vi, 159, [6]. Bibliographies. Index.

SIMPSON, JAMES *Hints on the Formation and Conduct of a General Model Normal School*, for training Teachers to supply the Demand of a National System of Popular Education. Edinburgh: Neill and Co, nd [?1835]. 8vo. Pp 8.

—Another edition. London: Saunders, Brothers, 1870. 8vo. Pp 16.   BM

—*The Normal School as it ought to be*; its Principles, Objects, and Organisation.

Edinburgh: Printed by Neill and Company, 1850. 8vo. Pp 10.

SOTHERN, ALAN 'The Life History of a P.T. (1855-1860)'; *Educ News*, 10 Feb 1911, **36**, 119-20.

'Training Schools in Scotland'; *The Museum*, July 1862, **2**, 199-208.

'Training Teachers'; *Chambers's Edinburgh J*, 18 Nov 1843, **12**, 351-2.

Professional Organisations

BELFORD, ALEX J *Centenary Handbook of the Educational Institute of Scotland*. Edinburgh: The Educational Institute of Scotland, 1946. 8vo. Pp vii, 430. Index.

—'Forerunners of the Institute'; *Centenary Handbook of the Educational Institute of Scotland* (1946), 1-29.

The Edinburgh Society of Teachers, 1737. Glasgow Schoolmasters' Society for Mutual Help, 1771. Glasgow Society of Teachers, 1794. The Calton and Bridgeton Society of Schoolmasters, Glasgow, 1804. Schoolmasters' Widows' Fund, 1807. Scottish School-Book Association, 1818. The Scottish Friendly Society of Governesses and Female Teachers, 1831. Aberdeen Society of Teachers, 1838. The Free Church Teachers' Associations, 1844. Glasgow Teachers Association, 1846. Association of Parochial Schoolmasters of Carrick, 1846. Society of the Parochial Schoolmasters of Kilsyth, Kirkintilloch, Campsie and Cadder, 1846. The Scholastic Association of Scotland, 1847.

BURGH AND PAROCHIAL SCHOOLMASTERS GENERAL PURPOSES FUND *Constitution and Rules*. Lasswade, 1852. 8vo. Pp 4.
EIS

—*Report*. 1855. Constitution and Rules of the Fund approved of by a General Meeting held on 18 September, 1846. np, 1855. 8vo. Pp 8.
EIS

—*Report*. 1856. Constitution and Rules of the Fund amended by a General Meeting, held on 19th September, 1856. np, 1856. 8vo. Pp 12.
EIS

DINGWALL, ALEXANDER 'A Forlorn Hope. The Roxburghshire Friendly Society of Parochial and Burgh Schoolmasters'; *SEJ*, 5 June 1931, **14**, 670-1.

EDUCATIONAL INSTITUTE OF SCOTLAND *Constitution of the Educational Institute of Scotland*, as arranged by the Revising Committee; to be submitted to the General Meeting in September 1849. np, [1849]. 8vo. Pp 16.
GUL

—*Record of the Proceedings of the Interim Committee of Management of the Educational Institute*, December 25, 1847. Edinburgh: Printed by Murray and Gibb, 1848. 8vo. Pp 16.
EUL

—*Royal Charter of Incorporation* and Rules and Regulations of the Educational Institute of Scotland. Incorporated 1851. np, nd. 8vo. Pp 16.
EUL

Printed in INSH, GEORGE PRATT *School Life in Old Scotland* (1925), 96-101.

'The Educational Institute of Scotland'; *Chambers's Edinburgh J*, new series, 25 Dec 1847, **8**, 409-11.

'The Educational Institute of Scotland: Its Origin, History and Objects'; *Tait's Edinburgh Mag*, Dec 1847, **14**, 807-10.

Reprinted in *Record of the Proceedings of the Interim Committee of Management, December 25, 1847*, 11-16.

'The Educational Institute—What is it? What *has* it *done* for the Profession? What is it *likely* to do?'; *Scottish Educational and Literary J*, Mar 1855, **3**, 123-7.

'Present Position and Duty of the Educational Institute of Scotland'; *Scottish Educational and Literary J*, Mar 1854, **2**, 255-61.

The Society in Scotland for Propagating Christian Knowledge

Proposals concerning the Propagating of Christian Knowledge in the Highlands and Islands of Scotland and Forraign Parts of the World. np, [Edinburgh], nd. [?1707]. Fol. Pp 4.

Her Majesties Letters Patent, erecting a Society in Scotland, for Propagating Christian Knowledge. Extract of the Act of the Lords of Council and Session, nominating the Members of the Society in Scotland, for Propagating Christian Knowledge. Act and Recommendation of the General Assembly of the Church of Scotland, for furthering the Design of Propagating Christian Knowledge. Edinburgh: Printed by the Heirs and Successors of Andrew Anderson, 1709. Fol. Pp 4.

The first two of these three documents were printed in BELSCHES, ALEXANDER *An Account of the Society in Scotland for Propagating Christian Knowledge* (1774), 54-8, 60-2, and in INSH, GEORGE PRATT *School Life in Old Scotland* (1925), 90-4.

Proposals by the Society in Scotland, for Propagating Christian Knowledge. np, [Edinburgh], nd [?1709]. Fol. P 1.

A Short Account of the Establishment and Progress of the Society in Scotland, for Propagating Christian Knowledge. np, [Edinburgh], 1713. Fol. Pp 2.

An Account of the Rise, Constitution, and Management, of the Society in Scotland, for Propagating Christian Knowledge. London: Printed for R Tookey, 1714. 8vo. Pp 35.   BM

—Second edition. Enlarged by a Member of the Society. Edinburgh: Printed for William Brown and Company, 1720. 8vo. Pp 48.

The State of the Society in Scotland for Propagating Christian Knowledge, anno 1729. Published by Order of the General Meeting of the foresaid Society. Edinburgh: Printed by William Brown and John Mosman, 1729. 12mo. Pp 48.   BM

Appeal for Funds. Edinburgh, 1729. Fol. P 1.

An Abridgement of the Statutes and Rules of the Society in Scotland for Propagating Christian Knowledge. Edinburgh: Printed by Robert Fleming and Company, 1732. 12mo. Pp 48.

A Short State of the Society in Scotland, for Propagating Christian Knowledge, anno 1732. Published by Order of the General Meeting of the foresaid Society. Edinburgh: Printed for William Brown, 1732. 12mo. Pp 32.

The Highland Complaint, transmitted by a Gentleman of that Country to his Friend at Edinburgh. Edinburgh, 1737. 8vo. Pp 42.

Second Patent, 1738. Printed in BELSCHES, ALEXANDER *An Account of the Society in Scotland for Propagating Christian Knowledge* (1774), 59-60, and in INSH, GEORGE PRATT *School Life in Old Scotland* (1925), 94-6.

PHILO-BRITANNICUS 'A Letter from a Gentleman in London to his Friend in the Country'; *Gentleman's Mag,* June 1739, 9, 286-8.

State of the Society in Scotland, for Propagating Christian Knowledge: giving a brief account of the condition of the Highlands and Islands of Scotland, and of the attempts that have been already made for the reformation of those parts, and what the Society has done, and have further in view, for their improvement in manual labour and industry, as well as in Christian Knowledge. Edinburgh: Printed by R Fleming, 1741. 8vo. Pp 75.   BM

WALKER, ROBERT *A Short Account of the Rise, Progress, and Present State of the Society in Scotland for Propagating Christian Knowledge.* With a sermon prefixed to it. Edinburgh: Printed by Thomas Lumsden and Company, 1748. 8vo. Pp 79.   stAUL

PLENDERLEATH, DAVID *Religion a Treasure to Men, and the Strength and Glory of a Nation.* A Sermon preached before the Society in Scotland for Propagating Christian Knowledge. To which is annexed, An account of the present state of the schools and missions supported by the Society: with reflexions on the usefulness and importance of the design and ends of their erection, drawn up by a Member of the Society. Edinburgh: Printed by Hamilton, Balfour, & Neill, 1754. 8vo. Pp 80.

State of the Society in Scotland for Propagating Christian Knowledge, in the year 1771. London: Printed for the Society, 1771. 8vo. Pp 34.

BELSCHES, ALEXANDER *An Account of the Society in Scotland for Propagating Christian Knowledge*, from its commencement in 1709. Edinburgh: Printed by A Murray and J Cochrane, 1774. 4to. Pp [2], 71.

'An Account of the Proceedings of the Society for Propagating Christian Knowledge in Scotland from June 1777 to June 1780'; in BLINSHALL, JAMES *The Evidence of the Future Publication of the Gospel to all Nations. A Sermon* (Edinburgh, 1780), 70-108.

'An Account of the Proceedings of the Society for Propagating Christian Knowledge in Scotland from June 1780 to June 1781'; in FRAME, JAMES *The Inscription on the Cross. A Sermon* (Edinburgh: 1781), 38-72.

MACFARLANE, JOHN *A Summary Account of the Rise and Progress of the Society in Scotland for Propagating Christian Knowledge*. Shewing the importance of the Institution; the benefits arising from it; the chief objects of the attention of the directors; and the aid necessary to enable them to carry out their beneficient designs. Edinburgh: Printed for the Society, 1783. 8vo. Pp 54.

HUNTER, HENRY *A Brief History of the Society in Scotland, for Propagating Christian Knowledge in the Highlands and Islands*: and of the Correspondent Board in London; from the Establishment of the Society in the year 1701, down to the present time. London, 1795. 8vo. Pp 77, 15.   EUL

An Account of the Funds, Expenditure, and General Management of the Affairs, of the Society in Scotland for Propagating Christian Knowledge: contained in a

report, drawn up by a committee of their number, appointed for that purpose. Edinburgh: Printed by J Paterson, 1798. 8vo. Pp 82.

A Short Account of the Society in Scotland, for Propagating Christian Knowledge in the Highlands and Islands. London: Printed by T Gillet, 1809. 8vo. Pp 24.

A Short Account of the Society in Scotland, for Propagating Christian Knowledge in the Highlands and Islands. To which is affixed, A Scheme of the Society's Establishment from 1 May, 1809, to May 1, 1810. London: Printed for the Society, 1811. 8vo. Pp 28.   BM

Short Account of the Object, Progress, and Exertions of the Society in Scotland for Propagating Christian Knowledge. Edinburgh, 1825. 8vo. Pp 7.

Case for the Society in Scotland for Propagating Christian Knowledge and Opinion of Counsel thereon. With an appendix, containing report on the constitution & practice of the Society, the Royal Patents, and list of members. Edinburgh, 1843. 8vo. Pp 17, 52, iv.   EUL
NOTE Counsel, asked whether the Society must dismiss those teachers who had left the Church of Scotland at the Disruption, advised raising an action in the Courts for declarator. This was done.

SIMSON, JAMES *Letter to the Lord Advocate, regarding the Schools on the Scheme of the Society in Scotland for Propagating Christian Knowledge*. Edinburgh, 1867. 8vo. Pp 10.   BM

ANDREW, IAN GRAHAM *A Brief Survey of the Society in Scotland for Propagating Christian Knowledge. A Statistical Addendum to the Survey*, by A G Cairns. Edinburgh, 1957. 8vo. Pp 24.

ENDOWED SCHOOLS AND HOSPITALS (SCOTLAND) COMMISSION 'Society for Propagating Christian Knowledge'; *Third Report* (1875), 137-40.

JONES, MARY G 'Scotland'; *The Charity School Movement* (Cambridge, 1938), 176-214, 377-83.

KERR, JOHN 'S.P.C.K. Schools'; *Scottish Education* (1910. Second edition, 1913), 181-91.

MAITLAND, WILLIAM 'The Society for Propagating the Gospel'; *History of Edinburgh, from its Foundation to the Present Time* (1753), 471-80.

MASON, JOHN 'Scottish Charity Schools of the Eighteenth Century'; *SHR*, Apr 1954, **33**, 1-13.

—'S.S.P.C.K.'; *A History of Scottish Experiments in Rural Education* (1935), 1-39.

RELIGIOUS INSTRUCTION (SCOTLAND) COMMISSION 'Society in Scotland for Propagating Christian Knowledge'; *Fourth Report* (1838), 318-22.

PP, 1837/38, xxxiii

RUSK, ROBERT R 'The Society in Scotland for Propagating Christian Knowledge'; *The Training of Teachers in Scotland* (1928), 17-23.

SIMPSON, IAN J 'The Aberdeenshire Schools of the Society for the Propagation of Christian Knowledge'; *Education in Aberdeenshire before 1872* (1947), 146-62.

U, C F 'Education in the Eighteenth Century [in a Hebridean S.S.P.C.K. School]'; *SEJ*, 14 Aug 1936, **19**, 1010-11.

WITHRINGTON, D J 'The S.P.C.K. and Highland Schools in mid-Eighteenth Century'; *SHR*, Oct 1962, **41**, 89-99.

Many of the annual sermons preached on behalf of the Society were later published and to most of them there was added an account of the Society at the date of publication. Three of these have already been given above. A list is now added of others that have been traced.

1755. ROBERTSON, WILLIAM *The Situation of the World at the Time of Christ's Appearance.*

1756. ERSKINE, JOHN *The Influence of Religion on National Happiness.*

1758. WITHERSPOON, JOHN *The Absolute Necessity of Salvation through Christ.*

1759. MAQUEEN, DANIEL *A Sermon.*
NOTE At p 57 are set out the qualifications desired in a schoolmaster and the duties required of him.

1763. RANDALL, THOMAS *Christian Benevolence.*

1769. BROWN, JAMES *The Extensive Influence of Religious Knowledge.*

1783. DUNCAN, ALEXANDER *The Evidence of the Resurrection of Jesus, as recorded in the New Testament.*

1784. FRASER, ALEXANDER *The Prophecies of the New Testament concerning the Man of Sin.*

1790. FLEMING, THOMAS *The Death of Christ an Atonement for Sin.*

1791. GERARD, ALEXANDER *The Corruption of Christianity.*

1794. LOVE, JOHN *Benevolence inspired and exalted by the Presence of Jesus Christ.*

1801. BROWN, WILLIAM LAWRENCE *The Nature, the Causes, and the Effects, of Indifference to Religion.*

1802. OGILVIE, JOHN *An Examination of the Evidence from Prophecy in behalf of the Christian Religion.*
KEMP, JOHN *The Character of the Apostle Paul.*

1804. BUCHANAN, WALTER *The Beneficial Influence of the Gospel.*

1805. DUNCAN, ANDREW *The Benefits of Christianity.*

1807. DALGLEISH, WALTER *The Importance of True Religion.*

1808. STUART, JOHN *The Blessedness of Giving, greater than that of Receiving.*

1809. MONCRIEFF-WELLWOOD, SIR HENRY, Bart. *A Sermon preached before the Society in Scotland for Propagating Christian Knowledge, at their Meeting on Tuesday, June 6, 1809*, being the Centenary Anniversary from the Date of their Charter in 1709.

1813. DICKSON, DAVID *The Influence of Learning on Religion.*

1814. CHALMERS, THOMAS *The Utility of Missions ascertained by Experience.*

1818. INGLIS, JOHN *The Grounds of Christian Hope.*

1819. WRIGHT, GEORGE *The Conversion of the World consequent upon the Improvement of the Church.*

1820. MUIRHEAD, GEORGE *The Divine Authority of the Scriptures.*

1821. DEWAR, DANIEL *God, the Chief Good, and the Chief End of Men.*

1822. THOMSON, WILLIAM AIRD *Preaching Christ Crucified.*

1823. GORDON, ROBERT *The Duty of Searching the Scriptures.*

1824. MACGILL, STEVENSON *Anniversary Sermon.*

1825. MACDONALD, JOHN *The Righteousness of God manifested.*

1826. MCFARLAN, PATRICK *The Influence of the Holy Spirit.*

1827. BROWN, JOHN *An Examination of the Sentiments of Socinians and Arians respecting the Meritorious Cause of the Forgiveness of Sin.*

1828. HENDERSON, JAMES *The Reception due to the Word of God.*

1829. LEE, JOHN *Anniversary Sermon.*

1830. BURNS, ROBERT *Jehovah the Guardian of his own Word.*

1831. MCLAGGAN, JAMES *Spiritual Views of the Divine Government.*

1832. PURVES, JAMES *Anniversary Sermon.*

1833. MANUEL, WILLIAM *The Ultimate Fulness of Christ's Church.*

1834. PAUL, JOHN *The Miraculous Propagation of the Gospel in the Apostolic Age.*

1837. BEITH, ALEXANDER *A Sermon preached before the Society on Thursday, June 1, 1837.*

1856. NICHOLSON, MAXWELL *The Duty of Building the Lord's House.*

1857. TULLOCH, JOHN *The Light of the World.*

1858. SMITH, WILLIAM *The Power of the Kingdom of God.*

1859. BOYD, A K H *Spiritual Insensibility. A Sermon preached before the Society in Scotland for Propagating Christian Knowledge on Tuesday, 6th December, 1859, being the Third Jubilee of the Society.*

NOTE The Minutes of the Society and other papers connected with it are now lodged in HM General Register House, Edinburgh.

Part Four

The Scottish Universities

ALEXANDER, WILLIAM LINDSAY *The University; Its Nature, Functions, and Requirements*. Edinburgh: Adam and Charles Black, 1859. 8vo. Pp 36.

ANDERSON, ALEXANDER *The Scottish University System*: Problem of reconciling the Elevation of its Standard with the Maintenance of its Public Utility: with a reference to the Question of College Fusion in Aberdeen. Edinburgh: Adam & Charles Black; G Davidson, 1859. 8vo. Pp 22.

ANDERSON, PETER J 'Records of the Scottish Universities'; *Scottish Notes and Queries*, Apr 1892, **5**, 162-3.

ASSOCIATION FOR THE IMPROVEMENT AND EXTENSION OF THE SCOTTISH UNIVERSITIES *Report by the Acting Committee*. Edinburgh: Printed by Robert Hardie & Co, nd [?1858]. 8vo. Pp 18. EUL

BLACK, ROBERT COOPER *Some Considerations on the Educational System of the Scottish Universities as compared with those of England*, with a particular reference to the Universities of Edinburgh and Oxford. With a Postscript containing Observations on an Article on 'The Scottish Universities' in "The North British Review" for August. Edinburgh: W P Kennedy; Glasgow: D Bryce; London: Hamilton, Adams, & Co; Oxford: Graham, 1850. 8vo. Pp 34.

BLACKIE, JOHN STUART *Classical Literature in its Relation to the Nineteenth Century and Scottish University Education*. Edinburgh: Sutherland and Knox; London: Simpkin, Marshall, and Co, 1852. 8vo. Pp 24.

—*On Subscription to Articles of Faith*: A Plea for the Liberties of the Scottish Universities. Edinburgh: William Tait; Aberdeen: Brown & Co, and L Smith; London: Simpkin, Marshall, & Co, 1843. 8vo. Pp 39.

—*'Scottish University Education—Entrance Examinations'*; *The Scotsman*, 25 Dec 1852.

—*'Scottish University Reform'*; *North British Rev*, May 1855, **23**, 73-112.

—*University Reform*: Eight Articles reprinted from the Scotsman Newspaper; with a Letter to Professor Pillans. Edinburgh: Sutherland and Knox; London: Simpkin, Marshall, and Co; Aberdeen: Lewis Smith, 1848. 8vo. Pp 67.

These letters, signed 'A', appeared in the *Scotsman* for 17 and 27 Nov, 4, 18, 25 Dec, 1847; 5 and 15 Jan and 2 Feb, 1848.

BLACKIE, WALTER G 'Competitive Examinations for the Public Service, and the preparatory Training in our Scottish Universities'; *Transactions of the National Association for the Promotion of Social Science, 1860* (1861), 318-21.

—*Remarks on the East India Company's Civil Service Examination Papers*: as illustrative of some defects in the course of academical education in Scotland. Printed at the request of the 'Scottish Literary Association'. For private circulation. Glasgow: W G Blackie and Co, 1858. 8vo. Pp 24.

BRISTED, JOHN 'The Scottish Universities touched on'; 'Ἀνθρωπλαμενος; or, *A Pedestrian Tour through Part of the Highlands of Scotland in 1801* (London: Printed for J Wallas, 1802), **2**, 536-633.

BROWN, WILLIAM *The Scientific Character of the Scottish Universities*, viewed in connection with religious belief and their educational use. Edinburgh: Adam and Charles Black, 1856. 8vo. Pp 52. BM

BRYCE, REUBEN J *Practical Suggestions for reforming the Educational Institutions of Scotland*: being an attempt to point out the necessity for desectarianising the schools and universities simultaneously; and the means whereby this may be accomplished. Edinburgh: William Oliphant and Sons; Glasgow: D Robertson; London: Hamilton and Co, 1852. 8vo. Pp 31.

BRYCE, WILLIAM MOIR 'The Blackfriars and the Scottish Universities'; *SHR*, Oct 1911, **9**, 1-9.

BUCHANAN, ANDREW *Of Monopolies in Learning*; with remarks on the present state of medical education, and on the constitution of the Scotch universities. Glasgow: Richard Griffin & Co, 1834. 12mo. Pp 24.   EUL

BUCHANAN, WALTER *The Parliamentary Representation of the Scottish Universities.* Edinburgh: Sutherland and Knox; Glasgow: Richard Griffin & Co, nd 1857. 8vo. Pp 12.

BULLOCH, JOHN MALCOLM *The Rectorship*: Its Origin, its Meaning, and its Practical Value. np [?Aberdeen], nd [1902]. 8vo. Pp 41. Plate.

CAMPBELL, LEWIS *The Scottish Universities. A Practical Suggestion for the Improvement of the Honour-System in the Scottish Universities.* Dundee: Frederick Shaw, 1867. 8vo. Pp 15.   EUL

CANT, RONALD C *Scottish 'Paper Universities'.* A Lost Chapter in Academic History. np [?Dundee], nd [1945]. 8vo. Pp 20.

Reprinted from the *Scots Mag*, new series, Sept 1945, **43**, 415-23; Oct 1945, **44**, 39-48.

CHALMERS, THOMAS *Letter to the Royal Commissioners for the Visitation of Colleges in Scotland.* Glasgow: Printed for William Collins, 1832. 8vo. Pp 80.

CHURCH OF SCOTLAND: PRESBYTERY OF ST ANDREWS *Case for the Presbytery, in the Libel against Sir David Brewster, K.H., LL.D.* Principal of the United College. Edinburgh: Printed by William Macphail, 1845. 8vo. Pp 68.   New Coll

—: — *Jurisdiction of the Church over Universities and Colleges*: or, A Statement of the Grounds on which the Presbytery of St Andrews refused to adopt the unsolicited Opinion of Counsel as to the Jurisdiction of the Church over Universities and Colleges. With an Appendix: containing the whole correspondence between the Counsel and the Convener of the Committee of Presbytery appointed to draw up the Libel, and a defence of his Conduct, acting under the direction of the Committee. Edinburgh: Macphail; *Journal* Office, Cupar; Fletcher, St Andrews; Gourlay, Anstruther; Cumming, Kirkaldy (*sic*), 1844. 8vo. Pp 44.   New Coll

—: SYNOD OF ABERDEEN *Report of the Synod's Committee on the Universities of Scotland.* Aberdeen: Printed by G Chalmers & Co, 1839. 8vo. Pp 20.   GUL

CLASON, PATRICK *Essays.* viz. I. On the Origin of Colleges, or Universities. II. On the Origin of the Custom of lecturing in Latin. III. On the Impropriety of this Custom, at present. Glasgow: Printed for Robert Urie and John Barry, 1769. 8vo. Pp 61.

'Classical Education'; *Edinburgh Rev*, July 1821, **35**, 302-14.

COISSAC, JEAN-BAPTISTE *Les Universités d'Écosse depuis la Fondation de l'Université de St-Andrews jusqu'au Triomphe de la Réforme (1410–1560).* Paris: Librairie Larousse, [1915]. 8vo. Pp 310. Bibliography.

CORMACK, SIR JOHN ROSE *Universities of Scotland Bill.* Remarks on the Condition, Necessities, and Claims of the Universities of Scotland: With an Appendix. By a Graduate. London: Edward Stanford, 1858. 8vo. Pp xvi, 72.   EUL

CUNNINGHAM, DANIEL JOHN *The Evolution of the Graduation Ceremony.* Edinburgh and London: William Blackwood & Sons, 1904. 8vo. Pp 51.   EUL

DALGLEISH, WALTER SCOTT 'University Certificate Examinations, or "Local Examinations", for Scotland'; *Transactions of the National Association for the Promotion of Social Science, 1863* (1864), 274-80.

—*University Certificate Examinations*, with suggestions for a scheme in Scotland similar to the English 'Middle Class Examination'. Edinburgh: James Gordon; Glasgow: Thomas Murray & Son, 1860. 8vo. Pp 40.

DAVIE, GEORGE ELDER *The Democratic Intellect*: Scotland and her Universities in the Nineteenth Century. Edinburgh: The University Press, 1961. 8vo. Pp xx, 352. Frontispiece and 8 plates. Index.

A Defence of the Universities of Scotland. By a Graduate. Edinburgh: Edmonston & Douglas, 1849. 8vo. Pp 15.

Demise of the Bill intituled 'An Act for the Visitation and Regulation of the Universities of Scotland'; *Aberdeen University Mag*, 24 Aug 1836, **1**, 267-73.

DEMOGEOT, J, and MONTUCCI, H *De l'Enseignement Supérieure en Angleterre et en Écosse*. Paris: Imprimerie impériale, 1870. 8vo.
The Scottish section occupies 345-509.

DOUGLAS, WILLIAM *The Ferguson Scholars, 1861-1955*. Glasgow: Published for the Trustees of the Ferguson Bequest Fund by Robert Maclehose and Company Limited, 1956. 8vo. Pp 367. Frontispiece.

DUFF, SIR MOUNTSTUART E GRANT *Inaugural Address on his Installation as Rector* [of Aberdeen University]. Edinburgh: Edmonston and Douglas; London: Hamilton, Adams, & Co, 1867. 8vo. Pp 50.

DURKAN, JOHN *The Scottish Universities in the Middle Ages, 1413-1560*. Unpublished PhD thesis, Edinburgh University, 1959. Typescript. 4to. Pp xxiii, 568, 204. Bibliography. EUL

ENDOWED SCHOOLS AND HOSPITALS (SCOTLAND) COMMISSION 'Bell Bequest'; *Third Report* (1875), 142-3; *Appendix to Third Report* (1875), **1**, 145.

—'Ferguson Bequest'; *Third Report* (1875), 131-7; *Appendix to Third Report* (1875), **1**, 172-4.

—'Maclean Bequest'; *Third Report* (1875), 141-2; *Appendix to Third Report* (1875), **1**, 143.

—'Supplementary Table of University Endowments'; *Appendix to Third Report* (1875), **1**, 428-9.

—'Universities'; *Third Report* (1875), 167-198.

FERGUSSON, ADAM WIGHTMAN *The Caird Travelling Scholarships*. Privately printed, for private use. Dundee, 1937. 4to. Pp 40.

FERRIER, JAMES F *A Letter to the Right Honourable the Lord Advocate of Scotland on the Necessity of a Change in the Patronage of the University of Edinburgh*. Edinburgh: Sutherland and Knox, 1858. 8vo. Pp 16.

[FLETCHER, ANDREW] *Proposals for the Reformation of Schools and Universities* in order to the better education of youth. Humbly offer'd to the serious consideration of the High Court of Parliament. np, [Edinburgh], 1704. 4to. Pp 11.

FORBES, PATRICK *Letter to the Right Hon. the Lord Advocate of Scotland, regarding Bills proposed to be brought into Parliament, by His Majesty's Government, for the Regulation of the Scottish Universities*, and particularly regarding a Bill to be brought in at the Commencement of next session, for the regulation of the Colleges of Aberdeen, in reference to the Recommendations of the Royal Commission of Visitation of 1826 and 1830. Aberdeen: Printed for Lewis Smith; Edinburgh: Maclaughlan & Stewart, and Thomas Clark; Glasgow: David Robertson; and Melville Fletcher, St Andrews, 1835. 8vo. Pp 27.

GEDDES, SIR WILLIAM D *Classical Education in the North of Scotland*. Edinburgh: Edmonston & Douglas; Aberdeen: John Smith, 1869. 8vo. Pp 69. EUL

—*Letter to the Commissioners for the Scottish Universities*. np [?Aberdeen], 1861. 4to. Pp 3. EUL

[GILLIS, JOHN] *An Inquiry, Whether the Study of the Ancient Languages be a necessary Branch of Modern Education?* Wherein, by the way, some Observations are made on a late Performance, intituled, *Essays on the Origin of Colleges, of the Custom of Lecturing in Latin, etc.* Edinburgh: Sands, Murray, and Cochran, 1769. 8vo. Pp xiv, 66.

GLASGOW, UNIVERSITY OF *Abstract of Evidence on Entrance Examinations* given to the Scottish Universities Commission in 1860. Glasgow: Printed at the University Press, by Maclehose & Macdougall, 1875. 8vo. Pp 46. GUL

GRAHAM, HENRY GREY 'Education in Scotland—The Universities—Their Life and Learning'; *The Social Life of Scotland in the Eighteenth Century* (London: Adam and Charles Black, 1899), **2**, 182-206.
The second edition, also in two volumes, which appeared in 1900, was identical with this.

— —(London: Adam and Charles Black, 1901), 448-72. EUL

This, the third edition, was in one volume. It was reprinted without change in 1906, 1928, 1937, 1950, and 1964, except that the issues from 1928 on were illustrated by eight plates.

GRAY, SIR ALEXANDER 'The Old Schools and Universities in Scotland'; *SHR*, **9**, 113-138.

GRAY, GEORGE H B 'Election Times at a Scotch University'; *Canadian Monthly and National Rev*, 1878, **12**, 160-3.
Not seen

The Grievance of University Tests as set forth in the Proceedings of the Presbytery of St Andrews. With an authentic Copy of the Libel in the case of Sir David Brewster. Edinburgh: John Johnstone; London: R Groombridge & Sons, 1845. 8vo. Pp 35.

HAMILTON, SIR WILLIAM 'Patronage of Universities'; *Edinburgh Rev*, Apr 1834, **59**, 196-227.
Reprinted with the title *On the Patronage and Superintendence of Universities*, in HAMILTON, SIR WILLIAM *Discussions* (1852) 348-85; (1853), 362-400; (1866), 358-96.

HANNAY, ROBERT K 'The Universities of Scotland'; in RASHDALL, HASTINGS *The Universities of Europe in the Middle Ages*, a new edition, ed POWICKE, F M, and EMDEN, A B (Oxford: At the Clarendon Press, 1936), **2**, 301-24.

HARROWER, JOHN *The Age of Entrance to the Arts Curriculum*. Aberdeen: The Rosemount Press, 1912. 8vo. Pp 8.   BM

'The Hebrew Chair. The Present Tests in Colleges and Schools'; *Free Church Mag*, Nov 1847, **4**, 352-5.

HORN, D B 'The Universities (Scotland) Act of 1858'; *University of Edinburgh J*, 1959, **19**, 169-99.

HUTTON, LAURENCE *Literary Landmarks of the Scottish Universities*. New York and London: G P Putnam's Sons, 1904. 8vo. Pp xi, 200. Frontispiece and 41 plates. Index.

INGLIS, SIR JOHN 'English and Scotch Universities'; *The Museum*, new series, 1 May 1866, **3**, 57-61.

INGLIS, SIR ROBERT HARRY, Bart. *Universities: Scotland*. Substance of a Speech,

delivered in the House of Commons, on Monday, the 14th July, 1853, against the Second Reading of the Bill to regulate the Admission of Professors to the Lay Chairs in the Universities of Scotland. London: Thomas Hatchard; J H Parker, London and Oxford, and W Blackwood, Edinburgh, 1853. 8vo. Pp 32.

INNES, ALEXANDER TAYLOR 'Open Teaching in the Universities of Scotland'; *The Museum*, Apr 1862, **2**, 49-55.

IRVINE, WALTER FORBES *A Letter to the Members of the Edinburgh University Council and the Edinburgh University Court*: being the Substance of a Speech on extended University Sessions and Entrance Examinations. Edinburgh: Paton and Ritchie, 1863. 8vo. Pp 16.

JARDINE, GEORGE *Outlines of Philosophical Education*, illustrated by the Method of Teaching the Logic, or First Class of Philosophy, in the University of Glasgow. Glasgow: Printed by Andrew & James Duncan, for Anderson & Macdowall, Edinburgh; Longman, Hurst, Rees, Orme, & Brown, London; and A & J M Duncan, Glasgow, 1818. 8vo. Pp viii, 3, 485.

— —; together with Observations on the Expediency of extending the Practical System to other Academical Establishments, and on the Propriety of making certain Additions to the Course of Philosophical Education in Universities. Second edition, enlarged. Glasgow: Printed at the University Press, for Oliver and Boyd, Edinburgh, and George B Whittaker, London, 1825. 8vo. Pp xv, 527.

KELLAND, PHILIP 'Scottish Universities— Professor Blackie's Inaugural Lecture'; *The Scotsman*, 22 Dec 1852.

—'Scottish University Education'; *The Scotsman*, 5 Jan 1853.
Two letters to the *Scotsman*, both signed 'A Southerner'. For the authorship see MURRAY, T *Greek Entrance Examination* (Edinburgh, 1855), 17, note 3.

—*The Scottish University System suited to the People*. Edinburgh: Adam & Charles Black, 1854. 8vo. Pp 15.

— —. Second edition. Edinburgh: Adam & Charles Black, 1854. 8vo. Pp 15. EUL

—*How to improve the Scottish Universities.* Edinburgh: Adam and Charles Black, 1855. 8vo. Pp 22. EUL

KILGOUR, ALEXANDER *The Scottish Universities, and what to reform in them.* Edinburgh: Sutherland & Knox; Glasgow: Richard Griffin & Co; Aberdeen: John Smith, 1857. 8vo. Pp v, 66.

—*University Reform.* Letters to the Right Hon. the Earl of Aberdeen on the Constitution and Government of the Scottish Universities. Aberdeen: Lewis Smith, 1850. 12mo. Pp 33. EUL
Five letters, each signed 'A Scottish Graduate', reprinted from the *Aberdeen Herald* of 13, 21, and 28 Oct, and 4 and 11 Nov 1850.

LEE, JOHN *Refutation of the Charges brought against him by the Rev. Dr Chalmers and others,* in reference to the Questions on Church Extension and University Education. Part I. With an Appendix, containing the Evidence of Dr Lee before the Commissioners of Religious Instruction. Edinburgh: William Blackwood & Sons, 1837. 8vo. Pp 107, 21.

—*Additional Refutation of the Charges . . .* University Education. Part II. Edinburgh: William Blackwood & Sons, 1837. 8vo. Pp 21.

LEES, GEORGE *An Address in reference to Courses of Instruction for Degrees in Arts,* together with a short plea for one general university in Scotland, for conferring degrees. St Andrews: Printed by J Cook & Son, 1865. 8vo. Pp 12. EUL

—'The Scottish University System, with suggestions for its further improvement'; *Transactions of the National Association for the Promotion of Social Science, 1863* (1864), 267-74.

LORIMER, JAMES 'Scottish University Reform'; *Edinburgh Rev,* Jan 1858, **107,** 88-121.

—'The Higher Instruction and its Representatives in Scotland'; *North British Rev,* May 1853, **19,** 219-42.

—'The Scottish Universities'; *North British Rev,* Aug 1850, **13,** 285-334.

—*The Universities of Scotland.* Past, present, and possible; with an Appendix of documents relating to the higher

instruction. Edinburgh: W P Kennedy; Glasgow: D Bryce; Aberdeen: G Davidson; London: Hamilton, Adams, & Co, 1854. 8vo. Pp viii, 88, 64. EUL
A second edition, identical with this, appeared in 1856. EUL

MACAULAY, THOMAS BABINGTON, LORD MACAULAY *Speech delivered in the House of Commons, Wednesday, July 9, 1845, on the Bill for the Abolition of Scottish University Tests.* Edinburgh: W P Kennedy; Glasgow: D Bryce; Ayr: D Guthrie; Aberdeen: C Panton, 1845. 8vo. Pp 9. New Coll
Reprinted in MACAULAY, LORD *Speeches, corrected by himself* (London, 1854), 402-20; (London, 1866), 192-201, with the title, *Theological Tests in the Scottish Universities.*

MCCRIE, THOMAS 'The Universities of Scotland'; *Life of Andrew Melville,* second edition (Edinburgh: William Blackwood; and T Cadell, London, 1824), **2,** 336-449.

MACFARLAN, DUNCAN *Substance of a Speech* delivered in the Presbytery of Glasgow, on Wednesday, the 25th Day of February, 1846, on bringing forward a Motion to petition both Houses of Parliament against the Abolition of University Tests in Scotland. Glasgow: John Smith and Son; William Blackwood and Sons, Edinburgh and London, 1846. 8vo. Pp 36. New Coll

'Management of Universities'; *British Mag,* 1 Jan 1836, **9,** 85-9.

MASSON, DAVID *Memories of Two Cities: Edinburgh and Aberdeen.* Edinburgh and London: Oliphant, Anderson & Ferrier, 1911. 8vo. Pp 317. Portrait. Index.

—*The State of Learning in Scotland.* Edinburgh: Edmonston & Douglas, 1866. 12mo. Pp 28.

MONCRIEFF, JAMES, LORD MONCRIEFF *Speech in the House of Commons, April 27, 1852, on the Second Reading of the University Tests (Scotland) Bill.* Edinburgh: Adam and Charles Black, 1852. 8vo. Pp 20. New Coll

MORGAN, ALEXANDER 'Historical Growth of the Arts Curriculum'; *SEJ,* 15 July 1932,

15, 890-1; 22 July 1932, **15**, 917-18; 29 July 1932, **15**, 930-1; 5 Aug 1932, **15**, 964-5; 12 Aug 1932, **15**, 980-1.

MUIR, JOHN *The Indian Civil Service and the Scottish Universities*; or, the New System of Appointment, considered, as it affects the Prospects of Scottish Students, and the Higher Education in Scotland. Edinburgh: W P Kennedy; Glasgow: D Bryce; Aberdeen: G Davidson; London: Hamilton, Adams, & Co, 1855. 8vo. Pp 27.

MUIR, WILLIAM *Speeches delivered in the Commission of the General Assembly, met at Edinburgh, on Thursday, 7th July, 1836, to consider 'The Universities Bill for Scotland'.* Edinburgh: Fraser & Co; London: Smith, Elder, & Co; Dublin: W Curry, Jun & Co, 1836. 8vo. Pp 28.
New Coll

Mr Rutherford and University Tests. By a Leal-hearted Scotchman. (From the *Glasgow Courier.*) Glasgow: Printed in the *Glasgow Courier* Office, nd [1845]. 8vo. Pp 8.
New Coll

NAPIER, MARK 'On the Progress and Prospects of Science in Scotland at the Close of the Sixteenth and Commencement of the Seventeeenth Centuries, as compared with the same at Cambridge a century later'; *Archaeological J*, Sept 1857, **14**, 221-62.

'The New Arts Curriculum in the Scottish Universities'; *The Museum*, new series, 1 Sept 1864, **1**, 201-5.

NICHOL, JOHN PRINGLE *Replies to Inquiries of the Commissioners regarding the Scottish Universities.* Glasgow: William Mackenzie, 1859. 8vo. Pp 30.   Mit

NICOL, JAMES *Our Higher Education*: Its Necessity and Nature. Aberdeen: D Wyllie and Son; London: Longmans & Co, 1868. 8vo. Pp 31.

Notes on the Constitutions of Universities. See WALKER, GEORGE.

'On Scottish University Tests'; *North British Rev*, Nov 1849, **12**, 265-82.

'One University for Scotland'; *The Museum*, Jan 1863, **2**, 437-44.

'Outlines of Philosophical Education'; *Blackwood's Edinburgh Mag*, July 1818, **3**, 420-4.

Oxford and the Scottish Universities. Reprinted from *The Scottish Magazine.* Edinburgh: R Lendrum & Co, 1848. 8vo. Pp 8.   EUL
Reprinted from the *Scottish Mag*, Oct 1848, **1**, 449-55, where the title is *English and Scottish Degrees.*

PILLANS, JAMES *A Word for the Universities of Scotland*; and a Plea for the Humanity Classes in the College of Edinburgh. Edinburgh: Maclachlan, Stewart, & Co; London: Simpkin and Marshall, 1848. 8vo. Pp 76.
Reprinted in PILLANS, JAMES *Contributions to the Cause of Education* (1856), 423-67.

A Plea for University Tests. By a Layman. Edinburgh: Paton and Ritchie, 1853. 8vo. Pp 21.

PLAYFAIR, LYON *On Teaching Universities and Examining Boards.* Edinburgh: Edmonston and Douglas, 1872. 8vo. Pp 37.

'Preparation for the University'; *The Presbyterian*, 1 Oct 1868, **1**, 1-2.

RAIT, SIR ROBERT SANGSTER 'Some Notes on the History of University Education in Scotland'; *Transactions of the Glasgow Archaeological Society*, new series, **5**, pt 2 (1908), 30-50.

RAMSAY, GEORGE G *Graduation in Arts.* Glasgow, 1870. 8vo. Pp 13.   GUL

RAMSAY, WALTER MARLOW 'The University of London and its Influence on Education in Scotland'; *Fraser's Mag*, new series, Aug 1876, **14**, 213-18.

RASHDALL, HASTINGS 'The Universities of Scotland'; *The Universities of Europe in the Middle Ages* (Oxford: At the Clarendon Press, 1895), **2**, pt 1, 295-315.

REECE, D W 'The Scottish Ordinary Degree'; *Aberdeen University Rev*, Spring 1962, **39**, 211-16.   EUL

'Remarks on the Principal Clauses of Lord Melbourne's University Bill'; *Aberdeen University Mag*, 21 June 1836, **1**, 191-212.

ROBERTSON, WILLIAM *The Church and the Universities of Scotland*: their Historical and Necessary Connection. Edinburgh and London: William Blackwood and Sons, 1853. 8vo. Pp 56.

'Royal Commission on the Universities of Scotland'; *New Scots Mag*, 30 June 1829, **1**, 437-43.

RUSSELL, MICHAEL *View of the System of Education at present pursued in the Schools and Universities of Scotland.* With an Appendix, containing Communications relative to the University of Cambridge, school of Westminster, the Perth Academy; together with a more detailed Account of the University of St Andrews. Edinburgh: Printed by John Moir, 1813. 8vo. Pp vii, 168, lv.

ST ANDREWS, UNIVERSITY OF *Scheme for the Extension of University Teaching by Means of Local Lectures and Classes*, in the counties of Fife, Forfar, Perth, Kinross, and Clackmannan. St Andrews: Printed by Johnston & Co, Dundee, for St Andrews University. 8vo. Pp 16. GUL

SANDFORD, SIR DANIEL K *Preliminary Lecture*, delivered in the Common Hall of the University of Glasgow, November the 7th, 1826; comprising a View of the Course of Study performed in the Greek Class. Edinburgh: William Blackwood; and T Cadell, London, 1826. 8vo. Pp viii, 32.

SAUNDERS, LAURANCE JAMES 'The Universities and the Professions'; *Scottish Democracy, 1815-1840* (Glasgow and London: Oliver and Boyd, 1950), 307-71.

'Scottish Universities Bill'; *British Mag*, 1 May 1836, **9**, 573-7.

SCOTTISH LITERARY INSTITUTE *University Reform.* np, 1857. 4to. Pp 4. Mit

—*Memorandum on University Reform submitted to Members of Parliament.* np, 1857. 8vo. Pp 2. GUL

The Scottish Schools and Universities. Three Articles reprinted from the *Scottish Press Newspaper* for October 13, 16, and 23, 1847. Edinburgh: *Scottish Press* Office, 1847. 8vo. Pp 29.

'Scottish Student Life'; *Scottish Rev*, July 1861, 252-62.

'The Scottish Universities'; *Tait's Edinburgh Mag*, June 1845, **12**, 375-9.

—; *Blackwood's Edinburgh Mag*, Jan 1858, **83**, 74-93.

SCOTTISH UNIVERSITIES AND EDUCATIONAL ASSOCIATION *Draft Report for Provisional Committee.* Prepared by Interim Acting Committee. Edinburgh: Andrew Elliot, 1866. 8vo. Pp 28.

SCOTTISH UNIVERSITIES COMMISSION, 1826 AND 1830 *Report.* October, 1830. Fol. Pp 436.   *PP*, 1831, xii, 310 CONTENTS General Report. Report on the University of Edinburgh. Report on the University of Glasgow. Report on the University and King's College of Aberdeen. Report on the Marischal College, Aberdeen. Report on the University and Colleges of St Andrews.

—*Evidence, Oral and Documentary.* Vol I.—University of Edinburgh. Fol. Pp xl, 637, 295. Index   *PP*, 1837, xxxv

— —. Vol II.—University of Glasgow. Fol. Pp xxiii, 576. Index.
PP, 1837, xxxvi

— —. Vol III.—University of St. Andrews. Fol. Pp xxiv, 433. Index.
PP, 1837, xxxvii

— —. Vol IV.—University of Aberdeen. Fol. Pp xxi, 342. Index.
PP, 1837, xxxviii

—*An Abstract of the General Report of the Royal Commissioners appointed to visit the Universities of Scotland.* With Notes and Tabular States relating to the state of these institutions in 1826. Edinburgh: Adam and Charles Black; James Brash and Co, Glasgow; Alex Brown & Co, Aberdeen; and M Fletcher, St Andrews, 1836. 8vo. Pp viii, 135, 43. Index.

'The Scottish Universities Commission'; *The Museum*, Jan 1862, **4**, 480-7.

'The Scottish Universities—Defects and Remedies'; *North British Rev*, May 1858, **28**, 376-402.

'The Scottish Universities reformed'; *The Museum*, Jan 1864, **3**, 444-51.

SCOTUS 'On the System of Education pursued in the Scottish Universities'; *Literary and Statistical Mag for Scotland*, Feb 1818, **2**, 21-3.

SELLAR, WILLIAM Y 'Scotch University Reform'; *Fraser's Mag*, Jan 1856, **53**, 116-26.

SHAIRP, JOHN CAMPBELL *Uses of the Study of Latin Literature.* Edinburgh: Printed by Thomas Constable, 1858. 8vo. Pp 28.

—*The Wants of the Scottish Universities and some of the Remedies*. Edinburgh: Thomas Constable and Co; Hamilton, Adams, and Co, London, 1856. 8vo. Pp 48.

STEWART, JOHN *A Letter to the Rev. Dr Paull of Tullynessle, on the Abolition of Tests in the Universities of Scotland*. Glasgow: David Robertson; Adam & Chas Black, Edinburgh, 1846. 8vo. Pp 14.

STRUTHERS, JOHN *How to improve the Teaching in the Scottish Universities*. Edinburgh: Sutherland and Knox; Aberdeen: John Smith; Glasgow: Griffin & Co, 1859. 8vo. Pp 36.

'Student Life in Scotland'; *Blackwood's Edinburgh Mag*, Aug 1854, **76**, 135-50; Oct 1854, **76**, 422-35.

—; *The Cornhill Mag*, Mar 1860, **1**, 366-79.

SWINTON, ARCHIBALD CAMPBELL *Legislation necessary on the Subject of University Tests in Scotland*. Edinburgh and London: William Blackwood and Sons, 1852. 8vo. Pp 27.

TAIT, ADAM DUNCAN *Letter to His Grace the Duke of Argyll on the proposed Abolition or Modification of the Tests affecting the Chairs in the Universities of Scotland*. Edinburgh: Paton and Ritchie, 1853. 8vo. Pp 56.

—*Letter to the Right Honourable the Lord Justice-Clerk on the State of the Theological Faculties in the Universities of Scotland*, with special Reference to recent Legislation; with Remarks on certain views propounded in a Letter to H.M. University Commissioners, by the Very Reverend Principal Tulloch of St Andrews. Edinburgh: Paton and Ritchie, 1859. 8vo. Pp 51.

TAIT, MATTHEW S *The Ferguson Scholarships*. Founded in 1860. Report to the Trustees of the Ferguson Bequest Fund, on the past Operation of the Scheme. Glasgow: Printed at the University Press, by Robert Maclehose, 1882. 8vo. Pp 30.   EUL

'The Theological Chairs in the Scottish Universities'; *Free Church Mag*, Aug 1847, **4**, 262-5.

THORBURN, DAVID *The Endowment of the Universities of Scotland an Object of National Importance*. With an Appendix. Edinburgh: Andrew Elliot, 1863. 8vo. Pp 48.

—*The University Endowment Movement*: Memorandum relative thereto. Edinburgh: Andrew Elliot, 1866. 8vo. Pp 41.

TULLOCH, JOHN 'Early Scottish University Education'; *The Museum*, July 1861, **1**, 137-46.

—*The Theological Faculties of the Scottish Universities in connection with University Reform*. A Letter to H.M. University Commissioners for Scotland. Edinburgh: Sutherland and Knox, 1858. 8vo. Pp 19.

'The Universities of Scotland'; *Quarterly J of Education*, Apr-July 1832, **4**, 21-43; July-Oct 1832, **4**, 234-68; Oct 1832-Jan 1833, **5**, 75-98.

Universities (Scotland) Act, 1858. *General Report of the Commissioners under the Universities (Scotland) Act, 1858*. With an appendix, containing Ordinances, Minutes, Reports on Special Subjects, and other documents. Edinburgh, 1863. Fol. Pp xlvii, 290. *PP*, 1863, xvi, [3174]

—. *Report of the Commissioners appointed under the Statute 21 and 22 of Her Majesty*, intituled 'An Act to make Provision for the better Government of the Universities of Scotland, and for the Union of the two Universities and Colleges of Aberdeen'; Edinburgh, 1860. Fol. Pp 19.   *PP*, 1860, liii, 198

The Universities (Scotland) Bill protested. (With remarks on Professor Ferrier's 'Letter to the Lord Advocate of Scotland'.) By a Scottish Graduate. Edinburgh: Bell & Bradfute, 1858. 8vo. Pp 22.   EUL

'University Reform'; *Aberdeen University Mag*, 13 Jan 1836, **1**, 3-12; 27 Jan 1836, **1**, 17-28; 10 Feb 1836, **1**, 33-41; 24 Feb 1836, **1**, 49-58; 9 Mar 1836, **1**, 65-73; 23 Mar 1836, **1**, 85-102; 6 Apr 1836, **1**, 103-15; 20 Apr 1836, **1**, 123-30.

'—', *Transactions of the National Association for the Promotion of Social Science*, *1863* (1864), 354-61.

'University Reform in Scotland'; *Scottish Rev*, Jan 1858, 53-67.

[WALKER, GEORGE] *Notes on the Constitutions of Universities*, with reference to the Rights of the Scottish Graduates. Aberdeen: Printed at the *Herald* Office, 1857. 8vo. Pp 68.

WALKER, THOMAS 'Scottish Education, 1411-1571'; *Cambridge History of English Literature* (Cambridge: At the University Press), 2 (1908), 367-71.

WILSON, GEORGE *The Grievance of the University Tests*, as applied to Professors of Physical Science in the Colleges of Scotland. Edinburgh: Sutherland and Knox; London: Simpkin, Marshall, & Co, 1852. 8vo. Pp 45.

Appendix A

This Appendix lists a number of writings to which references were found in other works during the compilation of the Bibliography but of which so far no copies have been identified or located. No more is known about any of them than what is given here.

Abstracts of Deeds endowing a Fund for Charitable Endowments in Banff. Banff, 1870.

BACON, JAMES *Report on a projected Academy at Kirkcaldy.*

BAINES, — *Report on Leeds Deputation to New Lanark.* Manchester, 1819.

BLACKIE, JOHN STUART *Academical Education.* 1858.

BLAIR, ANDREW *Can this last?* Edinburgh, 1869.

BOTHWELL, GEORGE B *Letter to the Working Classes of Aberdeen.* Aberdeen, 1859.

BRUCE, VICTOR A, 9TH EARL OF ELGIN *Secondary Education of the Future.* Ayr, 1870.

BUCHANAN, WALTER *Proposed Bases of a National System of Education.*

CANDLISH, ROBERT S *Public Education.*

CARMICHAEL, — *Recollections of Two Years in the Rector's Class* [High School of Edinburgh], *1809-1811.*

CUMMING, J E *Education in Scotland a Practical Movement.* Edinburgh, 1856.

CUNNINGHAM, ROBERT *Report on Studies prosecuted in the Edinburgh Institution.* 1835.

FAIRBAIRN, PATRICK *Thoughts on College Matters.* Glasgow, 1854.

FERGUSON, CHARLES *Speeches on the Universities Bill.* 1836.

FORFAR PUBLIC SCHOOL *Statutes and Regulations.* 1816.

FREE CHURCHMAN *The Free Church Education Scheme.* Edinburgh, 1851.

GIFFORD, WILLIAM *The Education Question considered.* 1869.

GORDON, JAMES *The Government Scheme of Education.* Aberdeen, 1847.

GORDON, THOMAS *Education in Scotland,* second edition.

GREY, HENRY *Report on Local Schools.* 1854.

JAMIESON, ROBERT *History of Agricultural Education in Aberdeenshire.* 1908.

Letters concerning a Plan for Rural Education.

LOWE, JAMES *Letters on Education.* 1845.

MACDONALD, ALEXANDER *Compendium of the Law relative to Schools,* first and second editions.

MILLIGAN, WILLIAM *Grammar School Curriculum.* Aberdeen, 1861.

MORTON, JAMES *On School and University Reform.*

MUIR, JOHN *Parochial Schools of Scotland.* 1815.

MUIR, WILLIAM *Speeches on the Government Plan of Education.* Edinburgh, 1839.

NICOL, JAMES *Letters on Infant Education.*

Observations on Public Examinations. 1825.

REID, JAMES B *Essay on Sabbath Schools.* Aberdeen, 1838.

Rules and Regulations of the Arbroath Academy. Arbroath, 1834.

STOW, DAVID *Memoranda,* or, Practical Hints on the Training System. Glasgow, 1835.

The System of National Education in Scotland. Aberdeen, 1839.

TOD, GEORGE *Sabbath Schools considered.* 1818.

Appendix B

In the Bibliography a number of pamphlets which are generally regarded as anonymous are assigned to particular authors. A list of these is given here with the names of the writers to whom they have been ascribed.

Analysis of a New System of General Education. See LAURIE, D.

Domestic Economy, Gymnastics, and Music. See FRASER, PATRICK.

Dr Clark's Spelling Reform. See BAIN, ALEXANDER.

Facts for the Consideration of the Governors of George Heriot's Hospital. See LEE, JOHN.

The Gym, or, Sketches from School [Chanonry House School, Aberdeen]. See ALLAN, J BUCKLEY.

An Inquiry, whether the Study of the Ancient Languages is a necessary branch of modern education. See GILLIS, JOHN.

Letter to the Lord Advocate on the Education Bill. See JOHNSTONE, JAMES.

Letters addressed to the Parochial Schoolmasters of Scotland, concerning the new method of tuition. See NORVALL, JAMES.

Milton's Plea for Education. See SCOTT, WILLIAM.

National Education and the Church of Scotland. See GREGOR, WALTER.

National Education in Scotland. See LEE, WILLIAM.

The Necessity of a Reform in the Parochial School System of Scotland. See FLEMING, JOHN.

Notes on the Constitutions of Universities. See WALKER, GEORGE.

Notes relative to Education in Scotland. See SIMPSON, ALEXANDER L.

Parish School Statistics. Means of Education in Scotland carefully revised. See COOK, JOHN (St Andrews).

Proposals for the Reform of Schools and Universities. See FLETCHER, ANDREW.

Reply, by Parens, to the Animadversions of 'A Sincere Friend to Children'. See IVORY, THOMAS.

Report by Sub-Committee of the Elders' Union of the Church of Scotland on the Lord Advocate's Bill, 1854. See SWINTON, ARCHIBALD.

The Revised Code. See KENNEDY, WILLIAM.

Scotland a Half-educated Nation. See LEWIS, GEORGE.

Statement and Representation respecting the Parochial Schoolmasters of Scotland. See DUNCAN, HENRY.

Statements relative to the City of Edinburgh. See LIDDLE, JOSEPH.

Appendix C

PART 1: A Note on Manuscript Sources for the History of Scottish Education before 1872

It is rare, in seeking out the history of Scottish schools in the period before the act of 1872, to find manuscripts of any antiquity or of much value in the schools themselves. (In the case of privately-founded schools there is a greater chance than there is with public schools.) In the public schools a few mid-19th century log-books have survived, however, kept by especially assiduous schoolmasters; and these may be found in the schools or in the local education offices for the areas concerned. A survey, being currently made by the Scottish Record Office of all local authority records, will shortly provide a complete listing of local holdings.

For the main groups of unpublished records which contain information about schools and schooling the researcher must look elsewhere. It is not surprising that the records relating to an institution should be generally kept by the person who or the body which has responsibility for it and control over it. In Scotland prior to 1872 responsibility for education was shared by the church and the state: in the three centuries before the 19th, they combined effectively in its support because their interests were compatible, if they were not identical. Thus at the time of the Reformation the church saw schooling as a major instrument in the conversion of the young to the new religion, and considered schoolmasters to be important members of the religious organisation: the reformed church was thus careful to extend and improve schooling where it could do so. When and where it met difficulties, it was ready to call on the state for support in the enterprise. For its part, the state was prepared to give this support—intermittently at least, and more readily in the 17th century than later; for governments recognized in education an admirable instrument for *their* purposes —the inculcation of morality, ' good manners ' and socially acceptable attitudes in order to provide for peaceful living under an agreed law; and, in the 17th and 18th centuries, a means of subduing and civilising such 'barbarous' and troublesome areas as the Gaelic-speaking Highlands and Islands. The public records of church and state, both local and national (including the records of burgh councils), are therefore clearly the primary sources to which historians of Scottish education will turn.

The great national records of state—acts of parliament, registers of privy council and privy seal—all contain important data about schools and universities before the parliamentary union with England, and of these only the acts of parliament are wholly in print. The register of the privy council has been printed up to 1691, that of the privy seal up to 1580; but, happily, in both series the unpublished gaps are being closed.

The unprinted privy council register (1692-1707) contains many references to schools, especially in the 1690s when vacant church stipends were gifted to the local community *ad pios usus* and were frequently used in school-building, for bursaries, etc. The privy seal register contains gifts of rentals from church or crown property for use as bursaries to grammar schools and universities and details of privileges which were accorded by the crown to schools, universities and their teachers. In these records it is possible for the researcher to confirm the existence of a school not mentioned elsewhere and to discover the name of this or that schoolmaster. Among other records of state, certain groups of financial records are important in providing similar information; for instance, the returns for hearth tax (1692-5) and poll tax (1694-9) comprise detailed lists of inhabitants in parishes throughout Scotland and include schoolmasters' names.

The records of courts of law, both local and national, may also be used in the identification of schools and their masters. The local feudal courts of barony and regality often registered reminders to a laird's tenants to pay their proportions of a schoolmaster's stipend, and they may also mention the local school and its teacher in other contexts. The printed digests of court of session cases are an invaluable quick guide to unpublished processes relating to parishes where the schoolmaster was party in a dispute; and the collected papers of these cases can include a range of information about local schooling not to be found elsewhere. It is also possible to discover schoolmasters' names from the witness lists to documents recorded in the registers of deeds and of sasines or in sheriff court processes, but this can be a lengthy and tedious task.

Three ranges of civil records, not mentioned so far, are also of considerable value: first, the minutes of heritors' meetings which dealt with the apportionment of schoolmasters' salaries among the local landowners and with the erection, furnishing and maintenance of school buildings; secondly, the minutes of the county commissioners of supply which frequently contain entries relating to masters' salaries —the commission received complaints about non-payment of salary by the heritors and about dilatoriness in providing accommodation, and could force stents on reluctant landowners for these purposes; thirdly, the Forfeited Estates papers (the records of management of estates under the crown after the rebellions of 1715 and 1745), which contain much information about Highland education, and which have been used, for instance, by Dr John Mason in his *A History of Scottish Experiments in Rural Education* (1935).

None of the series of records mentioned so far provides a large and distinct body of data on education, neatly collected together and easy to use: the clerks of privy council and privy seal, for example, recorded items in their registers as they came to them, and thus information about schools and universities is buried among the other voluminous decisions of state. The same is true to a large extent of the major church records: here educational matter is recorded, unordered, among the cases of discipline, notes about repairs to the church, lists of baptisms, collections for the poor or for communities hit by disaster, and so on. Occasionally, however, and more frequently in the later period, clerks to sessions and presbyteries did attempt to collect entries relating to schools in a separate book or part of a book: the church records in the Scottish Record Office contain a number of these, for example, for Dalmeny, Muckairn and Melrose parishes and for Elgin presbytery.

Although it is usual for educational data to be well scattered throughout the minute books of assemblies, synods, presbyteries and kirk sessions, these are nonetheless the historian's most extensive source. In these records of the established church, and in the parallel records of the seceding churches in the 18th century and later, he can expect to trace the extent and the nature of school provision over two or three centuries; to learn about the academic standing and perhaps the personal character of the masters (and schoolmistresses) employed by the parishes; to gain an insight into the educational idealism of a period from the conditions of employment which were laid down in contracts to new teachers, and from the rules which were adopted for the day-to-day running of the schools; and to plot the appearance, growth and multiplication, or stagnation of the various local schools   Not all session minutes, however,

will provide such information: occasionally the researcher will find records which over many years contain no reference whatever to schooling. But it is unwise to assume (as has sometimes been done) that lack of evidence means that no school existed. Entries relating to the local school may have been written up in a separate register now lost; or the long silence in the record may merely indicate that all was well with the school and that no minuted comment was thought to be needed (not least since the schoolmaster was also usually the session clerk). Where a session minute-book fails to provide information, it is well to look for a separate account-book of sessional funds, if it has survived; for these accounts will normally contain notes on the regular quarterly payments of poor scholars' fees and of other disbursements relating to the school, as well as registering incoming monies from gifts and mortifications for educational purposes. In default of any sessional records, it is the appropriate presbytery's minute-book which is most likely to produce the hoped-for data—the records of presbyterial visitations generally contain some mention of the various parochial schools and may include a good deal of information when complaints are made by or against the local schoolmasters.

Sometimes the available church records may be meagre and prove barren of educational matter, and the civil and legal records already mentioned also provide little or no information. One important source remains, and it is one far too often overlooked by historians of Scottish education: namely, the estate papers of families who owned land in the parish or county which is being investigated. These estate papers may contain extract minutes of heritors' or commissioners of supply meetings when the formal records of those meetings have been lost. But this is not their only nor their main value. Landowners in a parish were required in law to pay part of the schoolmaster's stipend (in proportion to the amount of land held in any parish); and their family papers very frequently contain bundles of receipts for payment of salary countersigned by the master. There are often quite long runs of these receipts (and of receipts for payment of bills for repair of school buildings), and it is possible from them to confirm the continuing existence of a school, to discover the names of school-masters and how long they served the school, to ascertain the amount of stipend paid at various periods, etc. The papers of families which owned large estates in one area of the country may include receipts which cover a large number of parishes; for example, the National Library of Scotland has Dundas of Dundas muniments which include school-receipts for numerous parishes in West Lothian, and in the Scottish Record Office there are such fine collections as the Biel papers (East Lothian and the Borders, 17th to 19th century), the Dunglass papers (Berwickshire, 17th to 19th century) and the very extensive Seaforth muniments (Lewis, mainland West Highlands, mainly 19th century).

Two large collections in the Scottish Record Office, which have not been sufficiently used as yet, must also be noted. The papers of the Dick Bequest, a 19th-century fund for the support of parochial schooling in Aberdeenshire, Banffshire and Moray, contain a great deal of important information about education in the north-east, much more than appears in the printed Bequest reports of 1835, 1844, 1854, 1865, 1890, etc. And the records of the Society in Scotland for the Propagation of Christian Knowledge (1709-1908) clearly deserve more attention than they have so far received (for example, in M G Jones' *The Charity School Movement: a study of 18th century Puritanism in action* (1938)): an exhaustive study of the sspck would indeed be an immensely valuable contribution to Scottish educational historiography.

The Scottish Record Office (HM General Register House, Princes Street, Edinburgh) contains the major holdings of the civil, legal and ecclesiastical records mentioned above. Certain legal and church records have not been deposited there and are still in the custody of ministers, presbytery clerks or sheriff clerks in the various localities. A very useful list of the holdings of Established Church records in Edinburgh has been published recently—*Records of the Church of Scotland preserved in the Scottish Record Office and the General Register Office* (Scottish Record Society publication, 1967: and appendix to vol xciv of the *Records of the Scottish Church History Society*, 1967). Many collections of family muniments have now been deposited in the Scottish Record Office, in the National Library of Scotland (George IV Bridge, Edinburgh) and in the manuscript departments of university libraries: short descriptions of the contents of family papers still in private hands are given in the reports of the National Register of Archives (Scotland). The Scottish Record Office has prepared source lists of those Established Church, family and other records in its possession which contain substantial educational material: these are printed below (parts 2 and 3 of this Appendix) with the permission of the Keeper of the Records of Scotland. There is as yet no similar list for the sro holdings of Free Church records for the period after 1843. Certain runs of the civil, legal and ecclesiastical records mentioned in this Note have been edited and printed, in full or in extract, by the Scottish Record Office or by record publishing societies; for these reference should be made, respectively, to *British National Archives: Sectional List No 24* (hmso) and to *Handlist of Scottish and Welsh Record Publications* (British Record Association, 1954).

Donald J Withrington

PART 2: Source List of Material relating to Schools in Private Muniments in the Scottish Record Office, December 1969

The heading to each group of items indicates the family or other collection which contains the relevant source material. The GD (gifts and deposits) and RH (Register House) references which follow each item should be quoted in all enquiries to the Scottish Record Office.

ABERCAIRNY

Letters from Dr David Doig, rector of Stirling Grammar School, 1776-81. [GD24/1/582.]

Letter from Dr Alexander Adam, rector of Edinburgh High School, on the subject of grammar, 1780. [GD24/1/588.]
Documents about Abercairney estate

affairs, including schools and schoolmasters' salaries, 1705-1801. [GD24/1/609.]

Papers concerning schools of Abernyte, Crieff, Blackford, Foulis, Buchanty, and Maderty, 1726-1859. [GD24/1/914-15.]

Notebooks by Henry Home Drummond in which he records his views on education at Edinburgh High School, Edinburgh University and Oxford, 1808-58. [GD24/1/1032.]

AILSA

Receipts for salaries of schoolmasters in Ayrshire parishes, and memorandum on education in Kirkoswald (19th cent), 17th-19th cent. [GD25/9/Box 2.]

Papers *re* school and schoolteachers of Maybole and Balgreen of Maybole, 17th-18th cent. [GD25/9/Boxes 13 and 44.]

AIRLIE

Letter from James Martin, schoolmaster in Perth, accepting 'Mr Walter' at his school, 1741. [GD16/34/342.]

Papers *re* payment of schoolteachers' salaries and upkeep of schoolhouses on Airlie estates, 1668-1883. [GD16/49.]

BARGANY

Letter from Ann Dalrymple about the fitness of Mr Hay to be schoolmaster at Ballintrae, nd. [GD109/3843.]
Letter from T F Kennedy of Dalquharran on maintenance of churches and schools in Ayrshire, 1825. [GD109/3847.]

BIEL

Papers on ecclesiastical affairs including references to salaries of schoolteachers and upkeep of schoolhouses (Lothians and Borders), 1545-1820. [GD6/1138-1246.]

BRITISH FISHERY SOCIETY

Letter about schoolmaster required for Tobermory, 1794. [GD9/34/5.]
Letters and other papers regarding SPCK and other schools at Lochbay and Waternish, 1793-1835. [GD9/114, 127, 129, 159/1, 182-3, 187/13, 196, 207 and 218.]

Letters concerning education at Pultneytown, 1804-20. [GD9/275 and 324.]

BROUGHTON AND CALLY

Plans, memorial and other papers regarding Gatehouse Academy, 1818-27. [GD10/1277-83 and 1421/369A.]

BUGHT

Letter about a subscription from India for the academy and infirmary at Inverness, 1809. [GD23/6/451.]
Letter from Mathew Adam, rector of Inverness Academy, to James Grant, chairman of the trustees of the Mackintosh Fund, relating to the removal of Duncan Mackintosh, bursar of the Fund, from his mathematics class because of insubordination, 1829. [GD/23/6/649.]

BURNETT & REID

Copy Petition regarding schoolhouse of Old Machar, 17 Oct 1825. [GD57/467.]

CAMPBELL OF JURA

Papers regarding schools in Jura, 1776-1887. [GD64/1/13, 110-14; GD64/3/119, 139 and 141-2.]

CLERK OF PENICUIK

Petition to Barons of Exchequer from William Young, schoolmaster in Glenalmont, for payment of arrears of salary, 1719. [GD18/2721.]

Papers concerning heritors of Penicuik, Lasswade and Glencorse including references to salaries of schoolteachers and upkeep of schoolhouses, 1658-1884. [GD18/2943-3101.]

Letter from D M Clerk to Sir George Clerk of Penicuik regarding Poor Law Assessment of schoolhouses attached to schools, 30 Sept 1841. [GD18/3411.]

Letter from John Gordon concerning petition from General Assembly Education Committee to Privy Council Education Committee, 7 Oct 1841. [GD18/3414.]

Offprint from *Edinburgh Evening Courant* of speech by Sir George Clerk on salaries of parochial schoolmasters, 2 Oct 1856. [GD18/3928.]

Papers on ecclesiastical affairs including references to schools and schoolteachers of Penicuik, Dalkeith and Glencorse, 1654-98. [GD18/3975-4008.]

Letters from Sir John Clerk to Mr Lesley, schoolmaster at Haddington, on the education of the writer's sons, 1728-30. [GD18/5033.]

Letter from John Love, rector of Dalkeith Grammar School, 1750. [GD18/5065.]

Letters from John Leslie, schoolmaster in Dalkeith, about the education of Sir John Clerk's son, 1730-8. [GD18/5380.]

Letters from Patrick Clerk while at school in Haddington and Dalkeith, 1731-4. [GD18/5387.]

Letters from John Douglas, schoolmaster at Haddington, William Wilkinson, schoolmaster at Lowther near Penrith, and others regarding the education of Sir John Clerk's sons, 1731-9. [GD18/5388.]

Letter from George Preston, Edinburgh, about proposals for taking in children to the Orphan Hospital, 1734. [GD18/5404.]

Letters regarding Penicuik schoolhouse, 1655-71. [GD18/5620.]

Subscription pamphlet for erection of a new High School in Edinburgh, 29 May 1777. [GD18/5834.]

CRAIGMILLAR AND LIBERTON

Letters concerning the school and schoolhouse at Liberton, 1811-12. [GD122/3/1419-20.]

CRAVEN BEQUEST

Demission by John Dischingtoun of his post as master of the Grammar School of Kirkwall, nd. [GD106/52.]

Note of school fees (Orkney), late 17th cent. [GD106/218.]

CUNINGHAME OF THORNTOUN

Letters from Anna Cuninghame, while at school in Edinburgh, giving news of her lessons, etc, 1822-3. [GD21/449.]

CUNNINGHAME-GRAHAM

Letters from various correspondents, the

subjects including religious instruction in schools, 1848-58. [GD22/1/371.]

DALHOUSIE

Programme of public meeting on education, held in Glasgow, with notes for a speech and other papers, 1854. [GD45/1/256.]

Letters concerning a petition on behalf of the parochial schoolmasters of Scotland, 1844-5. [GD45/7/30.]

Letters about Schools of Design, 1844-5. [GD45/7/31.]

Letter from George Milne, secretary to the directors of Dundee Public Seminaries, suggesting that the Committee on Education make a grant to help increase teachers' salaries, 1851. [GD45/12/446.]

Notes for Fox Maule relating to sums raised by the Free Church in providing churches, schools and New College, 1846. [GD45/13/396.]

Letters to Fox Maule from Dr R S Candlish, memorials to a committee of the Privy Council, and copy-reply concerning government grant to Free Church Normal Schools in Edinburgh and Glasgow, 1849. [GD45/13/398.]

Letter from Sir James Kay Shuttleworth enclosing copy-letter on public education in Scotland, 1851. [GD45/14/696.]

Petition by Andrew Fitchet, schoolmaster at Panbride, against an obligation to repair the school, *ante* 1781. [GD45/18/2323.]

Declaration (printed) by Sir David Cunninghame of London for the allocation of a sum bequeathed by Robert Johnstoun of London for maintenance of a grammar school at Kilmaurs, Ayrshire, 1658. [GD45/24/19.]

DEAN ORPHANAGE

Minute books, account books, letters and papers, 1733-86. [GD1/40/1-24.]

DICK BEQUEST

(*Educational trust for counties of Aberdeen, Banff & Moray*)

Excerpt from will of James Dick, 1827. Typed. [GD1/4/1.]

Copy Table of Rules and Regulations by James Dick, 1828. [GD1/4/2.]

Minute Books, 1830-1931. 3 vols. [GD1/4/3-5.]

Deeds relating to the Bequest, 1832. 1 vol. Printed. [GD1/4/6.]

Schemes of Division, yearly, 1832-90. 58 vols. [GD1/4/7-64.]

Abstract of Returns, yearly 1832-89. 57 vols. These give, by presbytery and parish, the name of schoolmaster, number of pupils, subjects and numbers studying each, salary, fees, repairs and remarks. [GD1/4/65-121.]

Abstract of Returns, 1852-62. 1 vol. Summary of above returns by presbyteries. [GD1/4/122.]

Abstract of Original Returns, Jan 1833. 2 vols. These give, by presbytery and parish, the extent of the parish, number of heritors, valued rent, real rent, population by 1831 census, number of scholars, number attending parochial school in summer and winter, number attending private schools, number of persons above 6 years of age unable to read, number above 8 years of age unable to write, accessibility of parochial school to all children in the parish, date of last presbyterial examination, hours of attendance in summer and winter, greatest distance from which scholars come, numbers present in January 1833, age of entering and leaving, number of scholars studying each subject and fees, name of schoolmaster, age, years as teacher, date of admission, years at college, family, assistants, salary, provision by heritors of school and dwelling house, annual value of accommodation, rooms, school fees, emoluments, endowments and fees of private schools and clergyman's opinion of schoolmaster. [GD1/4/123-124.]

State of claims on arrears, 1833. 1 vol. [GD1/4/125.]

Reports relative to Dick Bequest accounts 1833. 1 vol. [GD1/4/126.]

Record of teachers, 1833-53. 1 vol. This details, by parish, the name of teacher, date of birth, date of election, where educated, which university attended, number of sessions, subjects studied, experience as teacher, whether intended for any other profession, married and number of family, system taught, date and cause of leaving. [GD1/4/127.]

Visitation Books, yearly, 1833-90. 58 vols. These give short reports on teachers and progress made in the schools. [GD1/4/128-85.]

Report by Clerk of Trustees on operation of bequest, the state of the schools and the principle of division, 1834. 1 vol. [GD1/4/186.]

Reports on the Dick Bequest, 1835 to date. Printed. [GD1/4/187-254.]

Reports of examinations of teachers, 1835. 1 vol. [GD1/4/255.]

Examination papers of teachers, 1840-80. 6 vols. [GD1/4/256-61.]

Abstracts of General Returns, 1843-65. 3 vols. As for Abstracts of Original Returns, but population is given by 1841 census and details are given of school books used. [GD1/4/262-4.]

Scheme for administration of endowment, 1890. [GD1/4/265.]

Examination Results and Capitation Grants, 1902-8. 1 vol. By school, pupil and subject. [GD1/4/266.]

Excerpts from memorandum by Sir George M Paul, 1910. Typed. [GD1/4/267.]

Note by Sir George M Paul, 1918. Typed. [GD1/4/268.]

Trust Scheme, 1923. 1 vol. Printed. [GD1/4/269.]

Explanatory memoranda (3) regarding endowment scheme, 1929-32. [GD1/4/270-2.]

Minutes of evidence before Educational Endowments Commission, 1932. Typed. [GD1/4/273.]

Schedule of property and securities submitted to the Commission, 1935. Typed. [GD1/4/274.]

Scheme for administration of endowment, 1935. [GD1/4/275.]

DOUGLAS PAPERS

Petition to the town council of Haddington by Patrick Gray, schoolmaster there, 1726. [GD/98/XV/35/1.]

Papers *re* maintenance of scholars in Grammar School of Dundee, 1782. [GD98/Box 1/12.]

DUNDAS OF DUNDAS

Papers concerning Dalmeny school, 1729-34. [GD75/681-2.]

DUNGLASS

Papers *re* schools and schoolteachers in Berwickshire, 1691-1803. [GD206/2/214-216.]

ELIBANK

Account of disbursements by Mr Carlile, tutor to Lord Elibank, while the latter was a pupil at (Edinburgh?) High School, 1717-18. [GD32/24/6.]

LORD FORBES

Papers concerning schools at Keig and Alford, 17th-18th cent. [GD52/330 and 332.]

GILCHRIST OF OSPISDALE

Papers *re* churches and schools in Criech, Sutherland, etc, 1708-1854. [GD153/Box 8.]

GORDON CASTLE

Papers *re* schoolteachers' salaries (Banff and Elgin), 1828-61. [GD44/37/7.]

GUTHRIE OF GUTHRIE

Account of money spent 'upon Guthrie at the school of Aberdeen', 1696. [GD 188/Box 19.]

Extracts from records of session of Murroes *re* the school and schoolmaster, with other papers on the subject, 1703-97. [GD188/Box 24.]

HAMILTON BRUCE

Plans of school at Dunshalt, Auchtermuchty, 1861. [GD152/63.]

Printed letter to heritors of Kinghorn *re* the constitution of the parish school, 1844. [GD152/86.]

Applications and testimonials for post of headmaster of Dunshalt School, 1841. [GD152/133.]

HAMILTON-DALRYMPLE OF NORTH BERWICK

Letters from Lord Blantyre recommending Richard Dick as schoolmaster of North Berwick, etc, 1739-43. [GD110/918.]

Letters from John Suttie, 1739-57, including recommendation of a schoolmaster provided that he married as the heritors should direct him. [GD110/919.]

Letters relating to the election of a schoolmaster at Preston, 1741. [GD110/932.]

Letters from James Purdie concerning his decision to give up his school in Glasgow, etc, 1747-56. [GD110/995.]

Letter from Dr Hugh Reid, Sydserf, regarding the appointment of a schoolmaster, etc, 1748-56. [GD110/1001.]

HAY OF BELTON

Letter from George Moffat, Kelso, offering to accept Captain Hay's nephews as boarders and giving details of boarding and school fees, 1829. [GD73/5/9.]

HAY OF HAYSTOUN

Receipts for salaries of schoolteachers of Peebles and Libberton, 1704-43. [GD34/558.]

HAY OF PARK

Discharges and account by James Purdie, master of the Grammar School of Glasgow, for board and tuition, 1731-2. [GD72/602.]

HENDERSON

Papers concerning schoolmaster in Kinross, 1683-1772. [GD72/142-6.]

Contracts of appointment of schoolmasters in Linlithgow, 1592-3. [GD72/184-5.]

HOPE, TODD & KIRK, WS

Documents *re* Johnstone bequest for grammar school in Moffat, etc, 1639-1873. [GD246/Box 4.]

Minute book of patrons of the united parish and grammar schools of Moffat, 1831-46. [GD246/Box 4.]

Newspapers (2) containing reports *re* Caddonfoot School, 1868. [GD246/Box 21 Bundle 4.]

Plans and papers *re* alteration of school at Newhailes into dwelling houses etc, 1826-88. [GD246/Box 62 Bundle 2.]

HORSBURGH-PORTER MSS

Papers *re* church, manse and school of parishes of Hassendean and Innerleithen, 1650-1834. [GD178/3.]

IRVINE ROBERTSON

Answers to queries concerning the state of the establishment for parochial education in the parish of Fortingall, Perthshire, giving particulars from 1666 to 1 July 1825. [GD1/53/37.]

KING JAMES VI HOSPITAL, PERTH

Regulations by the managers of the Hospital of Perth for administration of the Charity School kept in the Hospital House, 1801: printed. [GD79/6/63.]

Register of Middle and West Kirk schools 1865-73. [GD79/7/58.]

Hospital Education Committee: minutes and lists of scholars—West, Middle and East Churches, *c* 1839-62. [GD79/7/63.]

Statement of sums received for setting up two schools in West Church parish, 1839. [GD79/7/68.]

KINROSS

Call by heritors of Dumbarny parish, Perthshire, to John Stewart, late schoolmaster at Kinfauns, to be schoolmaster in Dumbarney, 1724. [GD1/58/3.]

KINROSS HOUSE

Stent rolls of salary of schoolmaster of Kinross, 1647 and 1683. [GD29/104.]

Papers concerning salaries of schoolteachers of Anstruther Wester, Carnbee, and Kinross, 1673-90. [GD29/107, 111 and 112.]

LEIGHTON LIBRARY TRUSTEES, DUNBLANE

Papers *re* William Coldstream, schoolmaster of Dunblane, etc, 1746-1891. [GD1/392.]

LEVEN AND MELVILLE

Correspondence *re* Milton and Markinch schools, 1818-24. [GD26/12/36.]

Letter relating to the appointment of a schoolmaster at the charity school of Drummeldrie, 1756. [GD26/13/642.]

Correspondence concerning the school and schoolteacher of Monimail, 1803-4. [GD26/13/857.]

LOTHIAN

Letter *re* Mr Goudie, former schoolmaster at Jedburgh, 1690. [GD40/VII/35.]

LOW MSS

Papers *re* contracts with masters of the Grammar School of Montrose, 1637 and 1685. [GD1/47/1 and 2.]

MACGREGOR

Lists of scholars in Kinlochrannoch, 1772-83; in Finart in Rannoch, 1773-84; in Dalnamun, 1782-4; and in Strouan, 1778-82. [GD50/161.]

MACPHERSON OF CLUNY

Letters from Miss B Macpherson regarding her school in Edinburgh, 1789-1805. [GD80/927.]

MELVILLE CASTLE

Suggestions by Lady Glasgow for various aspects of social reform, including reform of schools, 1789. [GD51/1/13.]

Letter from Robert Johnston suggesting the formation of a marine school in Edinburgh similar to that at Greenock, 1816. [GD51/5/77.]

Letters regarding a new site for Edinburgh High School, 1823-5. [GD51/5/127 and 132.]

Letter from Rev John Kemp *re* charity schools maintained by SSPCK on former forfeited estates, 19 Dec 1789. [GD51/5/629.]

Letter from Earl of Cassillis enclosing memorandum on parish schools in Scotland and schoolmasters' salaries, 15 Apr 1802. [GD51/5/656/1-2.]

Letters from the treasurer of the Edinburgh Society of Teachers, 1808 and 1813. [GD51/5/664, 666 and 677.]

Letter from Rev John Paton *re* salary of schoolmaster at Lasswade, 3 June 1816. [GD51/5/682.]

Letter from William Tennant regarding his move from Lasswade school to Dollar Academy, 26 Nov 1818. [GD51/5/690.]

Letter *re* Mr Wilson, schoolmaster at Dunkeld, 1807. [GD51/9/275.]

Letter *re* schools proposed for the young laird of Dundas, 1809. [GD51/9/323.]

Letters from Archibald Hastie, Edinburgh, soliciting patronage for his private school, 1826. [GD51/9/435.]

Letter from Ebenezer Bell regarding arrears of salary due by Lord Melville to him as schoolmaster of Dalkeith, 27 July 1816. [GD51/11/118.]

MEY

Papers *re* schools and schoolmasters, 1650-1887. [GD96/680/4-5.]

MISCELLANEOUS DOCUMENTS

Copy-extract certificates of registration of the situation and description of schools in Argyll, 1799-1814. [RH9/17/216.]

MONRO OF ALLAN

Papers *re* school and schoolmaster of Fearn, 1767-1804. [GD71/469.]

MORTON

Copy-declaration by Patrick Smith of Braco *re* £1000 to be applied for support of the Grammar School of Kirkwall, 1649. [GD150/Box 59.]

Letters and papers *re* John Dishington, schoolmaster at Kirkwall, nd; and *re* Sandsting and Aithsting school, 1758. [GD150/Box 65.]

Accounts regarding schoolhouse of Aberdour, 1728. [GD150/Box 115.]

Papers concerning schools in Orkney, 1649-62. [GD150/Box 131.]

MURRAY OF LINTROSE

Accounts for the education of Helen and Anne Gray at Musselburgh, 1788-96. [GD68/2/74-6.]

NORTHESK

Papers regarding ground for Kinnaldie School, 1827-65. [GD130/Box 27.]

Applications for post of schoolmaster of St Vigeans, 1865. [GD130/Box 27.]

OGILVY OF INVERQUHARITY

Letters including a number from George Ogilvy, minister at Kirriemuir, *re* appointment of a schoolmaster, 1750-9. [GD205/Baldovan 229.]

Letter from Robert Colvill, minister at Kirk Yetholm about a schoolmaster's salary, 1715. [GD205/Portfolios 6-7.]

Letter from Thomas Chatto in Kelso *re* Sprouston school, 1717. [GD205/Portfolios 6-7.]

Letter from George Logan in Sprouston recommending a schoolmaster for Morebattle, 1721. [GD205/Portfolios 6-7.]

Letters from James Murray describing accident to the school at Kelso, etc, 1724. [GD205/Portfolios 6-7.]

Letter Wm Baxter in Morebattle *re* school of Yetholm, 1726. [GD205/Portfolios 6-7.]

A M ORR

Papers *re* schools in the presbytery of Dunoon, etc, 1658-1823. [GD1/456.]

ROSS ESTATE

Scroll minute of heritors of Kilmaronock regarding a schoolhouse, 1826. [GD47/388.]

Report (printed) by school board of Kilmaronock to ratepayers of the parish, 15 Mar 1909. [GD47/393.]

Letters from the schoolmaster at Lanark, Robert Thomson, about the education of James Buchanan, 1755-7. [GD47/547.]

Letter from John Beattie, Moffat Academy, requesting a testimonial for a situation in Coupar Academy, 1823. [GD47/611.]

SCOTT OF RAEBURN

Plan of school premises, Lessudden, 1808. [GD104/262.]

List of schoolmasters in the parish of Lessudden, 1720-1830. [GD104/288.]

SEAFORTH

Letters *re* election of a schoolteacher of Lochcarron, 1833. [GD46/1/187.]

Claim of schoolteacher in Stornoway, 1833-4. [GD46/1/194.]

Letters concerning conditions and standards in Torridon school, and the appointment of a schoolmaster, 1832-4. [GD46/1/378.]

Letters *re* education on Seaforth estates, 1832-49. [GD46/1/379.]

Letters *re* schools on Seaforth estates, 1835-6. [GD46/1/391.]

Letters *re* schoolmasters of Contin and Maryburgh, 1844-5. [GD46/1/399.]

Letters concerning salary of schoolmasters on Seaforth estates, 1820-2. [GD46/1/526.]

Letters *re* schools and schoolteachers in Lewis, 1828-35. [GD46/1/530.]

Letters *re* schools in Lewis, 1833-5. [GD46/1/539.]

Inventory of furniture in female school on Seaforth estates, mid-19th cent. [GD46/1/546.]

Volume of accounts, including school expenses and schoolteachers' salaries on Lewis, 1829-30. [GD46/1/578.]

Vouchers of receipts relating to schools, schoolteachers and schoolhouses in Lewis, 1830-1, 1833-5. [GD46/1/580 and 585.]

Letters *re* schoolhouse and schoolmaster of Glasserton, 1817-18. [GD46/2/74.]

Letter from Sheriff George Cameron regarding parochial schools in Scotland, 1852. [GD46/4/256.]

Receipts of salaries of schoolteachers in Lewis and Ross, 1785-91. [GD46/12/1.]

Papers on education in Scotland, especially in Highlands and Islands, 1800-53. [GD46/12/94-150.]

Letter from William McGregor concerning schools and schoolteachers on Seaforth estates, 28 Feb 1832. [GD46/13/184.]

Letters from Lady Dunmore *re* schools in Lewis, etc, 1830-44. [GD46/15/27.]

Letters relating to the proposed academies at Inverness and Fortrose, 1787-9. [GD46/17/4.]

Letters *re* Stornoway Grammar School, 1795-6. [GD46/17/15.]

Letters *re* Stornoway school, 1816-22. [GD46/17/43 and 60.]

Rolls of Gaelic school at Tailly and school of Uig; lists of literate and illiterate persons and education of all persons over 12 years of age in parish of Uig, 1819-25. [GD46/17/52 and 67.]

Note of literate and illiterate persons in Barvas, 1819. [GD46/17/53.]

Letters *re* school at Dingwall, 1822. [GD46/17/60-1.]

Papers *re* Stornoway Academy,1795-1825. [GD46/17/15, 64, 66 and 68.]

Letters *re* schools on Seaforth estates, 1797-1820. [GD46/17/14, 18, 48, 50, and 55-6.]

Letters concerning schools in Lewis, 1812-29. [GD46/17/41 and 69.]

Letters *re* school at Glenshiel, 1818-27. [GD46/17/44, 50, 57, 59, 64, 67-71, 73 and 80.]

Letters concerning school at Barvas, 1822-7. [GD46/17/60, 66, 70 and 72.]

Letters *re* SSPCK and education, 1819-20. [GD46/17/53-4 and 56.]

Papers on education, especially in Highlands and Islands, 1821-9. [GD46/17/59, 63-4, 66, 70-1, 73-5, 77-8 and 83.]

Papers *re* school at Maryburgh, 1825-6. [GD46/17/66, 68 and 71.]

Papers *re* a girl's school for Stornoway, 1825-6. [GD46/17/66, 68 and 70-1.]

Letter concerning a school for Ness, 1826. [GD46/17/68 and 71.]

Letter *re* a school at Byble, 1826. [GD46/17/71.]

Letters *re* schools at Back and Borve, 1827. [GD46/17/72.]

Letters *re* Dalkeith School, 1827. [GD46/17/72.]

Letters *re* school at Uig, 1827. [GD46/17/73.]

Letters concerning a Gaelic teacher for Carloway, 1827-8. [GD46/17/74.]

Letters *re* schools at Cross and Lochshiel, 1829. [GD46/17/77.]

Letters *re* schools at Ineclet, Shawbost and Lochs, 1829. [GD46/17/78-9.]

List of literate persons in Lewis, early 19th cent. [GD46/17/80.]

List of literate and illiterate persons in Lochs, early 19th cent. [GD46/17/82.]

SHAIRP OF HOUSTOUN

Receipts for salaries of schoolteachers in Haddington and Linlithgow, 1699-1789. [GD30/1528-34.]

SINCLAIR OF BRABSTER

Letter to George Sutherland of Brabster from J McHan [—] concerning a new teacher for the parish school, 23 Feb 1812. [GD1/55/49.]

SINCLAIR OF MEY

Papers *re* school rates, 1856-87. [GD96/657.]

Papers concerning schools and schoolteachers (Caithness), 1650-1887. [GD96/680/4-5.]

SOCIETY IN SCOTLAND FOR PROPAGATING CHRISTIAN KNOWLEDGE

Minutes of General and Committee meetings, 1714-1908. [GD95/1-2.]

Account books, 1709-1890. [GD95/6-7.]

Schoolmasters' salary books, 1766-9. [GD95/8.]

Volumes relating to administration of schools, including register of schools maintained by the Society, reports of visitations of schools, abstracts of schools returns, etc, 1710-1890. [GD95/9/1-13.]

Miscellaneous papers including proposals regarding erection and management of schools; reports of visitations of schools in Aberdeenshire, Moray, Inverness-shire, Orkney, Shetland, Caithness and Perthshire; regulations, reports and correspondence concerning the Society's schools and portfolio of returns by parish ministers on their respective parishes, 1708-1879. [GD95/10-11 and 13-14.]

TODS, MURRAY & JAMIESON, WS

Demission of school of Hawick by Robert Chisholm, 1720. [GD237/71/8.]

Memorial *re* schoolmaster of the parish of Ceres, 1770. [GD237/84.]

Plan of the schoolhouse at Darnick, 1853. [RHP5525.]

PART 3: Parochial Boards and Schools

This information is abstracted from the repertory of Church of Scotland records preserved in the Scottish Record Office. The appropriate CH reference should be quoted in all enquiries.

CH 2/2   ABERDEEN, SOUTH CHURCH OF ST NICHOLAS Kirk Session

20. Record of submission between Parochial Board and General Session of the parish of St Nicholas, 1865 (printed)

CH 2/86   DALMENY Kirk Session
14. School records 1792-1817
15. School records 1834-69

CH 2/144   ELGIN, Presbytery of
14. Reports on parish schools 1836-51
15. Reports on parish schools 1851-72

CH 2/173   GLASGOW, BARONY Kirk Session
30. Parochial Board minutes 1846-94

CH 2/319 ST QUIVOX Kirk Session
21. Whitelets School committee minutes 1827-72

CH 2/379 MUCKAIRN Kirk Session
10. 'School book'—account of payments and arrears 1812-34

CH 2/380 WALLS Kirk Session
1. Includes register for the charity schools of Sandness and Papa Stour 1742-9, 1754

CH 2/386 MELROSE Kirk Session
18. Personal details of schoolmasters within the Presbytery of Chirnside 1768-1842
Minutes of schoolmasters' meetings 1830-79

CH 2/400 FALKIRK Kirk Session
18. Includes record of Evening School attendances. 1787-9

CH 2/406 KINGLASSIE Kirk Session
17. School attendance books 1847-53
18. School attendance books 1853-9

CH 2/427 DAIRSIE Kirk Session
8. Parochial school board minutes 1860-85

CH 2/431 KIRKMAHOE Kirk Session
7. Parochial Board minutes 1845-86

CH 2/460 SHOTTS Kirk Session
1. Includes 'schooll wages' 1793

CH 2/470 TRAQUAIR Kirk Session
4. Parochial Board minutes 1846-56

CH 2/472 KINGHORN Kirk Session
16. Minutes of St Andrews Schoo 1835-9

CH 2/521 PERTH, ST JOHN's Kirk Session
32. Minute *re* erection of a school in Middle Church parish 1838

CH 2/529 MORTLACH Kirk Session
4. Heritors' minutes *re* schoolmaster's salary 1829-54

CH 2/535 GUTHRIE Kirk Session
1. Accounts (session and parochial board) 1842-60

CH 2/575 FARNELL Kirk Session
5. Accounts (including parochial board) 1829-76

CH 2/649 LOCHWINNOCH Kirk Session
26. Notes on schoolmasters nd

Index of Writers

(Here, and in the other indexes, a figure in brackets after a page number indicates the number of references on that page.)

A, A, 174
Adam, James, 179
Adam, Margaret, 140
Addison, W Innes, 73
Aitken, George A, 72
Alexander, William Lindsay, 201
Allan, J Buckley, 111
Allan, Mary D, 105
Allan, Patrick, 86
Allardyce, John, 71, 149
Allison, Mona, 157
Almond, Hely Hutchinson, 78
Alpha, 91
Alston, John, 85
Alves, Robert, 66
Anderson, Alexander, 179, 201
Anderson, Sir Alexander, 109
Anderson, Charles, 189
Anderson, George, 86, 179
Anderson, Helen Maud, 139
Anderson, James, 145
Anderson, John (1), 162
Anderson, John (2), 117, 121, 122, 173, 178
Anderson, Peter J, 71, 109, 111, 151, 165, 201
Anderson, R M, 73
Anderson, Robert, 112
Anderson, Thomas, 85
Anderson, William, 66, 67(2), 68(3), 69(2), 71, 72
Anderson, William James, 78
Andrew, Ian Graham, 196
Anglo-Scotus, 118
Angus, Marion, 73
Arbuckle, Sir William F, 169
Arkley, Patrick, 162
Arnot, Hugo, 115
Arnot, James, 66
Arnot, William, 90

B, *See* Thom, William
B, D, 68
B, J C, 67
B, J S, 186
Bache, Alexander D, 115, 117, 118, 119(2), 127, 144, 145, 162, 179
Baillie, Jamieson, 128
Bain, Alexander, 74
Bain, Andrew, 177

Bain, David, 178
Baird, Andrew, 173
Baird, Charles R, 163
Balcanquhall, Walter, 128
Ballantyne, James, 121
Balsillie, David, 117
Bannerman, Thomas, 108
Barclay, Hugh, 16, 90
Barclay, James, 94
Barclay, John B, 76
Barclay, William, 156(2)
Barnard, Henry, 192
Barr, James, 176
Barrett, Michael, 78
Barron, Evan M, 165
Barton, E, 70
Barty, James Strachan, 189
Beale, J M, 105, 160
Beaton, Angus John, 162
Beaton, David, 178
Beattie, James, 75, 179
Bedford, Sir Charles H, 129
Bedford, F W, 105
Begg, James, 80, 102, 179, 188
Beith, Alexander, 162, 198
Belford, Alexander J, 105, 194, 257
Bell, Alexander Melville, 179
Bell, Andrew, 94-5
Bell, George Joseph, 65
Bell, James, 145
Bellesheim, Alphonse, 15
Belsches, Alexander, 196
Billings, Robert W, 132
Biot, Jean Baptiste, 186-7
Black, Adam, 80
Black, Archibald Muir, 179
Black, George F, 15, 179
Black, John (1), 49, 109
Black, John (2), 179
Black, P Cameron, 91
Black, Robert Cooper, 201
Blackie, John Stuart, 74, 87, 95, 108, 201
Blackie, Walter G, 87, 201
Blair, P J, 111
Blamire, John, 137
Blanc, Hippolyte, 132
Blinshall, James, 196
Blundell, Odo, 78
Blyth, John J, 160

Index of Subjects

Index of Places

Addenda

BELFORD, ALEX J 'Foundation members of the EIS'; *SEJ*, 9, 16, 23, 30 Oct 1936, **19**, 1218-19, 1256-7, 1278-9, 1308-9; 30 Apr 1937, **20**, 546-8.

'Education of the people'; *Blackwood's Edinburgh Mag*, Jan 1830, **27**, 1-16.

'The Education Question in Scotland'; *North British Rev*, May 1861, **34**, 495-512.

MACKAY, A W *The history of the parochial school of Dalkeith from the Reformation to the 1872 Education Act*. Unpublished MEd thesis, Edinburgh University, 1969. Fcp. Typescript. Pp [3], iii, [1], 73, [9].   EUL

The Memorial of the Schoolmasters of Scotland, 18 September 1824. np, 1824. Fol. Pp 2.
                                                                                        BM

MILNE, IAN F *Educational provision in Greenock, 1800-1872*. Unpublished MEd thesis, Glasgow University, 1969. 4to. Typescript. Pp [4], 93, [2]. Bibliography.   EUL

'Popular education in Scotland'; *North British Rev*, Nov 1854, **22**, 57-83.

SCOTLAND, JAMES *The History of Scottish Education*. 2 vols. London: University of London Press Ltd, 1969 [1970]. Vol 1: Pp xix, 385. Bibliography, glossary, index, 8 plates. Vol 2: Pp xix, 294. Bibliography, glossary, index, 8 plates.

'Scottish schools for the middle-class'; *North British Rev*, Feb 1856, **24**, 359-85.

SMITH, JAMES V *The founding of the Society in Scotland for Propagating Christian Knowledge considered in relation to the trends in social and political history in the seventeenth and early eighteenth centuries*. Unpublished MEd thesis, Dundee University, 1969. 4to. Typescript. Pp [3], 78.   DUL

SMITH, ROBERT MURRAY 'Education'; *History of Greenock* (Greenock: Orr, Pollock & Co, 1921), 277-88.

SMITH, WILLIAM A Memorial for the established or parochial Schoolmasters in Scotland, addressed to the great men in Parliament . . . By William Smith, as Commissioner of said schoolmasters. London. 31 Jan 1750.   Not seen

STEWART, WILLIAM A C and MCCANN, W P 'Robert Owen and the New Lanark Schools'; *The Educational Innovators, 1750-1880* (London: Macmillan, 1967), 53-73.

Publications of the Scottish Council for Research in Education